Secure the Soul

Secure the Soul

*Christian Piety and Gang Prevention
in Guatemala*

Kevin Lewis O'Neill

UNIVERSITY OF CALIFORNIA PRESS

University of California Press, one of the most
distinguished university presses in the United States,
enriches lives around the world by advancing scholarship
in the humanities, social sciences, and natural sciences. Its
activities are supported by the UC Press Foundation and
by philanthropic contributions from individuals and
institutions. For more information, visit www.ucpress.edu.

University of California Press
Oakland, California

Library of Congress Cataloging-in-Publication Data

O'Neill, Kevin Lewis, 1977– author.
    Secure the soul : christian piety and gang prevention in
guatemala / Kevin Lewis O'Neill.
        pages   cm
    Includes bibliographical references and index.
    ISBN 978-0-520-27848-6 (cloth : alk. paper)
    ISBN 978-0-520-27849-3 (pbk. : alk. paper)
    ISBN 978-0-520-96009-1 (ebook)
        1. Gang prevention—Guatemala— Guatemala.
2. Church and social problems—Guatemala—
Guatemala.   I. Title.
    HV6439.G92G923 2015
    364.4—dc23   2014024593

Manufactured in the United States of America

24 23 22 21 20 19 18 17 16 15
10 9 8 7 6 5 4 3 2 1

In keeping with a commitment to support
environmentally responsible and sustainable printing
practices, UC Press has printed this book on Natures
Natural, a fiber that contains 30% post-consumer waste
and meets the minimum requirements of ANSI/NISO
Z39.48–1992 (R 1997) (*Permanence of Paper*).

To Sridhar, to Usha
For Archana, for Ignatius

Contents

Illustrations

I tore a page from my notebook, earnestly titled "Field Notes." Mateo rolled a joint with it as we finished our beers. On the outer edge of Guatemala City, with a volcano at our backs, we sat in a park. Grainy 1990s hip-hop music played from his cell phone, with the same song on loop, seemingly for hours. Nostalgia hit. "I'm sad, Kev." Mateo pulled from the joint. His hand, the very one pinching the blunt, looked different. The 818 once tattooed across his knuckles had faded. Both time and lasers were doing the trick. His monthly visits to a reinsertion program for ex–gang members looked like they were paying off. The former area code of his former Los Angeles was hardly visible. But the numbers faded faster than his memories. "Why you sad?" I asked. "You've got a good job, great kid, and Jesus. You always talk about Jesus." His eyes, swollen from the weed, teared up. "I know. I'm just sad, bro. I miss my family back in LA." I put my arm around him. "I know, Mateo. I know." The music then stopped, but only for a moment. The same song, that same goddam song, jumped off from the beginning. Mateo was right back where he had started.

Prologue

The streets were on fire. They were burning the devil. *La quema del diablo*. Every year, on December 7, at sunset, Guatemalans torch their trash. To purge the devil, some say. For spiritual purity, others add. Old newspapers, stained mattresses, and broken furniture—they set it ablaze in the streets, which is where I stood. Outside a small Pentecostal church, in an unplanned, undeveloped *zona* of Guatemala City, I stood with a pastor. The sun had set. Thick smoke gathered while dozens of bonfires cast shadows across otherwise unlit streets. He was on the phone with a young woman. Her sister had just been gang-raped on a public bus. The pastor struggled for answers. He offered prayers. He even promised to visit the very next day, on Monday; but for now, he said, he had a service to deliver, a congregation to minister. As he spoke, the flames grew closer. I turned away, only to find myself facing a red and black piñata. Shaped like the devil, hanging from a post, by the neck, it had been lynched. His feet were on fire.

The church was modest. A metal roof balanced atop four cement walls, while oversized, overused speakers pushed Pentecostal music past the seats and out the door. The streets seemed to push it back. Inside the church, toddlers toddled and children ran while young men sat with young women, and old women sat with their daughters. Fire or not, the devil or not, it was Sunday night, and they were at church for a service. Men and women squeezed into the space while flames licked at the windows. The church had begun to take on smoke.

FIGURE 1. La quema del diablo. Photo by Benjamin Fogarty-Valenzuela.

A greeting, a prayer, and then another song—the pastor kept to the script. So too did the congregants. But then the pastor mentioned a guest. He mentioned an honored guest. He, not the pastor, would deliver the sermon. He, not the pastor, would share his testimony. This young man, the pastor insisted, would share his testimony with anyone who would listen. The thought of it brought a smile to the pastor's face. "Will you listen?" the pastor asked. "Will you really listen?" Fireworks popped in the streets. Some turned to watch. "Listen to the young man," the pastor pressed, "because he is here to help you. He is here to save you. To save us. You need to listen to him." A stray dog poked his nose inside the church. A little boy kicked at it. "The gangs are too much," the pastor continued. "The violence in Guatemala is just too much."

Mateo, the young man, took to the pulpit. He was not tall, but he was obviously strong. He had broad shoulders, a thick neck, and a sturdy back. He could be mistaken for an athlete, a boxer perhaps, were it not for his gait. He walked like a gangsta. This is his word, not mine. He walked a little slower, a little more stridently than the average Guatemalan. Mateo had a kind of swagger that made him stand out. He knew it, and he liked it. The bald head, the baggy jeans, and the tattoos peeking out from under his collar—it all signaled a certain kind of time spent in the States. His stunted Spanish was also a tell. Mateo was not from Guatemala. Everyone knew as much. But, of course, he was. Everyone knew that, too.

Mateo spoke softly. "Thank you," he whispered, "Thank you, brothers and sisters." Mateo always spoke softly, at least at first. It was a bit of trick. "Get them leaning forward," he would tell me. "Get them on the edge of their seats," he would say. "Don't just yell at 'em. Make 'em work for it. They need to fuckin' work for it." He motioned for everyone to take their seats. "Sit, brothers and sisters. Please sit." As they sat down, Mateo stepped back. Taking a deep breath, he picked up the microphone and started slowly. "The word of God touches me. It touches me so much. I'm thirty years old. And I am alive by the grace of God." The whisper worked. It usually did. The young men and the young women leaned toward him. So too did the mothers and the fathers. The children still ran, and the toddlers still toddled, but the old women, the hardest of all to hook, shifted a bit in their seats. "The word of God touches my heart deeply," he said, with a cough. The smoke thickened.

"But let me back up," he said. "I want to start from the beginning." Mateo always started from the beginning. "When I was three years old, my dad and I left. We were here in Guatemala, but then we went to the United States illegally." He let that fact sit for a bit. "We left for the United States without papers. You see, my cousin is American. He was born in Guatemala but his papers are American. And when I was young, when I was still really little, I looked just like my cousin. But I wasn't him. We just looked the same. So I used his papers to cross the border." Mateo's pitch began to peak. He started to preach to the back of the room. "I arrived illegally . . . because my dad thought he was going to find something better. He was looking for what a lot of Central Americans are looking for." It was a familiar story. "When, really, this country, this Guatemala, is rich. Guatemala is blessed! Guatemala is a rich country!" Mateo yelled that last part. He always yelled that last part.

"Praise be to God!" the congregation erupted.

"Praise be to God!" Mateo echoed. A group of kids suddenly streaked past the front door. They dragged their piñata, their devil, with a rope. He was on fire. Bits of charred devil followed close behind.

Mateo started up before the faithful quieted down. Preaching over them at a clip, he said, "Guatemala is a beautiful country. God has blessed this country, but sometimes . . ." He slowed back down. "Sometimes we can't see beauty. Sometimes we can't even stand our own neighbor, our own land. Sometimes we don't know that God has already blessed us." He paused—to lower his voice, to stand in the moment. "Sometimes we're lost," he said. "Sometimes we're just totally lost." By this time smoke had filled the church. The smell of burning rubber and melting plastic mixed with the church's fluorescent lighting to create a surreal scene, one that toggled between a dream and a total nightmare. "Gang-raped on a public bus?" the pastor had asked, with a mix of compassion and disbelief.

"I've been lost," Mateo admitted. "I still get lost." His voice stiffened. "But the pastor is right. The gangs are too much. The violence is too much. That's why I'm worried. I'm so worried for the kids here, for the youth. I'm worried about this neighborhood. I'm worried about the people involved in gangs. Because if you choose that life, you're going to get yourself killed. You're going to find yourself in a bag. You're going to find one of your friends killed, hanged, with his head chopped off. You're going to find yourself doing time in prison." Mateo spoke from experience. "Look," he said, "I'm not here to tell you to get out of your neighborhood. I'm not here to tell you what to do, or how to live your life. I'm just here to tell you that God loves you. To tell you that there is a way out. To tell you that there are ways to heal all those cuts that you have on your heart." Now I started to cough. The smoke was too much.

Mateo leaned into his testimony. "When I arrived in South Central Los Angeles, I lived with my dad. I was young. Real young. And when I was like eight years old, my dad really started to get abusive. I'm not talking about anything sexual. No. My dad was tough with me. He's now a very caring man. He's older. He's wiser. He prays to God. And God changed him. But back then . . ." Mateo shook his head. He hated bringing it all back. "Back then he used to hit me. And I'm not talking about a father going to the closet and getting out his belt. I'm not talking about spanking a child two or three times to teach him something. No, brothers. No, sisters. My father hit me like I was twenty years old. He would punch me in the face. He would punch me like a man, and if I cried, he hit me more." The flames grew taller. Driven by curiosity as much as concern, I wrote in my notebook, "Does cement burn?"

Mateo's voice started to crack. "I didn't have a childhood," he preached, "I still remember this one time when I came home from school. And I was happy. I had done really well on a test. Like B+ or something. And I was happy." Mateo drifted a bit. On stage, in his mind, he drifted a bit. He lost himself in the smoke. But he came back. Stepping out from behind the pulpit, squaring himself to the congregation, he said, "My dad came home, and I said, 'Hey, Dad, look, I got a good grade.' But then he grabbed my homework and ripped it into pieces. And he grabbed me and he started punching me in my mouth, in my ribs, in my stomach. He started choking me." Mateo then stepped out of his narrative. He literally stepped to one side, to make a kind of parenthesis. "He wasn't beating me like you beat a child. He was hitting me like I was a man. He beat me like you beat a man." He wanted to make that point absolutely clear. "And he picked me up and opened the door and then threw me out. And I hit the floor with my back and my butt. And then I looked at him . . . I remember looking at him, and a teardrop started to fall out of my right eye. And I looked at him and I said, 'Dad, what's up? Why are you doing this?' Standing on the front steps of our apartment, in the middle of South Central, he tells me, 'Get out of here, you son of a bitch. You're not my son.'" They all sat in silence. Sounds from the streets jockeyed for their attention. Fireworks burst. Dogs growled. Babies wailed. The place was literally on fire. But these churchgoers did not stir. Mateo had their attention.

"I got up, I dusted myself, and he shut the door on me. And as I stood outside, in South Central, trying not to cry, I thought about what I was going to do. What was I going to do without a father? Without a family? Because at that time, brothers and sisters, I didn't know God. I didn't know anything about the Lord or about the Holy Spirit. I'm telling you, I didn't know God." One woman—a mother of many—called out, "But God knew you!" Mateo smiled. "That's right, sister. That is absolutely right. . . . Because I knew—deep down in my heart, under all the pain and the abuse—I knew that my blessed Father had my life in his hands." Mateo lingered on this last point. "During it all, and I'm serious, I always knew there was someone looking out for me. I always knew that there was someone knocking at my door, trying to open my heart. I just didn't know who it was. I didn't even know God existed. I didn't know he was trying to get my attention, that he was trying to restore me and to raise me up. I tell you, I didn't know God." He dropped his shoulders a bit. "All I knew were the gangs."

"I was growing up in the streets of Los Angeles," Mateo whispered, "seeing all the gangs and starting to see their sinfulness. And I would just watch them. The drugs, how they moved money, the cars, the guns, the prostitutes. But I also started to feel a part of a family. I felt . . ." Mateo was near tears—at the pulpit, in front of everyone. But he fought them back. He could usually fight them back. "I felt like . . . Oh, Lord. I felt like the gang was my family." He wiped a tear from his face. "And I remember that the gangs were really active at that point. It was all really tense. And everyone would talk about who had juice. Who had power. That dude is dangerous, they'd say. Watch out for that cat. But you know what, brothers and sisters, my heart was already destroyed by that time. I started skipping school and getting suspended." Mateo looked upward, toward the ceiling. "I was just so angry," he confessed, "I had all this hatred. So I started to get involved with drugs. The weed got me high. It did, but then I wanted something more powerful. So I started doing cocaine and crack. I started doing heroin and crystal meth. I smoked it. But I still didn't feel anything. It didn't do anything for me. And I was still so young and all I wanted was to feel something!"

"The gangs let me feel something," Mateo said. "But I was blind. I had like a bandage over my eyes, over my heart! I was angry. My heart was hard. All I knew was that I didn't want to let anyone in. I had this look in my eyes that screamed, 'Do not come in!'" Mateo pointed to the window, with its fire and its smoke. He pointed toward the devil. "All I could hear was the devil." Mateo flexed his voice, adding, "The devil is real. But the devil's not in the streets. Look at them. Running around, lighting stuff on fire. What are they doing? The devil is real but he's not out there. The devil is in our hearts. The gang was in my heart."

Mateo preached for another hour—about getting beaten into the gang, the Los Angeles riots, and fistfighting his way through the U.S. prison system. He also talked about finding Jesus, alone in his jail cell. "Did I do too much dope?" he asked himself in front of the church. "That's what I thought Jesus was. Too much dope. It was like three in the morning in jail and I heard this voice: 'Mateo, let me in.'" He cupped the mic with his hands for effect. "Let me in! Open your heart!" Mateo stumbled around the pulpit, acting it all out. "What's going on?" he asked, in a seeming stupor. Suddenly snapping out of it, he said, "And that's when I started to look for the Lord, brothers and sisters. And the Lord told me, 'Stop.' He told me that 'I'm going to lead you,' that I need to surrender to him."

At the end of the night, Mateo turned to his deportation. It made for a cold conclusion—because his new life in Guatemala, he said, had been hard. It had been lonely. "'Cause when Satan comes," Mateo warned, "he hits you. He strips you of all your belongings, and he leaves you half dead." As he spoke, the streets quieted; bonfires gave way to piles of soot. Families and friends turned in for the night. Yet the smoke lingered. The cool night, with its humidity, held it close. So atop some kind of carcinogenic cloud, Mateo returned, one last time, to his message. With the children asleep on their parents' laps, Mateo confessed, "The devil was in my heart. The gang was in my heart. But not anymore. Today I am free. By the grace of God, I am free."

Introduction

Mateo preached amid chaos. The flames, the fireworks, the devil—each added to the drama, but the real tragedy had been brewing for decades. New regimes of deportation, as well as a blurring distinction between the United States' War on Drugs and its War on Terror, combined with a multibillion-dollar drug trade to expand and embolden transnational street gangs throughout Central America. Guatemala got hit hard. And Mateo felt every punch. Following a thirty-six-year genocidal civil war (1960–96), uneven efforts at democratization and economic restructuring met a criminally negligent state to make postwar Guatemala the most violent noncombat zone in the world. The numbers are bleak. Guatemala City's homicide rate is more than twenty times the U.S. average. An estimated two-thirds of these homicides are gang related, and less than 2 percent of them result in a conviction. "This ain't LA," Mateo would say. "This place is fuckin' wild." And wild it can seem—as 24,000 police officers work alongside some 150,000 private security agents, three-quarters of whom are unregistered and all are armed. With the guns and the murders, in the shadows of all this violence, postwar peace and prosperity proved nothing more than bloodied banners.[1] Security is the new anthem.

La mano dura, or a strong-fisted approach to gang violence, has long defined the practice of postwar security. Its techniques include deportation, mass incarceration, and extrajudicial execution. The strategy is clear: stop the violence, for good. Yet, amid repatriation flights and

FIGURE 2. The daily news. Photo by Benjamin Fogarty-Valenzuela.

paramilitary death squads, overcrowded prisons and angry lynch mobs, an alternative definition of security has emerged. Industry experts call it "soft security." Its technique is prevention, and its hope is to stop the violence before it starts.[2] Mateo is one of its agents. He is also one of its subjects. For his testimony, his talk of transformation, braids together a growing commitment to soft security with a dramatic shift in religious affiliation. Once overwhelmingly Roman Catholic, the country is today as much as 60 percent Pentecostal and Charismatic Christian.[3] This confluence is crucial. In the shadows of an anemic postwar state, with unthinkable levels of urban violence, new forms of Christianity organize and underlie the practice of gang prevention. Jesus saves. And he also secures.

This book details the Christian dimensions of soft security in postwar Guatemala. It juxtaposes a set of ethnographies, each delineating how a church mission, a faith-based program, or an ostensibly secular security project traffics in Christian techniques of self-transformation. Much like Christianity, because of Christianity, soft security presumes that its subject is lost and must be found, that he has sinned and so must be saved.[4] Mateo's life evidences as much, but so too do the sites that assemble him: maximum security prisons (Chapter 1), reality television shows (Chapter 2), bilingual call centers (Chapter 3), child sponsorship programs (Chapter 4), and Pentecostal rehabilitation centers (Chapter 5).[5] Each faith-inflected intervention opens a window onto religion's knotted relationship with security. And this is the point. A range of scholars (in several disciplines) understand religion and security as distinct: religion as a threat to security or religion as a solution to insecurity.[6] Yet, the practice of soft security demonstrates that religion, observed here through various manifestations of Christianity, is neither the enemy nor the antidote. Rather, religion is a social fact deeply bound to the practice and to the construction of security, to the very idea of what it means to be secure.[7]

Mateo's life, assembled across these sites and braided between these chapters, evidences this entanglement in ways that foreground the fact that soft security is not so soft. Mateo knows this all too well. No matter how earnest the intervention, no matter how clever the effort, the outcomes often proved tragic. People died—spectacularly, in radically undignified ways. Death, dismemberment, and disappearance pierce every one of these chapters. "The programs are just fucked up," Mateo admitted, "They aren't organized. Nothing is nice and tight. So a lot of people die." But to conclude that these are mere misfires is to absolutely miss the point. Efficacy is not the issue. Productiveness is. For the practice of soft security, especially when hitched to Christian coordinates, targets the heart and the mind; it works on the soul, doing so in ways that distinguish between the lost and the found, the sinner and the saved, the worthy and the unworthy.[8] These moral distinctions have material effects. They set the conditions for visibility, segregation, and captivity—for who is seen (and who is not), who belongs (and who does not), who is free (and who gets tied up). Soft security can be brutal, this book argues, and Christianity makes it so.

The Christianity of interest here is neither a stable tradition nor a singular sect. It is an aspiration.[9] At the center of most every effort at prevention sits not Pentecostalism or Presbyterianism, but a piety built of sin and hope.[10] Make good with God, this piety insists, by turning inward, assessing your soul, and righting yourself with the Lord. "God was knocking at my door," Mateo confessed at the church that night, "God wanted to come inside. God wanted to raise me up." Both an obligation and an inspiration, evoking the cross as well as the empty tomb, Christian piety sits at the center of soft security. It demands from its person a commitment, at times a compulsion, to improve, to be better—to turn it all around. In doing so, this piety renders Christianity ubiquitous and undifferentiated, a Christianity best described as undenominated.[11] This is why this book moves beyond church histories and denominational ethnographies to see what the promise of piety makes possible.[12] In postwar Guatemala, with ruthless levels of social suffering, the promise of piety makes the solution to gang violence intuitive: secure the soul.

To appreciate this imperative requires some more detailed remarks on prevention and piety. The rest of this introduction does the rest of this work. It also frames Mateo's life history, which makes up the text between each numbered chapter. Edited for length and style, Mateo's life history evidences the social worlds that exist between each of these chapters as well as the cultural forces that bind them together. Yet Mateo's life history should be taken neither as mere evidence nor simple texture. Given his confessional logic and Christian techniques of self-transformation, his ambivalent relationship to being lost and having to be found, Mateo makes piety the perfect problem through which to see the politics of postwar security anew. Few life histories supply such a powerful demonstration of the violence and banality of transnational cultures, linking relatively mundane ministerial efforts to contemporary threads of religion and globalization; the politics of frontiers, borders, and boundaries; and deportation and democratization as lived practice. A patterned entity, embodying a story that is more than his own, Mateo is not incidental to some larger theoretical claim. In this book, for this analysis, amid a deeply interrelated set of ethnographies, Mateo is the thesis. He is the argument.[13]

. . .

A Soviet beachhead. This is what Guatemala would become, intelligence reports insisted, if the United States did not intervene.[14] In the early 1950s, the Truman administration watched as Guatemala transitioned from a military dictatorship to a democratically elected government. President Jacobo Árbenz Guzmán posed no obvious threat. His policies, in many ways, extended those of his predecessor. Yet, Decree 900 raised concerns. This new piece of legislation, passed by the Guatemalan Congress in 1952, redistributed unused land to peasants, in an effort to shift the economy from feudalism to capitalism. But the practice smacked of communism, at least to the United Fruit Company. This U.S. multinational corporation owned 42 percent of the arable land in Guatemala, some of it vulnerable to Decree 900. Two stockholders took charge.

They petitioned the president of the United States to intervene. Brothers in arms as well as actual brothers, they were Allen Welsh Dulles, the director of the U.S. Central Intelligence Agency (CIA), and John Foster Dulles, the U.S. secretary of state. They made their case well.[15]

In June 1954, under the Eisenhower administration, the CIA orchestrated a coup d'état against President Árbenz. It would become an infamous affair, with U.S.-trained revolutionaries on the ground and New York City advertisement agencies in the air. Both managed a message: President Árbenz was a communist. Sigmund Freud's nephew, Edward Bernays, authored the propaganda.[16] The results were disastrous.

The Guatemalan government became increasingly militarized until large-scale massacres, scorched-earth tactics, and massive numbers of disappearances and displacements riddled the country with what would later be understood as acts of genocide. At the helm of it all was Efraín Ríos Montt, a military dictator and a Pentecostal Christian. He delivered weekly radio addresses known as "sermons" and developed close ties to the United States' growing Moral Majority.[17] Dressed in battle fatigues and answering to the title of El General, Ríos Montt became Guatemala's quintessential Christian soldier. Yet, the net effect of his campaign, of the entire war, proved genocidal: 200,000 dead, 50,000 disappeared, and 1 million displaced.[18]

Many of the displaced marched north. They were not alone. El Salvador's civil war (1980–92), also backed by the U.S. government, coincided with Guatemala's, pushing tens of thousands of Central Americans to Los Angeles's poorest neighborhoods.[19] Once there, for reasons of belonging and security, the children of these refugees formed gangs to defend themselves against the city's already well-established Asian, African American, and Mexican gangs. Initially modest in reach, Mara Salvatrucha (MS-13) and Barrio 18 became transnational criminal organizations in the aftermath of the 1992 Los Angeles riots.[20] With a torched cityscape and a surging Moral Majority, increasingly strict antigang laws meant tougher prosecution, expanding the legal grounds for deportation to include such minor offenses as shoplifting.[21]

The tenor of it all was brash. Just months after the Los Angeles riots, presidential hopeful Patrick Buchanan spoke at the 1992 Republican National Convention. He crowed to a national television audience, "There is a religious war going on in this country. It is a cultural war, as critical to the kind of nation we shall be as the Cold War itself. For this war is for the soul of America." His speech was reactionary, filled with homophobic and racist statements as well as a Manichaean division

FIGURE 3. Los desaparecidos. Photo by Benjamin Fogarty-Valenzuela.

between us and them. It ended with an image from the Los Angeles riots: "The troopers [of the Eighteenth Cavalry] came up the street," he said, "M-16s at the ready. And the mob threatened and cursed, but the mob retreated because it had met the one thing that could stop it: force, rooted in justice, and backed by moral courage." Citing scripture (John 15:13, to be exact), Buchanan then set a tone for U.S. immigration policy that would last for decades. He announced, in militant Christian idiom, "[Just] as those [troopers] took back the streets of Los Angeles, block by block, my friends, we must take back our cities, and take back our culture, and take back our country."[22] This is a war for the soul of America, Buchanan insisted, rooted in force, justice, and moral courage.

The U.S. government led with force. The number of Central Americans deported annually tripled in less than a decade, rising from just over 8,000 in 1996 to well over 24,000 in 2004.[23] Following the events of September 11, 2001, the U.S. government began to confront MS-13 and Barrio 18 under the auspices of Immigration and Customs Enforcement (ICE), a new division of the Department of Homeland Security. In 2007, by routinely alleging unsubstantiated associations between these gangs and al-Qaeda, by stretching the War on Terror to its rhetorical limits, the U.S. government deported some 74,000 Central Americans to

Guatemala, Honduras, and El Salvador. In 2010, the United States successfully repatriated more than 31,000 Guatemalans, with 31.3 percent deported on criminal grounds.[24] Our goal, explained Secretary of Homeland Security Michael Chertoff, is to "return every single illegal entrant, no exceptions."[25] And when U.S. presidencies changed, U.S. policies did not. President Barack Obama issued more deportations in his first year in office than did President George W. Bush in his last year in office.[26]

The immigration laws that deported these Central Americans also banned U.S. officials from disclosing the criminal backgrounds of the deportees to their home countries. With a typical lack of coordination between the United States and Central American governments, hundreds of men, women, and children (but mostly men) stepped off of repatriation flights, walked onto tarmacs, and then hopped onto city buses—every day. No questions asked. Challenging already strained police, prison, and judicial systems, these deportees met minimum life chances, a complete lack of social services, and a glut of weapons left over from the region's civil wars. And, as men and women born in Central America but oftentimes raised in the United States, the youngest of these deportees did not speak Spanish fluently; they had no close family ties and no viable life chances but gang life.

These factors generated the ideal conditions for gang expansion. By 2006, with homicide rates that outpace even those of Guatemala's genocidal civil war, Central American gangs began to boast more than 100,000 members throughout the Americas—a population that continues to grow alongside a heaving drug trade.[27] In 2011, as much as 90 percent of the cocaine shipped from the Andes to the United States flowed through Guatemala.[28] For this reason, and for many more, members of Central American gangs have been spotted as far south as Argentina and as far north as Alaska.[29] In the end, a myriad of mistakes and misjudgments radically expanded the conditions of postwar violence, outpacing initial concerns of a Soviet beachhead. These gangs had gone global.

Central American governments answered with force, mobilizing paramilitary death squads and pushing prison systems past 300 percent of capacity.[30] El Salvador, in July 2003, rolled out its Mano Dura (Strong Fist) policy and then, months later, implemented more aggressive legislation named Super Mano Dura.[31] Honduras followed suit. Directly derived from Mayor Rudolf Giuliani's Zero Tolerance approach in New York City, the Honduran government launched Cero Tolerancia in August 2003. In January 2004, Guatemala enacted Plan Escoba

FIGURE 4. Guatemela City, Zona 3. Photo by Benjamin Fogarty-Valenzuela.

(Operation Street Sweep), effectively militarizing the country's police force, with off-duty police officers authorized to hunt down suspected gang members. The strong fist got even stronger.[32]

Central American governments, along with the United States, quickly admitted that a strong-fisted approach did little to curb the growth and influence of these gangs. This is one reason government agencies throughout the Americas began to pair *suppressive* policies—ones that favor incarceration and deportation—with more *integrated* efforts at gang prevention. An integrated approach synthesizes community policing efforts with youth programs and social services, creating a well-coordinated social net to catch those free-falling into gang life.[33] This was soft security.

Money started to move. Between 2008 and 2012, the U.S. Congress allocated $35 million in global International Narcotics Control and Law Enforcement funds for antigang efforts in Central America. In 2008, it provided an additional $60 million of support for antigang efforts through the Mérida Initiative, a $1.6 billion counterdrug and anticrime program for Mexico and Central America.[34] From 2009 to 2012, Congress directed $465.5 million through the Central American Regional Security Initiative, with $146 million delivered to United States Agency for International Development (USAID; for rule of law efforts and violence prevention projects) and the U.S. State Department (for cultural programs). Then others kicked in. The Inter-American Development Bank, the World Bank, and the United Nations joined with Germany, Spain, Switzerland, and South Korea to provide almost $2 billion between January 2009 and April 2012.[35] These funds supported soft-security projects throughout Central America.

Awash in money, with program officers scouring the streets in search of viable grantees, the integrated approach to gang violence quickly blurred any conceivable separation between soft security, international development, and corporate social responsibility.[36] The three suddenly shared the same end game. Good development became good security, which all became good business. Microloan cooperatives, after-school initiatives, and weekend soccer camps worked alongside community policing programs and private-public partnerships. Each crafted popular opinion, established coherence between aid and politics, and mitigated security threats by rebranding the opposition. Each project also placed people, rather than politics, at the center of security, intervening in the life of the individual for the sake of society.

Christianity, in this milieu, became a real political resource. Much of the reason is that the religion dominates civil society in Central America. No other social imaginary articulates change more persuasively than Christianity. No other institution has more legitimacy than churches. And no other set of actors connects better with people—with their hopes, their fears—than Christians. In Central America, especially in postwar Guatemala, Jesus is the answer, at times the only answer. Practically speaking, this meant that international aid agencies sought out Christian organizations to discuss, staff, and even implement soft-security projects, while Christians themselves jockeyed for growing amounts of money. The faithful pitched new projects and repurposed already proven programs. One-time acts of charity (the poor visit) morphed into development projects (mentorship programs) only to become soft-security schemes (anger management classes). Christianity, and often Christianity alone, was positioned perfectly to minister to the person, to administer security softly. An entrepreneurial buzz filled the air.

The result was countless Christian prevention programs. They were countless not because the number of Christian projects was actually infinite, but rather because counting some as Christian and others as not-Christian proved preposterous. The distinctions were imperceptible, even confounding. Ethnographically speaking, a so-called secular program staffed by Christians appeared just as Christian as a church project augmented by an international aid agency. Even the Guatemalan National Civil Police's own Office of Prevention, itself funded by the U.S. government, used scripture in its mission statement: "It is necessary to submit to the authorities not only because of possible punishment but also as a matter of conscience" (Romans 13:1, 6).[37] These elisions illustrate the argument made elsewhere that trying to disentangle the secular from the saved only performs the indeterminacy of secularism itself.[38]

Consistent through each of these efforts at gang prevention has been Christian piety. More ontology than cosmology, irrespective of theology, Christian piety is a persistent pull to work something out. That "something" is sin. Its "out" is salvation. "When I got out of prison in the United States," Mateo preached, "I just fell back into the same things." The problem is that Christian piety forever places redemption just beyond reach. "And then I got up," Mateo added, "dusted myself off, and then fell back into it all over again." For Christian piety assumes a radically imperfect world populated by radically imperfect people as well as a God hell-bent on perfection. Frustration and failure are inevitable. "And then I fell again and again and again," he added, "That's how I got deported." But resignation is not an option. It never has been. Not only is capitulation not Christian, but impiety is also *the* justification for intervention. It can also be *the* rationalization for abandonment.[39] "But I do not quit," Mateo beamed, to himself as well as to the faithful who filled the church that night. "I never stop trying to change myself."

Clear articulations of this piety emerge in the church setting. Mateo often pleads for parishioners to change. But this piety needs neither a pastor nor a priest. There is no church of piety.[40] A mash-up of self-esteem, motivation, and liberation draped across the ruins of disciplinary infrastructures, these faith-inflected efforts at gang abatement constitute the affective infrastructure of postwar security, fusing Christian practice, moral ambition, and behavior modification to the dialectics of local empowerment and transnational delinquency.[41] Be better, these programs insist. For you are fallen, they remind. The ultimate effect is an everlasting effort at sanctification, as the sinner struggles to bridge the chasm between perfection and imperfection, between God and himself. And so things get done. Sinners strengthen their will, examine their conscience, and comport their bodies. The pious also intervene in the lives of the uninterested, if only to strengthen their own sense of self. These practices, beyond Christian denomination and bound to ideologies of transformation, constitute embodied horizons of absolute uncertainty.

This uncertainty has a history. Piety and prevention have been bedfellows for centuries. In the early twentieth century, the influential Chicago School of urban thought argued that when communities do not transmit the right values to their youth, those youth go crooked.[42] They loiter in alleyways; they run with the wrong crowd. They join street gangs. As this logic gained an audience in the 1940s, as the welfare state grew, antigang initiatives in the United States worked to strengthen communities. This meant that government-funded social workers intervened in the lives of youth while Protestant ministers, inspired by a then-popular Social Gospel, followed suit. These moral technicians walked the streets, talking to disillusioned youth about earning an honest wage in what was then a thriving urban industrial economy. This was the so-called social work approach to fighting gangs, and it lingered at the level of individual behavior and personal values.[43] It placed supreme confidence in the idea that if young men and women received the attention they deserved, then the problem of street gangs would dissipate, and security would follow.

This approach to gang abatement worked mostly because social workers and Protestant ministers targeted men and women aging out of gangs. Given that adolescents largely constituted U.S. street gangs in the 1940s and 1950s and that the street gang's primary activity in this era was inactivity, gang members eventually needed to find work.[44] Gang membership, in a sense, had a life cycle that social workers and Protestant ministers helped to complete.

Much has changed since then, of course, about gangs and the economy.[45] Neoliberal economic reforms, along with a concomitant decline of the welfare state, have radically limited the kind of work available to those young men and women who might otherwise have aged out of gang life.[46] Migrant labor circuits, the War on Terror, and new regimes of deportation are other processes that have made the social work approach rather ill equipped to address the problem of gangs. Yet antigang strategies across the Americas still draw on some of the Chicago School's most basic assumptions about prevention and piety while at the same time coordinating with Christian notions of sin and salvation. This rather potent mix of idiom and affect amid a politically unstable context has significantly reordered piety's relationship to prevention.

For one, the place of piety has changed. For centuries, piety got under the skin of its subject within clearly demarcated places. Nineteenth- and twentieth-century efforts at discipline placed people inside of buildings—to mold them, to make them docile. Prisons, factories, and hospitals as well as asylums, seminaries, and schools served as principal sites of correction. The social work approach to gangs pivoted on this fact. Meticulous regulation, methodical schedules, and elaborate inspections did their best to turn the peasant into the soldier, the misfit into the altar boy.[47] All of these efforts, bolstered by the built form, disciplined the body.

But the built form is no longer necessary. Discipline is not dead, of course, but the closed, contained space of the prison, factory, and asylum has given way to emergent configurations of innovation, ethics, and good will. The difference between the two is critical. While the prison, factory, and asylum offer concrete, architecturally specific sites of intervention, the experience of piety and prevention today—of soft security—is opportunistic. It is fleeting. One does not enter or exit a reality television show or a child sponsorship program the same way one enters or exits a nineteenth-century prison, even if each works to stem the tide of gang violence. The prison is heavy, its logic established, with blueprints that clearly define its ethics. The reality television show and the child sponsorship program, in contrast, are lines of flight.[48] Here one moment, each are gone the next. The child sponsorship program might overlap with an after-school program, which might then bleed into a community policing unit, which ultimately might dovetail with a back-to-work program run by a local church and sponsored (in part) by a multinational corporation. The program might also lead to absolutely nothing. While the experience of discipline is of being inside a building (or not), the phenomenology of Christian piety is of being a part of something (or not). For in postwar Guatemala, when it comes to soft security, there are no blueprints. There is no stability. Nothing is heavy. Everything is open, even the prison, the factory, and the asylum.

The life of Mateo makes this point. He starred in the reality television show detailed in Chapter 2. Soon after the show, by way of some contract work, he volunteered as a prison chaplain (Chapter 1), drawing on his own experience of incarceration in the United States, while also moonlighting with a child sponsorship program (Chapter 4). Alongside all of this, Mateo worked for call centers (Chapter 3), often trading his paychecks for weeklong benders that would sometimes land him in a Pentecostal rehabilitation center (Chapter 5) or a maximum security prison (Chapter 1). "I'm not perfect, Kev," Mateo would tell me. "No one is." This might be true, but Mateo is still alive, which is more than can be said for the thousands of other men who shuttled between prisons, call centers, and rehabilitation centers while some-

FIGURE 5. Grim reaper. Photo by Benjamin Fogarty-Valenzuela.

times coming into contact with back-to-work initiatives and sponsorship programs.

Mateo's longevity has a lot to do with his history. With the help of Christianity, he left his Los Angeles-based gang while in a U.S. prison. And so he returned to Guatemala with few complications. No one there expected him to join a gang nor was immediately offended that he had left one. "I never walked the streets in Guate," Mateo said, "so that helped me out—'cause those other people, you know, they're dead." His father also continued to work a steady job in the United States, sending support when he could. So there is a logic to his relatively long life. There is also a lesson. True to Christian piety, Mateo wants to be better. In his home, pinned to a wall, hangs a piece of paper. Picked up at a call center, or maybe a church, obviously crumpled up but then smoothed out, the flyer presents a constellation of words. They overlap: *sincere, confident, healthy, generous,* and *loyal.* There are others: *peaceful, secure, forgiven, ambitious,* and *righteous.* At least fifty more words fill the page. But at the top, in his own writing, Mateo scratched a note to himself. "Take 100% responsibility for your life," he writes, "No excuses. No blame. It is in you. Choose your feelings carefully. Connect with love. Be at peace. Act as if [you are at peace] and you will soon feel those vibrations." It is this sincerity, this ambition, especially this sense of having been forgiven, that makes Mateo such an intriguing figure. He strives. He falls. And Christian piety is one of his only tools to get back up again, making radiantly clear just how intimately linked the identification of a problem really is to the availability of a solution.[49]

Mateo's anger is also important. So too is the drinking and the drugs. They ground this book, upsetting any kind of narrative arc that could place Mateo on some kind of teleology, one with a clear before and an obvious after. Augustine's *Confessions* is good to think with; it casts a long shadow, especially over this book, but the bishop's story is pure fiction.[50] Mateo embodies Christian piety; he speaks with an Augustinian accent, but the ethnographic method upends normative questions of success and failure. Is Mateo actually pious? This is a terribly unhelpful question. More interesting, more honest to the life of Mateo as well as to the politics of soft security, is a different set of questions: What counts as piety? Under which conditions does piety emerge? And to what effect? When one asks these questions with an eye to soft security, it is obvious that Christian piety does a great deal. It provides the imperative to improve as well as the metrics to assess this improvement. This piety also helps to parse out who gets to live and who is allowed to die. The pious receive attention. The impious do not. For while the problematic of modern governance is often characterized as those processes by which authorities make live and let die, it is the impulse of Christian piety that structures this distinction.[51]

The effects are observable. Christian piety provides both the agents and the subjects of soft security with an embodied set of coordinates that answers some rather fundamental questions: Who is worthy of intervention (and who is not)? Who is open to the promise of piety (and who is not)? And who is in search of redemption (and who is not)? The answers to these questions set the conditions for life itself—for who gets to live (and who is allowed to die). Christian piety distinguishes between the ineligible and the eligible, the delinquent and the citizen, the lost and the found.

At the center of these distinctions, at the core of Christian piety, is a struggle between sin and salvation. This is why neither an absolutely perfect person nor a recklessly failed subject would be able to tell the embattled story of Christian piety in postwar Guatemala. They could not communicate the effects of soft security. Only an honestly ambivalent subject, a divided person, one torn by Christian piety's own extremes, could do justice to this confluence of piety and prevention in postwar Guatemala. That person is Mateo.

. . .

We sat at a table, in a roadside eatery. The traffic often drowned out our conversation. Mateo seemed nervous. I was too. "So the book would be about me?" he asked. I sat up in my chair. "No, not really," I explained. "Your story would sit between more formal chapters." I drew a table of contents on the back of a napkin. "The reader would read about you and then read about the prisons. Then he'd read more about you and then read about the reality television show. And so on." Mateo nodded. "But why?" he asked. I fumbled the answer. I mentioned something about chapters 1, 3, and 5 marking a self-conscious effort to rethink the postwar prison, factory, and asylum. They work differently today than they did in the past. "They're all so fluid," I said. As I spoke I redrew the table of contents, connecting these three chapters with arrows. I then added that chapters 2 and 4 would focus on bodily comportment and etiquette. "Like being polite and sitting up straight," I said, as I connected those two chapters with more lines. Mateo stared at me. "No, bro," he said, with waning patience. "Why me?" That was easier. I told him that his story connects the dots. "These five sites are going to seem pretty random," I explained, "but they are totally obvious to you. And to all the guys sent back from the States. These are the kinds of places and projects that engage you and that you engage." Mateo nodded.

Over the sound of traffic and the smell of diesel fume, I then wanted to add (though could not yet get my head around) the idea that these five chapters, when read alongside Mateo's life story, map the affective infrastructure of postwar security. The prisons are porous. The call center industry rose but will relocate (most likely to El Salvador). And the rehabs close and reopen at a surprising rate. The reality television show came and went while the child sponsorship program floats atop a fickle donor base. Prevention is impermanent, I wanted to explain. And yet underneath it all, structuring these institutions and imperatives, sits a Christian piety that empties the present and eviscerates the future. The book, I wanted to say, maps ethnographically this ever-morphing assemblage.

But I said none of this. I couldn't. I didn't know enough yet. Instead we both stared at my digital recorder until I went to turn it on. "You cool with this?" I asked. "Yeah," he shrugged. So I pressed the record button. And then he stopped me. "I wanna start with a prayer," he said. "Do it," I encouraged. Mateo then closed his eyes, bowed his head, and started to pray. "Father God," he whispered, "when I speak, I pray that it'll be you who gives me the words to speak and speak of my . . . of what I've been through, and what I've suffered, and what I'm doing now. And give me the exact words to say, so that people that's gonna be listening to me will be touched by your Holy Spirit, will be touched by your presence, will be touched by your grace and mercy. Thank you Lord for allowing me to see another day, and I pray for all of those that are gonna read this, that they will recognize that God is the only one. Amen." Amen.

Forgiveness

Mateo's father works a forklift in Arkansas. He has done it for years. When the paychecks added up, he bought a modest townhouse about thirty minutes south of Guatemala City. Made of quick but sturdy construction, repeated thousands of times across a now-sprawling metropolitan area, the house echoes in uncanny ways Los Angeles, California, in the 1950s. Southern California in that era found itself bulldozed into cul-de-sacs, with single-family, tract housing defining much of the San Fernando Valley. These massive developments, spurred by the GI Bill and stoked by industrial production, were manufactured with a kind of pre-urban nostalgia for open fields, though one articulated by white picket fences and manicured lawns. The racial overtones were obvious to most everyone. White flight, people called it.

A similar impulse hit Guatemala City a half-century later, with middle-class *capitalinos* seduced by the promise of a slightly different kind of pre-urban nostalgia. Again, the racial overtones were obvious to most everyone. Security, people call it. Guatemala City's congested city center, with its rising homicide rates, inspired landed families from economically average neighborhoods to look beyond the city limits. Hundreds of billboards helped them. Dotting almost every Guatemalan road, these signs are not subtle. They invoke the spirit of Los Angeles, for sure, with blue skies and green grass, but the images are grounded with razor wire, armed guards, and concrete fences. All of it fortifies well-dressed families against the perils of Guatemala City. "This could be you!" these advertisements promise.

These images caught the imagination of Mateo's father, who ultimately found it more appealing to buy a piece of the American Dream on the outskirts of Guatemala City than in the American South. He always considered Guatemala to be his real home. And Mateo is happy he does. The house is a blessing. Mateo watches over it, living there nearly free of charge, which helps when he is between jobs. While others in his situation have to hustle to keep a roof over their heads, this pied-à-terre lets Mateo take his time—to rebound from missed opportunities, to find the right job, to heal from old wounds. It even lets Mateo imagine from time to time that he still lives in California.

It is the third of July and Mateo is taking his time. Between jobs, with no real prospects on the horizon, we sit on a couch in his living room, with his front door ajar. The house is mostly empty, except for the couch and a television. A cool breeze sneaks in while some American-made gladiator movie dubbed into Spanish plays in the background. A teenager from the neighborhood sits on a chair in the corner, working through a fist-sized stash of weed. He is separating seed and stem from leaf. But there is no rush. Mateo has all day, which is how we got to talking about healing and forgiveness, about the power and the problem of leaving it all behind.

"Could you ever forgive—really forgive—your father?" I asked Mateo. His answer unfolded over the course of an afternoon, beginning and ending with stories from prison, weaving in and out of his own gladiatorial tales, and ending with sadness that he smoothed out with a joint.

"I was doing a six-year term in California when I called my dad." Mateo's right hand crept up his left arm, his fingers tracing the contours of a tattoo. "I was already going to church. I wasn't really into it, but I used to go just to get out of my cell. But from listening to the Word, I started feeling something in my heart. And I remember that I called my dad in Arkansas." The teenager, in the corner, mumbled something to himself. He was obviously pissed. "This is a pile of shit," he said. He was frustrated by how little leaf there actually was. But Mateo did not pay him any attention.

"And I remember my dad answered the phone," Mateo said. "I hadn't talked to him in years. Because I was really mad. I was still hurt, even though I was already grown up. I was always crying, but not in front of the homeboys. Because you were not allowed to cry in jail. They would give you a beat-down." I nodded, absolutely engaged but also slightly distracted by the movie. Cartoonishly muscular men swung swords at each other. "I remember I called him, and I forgave him." His fingers kept tracing the tattoo. "It was hard for me to call him, but I remember that God was molding my heart."

A scene from the movie then stole Mateo's attention. He had seen it before—we had both seen the movie before—but he loved this one part. In the arena, in front of a crowd, some gladiator plunges a sword into some other guy's chest. He then cuts the guy's head off. It is all done in slow motion, with music to match. The blood spurts. The head rolls. The gladiator then turns to the crowd—to the sovereign, really, if you follow the storyline—asking, "Are you not entertained?" He screams, "Are you not entertained? Is this not why you are here?" The violence, the victory, the showmanship, grabbed Mateo. It always grabbed Mateo. "Fuckin' bad ass," he said, lifting a finger toward the screen. "That's the way you fuckin' do it."

Our conversation rolled on. Mateo's focus returned. Picking up where he had left off, he explained, "There was a meeting every week. There was like a church service, and one day I went because the guy who came to talk was a homie. He was a Sureño and an ex–drug addict." Mateo sat up, obviously moved by the memory. "The homeboy was an ex-addict, a gang member from the streets. He did prison time. And he was big. I mean strong. And what was weird was that all the homies wanted to go. Everyone was like, 'Hey, wanna go to bible study? El Pastor is coming to preach.' That was his nickname. People called him El Pastor." The breeze pushed the front door open a bit more. A mother and her two children walked past. Mateo waved. The young woman waved back with a smile.

"This guy was different," explained Mateo. "He didn't talk like us. His words were different. He was all, 'What's up, brothers? God bless you, compadres. How are you, my brothers? How is everything?'" Mateo performed El Pastor in a lower register, pushing his chest out and his shoulders up. His entire body straightened. "But for real, he was different. He looked clean, bro. When he talked, I felt like it wasn't him. He talked, but it felt like he had the voice of a trumpet. I trembled when that guy talked, and something inside me . . ." Mateo leaned back. Caught in the memory, staring somewhere above the television, he said, "Something was restless. I wanted to get out."

"Out of where?" I asked.

"I don't know. I just started noticing shit, and his voice spoke to me. That's when I understood. I understood that when someone talks to you about God, you get restless." Mateo seemed startled by the memory. "I remember it made me feel bad. And I asked the Pastor why that was: 'Why do I feel so bad?'" Turning toward me, Mateo said, "You know what this guy tells me? He tells me, 'Because you have a lot of broken-ness.'" Mateo crumbled up his face in disbelief. "I was like, 'What? What you mean? What's that mean, dawg?' Then El Pastor says, 'You don't understand because you're still of the flesh. You haven't learned the lesson yet, and that's why you live the way you live.'" The teenager asked what he should do with the weed. "Just bag it, bro," Mateo said.

Mateo seemed disbelieving. Building a case for himself, ready to give witness, he said, "But look, dawg, in prison—it was scary in there. It wasn't like you could just walk around with a bible and shit. You could feel the spirit of death there. You felt the spirit of hate, of loneliness, of sadness—all those yokes, all those spirits, homie. It feels bad. It's dead in there! And everybody in there is fighting for their lives, defending their piece. And that's what's so hard." Insistent, almost exhausted, Mateo made his point: "You need to run with somebody, because if you're alone . . . If you do wrong, then your own people will reject you, and that's when you become a victim. If your people reject you, then everybody else is like, 'What's up, honey? We'll take care of you.'" Mateo evoked rape in falsetto. "I saw things like that. It's scary, homie. It's scary. It's real scary, dawg. So you just got to fight."

And fight he did. Maybe it was the movie or the prospect of getting high, or maybe it was to balance some kind of emotional ledger, the sensational counterbalancing his sentimentality, but Mateo then leaned into stories about prison fights. "What happened was, we went to chow time, right? It was dinnertime. So at dinnertime, we went into the big cafeteria, and I sat down at my table." Mateo hopped to his feet to act it out. "'Cause in the prison, tables are metal and the seats are made of metal, and the guards had it all programmed—like in every seat, at every table, you had to have a black, a Hispanic, a Colombian, or some-thing like that, right?" Mateo set an imaginary table. "But usually we tried to sit together. Our people, you know? Our gang. The blacks did too. And, look, there is always problems when you sit with a black or something like that. And that day I sat down. Another homie was there, and some other dude was there, and a black sat down here. And I had my tray in front of me, and the black moved my tray. The black dude moved my tray and that was disrespectful, you know?" Mateo looked at me, to make sure that I understood the infraction. "There are a lot of politics," he said, "and there are a lot of rules, and that's why there are a lot of riots. 'Cause you break a politic, you break one rule, and it gets all fucked up." Mateo put his hand to his head in sheer disbelief. "Homie, like fuck, dawg, that fool moved my tray." He pushed the story forward, "I tell him, 'What's up, dude? Wassup? Whatcha move my tray for? That's my tray, dawg.' He says something like, 'Well, 'cause.' And I says, 'What you mean, "'Cause"?' And I socked him. I hit him." Mateo acted this out, swinging in slow motion. "Pah," he blurted on imaginary contact with the guy's face.

"They took me to the hole. Two weeks of punishment. And then they took me back to my cell. After that the homies ask me, 'Whatcha gonna do?'" Mateo started to shake his head with a mix of shame and pride, with a smile that admitted what he did was wrong but also signaled that he would do it again. "We did him up, man. We jumped him. Me and another dude that I met in jail. We found this couch and there was metal there. On the bottom there was like wood, and there were screws sticking out of the wood, and with that, we hit that dude. We opened his head." Mateo used his own head as a map. "It opened here. And here. And we fucked him up here." Most of this guy's face seemed to have been torn apart. "They gave me six months for that. Half a year in solitary time. I didn't go outside at all. Half a year without sun, without anything. No breeze. Nobody, bro. Only the fuckin' crickets sang to me at night." "Are you not entertained?" the movie had asked. "Is this not why you are here?" Mateo seemed to echo.

Mateo settled down. He sat down, saying, "Kev, man, homie, it's like, I see myself here in Guatemala and I'm like, damn, I'm alive. I mean, I hurt people. They hurt me. I don't feel good about what I did. I'm not happy about it. But I also changed in prison. I changed a lot." The teenager dropped the bag of weed on the coffee table as Mateo's thoughts moved back in time. "I mean, when I met El Pastor, I remember saying to myself, 'Damn, homie! I wanna be like this dawg. I wanna have that power.' But bro, to be a Christian in jail? That was hard, man. But that dude never gave up on me. He says to me: 'If you don't straighten up, don't get right with God, you're headed for a life like these guys. A life in jail. Some of these guys are never getting out. They've left their kids and wives on the outside. Some leave and don't come back. Some are lost in the streets because of their addictions. What do you want, brother?'"

The question had stuck with Mateo. "'What exactly is it that you want?' That's what he asked me. 'You want to always live the way you're living now?' The way he talked to me . . . Oh holy fuck, I started to believe what he was saying, and I started feeling the Lord, homie. It's like, God was knocking at my door, for real." Mateo closed his eyes and slipped into a bit of a prayer, narrating what he felt God was telling him: "'Let me in, man. Let me in there. Let me be your father. Let me talk to you. Let me show what I got for you, man. Just like I love my son who's speaking through me, I also want to lift you up. I want to bless you, man. I want to clean your blood. I want to clean your blood, your spirit, your soul! I want to heal you, man.'"

Mateo pressed on his chest, digging his fingers into his heart. "I was scared," Mateo confessed. "I was confused, but at the same time, I wanted it. And so it happened. I started going to church in there, dawg. In prison, homie. But I still kicked it with the homies and shit—all the homies. I was always with the homies. But those homies said to me, 'Hey dawg, hey man, it's good. Do it right. Do it right. It's good what you're doing. It's good, because we all have an ugly past, and some of us still do.' Some were already veterans, and with them at the table, the guys gave me that kind of encouragement. 'You're still young. Don't get comfortable,' they told me. 'You've been institutionalized, homie. You have to break that chain,' the brothers told me." Mateo fingered the weed through the bag, rolling the leaves as if lost in meditation.

"All of it, bro, got me involved with God and the Bible and the church. It let me forgive my father. It was real powerful, man. Like I said, we were on the phone. And he started crying on the phone. And I asked my dad this question: 'Dad, why did you treat me like that? Why did you beat me up like that? I want to understand your discipline . . . because your discipline was out of bounds. You got me like a grown-up; you beat me up like I was a grown-up, like I was your enemy. I was only a child. I never enjoyed a young life. I never had what the other little kids had: a toy, or a hug, or a kiss from you. You used to send me to bed bruised up without supper, or without lunch.'"

Mateo pressed his fist to his cheek, as if speaking into a phone, leaning forward toward me, as if I was in on the call with him. "And he asked me this: 'Son,' he asked me, 'forgive me. I dunno why I did it.' And he broke down crying on the other side of the phone. And I was gonna cry, but I remember the cop was looking at me, you know, you kinda . . . you shy when someone . . . you know. And I stayed quiet, Kevin. I was like, 'You know what—it's hard for me to do this, Dad—but forgive me. Forgive me if I did something wrong.' And he answered, 'No, you didn't do nothing wrong. It was me. I wanna ask you to forgive me.' 'I forgive you, I forgive you, Dad.' And I remember, when I went to my cell block 'cause my time was up on the phone, I started crying, Kevin. I couldn't hold no more the tears. I cried. I cried, I cried . . . I cried like a baby. And I know now, knowing the Lord, that God was touching my heart at that moment. That God was cleaning out my heart. That I was taking out those roots, and those bad memories."

The question remained that day, but also years after, whether those roots, those bad memories, could ever really be removed. The townhouse, surrounded by other townhouses, reminded Mateo, when mixed with weed, of California—of South Central Los Angeles. And although the weed was bunk, it jogged his memories enough to confuse the issue—to lock Mateo perpetually between past and present without really invoking the future. With the gladiator movie long over and the sun setting, with Mateo's right hand once again tracing the contours of a tattoo on his left shoulder, he reached for some papers to roll another joint. "I mean, when I met El Pastor," Mateo waxed one last time, "I remember saying to myself, 'Damn, homie, I wanna be like this dawg. I wanna have that power.'" Mateo then winced, "But I'm still of the flesh. I haven't learned the lesson yet."

Mateo looked down at the bag of weed, sighing, "This *is* a pile of shit."

CHAPTER I

Insecurities

The phone call was rushed, near frantic. From inside Boqueron, one of Guatemala's maximum security prisons, a known gang leader pleaded with Pastor Morales via cell phone to do something: contact the press, notify a human rights office, intervene. A member of Mara Salvatrucha (MS-13), Gustavo explained to Pastor Morales that he was being transferred to Pavoncito, a notoriously insecure prison that houses members of the Paisas. The Paisas are an association of prisoners that controls much of the Guatemalan prison system. Many are former soldiers, with extensive combat experience in some of Central America's longest and bloodiest civil wars. From behind bars, they smuggle drugs, participate in human trafficking, and run prison systems, all while state officials offer failed responses. "The Paisas are becoming a criminal organization," conceded one police officer, "maybe even taking orders from outside the country."[1] More immediately relevant to Gustavo's phone call, however, is that the Paisas and MS-13 are enemies. They compete for turf, for contracts, for respect. Pastor Morales, a minister and part-time prison chaplain, immediately understood the stakes of Gustavo's transfer. As many would comment later, such a move from one prison population to another "*es igual a la pena de muerte.*" It is the same as a death sentence.

Although Pastor Morales called anyone who would listen, bringing both a municipal judge and Gustavo's mother to the prison gates, Gustavo entered Pavoncito shortly before 4:00 A.M. with four other members of MS-13. Prison officials placed these five men into a "secure" cell for their own protection, but their presence within the general prison population sparked a riot that culminated around 6:30 A.M. At this early hour, a mob of prisoners broke into Gustavo's cell, ripping the door off its hinges. They then dragged him and his fellow gang members into the prison yard and decapitated them, one by one.[2] With night turning to day, with sunlight revealing what only darkness could permit, Gustavo's head sat on a pike while the prisoners set his body on fire. "Kill the dog, kill the rabies," members of the Paisas chanted. One even hoisted a decapitated head above his own. "Cholo enters, cholo dies," they screamed.[3]

Only days after images of Gustavo's severed head circled the World Wide Web, the director of Guatemala's central morgue reflected aloud to me during an interview, "It's not like scissors cutting through paper, you know. Decapitation is tedious work (*trabajo tedioso*), a kind of sweaty (*laborioso*) work." For effect, the director ran his fingers across his own cervical vertebrae, demonstrating the physicality of it all. He sighed. Overwhelmed and overworked, haunted by a mercilessly dark job in a ruthlessly violent country, he adjusted his glasses, adding, "It's actually quite difficult to match the right head to the right body." With each body having been burned almost beyond recognition, with their heads kicked across the prison yard like soccer balls, it took all of the morgue's expertise to piece these bodies back together. "You need to study the articulations of each cut. You need to make sure that the cuts from the head match the cuts from the neck." The director seemed to stare past me.

In contrast to such a clinical appraisal, Pastor Morales focused not on Gustavo's broken body but on his soul. He mourned Gustavo as an unfinished work, because he knew "what an incredible thing was happening in Gustavo's heart." With the cadence of a eulogy, Pastor Morales explained: "On the outside he was incredibly intimidating, with scars from stab wounds and bullets. On the inside, I came to love Gustavo, who became my friend. In private, away from the piercing eyes of his other homies, it was easy to note his softening heart. During a bible study, Gustavo turned to me to whisper, 'It's great to feel such a deep presence of the Lord here with the homies today.'" Amid such rabid insecurity, with heads ripped from bodies and bodies burnt to ash, Pastor Morales's grief remained trained on Gustavo's heart, his softening inner world, his ability, in the words of Gustavo, to *feel* the Lord's presence *deeply*.

The distance between these two responses, between the morgue director's morbid despair and the pastor's ministerial disquiet, deserves

FIGURE 6. Prisoner transport vehicle, Pavoncito. Photo by Benjamin Fogarty-
Valenzuela.

attention. For it accentuates the Christian production and the consequences of postwar insecurity. In this bloodied context, with a prison
system swollen to past 250 percent capacity, postwar insecurity carries
a double valence—not only for prisoners and their chaplains but also
for liberal, democratic, and ostensibly secular security officials.[4] The
first meaning relates directly to gang violence. MS-13 and others render
the postwar prison insecure.[5] "These prisons," warned Pastor Morales,
"are out of control. The guards aren't in charge. The prisoners are." The
second meaning, related to the first, is more of an affect than an effect.
Insecurity, in this sense, is the feeling of rejection and isolation, of anxiety and hostility.[6] "Gustavo texted me when he was being transferred,"
Pastoral Morales remembered, vibrating with emotion, "he texted me
that they were going to kill him. That he was a dead man."

Pastoral Morales and his colleagues in Christ routinely connect these
two meanings of insecurity by reading the first as a result of the second,
by understanding a failed sense of self as directly responsible for a nearly
failed prison system. Correcting this consciousness and, in turn, this correctional system has become the work of Christ. "I texted back Gustavo
some scripture," Pastor Morales added. "It was a few lines that came to
my heart, that I wanted to share with him at such a terrible moment."
For in the shadows of prison riots and public decapitations, of wailing

women waiting at prison gates, the practice of prison chaplaincy announces with a bold kind of clarity that society must be defended— one sense of security at a time. This means suturing the soul to the social. And in doing so, the pious production of postwar insecurity shuttles between Gustavo's severed head and his softening heart, between the materiality of prisons and the morality of Pentecostalism, emphasizing pastoral interventions but ending, as did Gustavo, in pieces. Insecurity defines the postwar prison, and Christian men like Morales make it so. How, this chapter asks, and to what effect? The answer begins and ends with one particular manifestation of Christian piety: self-esteem.

SELF-ESTEEM

The wall was cool to the touch. Pressing my palm against its uneven surface, absorbing a bit of the mid-morning chill, I stopped to consider, to really meditate on, Gustavo's last hours. I was in Pavoncito with Pastor Allende, a Pentecostal prison chaplain who works separately from Pastor Morales. In the middle of rounds, we found ourselves in a part of the prison called Alaska, named for its isolation. This is where Gustavo and his fellow members of MS-13 had waited for death, most likely pacing the length of their six-foot-by-six-foot cell as a mob approached. None of them would have seen anything. The cells have no exterior windows. But they would have heard the Paisas approaching, with their screams and their taunts. At the far end of a long corridor, on the only floor of this one-story structure, dozens of Paisas rushed their door. At the same time, dozens more pounded a sledgehammer to the cell's exterior wall. What must Gustavo have felt, I thought to myself, with each thud of the hammer, with each tug on his cell door? Prisoners later put the number of Paisas involved as high as sixty. To this day, a sloppy repair with a rushed paint job marks the headway that this mob made. A human-sized hole aligns exactly with the cell. No one can confirm whether the mob dragged these five men through the wall, out the hole, or whether they pulled each of them through their cell door. The only real evidence of the event was the two Paisas that Gustavo and his comrades killed during the struggle. Their bodies left Pavoncito with Gustavo's later that same day, as did photos. Stumps of charred flesh, a basket of severed heads, each facing a different direction, and a stripped corpse with a broom handle plugging the anus.

With my hand still pressed against the wall, at the very spot where the Paisas had swung their hammer, I asked Pastor Allende why the wall was still broken. He mumbled back something about everyone inside of this prison being broken, being in need of repair. "And you know what?" he added. "The prison of the heart is worse than the prison of Pavoncito. And so I go inside this prison, inside all prisons, to open the gates but also to open minds and to transform people." This impromptu sermon, one of hundreds I would absorb over the years, reminded me that Gustavo's beheading was not merely gratuitous assault. It was conducted in a context of certain soteriologies of self.

By "soteriologies of self" I mean simply the ethnographic fact that the loudest, most observable, most pious Christian therapy employed by chaplains within the prison context is self-esteem. The Christian promotion of self-esteem saturates the prison system where Gustavo died; the practice of esteeming the self guides much of what prison chaplains do and say. The idea and promise of self-esteem provide both the pastors and the prisoners with a set of moral coordinates for who they are and, more importantly, what kind of people they want to become. In contrast to other available approaches to reform, it is self-esteem that stars in these Christian settings wherein the incarcerated might choose Jesus Christ over MS-13, leading one of Guatemala's more experienced prison chaplains to announce, in seemingly uncomplicated ways, "The greatest need here is to continue working with gangs, but we also need to support human development (*fortalecer la formación humana*) in order to recover self-esteem. We need more psychologists than educators here in Guatemala." By way of Christian authorities but within monuments to modern imaginations, prison chaplains work to esteem the self in the name of security.

"To raise your self-esteem," yet another prison chaplain had explained during an earlier set of rounds, "is to create a shield against bloodthirsty enemies." I remembered this musing as I leaned against the ruins of Pavoncito, at the very site of Gustavo's murder. Its promise rang hollow, at least to me. A shield? I thought. The sledgehammer must have sounded like war drums to Gustavo, a veritable death march. Yet, Christian support groups, moral manuals, testimonials, and bibliotherapy (the practice of narrating one's broken self to oneself) work to equip incarcerated gang members with the tools necessary to patrol their inner worlds, to esteem their selves, to recognize the moments when they *feel* the Lord's presence *deeply*.[7]

THE PRISON

To appreciate the practice of self-esteem, one must first assess the prison, if only to dislodge self-esteem from its bourgeois North American roots, from middle-class concerns over weight loss and social anxiety, from a largely gendered interest in a certain personal fulfillment and achievement.[8] Guatemalan prisons, for one, are not total institutions or supermax structures but rather warehouses of violence.[9] Prison cells designed to house four individuals at a time hold up to eighteen, for sentences that stretch more than 30, 40, and even 50 years. What may first appear as holding cells, dark spaces in which prisoners linger a day or two before prison personnel find more appropriate accommodations, are in fact where active gang members live until their release or, just as likely, their death. In the overcrowded cells, their walls slick with phlegm, constant noise meets a stunning lack of natural light to form a haunting echo chamber. And while the prison tower, which the philosopher Jeremy Bentham dubbed the panopticon, continues to resonate as a metaphor for power's entangled relationship with knowledge, it is painfully obvious that no one is really watching—and the prisoners know that they have been left alone. Prisoners do not decapitate fellow prisoners because of just a brief lack of oversight. Guards never enter the cell blocks that house active gang members, and the incarcerated take advantage of perforated boundaries to traffic a steady flow of drugs, cell phones, and sex workers. In many ways, this is how and why prison chaplains, men and women of faith who range from apocalyptic neo-Pentecostals to mainline Charismatic Christians, have become such a valued political resource. With no one else watching, these pastors pray that active gang members, through the saving grace of Jesus Christ, can become capable of watching themselves.[10]

This effort is audacious, even if it is familiar to the history of American prisons. These institutions have always had a certain religious, even monastic, quality to them. The very language of prison reform is littered with religious imagery: the cell, the penitentiary, the reformatory.[11] In the North American context, learned men of faith guided the construction of the modern prison in the early nineteenth century, developing undeniably Christian efforts at moral improvement. The Quakers, who authored Philadelphia's Walnut Street Prison, argued that exclusive contact with moral administrators could straighten crooked souls. Here, the iconic drawing of the kneeling prisoner, the very one that illustrates Michel Foucault's discussion of Jeremy Bentham's panopticon in *Discipline and Punish*, captures solitary confinement's Christian dimensions. At the same time, Calvinism inspired New York's Auburn Prison, which structured moral reform around congregate labor during the day and solitary confinement at night. This "method of discipline" consisted of "downcast eyes, lockstep marching, absolute silence, supervised work, [and] an unsparing use of the whip."[12] Asylums had to be built nearby for those prisoners driven mad by the prison's "eerie silence."[13] Yet sometimes the asylum also proved too little, too late. Prisoners often escaped—life, not judgment: "That prisoners in perpetual solitary confinement often hanged themselves or battered themselves to death," notes one critic, "was attributed to insanity induced by masturbation."[14] Prisons often pushed prisoners beyond their limits.

Auburn Prison and Walnut Street Prison are important not simply as monuments to a Christian logic or as examples of the observation made elsewhere that architecture is a moral science, but because these penitentiaries served as the preeminent models for prison reform in Latin America.[15] The Walnut Street Prison and the Auburn Prison laid the foundation for the prisons that Alexis de Tocqueville and Gustave de Beaumont visited in antebellum America, the kind of prison that, in the words of Tocqueville, "does not break men's will, but softens, bends, and guides it. It seldom enjoins, but often inhibits, action; it does not destroy anything, but prevents much from being born; it is not at all tyrannical, but it hinders, restrains, stifles, and stultifies."[16] This French delegation, the archive tells us, were not the only foreign visitors. Tocqueville and Beaumont stood shoulder to shoulder with Latin American delegations eager to add prison reform to their liberalization to-do list. For over a century, an array of Latin American countries, from Brazil to Cuba, re-created North American prisons brick by brick— with blueprints purchased from afar, architects brought by boat, and the promise of progress standing guard in the watchtowers that they constructed.[17]

This effort at reform proved uneven. Underfunded and overcrowded, with a history of slavery and debt peonage informing the effort, these correctional facilities melted into something far more brutal. Modern prisons became colonial whipping posts. And while authoritarian regimes throughout Latin America eventually co-opted these structures in the twentieth century for torture rather than moral reform—for punishment instead of discipline—the jails themselves still hint, architecturally speaking, at a Jacksonian notion that curing criminals means "inculcating in them healthy habits."[18] This is one reason why constructing Bentham's panopticon within the criminal's soul can seem so very intuitive for contemporary prison chaplains in Guatemala, and why the psycho-theological promise of self-esteem can appear so logical—even when the prison itself has become a never-ending crime scene.

RIOTS

"The Paisas were able to basically take over Pavoncito," Pastor Morales remembered. We sat side by side in his car, cruising the capital city en route to Pavoncito. Visceral memories cascaded, wrought by disbelief. "It turned to utter chaos. It was on the radio, the news station—we turned the radio on—you could hear screaming, yelling, and chaos and riots and sirens. They were playing it live over the radio." Raw emotions pushed the narrative as traffic seemed to both stand still and whirl past us. "It was really early in the morning," he remembered. "On the day of the killings, after their transfer, a couple of hours went by and then things got bad. When the guards changed their shift, the Paisas attacked the section where the MS-13 guys were." Pastor Morales trailed off. Sipping some coffee while collecting his thoughts, he let the city and its half-made streets distract us. He needed a moment. For the riot and its effects were unthinkable and yet totally predictable. These prisons have been battlegrounds for years.

A little more than five years before Gustavo's murder, prisoners had seized control of Pavoncito. They had run the prison since 1996, with the police and military securing only its perimeter. But on December 24, 2002, Pavoncito jumped the rails. On that day, seventeen prisoners ended up dead and some thirty more were injured as inmates struggled over prison territory and limited resources. Independent reports stated clearly that many of the recovered bodies had been burned and mutilated. One inmate had even been decapitated, the head quickly coveted by the offenders as some kind of trophy.[19] And amid the melee, prisoners demanded better living conditions while the Guatemalan military lobbed cans of tear gas from just outside the prison gates.

A survivor of this particular riot recounted to me years later how he had stayed alive by keeping his head down, minding his own business, even when he stumbled into a part of the prison where men were cutting other men into pieces. Born in Guatemala but raised in Los Angeles before being deported "home" and then arrested by the Guatemalan National Police on trumped-up charges, he experienced the stark distance between prisons in the United States and Guatemala. "That place really got wild," he shook. "You wanna get wild, then let's get wild," he conceded, "but these guys started killin' each other, cuttin' up each other, and tryin' to stuff the pieces down the drain."

The government responded, years later, by raiding Pavoncito with thousands of Guatemalan security forces. It was a spectacular event.

Army helicopters flew overhead and armored cars waited at the prison gates while masked soldiers imposed a local state of emergency. Local news stations witnessed it all. The government had invited them. Inside the prison, police seized hundreds of firearms while the director of Guatemala's prison system, Alejandro Giammattei, green-lighted the execution of seven imprisoned gang members. Without judicial oversight, perceiving himself beyond the reach of public scrutiny, Giammattei had some of the most influential gang leaders murdered in the middle of a police action.[20] Justice served.

Each of these actions, and their corresponding prison riot, anticipated Gustavo's fate. There had always been a tit for tat, a tug of war, over prison space—with prisoners battling the police every step of the way. And so while Gustavo was being transferred from Boqueron to Pavoncito, steadfastly texting his pastor along the way, no one was surprised to learn that Boqueron was burning. "To this day in Boqueron," Pastor Morales whispered as we waited at a red light, "the crossbeams are bent because of the fire." When the prison guards entered Boqueron to transfer Gustavo and his fellow MS-13 members to Pavoncito, they took the prison by force, opening Pandora's box. For parts of Boqueron's prison yard, which is like a courtyard, are capped with a grate. Walls on all sides, bars on top, the metal cuts the sun while allowing armed guards to patrol on top of the prison population. The entire structure makes the prisoners feel (because they literally are) underfoot. Looking up, straight up, all one sees is the sun, the striated sky, and the bottom of boots. "The grate contains the guys," explained one guard.

Not too long before the Pavoncito riot, the one that started with Gustavo's murder, four police officers, being held in Boqueron in connection with the killing of three Salvadoran congressmen, were shot dead.[21] No one saw a thing, the story goes. But, of course, the prisoners knew it all. "That's where they died," one of the prisoners told me. "Right over there," he pointed. I stood in Boqueron, in a dark, windowless hallway, damp with mold. Pastor Morales stood next to me. There, prisoners had executed these four police officers. The chaplain prayed. The murder of these policemen had sparked a twelve-hour prison riot, with some three hundred national police officers and soldiers waiting outside for things to quiet down.[22] "The grate keeps a lid on things," the guard had insisted.

And so on the morning of Gustavo's transfer, long before any of the prisoners were awake, armed guards raided Boqueron. They quickly took the five men for transfer, but then they sent a message. "The guards went on a rampage," Pastor Morales explained, his hands on the steering wheel, eyes on the road. "They just beat these guys down. They put their mattresses in the middle of the main prison and piled all their clothes on top and just set it all on fire." The heat of it all warped the grate as well as any sense of justice. "They were limping," Pastor Morales remembered. "These guys were in boxer shorts or towels. Some of them were naked. A lot of them had nothing but bath towels wrapped around their waists. I have never seen—it was like a war zone inside Boqueron prison."

The reason for the raid hinged on Gustavo's suspected involvement with the police murders. "We talked about it," Pastor Morales admitted, "directly with Gustavo. And there was . . . he didn't deny it or . . . but you could tell it was a different part of his life." Pastor Morales tried to reason through Gustavo's compartmentalizing his emerging Christianity from these killings. It was a different (meaning parallel, rather than past) part of his life. The distinction proved too tedious to explain. Pastor Morales stammered on, "Regardless, he was a marked man because he was the one who had done the killing of those guys there." And so violence begat violence.

Late into the night, soon after the Pavoncito riot had ended and the bodies had been removed, Pastor Morales ministered to the prisoners of Boqueron. "I have to thank you for supporting us," a member of MS-13 told Pastor Morales. The prisoner was shaking with emotion. His voice wobbled. He waited for a moment, eventually explaining to the pastor: "I don't know what else to do except kill. We are going to start killing cops. What else are we going to do? We are going to start killing cops in the street." The prisoners were furious. "Listen," Pastor Morales reasoned, "you got to do what you got to do. I can't tell you what to do. But I want you to know that if you do that, if you start killing police officers, that is exactly what everyone is hoping and praying you will do." Pastor Morales let this point sit—for spectacular moments of gang violence ultimately legitimate equally spectacular moments of state violence. States of exception have become the rule in postwar Guatemala.[23] "The government will sacrifice a bunch of police officers in a second," Pastor Morales reasoned aloud, "to have the license to kill all you guys. They would love it. You go kill police officers: then you're cop killers in a concrete way. They can do anything they want and not have any repercussions at all."

Pastor Morales then shifted into a more explicitly Christian register. "Vengeance is mine, sayeth the Lord," he quoted from Psalms.[24] In near darkness, with ash under their feet and warped metal over their heads, the men naked and bruised, they talked scripture. "The bible study wasn't planned," Pastor Morales later insisted. "It just became a conversation between me and some of the core leaders of MS-13. It got us all thinking and talking, about playing into the hands of the police." Through an intimate exchange between prison chaplain and active gang members, in the immediate aftermath of extraordinary violence, decisions had been formed. "A big part of it," Pastor Morales remembered, pulling the car to a full stop, parking both the vehicle and his memory, "was to say if God is who he really is, then those police got what's coming to them far worse than you could ever give. If 'vengeance is mine, sayeth the Lord,' then you don't need to do God's job for him." Tempers seemed to soften. Rage seemed to subside. "These guys from MS-13 literally told me that day, 'We are going to pull the plug. We are not going to kill police officers.' They decided they weren't going to play into the hands of the government."

Pastor Morales considered his counsel a victory but the death of Gustavo a total defeat. "What a loss," he sighed. "Here is a guy who is on the verge of causing major transformation. If the officials had ever done anything to find out what was actually going on in the prison, that Gustavo was on the verge of a major transformation . . ." Pastor Morales trailed off, pulling the keys from the ignition. "They killed the one guy with the potential to change. They killed the guy in whom that transformation really had begun to occur." Gustavo's individual change could have inspired others. But how?

TAXED

"The prison system won't change them," admitted Pastor Morales with a sigh. Standing outside the gates of Pavoncito, with one hand propped against a chain link fence, he added, "Most of these guys, if they don't change their hearts, they are going to go outside and commit the same thing. I see that in so many of them. They go out, and thirty days later they are back again." Pastor Morales leaned against the fence, shielding his eyes from the sun with a raised arm. "That's why we are here. We can teach them. We can tell them that they can have a better life. That they can be better people. And can walk with them. We can be a companion to them." Because no one else will. "The government doesn't do anything." Pastor Morales nodded at the guards, laying blame at their feet. "They don't bring any therapies inside this prison. They don't help to restore lives. The government doesn't believe in rehabilitation. They

FIGURE 7. Pavón. Photo by Benjamin Fogarty-Valenzuela.

say these guys are animals; they are maniacs; they are not human. The government doesn't want to spend money on these guys. And that's why Jesus is the only answer. Jesus is the only way to restore these guys." A guard tower loomed above us. Others punctuated the horizon. Each was obviously empty.

Pastor Morales was at least half right. Maximum security prisons in Guatemala do not offer prisoners access to therapists, psychiatrists, life coaches, social workers, teachers, medical doctors, or psychologists. The only moral technician available to the prisoner—the only available agent of change—is the prison chaplain.[25] Pastor Morales and his colleagues, in these settings, have a monopoly on morality, making Christianity the vernacular through which gangs like MS-13 get to be questioned, analyzed, classified, and regulated at specific times and under specific circumstances.[26] Alone before God, so to speak, these prison chaplains struggle to turn active gang members into self-governing subjects—into men who can step back, take a deep breath, and decide not to kill police. But this ability to govern the self, depends on recognizing oneself as insecure, in desperate need of intervention.

The internalization of this insecurity takes place at the everyday level of prison chaplaincy, which Pastor Morales pursues alongside dozens of other committed men of faith.[27] It is a kind of pastoral care that invites the active gang member not just to know thyself but also to secure thyself—"to detach from the self, establish it as an object, and reflect on it as a problem."[28] The emphasis on Christian inwardness has stuck (and continues to stick) in part because of an underfunded postwar government, several U.S. administrations attracted to faith-based initiatives, and North American churches flush with goodwill. Also aided by a growing financial commitment from international aid agencies, prison chaplaincy, with its confessional logic and Christian technologies of self-governance, constitutes active gang members as subjects of self-esteem.

The work is real. Amid thick plumes of weed and reggaeton's thumping bass, punctuated by phone calls received on black market cellulars and propositions made by sex workers, prison chaplains sit with incarcerated gang members made blue with ink, with 18s and 13s tattooed across their faces. In the yard, in their cells, while on walks, these chaplains engage active gang members. Spiritual direction, bible study, and fellowship—"all of this is to lift up their self-esteem," explains one chaplain. "It is not a simple process. It is a long process, really, but that's why we are working with these guys. That's why we keep telling them they can do it, that they can change. We'll do it until one day they have their freedom. Free from the prison but also free from themselves." Pastor Morales works hard to deliver this freedom—not only to each active gang member but also to postwar Guatemala. In the prison, through a purple haze of sorts, Pastor Morales poses the big missionary problems: "Who am I (¿Quién soy?)?" "Why am I the person that I am (¿Por qué soy como soy?)?" He riffs on biblical stories like the parable in which Jesus befriends tax collectors (Luke 18:9–14). Pastor Morales guides the incarcerated, seated in a circle on moldy mattresses or plastic chairs, to understand that Jesus ate with tax collectors (Mark 2:16), that he offered them salvation (Luke 19:9), and that he even chose a tax collector to be one of his twelve disciples (Matthew 9:9).

"During one bible study," Pastor Morales remembered, "we looked at Matthew, the tax collector. Gustavo was there, and we were talking about how Matthew was a thief. He was collecting taxes but taking all the money for himself. He was extorting people." It is a story that resonates with many of these prisoners. It resonated with Gustavo, for impuestos, or self-styled taxes, constitute MS-13's greatest source of income. Bus drivers, shopkeepers, even homeowners routinely pay considerable sums of money to MS-13 for protection. Some parents even pay what is called a "rape tax" so that their daughters are not violated. The incarcerated often manage these extortion efforts from jail by way of black market cell phones, flexing their own brand of punishment while they themselves become subject to new technologies of discipline. Amid this context Pastor Morales routinely shifts the conversation toward something more reflective. "And this is the point," Pastor Morales insisted, "because this is what Christ did for me. He shared his life with me. He not only said, 'I love you,' but he proved it by dying for me on the cross. We need to give hope to these prisoners, to these gang members. We need to ask the big questions. And more importantly we need to get *them* to ask the big questions. 'Am I a real follower of Jesus Christ?' This is the question that they need to ask themselves." This question, posed to oneself, problematizes the self. It makes the self not simply a topic of debate but also a site of intervention.

The question stirred Gustavo. "I asked the guys," Pastor Morales remembered, "'Who are today's Matthews in Guatemala? Who extorts money from people? Who's taking everyone's money?' And of course they all started laughing. Gustavo and the other key guys had these big smiles on their faces about who that meant." Pastor Morales then read aloud: "As Jesus went on from there, he saw a man named Matthew sitting at the tax collector's booth. 'Follow me,' he told him, and Matthew got up and followed him" (Matthew 9:9). In the circle, with intimacy mounting, Morales let the verse sit. Then he quoted another: "Those who are well have no need of a physician, but those who are sick [do]" (Matthew 9:12). "I asked them if any were offended that people think of them as sick. And they were not. Because my question created an opening. It created an incredible conversation. It turned the tables. They weren't seeking Jesus's approval. Jesus was seeking their approval. Suddenly each of them had a decision to make."

Turning the tables, as a strategy, sits at the center of prison chaplaincy. Questions, not answers—this is the focus. Problems, not solutions— this is the intent. Each constructs gang membership into something that can be discussed, questioned, and considered through Christian idiom and salvific affect. Pastor Morales continued, "You don't see Matthew in church after he joins Jesus. You see Jesus in Matthew's house. Jesus went to Matthew; Matthew didn't go to Jesus. So the idea is—the idea that we talked about is that maybe Jesus wasn't interested in getting Matthew to join him. Maybe Jesus was more interested in connecting with Matthew and becoming a part of Matthew's gang." An abstract narrative became a concrete problem. Morales then guided these prisoners through some of its implications. Would Jesus eat with members of MS-13? Would he offer a member of MS-13 salvation? And would Jesus ever consider a member of MS-13 to be one of his most trusted disciples? The questions peaked. Pastor Morales asked, "Would you allow Jesus to join MS-13?" Through this question, Pastor Morales tried to shift these gang members' allegiance from MS-13 to Jesus Christ. It is a question that ultimately prompted Gustavo to turn toward Pastor Morales, to whisper in his ear words that will stay with this minister for a lifetime: "It's great to feel such a deep presence of the Lord here with the homies today."

Months after the riot, Gustavo long dead, Pastor Morales winced yet again at the memory: "Here was the potential for some major transformation. One of the key leaders of MS-13 was beginning to change. He wasn't the number one leader but he was in the top five and he was clearly changing. He had the potential. He had the desire for transformation in the gang." He could have changed himself, his gang, and maybe even the prison.

WEARY

This effort at change takes place through a relatively sleek logic that pivots on original sin as a theological fact and the promise of self-esteem as a modern-day manifestation of grace. Largely authored by Pentecostal and Charismatic pastors in Southern California and Colorado Springs but repeated by prison chaplains in Guatemala, theological therapy goes something like this: Men and women join gangs because they have low self-esteem.[29] Active members lean on gangs to provide the kind of emotional support that they never received from parents, and they have thus fallen into a delinquent lifestyle while in search of acceptance. Weary, tired, with a deflated sense of self, young men and women use these gangs to prop up their selves. Their criminal activity and excessive tattoos evidence an inward struggle between sin and salvation. Prison chaplains, in response to a narrative that they themselves propagate, further suggest that gang members will always be half-made—that sin has always strained the human condition—but that Jesus Christ, not MS-13, should buttress every person.

Pastor Allende narrates this now-familiar logic:

> Their self-esteem, practically speaking, needs to be raised up, and this is what I try to do through my ministry. From the moment I begin to work with them, I begin to instill in them [the idea] that they are important and that they can become valued members of society. In my own case, I was really mistreated when I was 7 or 8 years old. I was always told that I wasn't worth

anything (*inútil*) and that I was stupid (*torpe*). People said stuff like that to me, and those words were just growing in me. And so when I was growing up, I thought that I was worthless and this is why I turned to drugs and alcohol. This is why my self-esteem was so low.

Pastor Allende then performs the very change that he advocates:

> Then, when I came to know our Lord Jesus Christ, I got this new idea that each one of us is really valuable. This made me feel like I had more value myself, and my self-esteem began to increase little by little. So much so that I began to think, "I can (*yo puedo*). I can. I am valuable. I can. I can be a person who doesn't need to rob others and do stuff like that. I can work. I can do something with my life."

Pastor's Allende's narrative glosses the self-esteem manuals that prison chaplains commonly use, manuals that announce: "When people possess high levels of self-esteem, they are able to overcome problems easily. . . . But to improve our self-esteem, it is important to complete a detailed analysis of what we want to change about ourselves, taking into account those aspects that are susceptible to change." As part of his ministry, Pastor Allende guides the incarcerated through spiritual exercises that allow them to assess their esteem—to map the parts of their selves that need work, which might include, as per the manual, the "inability to dream," "anxiety over the future," and the tendency to "idealize other people."[30] "Address your weaknesses," suggests one exercise. For "they imprison us," the text explains. "So find the perfect motivation for changing these aspects in your life and don't expect a sudden miracle. Your habits will not change overnight. But rejoice when you make a tiny progressive change." Action is the impetus. "Deal with low self-esteem today," the manual insists, enumerating a series of action items: "(1) Sit down and examine yourself. (2) Make a list of strengths. (3) List your goals and be sure to create milestones going there. (4) Break down each goal in stages. (5) Maintain optimism. Plan carefully and be firm in what you want to achieve. (6) Make a time frame of what you hope to achieve in a specific period of time. (7) Think about how people could help in reaching or achieving your goals." Faith in Christ guides this introspection, and Jesus provides the stimulus. So too does prayer.

On one occasion, while walking the grounds of Pavoncito, Pastor Allende entered Alaska. Still a site for solitary confinement, he kneeled in front of a locked prison cell. Lowering his head, folding his hands, he prayed for the prisoners. Although he was unannounced and lost in prayer, silent in most every way, the jailed prisoners eventually spotted

Pastor Allende. Confusion met contempt as they began to heckle him. "Are you fucking kidding me?" one huffed. "Leave!" another shouted. Pastor Allende did not budge. Inches from the cell door, he aimed his efforts into an otherwise unlit room, as the prisoners stirred. Pastor Allende would later explain, "I am trying to change them because their gang tattoos can't be erased and their attitudes are really negative, but they can change their thoughts. It's just that it takes a specific kind of spiritual work to change their thoughts and to change their attitude." As Pastor Allende weathered the taunts in the name of Christ, eventually dusting himself off while blessing the men, a prisoner muttered again, "Get the fuck out of here." Walking out of the prison, with sneers at his heels, he declared, "They need to change but they don't think they can. It's their mentality. It's the mentality of people like those guys that keeps them from changing." He then leaned against the very wall that had once separated Gustavo and his fellow members from their eventual decapitations. "I'm just a messenger of change, of transformation," he explained, "because when someone's self-esteem is so low, then they are dead. They are going to die. Because they don't want to change. Because they cannot change. So we come here with hope, the gift of hope. We pray for them. We pray with them. Until they want to pray with us. We give them hope."

The promise and power of self-esteem tends to enter the lives of prisoners when they are at their lowest, when Christ appears as the only answer. "I was a total coke head," confessed one prisoner. Behind bars in Pavoncito, months away from his release, he explained, "I like cocaine. I mean I love it. I would do mountains of it in here. I was all tweaked. Totally paranoid." He leaned into his conversion story, "And I had this gun and I was just waiting for something. I didn't know what. I was just waiting. Because inside—inside here, there's everything. You can buy anything in here." Sitting up and then tilting forward, whispering and then raising his voice, he shared, "But one day I went to buy some coke. They were selling it just over there. I bought it, started doing lines, but I didn't feel anything. I mean I didn't feel a thing. Nothing. It didn't get me high. It didn't get me anxious. It didn't do shit." Taking this as his road-to-Damascus moment, his moment of being knocked from his horse, he turned toward God: "So I started searching for God. It was time to search for God. So I was opening myself up to God. I was screaming, 'Help me! Help me!' I wanted out of it all. And I'm alive today because God wants it. I mean, really I shouldn't be alive. I should have died a long time ago." But much of his new life demands steady work, a thoughtful kind of spiritual labor.

Self-esteem is that labor. "You have to lift your self-esteem up, actually lift it up," explained Pastor Allende to me but also to this born-again prisoner. "These guys have been tossed aside by society as trash. They get seen by everyone as dirt. No one values them. Society hates them. And then they don't value themselves. They kill people and commit crimes. And they do it just to make themselves known." So much of the narrative pivots on self-acknowledgement and self-recognition, on announcing to the world that they exist. "Each violent act is their way of saying 'Here I am,'" Pastor Allende explained. "'Really, here I am. I know people don't want me, but I'll show you.'" These efforts at self-identification aim at both self and society. In fact, nowhere does gang ministry as political rationality meet the everyday level of prison life more vividly than when chaplains instruct active gang members to explore their inner worlds for the sake of not just self-identification but also public security. The two—salvation and security—often melt into each other. "People behind bars often dream of a better life," one manual reads.[31] "And people who experience low self-esteem feel imprisoned. But there is a likelihood that their prison doors will swing wide open. No one keeps them there but low self-esteem." Yet, important to this confluence is a curious slippage in technical registers on which Pastor Allende's ministry rests, and this sustained confusion contributes to the Christian production of insecurity.

THE WILL

This slippage begins with material developments rather than theological assumptions, with money rather than conviction. Pastor Allende, to explain, spent two decades running a Christian rehabilitation center for alcoholics and drug addicts in Guatemala City. Having, in his words, perfected the art of "straightening crooked souls" with biblically infused group therapy sessions, Pastor Allende has expanded his services to include *delincuencia,* or the problem of gang membership. And although the pastor speaks passionately about how this ministerial decision is a response to God's ever-growing call to act in this world, to respond to the problems of both his city and his nation, he sheepishly admits from time to time that he is also following the money, that new streams of funding from North American churches continue to appear for those ministers able and willing to "rehabilitate" active gang members from a Christian perspective. Given a sustained relationship between the insecurity in Guatemala and the insecurity inside Guatemalans, a growing number of international funders promote a Christian response.

As the critical student of development might anticipate, however, increased streams of international monies carry a range of unintended consequences.[32] Inside faith-based development offices, the increasingly obvious (that is, humane) response to gangs such as MS-13 is an integrated approach. The only other sustained response has involved the criminalization of Latinos by way of draconian deportation policies, racist community policing programs throughout Central and North America, and death squads keen on reliving the civil war's extrajudicial liberties. Yet, instead of solving the problem, more money to support more-integrated approaches has simply changed the way gangs have come to be understood as a problem—not only because gang ministry places self-esteem at the center of security debates but also because of the kinds of ministers that have responded to this windfall. Pastor Allende spent over two decades training his ministerial craft on the Christian war against alcoholism and drug addiction. And much like Pastor Allende, those who are proficient in the language of Christian rehabilitation—those able to respond to these funding programs—are almost exclusively Pentecostal and Charismatic ministers with both training in and experience with drug and alcohol treatment.

Above Pastor Allende's desk sits a poster. A heroin user is on his knees, with his left arm extended and his right hand searching for a vein. Jesus kneels behind the man, leaning over his back, in such a way that Jesus's left arm becomes the user's left arm. The confusion is intended. The poster reads, "While you think you are just having fun, someone else is suffering for you." Pastor Allende, in reference to the poster but also the gangs, in a way that makes the one appear to be the other, explained, "It's all so self-destructive. Getting high, running with gangs—it hurts God. It hurts you. It hurts the family. Evil thoughts. Negative thoughts. It's all going to kill." The problem, however, is that few pastors have any working knowledge of gang culture. So while Pastor Allende argues convincingly that one cannot separate substance abuse from gang membership—that a recovering gang member is almost always also a recovering alcoholic or a recovering drug addict—this sustained confusion between addiction and gang membership (between substance abuse and *delincuencia*) has certain rhetorical effects. This slippage makes gangs such as MS-13 a "disease of the will" and thus frames Jesus Christ as "the divine physician," ultimately understanding self-esteem as an inoculation for both the soul and society.[33] Simply put, prison chaplains often treat members of MS-13 as if they are addicted to gangs.

This slippage has a history. In nineteenth-century North America, alcoholism too became understood as a disease of the will. Alcoholism, from this perspective, evidenced an atrophied will, a palsy of the will, a will that simply could not govern. The liberal imagination's division of the human condition into problems of the body (the domain of medicine) and problems of the mind (the domain of psychology) eventually obscured the will.[34] The will got lost in the shuffle—made unintelligible by advanced medicine, abandoned by psychology, and snubbed by modern philosophy. Yet two discourses (intertwined today) consistently kept the will at the center of their analytical interests: first, Christian theologies of the Calvinistic, Pentecostal kind and second, self-help discourses.[35] Both recognize the will as a tangible force in the world—as both a cause and an effect. Both allot the will a kind of ontological status; for both Pentecostal theology and self-help, the will tends to be both expansive and shadowy, with nooks and crevices that constantly need to be swept clean. For both, the will is something that can be examined, mapped, manipulated, and strengthened.

In both discourses, the will is also a major dilemma. Just ask Augustine. When read by way of Calvinism, the bishop of Hippo articulates what is so central to contemporary Charismatic and Pentecostal theologies: the idea that sin frustrates the whole of creation and that sinners must achieve salvation against their reckless will. Augustine contends that carnal sensations mislead the will away from God, blurring the believer's vision in much the same way that a cataract might distort one's eyesight.[36] Because of this moral shortsightedness, Augustine notes, we have lost control of ourselves. This is why Pastor Allende and his colleagues in Christ employ an array of techniques such as self-esteem: not simply to corral a gang member's delinquent will but also to strengthen that will, so that one day he or she might be strong enough to choose Christ over MS-13.

Prison chaplains advance this logic with self-esteem manuals that have been adapted—sometimes inelegantly—from Christian materials developed for alcoholics within the North American context. These manuals prompt their intended readers, in all their middle-class whiteness, to assess their level of honesty, count the times they have lied in a given day, and make three goals for the week—goals that will ultimately result in a greater sense of self, a higher level of self-esteem, and a stronger will. Prison chaplains have unsystematically downloaded many of these self-help therapies from the World Wide Web—therapies taken from Alcoholics Anonymous sit awkwardly alongside biblical passages as well as decontextualized quotes from Dr. Phil. "Ask yourself these questions," one manual orders. "Is your self-esteem based on what others think of you? Do you do things to make other people happy, even if it makes you feel bad? Do you have a hard time being happy for others when they succeed? Do you call yourself names like 'stupid' or 'dummy' when you make mistakes—or sometimes even when you don't? Do you have a hard time taking risks?"

In the wake of these internal dialogues, the actual practice of prison chaplaincy tends to pathologize low self-esteem as a kind of sickness, constantly placing each member of MS-13 at odds with his or her atrophied will. One manual, citing scripture (Samuel 31:4), speculates on the dangers of having low self-esteem: "It is almost impossible for people to reach their full potential," the manual reads, "if they do not have a healthy level of self-esteem. King Saul frustrated God's plan for him and did not let God take Saul where God wanted to take him. His poor self-image did not allow him to believe that God would support him. And so Saul died before fulfilling God's purpose." This analogy is why Pastor Allende could reflect aloud to me about the relationship between his expertise and the prison population that he serves:

> Who is *the* doctor and surgeon? The answer is Jesus Christ, right? The doctor of all doctors is Jesus Christ. He is the doctor of the soul . . . because we know perfectly well that drugs, alcoholism, and gang membership are only ways for people to escape problems and emptiness. But when we come to Jesus Christ, we know that Jesus Christ will be able to fill this void. He gives us the ability to get stronger, to move on. He helps us get better.

Pastor Allende continued:

> And one can also say that the heart is [Christ's] surgical field. When one speaks about Christ's surgical field, one speaks about the heart. The Bible tells us that it is all about the heart and the word of God. And that within the heart emerges everything that is bad—adultery, robberies, homicides, everything. And so this is where the Lord begins his work.

To extend this metaphor, the practice of self-esteem would be not just inoculation but also a scalpel—an instrument that allows pastors like Allende to carve and to cut the soul, to perform a kind of spiritual triage for those gang members whose wills have become weak and, at times, paralyzed. This, to use Allende's words, is "the Lord's work." This, for better or for worse, contributes to the production of postwar insecurity, prompting a specialized cadre of ministers to apply their therapeutic skills to gangs. Relying on the promise of self-esteem, these ministers have placed the problem of gangs in the soul rather than on the streets, training a growing number of eyes on atrophied wills that only the saving grace of Jesus Christ can strengthen.

PRISON GATES

"What began to happen," Pastor Morales told me, "was that family members began to show up. They were mostly women, mostly sisters and mothers of the gang members. They came and we just waited." They came down a long dirt road and then waited for hours, leaning on Pavoncito's front gates. "The entire prison was out of control. The guards didn't know what they were doing. It was a feeling of total loss of control. Total insecurity. We couldn't see it. But that's where the decapitations happened. The reports were that they were playing soccer with the heads. And that they had put them on poles and marched them around kind of in a biblical Jericho model." Pastor Morales continued, "There were no men around. These were all sisters, girlfriends and mothers at the gates, at the morgue. It was kind of like the cross: all the disciples took off, but the women stood right there." He ministered to the women throughout the day, pushing the events through Christian idiom, rendering visible two effects of gang ministry's inward turn while also returning to where this story began: with a frantic phone call and a failed effort, with Gustavo's head sitting on a pike while his mother held vigil just beyond the gates. To what effect?

The first effect is that prison chaplaincy's production and promotion of self-esteem within the very prison system in which Gustavo died marks a novel relationship between space and security. Put simply, the practice of self-esteem effectively shifts the terrain over which security officials wrestle from the streets to the soul—from material conditions to the "vast and unbounded inner chamber" that Augustine narrates so vividly in his *Confessions* and that has subsequently inspired so many missionary intimacies.[37] This relationship between space and security is less material but no less tangible than efforts at securing or even disembedding the city through new modes of segregation and the neoliberal privatization of security.[38] Through the spatialization of security, the practice of self-esteem evokes a uniquely private, historically contingent space that takes shape amid explicitly Pentecostal and Charismatic efforts at prison chaplaincy. Located somewhere between desire and the will, this inward terrain is an ever-insecure space tethered to a theological anthropology that prompts the believer to enter the inner world of

the self before gazing upward at the divine.[39] Pastor Morales's ministerial relationship with Gustavo, for example, his concern for Gustavo's
heart amid the flux of bodies and terror, evidences a mode of Christian
governance that polices the soul above and before the streets, "extending [a range of security officials] away from political institutions and
economic relations" and "towards the terrain of the self."[40] Public concern gets mapped onto rather private spaces.

The second effect, related to the first, addresses the politics of visibility while also saying something about the sovereign's relationship to
Christian efforts at self-governance. Michel Foucault famously begins
Discipline and Punish with two contrasting narratives. The first is a
graphic retelling of a public execution from 1757—of a man named
Damiens, who was stripped, tortured, and eventually quartered for the
crime of regicide. "This last operation," Foucault's sources note, "was
very long, because the horses used were not accustomed to drawing;
consequently, instead of four, six were needed; and when they did not
suffice, they were forced, in order to cut off the wretch's thighs, to sever
the sinew and to hack at the joints."[41] Foucault contrasts this public
execution with a decidedly boring prison schedule from the mid-
nineteenth century: "At the first drum roll, the prisoners must rise and
dress in silence. . . . At the second drum roll, they must be dressed and
make their beds. At the third, they must line up and proceed to the
chapel for Morning Prayer. There is a five-minute interval between each
drum roll."[42] Tragically, the prison riot at Pavoncito allowed this chapter's opening vignette to parallel Foucault's introduction to *Discipline
and Punish*. Both Damiens and Gustavo suffered spectacular deaths—in
front of crowds, for the sake of order, and within earshot of loved ones.
And the Guatemalan morgue director's comments about decapitation
echo Damiens's botched quartering. Dismemberment has never been
like scissors cutting through paper; it has always been tedious work, a
sweaty kind of labor. Nineteenth-century efforts at prison reform, moreover, with their rigid schedules and moral intentions, seem uncannily
similar to Pastor Morales's work, even if the language of self-help is
more recent.

Foucault's first vignette gives way to his second. His is a genealogical
argument tethered not so much to an idea of historical progress as to
the possibility of change, of breaks in the order of things.[43] For Foucault,
the archive reveals the emergence of disciplinary forms, a noticeable
shift from body to soul, which unfolds primarily at the level of the state.
This shift is not one of succession, from the body to the soul, but one of

blending together—an unstable relationship between sovereignty, discipline, and governance.[44] MS-13 and its ministries evidences as much. Within postwar Guatemala, punishment as spectacle coincides with mundane efforts at reforming the prisoner from the inside out. The only difference is that non-state actors now do the work of the state. Freelancing Charismatic and Pentecostal ministers funded by North American church organizations secure the soul while members of the Paisas execute members of MS-13—and vice versa. The only thing that the Guatemalan government seems to provide is a theater for this moral drama, meaning the prison.[45]

Yet, this relationship between space and security, this inward turn by way of prison chaplaincy, obfuscates the place of the body amid the mounting concern for the soul—and in locales that extend far beyond the prison gates. More than a year after Gustavo's murder, for example, at about 5:00 A.M., as men and women began their weekday commutes through Guatemala City, an unfortunate few stumbled upon a severed head—in four different parts of the city. One was perched near a shopping center. Another was found in a comfortable, middle-class neighborhood. A third appeared in front of a fire station. The fourth rested on the steps of the Congress building. An early-morning streetwalker found this fourth head. It was tucked inside a black plastic bag along with a handwritten note. Damp with blood, with words smudged and corners bent, the letter railed against postwar impunity and Guatemala's prison system. A strange missive inside a morbid bottle, the letter evoked the old adage that violence begets violence: "This is happening because of the mistreatment and the injustices in the country's jails," the letter reads. "If you don't do anything about these mistreatments, what happens from now on will be the fault of the government and the prison system, who are the ones abusing their authority."[46] Gustavo's fellow gang members had sent a message.

Growing interest and support for gang ministry and increased optimism about incarcerated gang members' ability to watch themselves tend to blur the corporeality of prison life as well as the fact that no one is watching. Again, prisoners do not decapitate fellow prisoners (and severed heads do not litter city streets) because of a brief lack of oversight. As the language of postwar security continues to lean toward the terrain of the self, toward so-called integrated approaches rather than a range of suppressive antigang policies, this shift accomplishes cultural work. While certainly not a zero-sum game, the emergence of the self as a viable terrain on which to secure postwar Guatemala does distract from (if not displace) a concern for the historical and material conditions that have contributed to the rise of gangs such as MS-13. The self also muffles an empathetic cry for those men and women "green-lighted" (meaning marked for death) amid all this talk of the self.

Although charges could be brought against those who ordered Gustavo's transfer from one prison to another, prison chaplains, along with their governments, tend to remain concerned for prisoners' hearts—even at the expense of their bodies. "One thing I will remember," mentioned Pastor Morales, "was the complete passivity. Not once did I hear one member of any of those families say anything. . . . They did not expect any kind of investigation, any kind of arrests to be made. It wasn't even expected nor even desired. It was a complete passivity and victimization. 'There is nothing we can do about this,' they seemed to say." The effect was a palpable, deeply layered sense of insecurity for both pastor and parishioner. And, this, to borrow the language (but probably not the logic) of Pastors Morales and Allende, is the sin worth exposing.[47]

Hamsters

We met up at the mall—a beautiful new mall. While the shopping center had all but died in the United States by then—the media widely reported that none had been built there between 2007 and 2012—investors in Guatemala saw malls as flagships for urban development. "Beacons of hope," they called them, with greenfield developments on the urban fringe. We sat inside one of them. Mateo ate from a plate of nachos. I sipped a bottle of water. We watched a merry-go-round loop kids at a painfully slow pace while overhead speakers piped in English-language hits from the 1980s: Phil Collins, Michael Jackson, and Duran Duran. With the stores nearly empty and the retail prices well past reasonable, the entire effort seemed unsustainable. But the space was familiar to Mateo. And this is what counted. It was smaller than the malls in Los Angeles, for sure, but the angles were all on point. The architects obviously had a model in mind. The stores were more petit, the doors lower, and the walkways narrower than their sister structures in the United States, but the mall was formally complete (cineplex, food court, glass elevators). It just was not as big. But Mateo did not care. If the experiment failed and no one bought stuff, if the mall died, like they do in the United States, then so be it. That was not his concern. Not at that moment. He just wanted to lounge a little bit inside this undersized echo of American excess.

Amid the nachos and the music, the merry-go-round and the memories, Mateo spoke about a different experiment in development, one that hit even closer to home than the mall. And he was pissed. "They would interview us," he said. "They would talk to us. They would make us work out. They would wake us up early. They were trying to make us disciplined . . . to see how we would react." Mateo shook his head, digging into his nachos with a bit of force: "We were like hamsters in a mothafuckin' cage. In a mothafuckin' laboratory. That's what the fuck we were. Let's be honest, homie. Let's stop the bullshit. That's what they did. They grabbed ten hamsters, all from rival gangs, and stuck 'em in one fucking house. They didn't give a fuck. And things got outta hand." Things did get out of hand.

Mateo was speaking about an experiment in soft security. The project took ten former gang members, split them into two teams of five, and provided them with seed money to start two small businesses. One group tried its hand at a shoe-shining collective. The other started a car wash. To add absurdity to insult, development officers filmed the efforts, editing them into a reality television show that aired in Guatemala City. Their intention was to show the viewing public that a man like Mateo could change. He could work for an honest wage. He could be a proper citizen. The effect was absolute chaos.

Mateo had only just been deported. "The judge got tired of me," he admitted, scraping the last bits of processed cheese from his now limp paper plate, "so they suspended my residence card and deported me." He was held in Texas and then in Arizona, flown from Houston to Phoenix, for months before the inevitable happened. "When I came here, it was real hard: My tattoos on my back, and stuff like that. And these little tattoos on my arms. No family. I didn't have no friends. Nothin'. But I remember the whole time that the powerful hand of God was with me. God was with me. I was in God's hands." Mateo wrung his own hands while talking. "I was just too blind, 'cause I was still involved in other things. I was not opening my heart to God." Those other things included drugs, drinking, and an inability to totally extract himself from gang life. "It's not like flippin' a switch," he told me.

Mateo's return to Guatemala proved difficult. He had left Guatemala a toddler and returned a man, with no contact in between. "I came here in 2005, in February, to Guatemala." He landed at the national airport with hundreds of other guys—in hand restraints and no shoelaces. Herded from the plane to the tarmac to an anonymous meeting room, Mateo was set free—into the city. "Once they touch Guatemalan soil," an attaché for U.S. Immigration and Customs Enforcement (ICE) explained to me as we stood on the tarmac, "they are in the hands of the

Guatemalan government." Twice a day, hundreds of men walk out the door and onto the streets of Guatemala City. "ICE has absolutely no responsibility for these guys," he stressed. One strode out the door on crutches, while we watched, vowing to head back to the United States as soon as he had the money. His nine-month-old daughter was waiting for him, he said, in Allentown, Pennsylvania. He just needed the money and his leg to heal. He had broken it while literally climbing over the U.S.-Mexico border.

"I went to live with an aunt," Mateo said, "[but] I started having problems there with my aunt's kids. Sometimes they would give me faces."

"Like how?" I asked, both of us now leaning back in our chairs, taking in the sight of the food court.

"Like, I would ask my aunt for a plate of beans. And sometimes her kids would give me bad looks, like 'What's up with this guy?' And that would make me feel like, bad, you know?" The transition proved near impossible. "My family lives in Esquintla. It's kinda far from the capital. It's a tropical area. Rivers and trees. It was so different from LA." Mateo's shoulders slumped. "And my Spanish sucked. It was poor, man. It was like—from 1 to 100 percent—it was maybe at like 13 percent. It was real bad, man. And I remember people were laughing at me. When I went to the store or something, people would steal from me 'cause I don't know how to use the money."

Out of place, out of sorts, and getting run around town, Mateo did his best to turn a corner: "But then I was like, 'What's goin' on with me? I'm smart, man. I need to learn quick. I need to do something quick!'" Mateo started snapping his fingers, acting out his ambition. "So I started practicing my Spanish, reading books in Spanish. I started asking around about the bills, and that's how I started learning." A street kid came up to us, in the mall, asking if we wanted to buy some candies. A security guard rushed him away, pushing him back to the streets. The mall music kept on playing. This time it was Cyndi Lauper.

"And my first job here," Mateo remembered, "was rough. 'Cause I couldn't work like in a company 'cause of my tattoos. So I started working as a helper . . . carrying dirt, rocks . . . you know, heavy jobs. Hard work, brother." Working manual labor, in the tropical heat, Mateo lost hope. "I used to come home late, dirty, tired . . . just to win 15 quetzales [US$2]. From seven in the morning to like six in the afternoon."

Years later, Mateo could spin the work into a kind of Christian redemption tale: "But God was showing me something. That all that money that I was winning for selling drugs in LA . . . God was telling

me, 'Look, I'm gonna build you. I'm gonna construct you. I'm gonna
show you, and you gonna understand why.' But I still didn't know why.
And there were moments when I felt depressed. There were moments
when I felt scared. There was a moment that I cried in my aunt's house."
Mateo dropped to a whisper, letting the mall music compete with his
memories: "There was no one around. And I was scared. I started crying. I got on my knees and I said, 'God, why? What's gonna happen? I
wanna go back. I don't know nobody here. I don't have no family.' And
I was real confused. I started drinking." *Química,* or rubbing alcohol,
proved the cheapest. For a few dollars, Mateo could stay drunk all day
long. And so Mateo did.

"A real, real depression came in my heart, in my life. A real spirit of
worriness, like, 'Oh, man, I wanna get out of here. I wanna leave. I want
to go back to the States.'" Mateo fidgeted, his foot bouncing well past
the pace of any music within earshot. "'Cause all of my cousins, grand-
parents, family was there. But when I was here in Guatemala, I feel like
my family forgot about me because nobody called me. Nobody helped
me." Mateo's father did not buy his townhouse until 2009, and so
Mateo bounced around for years. "The only person that maybe helped
me once or twice was my older sister and my dad. But I didn't feel that
in my heart . . . I was like, 'Man, I don't want this. I wanna get out of
here.'" Mateo then admitted to still wanting to get out of Guatemala.
"I'd go back to LA in a second, Kev," he said. "In a second," he stressed.

But Mateo fought for work. "I tried to look for a job. But they always
rejected me. The Koreans . . . 'cause there's Koreans here in Guatemala.
They got a lot of factories, like doing T-shirts and shit. But they're
fucked up. They slap the Guatemalans. They treat them bad." Mateo
remembered one story when the manager of one factory pushed a
worker around, screaming at him in Korean. "They used to bad-mouth
them. Mistreat them. And the Guatemalans there would be humbled
'cause that's the only job they got. So these Koreans would take advantage of them." The tensions between the Guatemalans and Koreans
sounded epic. "One time, I went to look for a job, again. It was like my
fifth time. And I remember this Korean came out." Mateo paused to get
his thoughts in order. "And I went and suited up nice. Suited up like
with a necktie, with a nice long-sleeved shirt, and I shined my shoes.
And I remember, he came out with my papers and identification. He
gave them to me and he said, 'You know what, we sorry, man, but you
have the face of a gang member and we don't want people like you
here.' And I remember that I looked at him and I wanted so much to

grab him and beat him down. But God was like . . . holding my hands . . . like, sustaining me . . . like, 'Relax, I got your back.'" Absolutely nothing opened up for Mateo. In a municipality with just over 100,000 people, in an area with Korean factories and fields of sugarcane, Mateo struggled to stand on his own feet.

"I remember I grabbed my papers and I walked away. And I remember when I was going back to my aunt's home, I started crying, and I asked God, 'Please help me. Please. I'm tired of this. I don't wanna go back to robbing. I don't wanna go back to selling drugs. I don't wanna go back to using drugs.' And I remember, I started going to church and stuff like that again. And I started getting more involved with God again." Always a quiet port in Mateo's stormy life, the church, any church, gave Mateo a space to relax, to catch his breath. "And God started talking to me. And through a church, a pastor helped me out. He gave me a job. No salary. Just he used to give me my lunch, and maybe he would give me like Q15 [US$2] or something. But it was not a job. It was just to do something so my mind could be occupied." Knowing Mateo, having a sense of how much stimulation he needs to feel occupied, I considered just how painful—how downright boring—his work at the church might have been.

"After a while, the pastor came to me and told me, 'Mateo, I got blessings for you. I got blessings for you. Listen, there's this program called *Challenge 10*. They're interviewing ex-gang members like you. And God has placed in my heart to let you know that this is for you. There is something about this job that is gonna help you guys out, and I feel like you should go for it.'" No matter how one tells Mateo's story, this is a major turning point. "I got happy. I got excited! I was like, 'Lord, thank you. You answer prayers . . . awright, I'll do it!'" Mateo got himself together: "I went to go dress up. I got my tie. I got suited up . . . And I remember, I went to this program and I met these people from *Challenge 10*. They interviewed me. And I was honest with them—all the questions they asked me—I answered them with all honesty. And it worked, 'cause in my mind I said, 'No, I need to start to be honest. I need to stop lying and stop playing the part. Stop trying to get over people. I need to start living a true life now.'" Mateo's commitment to truth, his interest in living a pious life, seemed to have set him apart.

"And out of me there was like fifty more ex-gang members, and only ten got picked, brother. And guess what—I was one of the ten, brother! I got picked! That's a miracle, man! That's a blessing! Out of fifty, only ten got picked, and I was one of those ten. It's like when you go to the

Latin American Idol—you know what I'm saying?" Even years later, with all that had happened, his selection, among all the others, still excited Mateo: "Give me some love, brother!" Mateo yelled, drawing some attention in the food court. "You know, that's how it was, and I got picked! And it was a blessing. And I remember, they got the list and they said, 'These was the people that got picked.' And when they said my name, I was like, 'Yeah!' I wanted to shout! But there was a lot of people, so I was like . . . I was kinda acting all hard . . . but inside I was like, 'Hey, that's cool!'" Mateo beamed. Years later, he still beamed.

But his excitement eventually faded. He remembers the first night on set, in the house, with his fellow participants. "I was sleeping next to a MS. I was sleeping next to an 18th Streeter, and I was even sleeping next to a White Fence. White Fence is a gang out there in LA, White Fence 13. And wow, it was fucked up for me to be with them. These guys were *mareros* from here, and I was from the States. And these guys could have shot me up. They don't like the deported. We're not always welcome by these gangs out here. We're not."

The program buried the guys in tedium, at least at first: "They did all kinds of programs. They did all kinds of exams. They interviewed us about our past. How did we got into the neighborhood? How we got out? And why did we choose to get out of there? Why did we went to the neighborhood, and why did we fight it? Things like that, you know." Mateo remembered, "They even bought each and every one of us, all of our families, like 400 quetzales [US $50] of groceries. Things like that. They bought us shoes. They took us to nice places, and they bought us nice clothes. What they tried to do is they tried to make us look and dress differently. That's what they trying to do."

And they made them sweat, waking them up each morning for a 6 A.M. workout. "I don't know where the fuck that shit came from," Mateo said in complete disbelief. "I thought I was in prison with that shit. I was like, 'What the fuck?' Shit, I did this shit in prison, man—now I gotta do this shit in here? I was like telling them, 'You gotta be fucked up, man. Man, you twisted, brother.' They make us run around, do push-ups, and shit like that. And then they had a time to eat lunch, breakfast, any meal, man. They always had a schedule." Mateo cut the program a break. The idea was to mold these gang members in front of society: "That's what it was about. There was a therapy involved—there was a lot about . . . breaking the ice with society, then having a communication with the business leaders, people real important in the companies here in Guatemala—and that's what it was all about."

But the program ended as quickly as it had started. "The contract finished. They took off . . . these people from the program, man. They helped us out, but in the same way, they abandoned us. They abandoned a lot of people. They abandoned us. The head guy is a punk. He pooped out on us. He pooped out. That really hurt my feelings. I really trusted him. I really respected that dude." Mateo sat crestfallen. "To me, all these guys pooped out on us. They left the program. They left everything. They dropped everything. They even left gang members here that were already off the gang. They left them, and left them with false promises. So half of those guys are dead—a lot of people died. After this program, a lot of people started dying." Mateo recounted the life or death of each former participant. More were dead than alive. "The program's just fucked up. It wasn't organized. Nothing was nice and tight. But the agents out there, they had everything nice, throwing meetings, throwing councils. But most of the people that were helping us were not even really trained to hang around with people like us. They were just thrown there, like 'We'll see what they do,' and I didn't like that. They had people working there just for the money, taking things—computers and shit like that."

Mateo described what tends to happen when development projects and security schemes get an influx of cash. "All I know is that this project did wrong for not having it real organized, for not having professional people. They would just pick people up because they were important people in companies in Guatemala. It's not like that you have to have people with our lives. But you can't get a fuckin' . . . a fuckin' little bitch who's never ever suffered in his life. You can't throw that kind of person with people like me."

Mateo and I sat in silence while overhead speakers continued with English-language hits from a not-so-distant past. And I thought about what Mateo had said. "Fuckin' hamsters," he had told me, "in a mothafuckin' cage. In a mothafuckin' laboratory."

CHAPTER 2

Reality

The eye masks looked ridiculous, and the guys knew it. The shiny strips
of plastic made them look like old-fashioned bandits or, worse yet,
dopey superheroes. A former member of Mara Salvatrucha (MS-13)
complained into the camera, appealing to a public that he assumed was
already laughing at him, "This thing makes me look like Batman or
something. Or, no, like a little Batgirl, right?"[1] The masks didn't even do
a good job of obscuring their faces, which was their ostensible purpose.
The masks were supposed to protect the identities of ten former gang
members while they participated in a reality television show cospon-
sored by the United States Agency for International Development
(USAID) and titled *Desafío 10 (Challenge 10)*.[2] Recruited from local
churches, in which many of these former gang members hid for their
lives, the ten men were split into two teams, each of which was expected
to build a sustainable business within Guatemala's formal economy.[3]
One team used its seed money (approximately US$3,200) to start a car
wash, while the other team began a shoe repair service. Successful Guatemalan executives mentored both teams from start to finish, nurturing
and nudging these men toward entrepreneurial self-sufficiency.

Desafío 10 aired in Guatemala in March 2006. An experiment in soft
diplomacy, this reality television show enjoyed international coverage
while battling local indifference.[4] Few Guatemalans watched the show.
Aimed at a wide audience from at-risk youth to middle-class *capitalinos*,
the show's most recognizable viewers turned out to be active gang

members drawn by the spectacle. And a spectacle it was. Drawing heavily on North American programming, taking cues from such successes as *The Apprentice* and *Queer Eye for the Straight Guy*, *Desafío 10* provided the viewing public with dramatic examples of self-transformation. Harold Sibaja, a self-professed Christian and the show's executive producer, insisted that *Desafío 10* would "sensitize the entire population to the fact that ... once [gang members are] rehabilitated, they need a chance, an opportunity to become responsible citizens, wage earners and would-be consumers."[5] These men can work, each episode pleaded. They will consume. This is why, amid the show's pomp and circumstance, its silly graphics and slow-motion montages, *Desafío 10*'s narrative arc bent toward the productive citizen—from criminal to Christian to consumer.

Over the course of five hour-long episodes, the ten ex–gang members crafted themselves (or, more accurately, allowed themselves to be crafted) into paragons of citizen-workers by day and consumer-citizens by night.[6] They participated in early-morning workout sessions with personal trainers, wept late-night confessions into shaky cameras, shopped in some of Guatemala City's more exclusive malls, and dined with local celebrities. Very little of the show, in fact, addressed either of the two business ventures, which made *Desafío 10* at times seem more like a reward than a challenge. The amount of swag that each contestant received quickly approached the comical: new shoes, all-you-can-eat buffets, sets of luggage. After one shopping spree at an upscale mall, Chejo, another former member of MS-13, poked his head into the camera's frame, matching the viewer's presumed disbelief with a thumbs-up: "335 quetzales [US$43] for a pair of pants? That's a lot! What a blessing, no?"[7] Cars were washed and shoes were repaired, to be sure, but little was made of either enterprise.

The real drama—the one that seemed to preoccupy the producers as well as the USAID development officers funding the effort—took place along the thin border between the ex–gang member's visible body and his raucous but redeemable interior. It is a divide with a venerated history in the Christian tradition, which the show's flashy introduction evoked with rumbling evangelical questions: "Who will have the courage? Who will have the strength? Who will dare to change his life?" Answering these questions, staking a claim on a life in need of management, the show assured its viewers that a kind of conversion awaited these ten men. All of the former gang members would become, in the words of Harold Sibaja, responsible citizens, wage earners, and consumers.

This pious commitment to self-transformation, with its Christian images and imperatives, structures not just this audacious effort at reality but also its effects. Of particular interest is what I call the formalization of delinquency. This is an entrepreneurial, deeply pastoral effort at governance that is first and foremost interested in the formal economy. *Desafío 10*, at its most basic, recognized that postwar gangs are commercial enterprises and that gang prevention and intervention must provide gang members with the opportunity to earn a legitimate income within the mainstream economic market.[8] As an active member of MS-13 once told me, "Leave [the gang]? Where else am I going to make 25 quetzales [US$3] a day?" The formalization of delinquency also includes great concern, as observable on *Desafío 10*, with the state of being formal, with proper etiquette and genteel behavior, with adorning the once aberrant subject in morally righteous products (pressed slacks, starched shirts, shined shoes). Proper clothes, when paired with the appropriate table manners and confessional practices, provide "an effective means of working on the self and a fitting medium for signaling its interior improvements."[9] Be punctual. Sit up straight. Tuck in your shirt.

Both meanings of formalization make this ostensibly secular security project depend upon a structure that shuns delinquency for more manageable habits of living—for what the apostle Paul would have called "moral fitness."[10] The reformed gang member will dress the part; his interior rejuvenation will be outwardly evident—by way of his manners, morals, and modesty. This will to improve, this variation on Christian citizenship, animates the everyday relationships that exist between piety and prevention by way of the body and the soul—by way of an ex–gang member's "sign-carrying, sign-wearing body" and his moral righteousness, his work ethic, his willingness to be a formal member of society.[11] Security through sanctification—this is the aim.

This sanctification traffics in some rather subtle signifiers. Take those strange little masks, the ones that marked these gangsters as bandits. Their eventual removal allowed *Desafío 10* to mimic its North American reality television counterparts without having to spend thousands of dollars on surgical bills or home repairs. Pulling off his mask early into the second episode, giving the viewing public its much desired before-and-after shots, Carpintero (a former member of MS-13) sighed, "I'm not going to hide behind this thing, because the truth is that I am happy with the way God has remade me." Pintor, a onetime member of Barrio 18, then removed his mask, adding, "Yeah, I'm going to take this mask off also. The truth is that I am a son of God and I don't need to wear this thing." Children of God, Carpintero and Pintor had already changed; they had been remade. We learn elsewhere that in fact they arrived to the show already born-again Christians, shepherded toward *Desafío 10* by Pentecostal churches and an underground network of gang ministers.[12] The work that needs to be accomplished, the work that each contestant seems to shoulder freely throughout the show, is not one of holy revolution but of discipline—of masculine self-mastery. The challenge for these men is to match their born-again bodies to the moral demands of advanced capitalism—all for the sake of postwar security.

MAKEOVER AS TAKEOVER

Desafío 10's initial pitch was met with modest skepticism rather than complete disbelief. Harold Sibaja first called the idea "off the wall," while José Garzón, USAID's chief of Democracy and Governance in Guatemala, played the part of virgin: "My first reaction was 'What?' My second reaction was 'Let's try it out.'" In this postwar era, one in which gangs use extortion and racketeering as well as a brutal homicide rate to turn a profit, no effort at security seemed too silly. Nothing was off the table—not even reality television.

From a certain perspective, security by way of reality programming is not a totally absurd idea. Beyond the fact that 69 percent of television programming worldwide (cable and broadcast) is devoted to reality television, this genre of entertainment has long modeled active citizenship by way of self-disclosure and self-improvement, making innocuous (at least within the context of primetime programming) the language of individual responsibility and self-transformation.[13] Reality television teaches us that Paul's conversion on the road to Damascus can happen like clockwork—given the right framing device, the right product placement, the right lighting. Self-making as self-regulation is reality television's key formulation. The entire genre, in fact, pivots on its ability to reveal an individual's inner beauty by way of "spectacular subjectivities" and "disciplinary intimacies" while at the same time producing a docile body willing to do, wear, say, or eat whatever it takes to improve— to win at life.[14] "'Winning' [in the context of reality shows] is predicated not on achievement but on surrender," one critic smartly observes. "It is a makeover that requires takeover."[15] This consistent gesture toward makeover as takeover allows reality programming's optimism—whether regarding weight loss or gang abatement. Such programming ultimately promotes a pedagogy of the soul, providing contrived contexts in which each contestant does not just learn but also experiences life lessons about how to properly care for his or her self: chew slowly, journal often, strengthen your core, be punctual, starch your collar.[16] Reality programming invites each contestant to cultivate his or her "best life ever" in a way that makes reality programming itself a part of postwar policing rather than a mere derivative or complement of it.[17]

What is maybe even more obvious is that reality programming, especially in the case of *Desafío 10*, has always been as much about the viewer as those viewed, generating morality tale after Solomonic parable, for a voyeuristic audience presumably in need of schooling.[18] This is what made *Desafío 10* so very interested in "working on individual bodies and on whole populations."[19] *Desafío 10*'s explicit focus was never just ex–gang members, though Sibaja indulged in a kind of ethnographic attachment by the show's fifth episode. A competing focus was the viewing public. Garzón emphasized, "I hope that the show sensitizes the Guatemalan public to the idea of rehabilitation [and] not jail. . . . We're trying to make the public aware that there are other solutions out there." The logic sticks. "Killing [gang members] and making them disappear is not the solution," Sibaja added, "Nor are there sufficient jails to put them all behind bars. So we have to give them a chance." *Desafío 10* provided an opportunity.

With the format of reality programming trending toward imitation, one aim continues to be for viewers to do unto themselves what they see done unto others.[20] *Desafío 10* wants Guatemalans to learn a thing or two as they watch young men primped and preened into genteel subjects. This is why, as per the rules of *Desafío 10*, as per each carefully edited episode, each team learns to produce market research, a feasibility study, a business plan, a strategy for implementing these plans, and a schematic for how they would eventually launch their business. The Excel spreadsheets, dry erase boards, and conference tables in the background make the ubiquitous language of investment (whether in terms of morality or markets) somewhat predictable. "You can really mobilize the private sector," Sibaja explained, "if you give them a win-win situation. [*Desafío 10*] is a cost that has a social impact and [that] serves also as good publicity for the private sector." Everyone wins, *Desafío 10* insisted, when the delinquent formalizes. Everyone is safer when criminals learn how to better manage themselves. "It's a fantastic story," Garzón bubbled. "At the inauguration of the businesses that the former gang members created[,] . . . one of them apologized for the crimes he had committed." Suddenly straddling registers, finding himself waist-deep in Christian imagery, Garzón concluded wistfully, "The fact that you can save some, even if it's only ten . . . We have to try to save those we can." Amid this effort at salvation, *Desafío 10* scripted the formalization of delinquency onto larger narratives of regional security, electing reality programming as an intuitive medium to discipline bodies while also corralling a population. It was a hard-fought effort advanced by way of clothing, cuisine, and confession.

BORN-AGAIN BODIES

Desafío 10 dripped with Christian content. On camera, participants routinely thanked God by name—in ways that went beyond simple platitudes. One former member of MS-13, with chickens underfoot and corrugated metal overhead, a yellow mask affixed to his face, announced early in the first episode, "I love God in an unimaginable way. God helped me leave the gang, and for years he helped me stay out of the gang. Because of God, I am still alive today." A Pentecostal pastor, late in the fourth episode, delivered a wordy, tearful testimony, wiping his face and thanking Jesus for what he provided these men: "And many of these ex–gang members said they wanted to leave gang life, but they couldn't. They needed something stronger to get them out. They needed someone who could open their heart and love them; they needed someone to care for them, the love that they couldn't get in their own homes." In several of the episodes, the ten even bounced to Christian hip-hop— in episode 2, for example, to a song titled "Extend a Hand to the Fallen"—while en route to their work stations, making the religion relevant but also catchy for both participant and viewer. The music's heavy bass skipped alongside the lyrics, with the ex–gang members singing along: "You forget that Jesus Christ / showed mercy before he died. / And sadly this is the reality of a nation without food: / if we don't understand our role, we won't get to heaven."

Behind the scenes, away from the cameras, *Desafío 10*–organized support groups provided a space for this Christianity to come into clear relief. In these intimate settings, where ex–gang members discussed the lurking chance of recidivism, Pentecostal and Charismatic pastors delivered passionate sermons on the theme of redemption; participants read aloud from bibles, quoting what they believed to be important passages for a life after gangs. These men laid hands on each other, asking Jesus Christ to steady their shaky lives, while group leaders played clips from Mel Gibson's *Passion of the Christ*. They asked small reflection groups to discuss, for example, why Jesus forgave a pair of criminals as he died ever so slowly and painfully on the cross. Why were thieves closest to Christ when he breathed his last breath?

Less obviously theological (but no less Christian) passageways for moral governance drove *Desafío 10*'s formalization efforts, avenues that profoundly altered how an ex–gang member's body should be adorned for (and oriented toward) the formal economy. The show's focus on "making over" each ex–gang member, for example, with shiny shoes, fresh underwear, and fancy clothes, drew from reality television's well-established repertoire of attention-grabbing stunts while also reso- nating deeply with the missionary tics of certain Protestant Christiani- ties. Dressing the part, formalizing one's appearance, has always been central to a new Christian lifestyle. As anthropologists Jean Comaroff and John Comaroff noted in the South African context, "standards of Christian decency applied to dress, and converts had to ensure that their distinction from their fellows was shown in their attire."[21] A refined appearance delivered "a newly embodied sense of self-worth, taste and personhood."[22] And so it comes as no surprise that following an all-you- can-buy trip to the local supermarket—a shopping spree in which ex– gang members strolled up and down aisles of North American merchan- dise, stopping to sniff flowery shampoos ("This smells amazing," sighs an ex–gang member, "really excellent")—the show rushes the ten par- ticipants to a high-end shoe store, one that specializes in North Ameri- can brands. A disembodied narrator intones, "Calzado Cobán, another businessman working with *Desafío 10*, has given each ex–gang member the opportunity to choose a pair of formal shoes."

Its opportunity begins at the level of need, to be sure. These ex–gang members are of modest means and had never bought formal shoes within the formal economy, buying instead locally manufactured shoes that pirate North American styles.[23] Gang life is not lucrative. Deep into the third episode, Promotor, a former member of the LA-based gang White Fence, declared, "I understand that gang life is not a good life. But let me tell you, I'd steal a half-dozen eggs for my family. Can you understand that? I'd look at my brothers, and their stomachs would be huge from gas . . . Man, it's something. Before coming to *Desafío 10*, I hadn't had anything to eat for two days." From appetite to opulence—this is the opportunity, it would seem. Yet this trip to the shoe store was more than just a flashy gift or a search for footwear that would make these men look legit as they strolled into the formal economy. This outing was also an experience now essential to the makeover genre—one that tends to evoke moral clarity by way of unexpected prizes. The "give," followed by the "wow," yields a space for reflection—about promises not yet kept, self-improvement schemes to be tried again, and goals to be conquered. New shoes yield a new perspective. Oprah Winfrey does not just give cars for the sake of giving cars; she gives such extravagant gifts partly because the experience of receiving a new car, especially when one needs just any old car, motivates the new car owner to see life anew—to drive down her best life.[24]

The same sugary gimmick, with all of its religious inflections and its come-to-Jesus moments, defined much of *Desafío 10*. Hopped-up on free stuff, Pintor spoke excitedly into the camera, for example: "I've always wanted boots. And when they said that we can choose a pair of formal shoes, I said, 'Aw'. I looked for boots anyway and screamed out loud [when I found a pair I liked]. And I cried and said, 'These are mine.' And so when they said we can get a pair of formal shoes as well as another kind of shoe, I went right back to these boots . . . I told the others, 'These, these are going to be mine.' And when I saw the price! Ugh! I thought, 'No way!'" Through the magic of product placement, a production strategy that helped fund this reality show, the impossible became possible, prompting Pintor to testify (in classic Christian fashion) about his experience.[25] Of interest is the righteous turn his testimony took, how materiality and morality melded into a single discourse. Staring into the camera, standing a little taller than before (literally and figuratively) because of his new shoes, grounded by a thicker sole/soul (literally and figuratively) because of his new shoes, Pintor testified, somewhat out of context but somehow not: "For real, I am serious, that if you smoke weed, if you are doing drugs, taking anything, if you have any real vices, just stop them, because in the end they are just going to kill you." Pintor had seen the light. He had begun to realize that "prosperity was itself the reward of a pious heart and a disciplined body."[26]

Desafío 10 did not stop at shoes, of course. Reality television shows, much like gospels of prosperity, gain sustenance through a contagious kind of excess—from glut in the face of absence. Righteous pastors, at least within the Guatemalan context, do not rent simple church spaces; they build megachurches. These men of faith do not drive used cars; they sit behind the wheel of brand new sports coupes and luxury sedans. Rather than being seen as ostentatious, this Christian approach to prosperity correlates one's morality and one's materiality.[27] To the virtuous go the spoils. This is why the show handed ex–gang members not one pair of shoes but two. This is also why their experience at an upscale

FIGURE 8. Siman department store. Photo by Benjamin Fogarty-Valenzuela.

shoe store was only the beginning. The show's narrator announced, only moments after the men finished cinching up their laces, "Now, the participants of *Desafío 10* have been invited to Siman [a chic department store] so that they can select a formal suit, casual wear, and fresh underwear." The makeover had only just begun.

The scenes that follow can only be described as surreal, especially for those familiar with Guatemala City, a violent capital that tags as taboo anyone who appears to be related to a gang. In one scene, masked participants with baggy jeans swaggered through well-lit dressing rooms; in another, middle-class saleswomen of the genteel kind measured inseams and suggested color palettes. Yet another scene provided a quick shot of half-dressed ex–gang members trying on shirts with sleeves just long enough to cover their tattoos. All of these scenes, when stitched together, helped to establish a "before" to this shopping excursion's eventual "after," pressing by way of conspicuous consumption a Christian relationship between the clothed body and the converted soul. The proof of this conversion came in the form of bewildered gratitude. Holding bags of merchandise, prompted to say a few words, Chejo sighed in disbelief, "I never thought I could buy 2,426 quetzales [US$300] worth of clothes. I mean, I'm not buying it, but they're giving it to me. And because of this, I'm really happy, really, because the people here have been so nice. They have had such a good attitude and have treated us so well. They've given us the best they have. Really, they have." New York, a member of MS-13 for some eleven years, came to the same conclusion, appreciating the salespersons' generous attitudes while also savoring the choices that he was allowed to make. He added, "Me? I really like this place. I've liked it since the moment I got in here. It's the attitude. They have a nice way of being. They keep asking me what I like. Do I like this or that? Or how about that? I keep saying things like, 'No, not that one. I don't want that one. I want the other one.'" This lifestyle, this way of being, this finicky parade of dry-clean-only slacks, spoke to New York. This experience presented him with an alternative to gang life, with a different way of being in the world, with a generous taste of formality.

This collective appreciation peaked in a somewhat clichéd gift exchange. At the very end of the shopping spree, to show their gratitude, the participants literally gave the salespersons the shirts off their backs, trading *Desafío 10* T-shirts for bags (and bags) of belts, socks, slacks, shirts, boxers, and briefs. A comforting, overwhelmingly generous portrait of peace and equality emerged, with middle-class *capitalinos* bonding with desperately poor and deeply marginalized ex–gang members. It is a scene that could not have been scripted any better—because scripted it certainly was. Not only had the show's participants been chosen from dozens of eligible ex–gang members by way of in-depth psychological evaluations and arcane personality tests (the producers wanted the ten most affable men possible), but the applicants' bodies had also been closely studied and fastidiously documented. Photographs of each candidate's bare chest and back, his arms and his neck, had been pooled in a digital archive, allowing the selection committee to assess which men had enough tattoos to look authentic and which had too many for a pressed shirt to hide. Which bodies, the archive begged producers to ask, looked sufficiently deviant to warrant concern but not too delinquent so as to seem forever lost? Which bare chest might provide the best contrast when placed in an upscale dressing room?

Of course, the appearance of change was always *Desafío 10*'s ultimate intent. How could it not have been, given how underfunded this project was, given how little time program officers actually spent with these ten men, given that reality television is first and foremost about the circulation of images? In the end, an "economy of appearance" is what this show guarded by editing out a misdemeanor that has since been explained away as a misunderstanding.[28] During production, one of the ten ex–gang members, one who will remain anonymous, lifted a pair of pants from the store. With so many bags shuttling throughout the store, with so much excitement to distract, with piles of overpriced North American styles towering over everyone, who would miss a pair of trousers? But he was eventually caught. The editorial decision to cut this event from the show—to flatten reality for the sake of reality— allowed the producers to maintain the show's narrative arc, one that pulled ten ex–gang members from obscurity, dressed them in proper churchgoing clothes, and sent them into the formal economy to earn a suitable living. It is a narrative arc, as one might expect, with more than just one crack in it.

EVERY MEAL IS A LESSON LEARNED

Social disorganization is the cause of street gangs. This is what Clifford Shaw and Henry McKay argued, as did Frederic Thrasher in his seminal study of 1,313 Chicago-based gangs. When communities do not trans-mit the right values to their youth, those youth run astray.[29] For the self only develops through social interaction, they argued, with individuals and groups adapting to their environment and competing for space in the city.[30] And the place is important, they insisted. Distinct environ-ments have observable effects. There are regions, Robert E. Park wrote in 1924, where there is "an excessive amount of juvenile delinquency, and other regions in which there is almost none."[31] To correct for this dereliction, for the production of hobos, delinquents, and gang mem-bers, one need only to manipulate the environment. One need only cre-ate contexts in which individuals can become a different kind of human through different kinds of interactions. Context is key. Social life, this brand of thought argued, is made up of real-life encounters, which is why so much of reform, in this era, shepherded young men from the streets into the factory. Industrial work provided an organized environ-ment that could shape disorganized behavior.

In the absence of factories, bereft of work, *Desafío 10* made do—by foregrounding some of the show's more curious plot twists. New con-texts could generate new behavior, producers hoped. Different spaces could yield different attitudes. This is why the show routinely placed these newly re-made men, with their shiny shoes and pressed slacks, in some of Guatemala City's most exclusive restaurants—to squirm in their seats and to fumble over silverware, to pick at side salads and to mumble appreciations to the wait staff. As a qualified return to the so-called social work approach to combating gangs, *Desafío 10* worked to transmit the right values to its ten participants but consistently did so through a flashy neoliberal logic of excess tempered only by a Christian commitment to moral righteousness—to sitting up straight and giving thanks for every dinner roll offered.[32]

The ten routinely found themselves in these formal settings because *Desafío 10* was a contest (lest there be any question as to how producers structured reality), at each stage of which Harold Sibaja evaluated each team's performance (lest there be any question as to how producers structured subjectivity). "We are going to evaluate you," Sibaja explained. "Some will do better than others." He braced his men for his judgment: "Your mentors and I have talked. We evaluated the success and the failures of each of the groups. Are you ready to hear the assessment?" The reward for small victories was a luxurious dining experience—meals that routinely brought to life the Victorian proverb that "every meal is a lesson learned."[33] If the show's graspy makeover of these ten men prompted many to see their lives anew, to gain some kind of moral clarity about their respective futures, then those evenings spent in five-star restaurants rattled that wide-eyed optimism with a firm jolt of order and discipline. Fish out of water, invited to dinner only to be taken to church, the only thing these ten men could do was chew softly and nod in agreement while restaurant owners, local celebrities, and successful businessmen delivered sermon after sermon about values and morality.

Juan Carlos Paiz, the president of Guatemala's most influential business association and one of the principal architects of the Central American Free Trade Agreement, joined the participants for a meal at the Quinto Real, a hotel adorned with marble, white linens, and crystal. Leaning back in his chair as the ex–gang members leaned forward in theirs, Paiz waxed, "The people here want a change. And the project that you are a part of, for me, is the most important project of them all. Because the biggest problem for people—and this is according to the people—is fear and insecurity. And if this project can show them that people like you can become businessmen . . . well, that's the dream." Comfortable in his environment while the participants fidgeted in their seats, Paiz referenced "the people" as object and subject, recipient and agent, source of opinion and object of opinion. He argued, "The dream is that you will be able to achieve your dreams. That's it. Just like me! Thousands upon thousands of people need that kind of change. And if you can make that change, it will be the first step in this larger process. And what we are doing here will be the beginning. Guatemala will

FIGURE 9. Hotel Camino Real, Guatemala City. Photo by
Benjamin Fogarty-Valenzuela.

change and so will all of Latin America." Tightening his narrative,
returning to the men who sat at his table, Paiz concluded, "I want to tell
you that . . . that I admire you very much. I have heard your stories . . .
they are hard stories, stories that will haunt you your entire life, but a
future . . . [There is] a future in your hands, a future for you." True to
Desafío 10's entrepreneurial spirit, its Christian commitment to change
and optimism, to hard work and reward, the future waits for these ex–
gang members in reach of their very own hands.

And yet it was their hands that sometimes shook under the pressure—
of the cameras, the special guests, the unspoken etiquette. The show had

them laughing, of course, enjoying their meals as one would hope. But there was also an observable uneasiness with how these ex–gang members navigated their new surroundings, making salient Mary Douglas's observation that manners encode social events with hierarchy and boundaries.[34] In one scene, for example, at El Camino, Guatemala's premier hotel, these men enjoyed an elaborate buffet. As their team mentor, Carlos Zúñiga, explained how a buffet works—that you can go back as many times as you like but that you should get a fresh plate each time—a cameraman asked Carpintero what he was eating. Observable on film if not readily apparent from the transcripts, a palpable uncertainty twanged in Carpintero's voice as he answered the question sheepishly:

> *Carpintero:* Hmmmm . . . They told me this is tacos al pastor . . . *(Asking a waiter:)* Excuse me, sir, what do you call this? Tacos al pastor, right?
>
> *Waiter:* Tacos al pastor.
>
> *Carpintero:* Ah, yes. Thank you. They are tacos al pastor. They look . . . they look delicious, right?

Carpintero's bodily disposition, his visible discomfort, illustrates Pierre Bourdieu's obliquely Christian point that "uprightness" and "firmness" communicate states of virtue as well as posture.[35] These are the embodied semiotics of not just class but also piety, of wearing one's inner transformations on top of the skin. By highlighting this moral/corporeal disquietude, by editing these scenes so that Carpintero's nervousness becomes visible, *Desafío 10* created a distance, if not a continuum, between this yet-informal ex–gang member and his more formal dinner companions. Shoulders slumped, elbows on the table, even mouth agape—it all created friction between host and guest while signaling to a viewing public just how unmade these men really were. In fact, these meals accentuated this moral distance between formality and informality, providing opportunities for the formal to school the informal on etiquette and asceticism—on proper ways of being.

Some found themselves awash in gratitude. New York's voice cracked as he sat across the table from a professional soccer player and local celebrity. The athlete had already made the contrast. "I had parents who supported me," he said to the table. "They gave me an education and ultimately because of them, my life is set." He offered his best wishes. They seemed sincere. "I hope you can reintegrate," he stressed. But all of this just set up New York. Putting his water glass to the side, clanking it awkwardly against his cutlery, New York confessed, "Believe me when

I tell you that it is a real pleasure to be here with you, to be this close to you, to share this table with you." New York began to wipe tears from his eyes. "For real, it's a really important moment for me. It's filling my heart up to be a better person. Really. Do you understand? I mean, what a great guy you are to accept this invitation." Leaning toward his dinner mate, bridging an observable gap between the formal and the informal, this street-tough ex–gang member, the very man who wanted to leave the show the very first day because he struggled with his illiteracy, offered himself not just to a soccer player but to Guatemala: "I want to learn from you so I can empower my son and move forward in my life with my wife. Believe me. For real, this is a really big day for me." Education was the order of the day.

But the gaffes mounted. The owner of an upscale Thai restaurant, in another scene, sermonized to a group of ex–gang members who had absolutely no idea how to use chopsticks. This physical and cultural inelegance—this understandable but nonetheless awkward fumbling—communicated a kind of moral clumsiness, creating a space for the restaurant owner to fill. He started with choices. "Our restaurant includes an Asian food station, with a *wok.*" He then slowed down to spell out the options. "Each person chooses the ingredients that they want. There is seafood and meat. And you can mix this with rice or pasta. There are a variety of vegetables to meet your taste. Then for the main course we have a skewer, with frog legs, lamb, and steak, if someone likes exotic food, and there is also something we call a boat of steaks. In it, there is lamb and salmon." The men nodded. He then preached, on a different set of choices, "And I hope that you really like the restaurant, and that you keep moving forward in your lives. God is great and all powerful, OK?" The group replied in unison, "Amen." The owner continued, "And life is very precious, right? And you know that we are on a straight path. We always need to be on a straight path . . . God is great. He will help you. He will help you and is going to make sure you travel on a straight path." Amen.

This straight path was the focus of not just this meal but also the reality television show as a whole. As the moral opposite of crookedness or queerness, straightness emerged as the less than subtle subtext to the show's take on security. There is the path of the righteous, of the pious, that follows directly to God. Do not deviate from this path. Do not go astray. Think John Bunyan's *Pilgrim's Progress:* "This hill, though high, I covet to ascend; / The difficulty will not me offend."[36] This Protestant rectitude, rooted in the Christian tradition, contributed toward gang abatement by way of a straight path, a steady hand, and deft knowledge of a bourgeois, vaguely Victorian kind of table etiquette. For the hill to climb, the mountain to ascend, often proved to be a struggle over bodily comportment. Yet, for all of the fuss directed at each ex–gang member's body and how he managed that body, it was inevitable that the show would turn inward from time to time.

THE TURN WITHIN

Mexican Boy was crying. At the very beginning of the third episode, with a tear-stained face, he shared a deep fear with Harold Sibaja: "We want something better for Guatemala. Do you understand me? We don't want so much violence, but like I told you, I don't know if the people are ever going to accept us. I don't know if they'll ever see us as equal."

Obviously thrown by Mexican Boy's candor, Sibaja stammered, "Here, the . . . What they are going to see here . . . Here everyone is going to win. Business is going to be for everyone. This is just the start. And it's an education." Mexican Boy nodded in agreement. Sibaja continued with momentum, "The idea is that you come to understand things like punctuality, leadership—do you see this? You are learning here. Maybe it hurts in this moment, but you are learning something. That is what we want for you."

"Yes," Mexican Boy sighed, "discipline."

Surprised, it would seem, by how well Mexican Boy read his curriculum, Sibaja perked up, "Exactly! That's it! Now motivate the others and don't feel so bad, because there is no reason to. I know it's hard, but here we are all winners. These are just baby steps (*pasitos intermedios*)." Baby steps, indeed, but in which direction?

A large part of *Desafío 10*'s direction—its teleology, its willingness to read Mexican Boy's tears as growing pangs—is familiar to any student of colonialism. Civilizing missions, as they were called, justified the violent taking of foreign lands with a theological language. For centuries, throughout Latin America, Christians have understood the use of force as unlawful unless non-Christians proved incapable of governing themselves. Indigenous nakedness, perceived laziness, alleged cannibalism—this was evidence enough (for both church and crown) to prove inherent incapability.[37] Thus, the taking of land by force, the bringing of Christianity to the Americas allowed colonialists to steward Christ's flock, to save non-Christians from themselves. From this perspective, Mexican Boy's painful, tearful education in "discipline" could be read as simply one moment in global Christendom's extended effort at advancing humanity. Yet colonialism's accoutrements have changed.

Instead of a single (holy) book, now there are multiple books. There are hundreds of books, to be precise, about leadership, entrepreneurialism, financial intelligence, and related topics. In the middle of the fourth episode, the upscale Guatemalan bookstore Editorial Santillana donated reading materials to the men. Blind to the fact that the group's reading proficiency trailed behind the books (New York could not read at all), María de Carmen de Ola, a dignified woman of obvious means, presented these men with tools for personal transformation. The first was a Spanish translation of Robert Kiyosaki's *Rich Dad, Poor Dad*. A stream of parables, this *New York Times* best seller advocates financial independence through investing, real estate, and owning businesses. "We all have tremendous potential," Kiyosaki writes, "and we all are blessed with gifts. Yet the one thing that holds all of us back is some degree of self-doubt."[38] The second was a Spanish translation of David Fischman's *The Path of a Leader*, which mines the ancestral worlds of Chile, Japan, Africa, and India for kernels of wisdom. "I was [a] neurotic, materialistic, egocentric person," Fischman confesses; "however, I was fortunate enough to find a few people who helped me put true meaning and . . . [I wanted] to show [my reader] that change is possible as long as there is desire to improve."[39] The third book was a Spanish translation of Ann Cameron's *The Most Beautiful Place in the World*, which tells the story of a young Guatemalan boy who fought for an education rather than remain a shoe shiner for the rest of his life. "I was sitting in the dust all smeared up with shoe polish," the book narrates, "and [the other kids] were all neat and clean, with their pencils and notebooks, going to school."[40]

With these books in lieu of an education, *Desafío 10* angled half of these men toward the life of a shoe shiner, the other half toward that of a car washer. And it did so by encouraging its participants to turn inward—with regimes of emotional etiquette and a parade of therapeutic imperatives.[41] The show's reliance on the confession, for example, on those moments when ex–gang members opened up to each other or the camera, allowed each participant to confess (and thereby help constitute) a sense of self that could be monitored, measured, and motivated. Through psycho-theological techniques of self-making, ones in which the language of conduct and attitude figure prominently, *Desafío 10* made the inward terrain of each participant a particular domain of government.[42] Again, it had to.

In a country with the hemisphere's second-lowest tax revenue (next to Haiti) and the lowest tax collection base in Central America, in a country that has been consistently outmanned and outgunned—outfinanced ten to one—by transnational criminal networks, *Desafío 10* directed its participants inward largely because state and nonstate security forces do not have the resources to protect the citizens.[43] Sixty percent of the country, by 2012, had effectively fallen under the control of drug traffickers.[44] So police from within, *Desafío 10* preached; govern the soul.[45] In the face of gang violence and a lackluster state, *Desafío 10* promoted a decidedly Christian program for regional security: self-transformation.[46] This effort peppered each episode with moving testimonies—many spoken directly into the camera, most colored with tears. A young man nicknamed California, a former member of an LA-based gang, leaned into the camera. "I want to thank God that I am here . . . Because when I was trying to look for a job, they told me that I couldn't get one because of my tattoos and because I look like a gang member." Producers backlighted his testimony. His face obscured, with dramatic instrumental music threatening to drown out his words, he continued, "And that made me real sad. It's not easy. But let me tell you: if you want to change, you better do it sooner rather than later. And so I want to send a message to those watching, to those who want to change but think they can't. You can change! Of course you can change! Here I am telling you because I lived that life." California stared to tear up. "I know gang life. I'm not lying to you. I'm alive. And now I live a totally different life. It's a struggle. Day after day, I struggle. And this program [*Desafío 10*] is opening my eyes to using my mind, to thinking well, to analyzing things, to appreciating stuff." You must change, California insisted, and do so from the inside out—use your mind, think better, analyze things, appreciate stuff.

Desafío 10 also prompted participants to turn inward during moments of formal evaluation. As mentioned before, the show graded each contestant at different stages of the competition, providing each man with a detailed assessment of five seemingly immeasurable virtues. They were qualities gleaned from the world of business administration: leadership, punctuality, teamwork, initiative, and creativity. In many ways, this evaluation represented an old current in Protestant thought, one in which the confession proved instrumental for the care of both body and soul. To be judged, to be evaluated, each man had to speak at length about his life and his experiences, about his desires and accomplishments. Yet *Desafío 10* as reality programming gave the confessional an unusual and distinctly neoliberal twist. No longer was the confession meant to purify oneself for a mysterious God. Rather, the point was to align oneself with the rational workings of the market economy. This is the arena in which leadership, punctuality, teamwork, initiative, and creativity become critical to success. And, as participants confessed their feelings and narrated their lives, producers assessed each participant—not necessarily caring who was more punctual or more creative than another but rather how many of the ten were even capable of being punctual or creative. These evaluations sought answers to the show's own explicitly evangelical questions: Who will have the courage? Who will have the strength? Who will dare to change his life?

The style and structure of each evaluation quickly standardized, with a substantial chunk of every episode devoted to these drawn-out inquisitions. The first formal evaluation took up almost twenty minutes of the second episode. Picture a long oak table inside a shadowy boardroom. Imagine Harold Sibaja at the table's helm, with each team's mentor flanking him. The ten ex–gang members fill out the rest of the seats. Dressed in their Sunday best (their mall prizes), all sit quietly with their hands folded neatly in front of them. They wait patiently, in silence, to be judged. Sibaja breaks a long stretch of silence: "We're going to evaluate what you've done so far. We asked each team to complete a market assessment. Some of you did better than others. But, for now, we basically want to listen to you. We want to know what you are feeling about this experience." This emphasis on experience—on what each participant *feels*—primes the men to compete not at the level of outcome so much as introspection. Security by way of entrepreneurialism relies a great deal, *Desafío 10* established, on one's ability to know oneself and, by extension, to govern oneself like a proper Christian.

Chejo speaks up. With a crack in his voice, he explains, "My experience of working with this group has been excellent and what has impacted me the most has been how business works. We [as a group] have been really fragmented and it has hurt us a great deal . . . excuse me." Chejo collects himself. "I'm someone who cries a lot, which is why I am tearing up [weeps openly]. I'm giving all that I can, and I am learning all that I can. The support of my team has been excellent."

Sibaja, unfazed by this show of emotion, waits for Chejo to continue. "And so you are content with your team," Sibaja clarifies.

"I'm content with all of them," Chejo responds, "and the truth is that if we lose this battle, we're not going to lose the war. We're aware of . . . we know that there are a lot of doors opening up for us." Sibaja nods slowly as if tabulating huge numbers in his head.

Carpintero then adds, "I've learned so much from these guys. I feel really proud to speak here because we have really been depressed up to this point, but I think everything is now within our reach. I think we are not perfect, right. We have all had our low moments . . . but we're moving ahead, little by little. Whether we win or not . . . I think we are all winners because of the kind of effort we are all making." Moral progress, forward and inward—no one is perfect but surely everyone can improve.

Sibaja, arranging a set of files in front of him, quickly clarifies that there are, in fact, winners and losers. "In terms of leadership: we feel that Group A had strong leadership from the beginning, while this wasn't the case with Group B. Each one of us has distinct qualities. Some are good at some things more than other things. There are innate leaders and there are others that are not. We are all part of a team and all of us need each other." Sibaja pauses to turn to the young man that the show named Bibliotecario, adding, "But your team's success is really due to your motivating them in a certain direction. Without a doubt, you led them in a way that made sense. And because of this leadership, we have decided that Group A has [more leadership than Group B]."

All the men seated around the table applaud politely. Half of the men accept the victory modestly, smiling sheepishly, while the other half concede defeat with aplomb. When the applause ends, the men once again fold their hands and wait patiently for Sibaja to evaluate them on punctuality, teamwork, initiative, and then creativity. The rhythm of these evaluations—the questions, the answers, the posture, the folded hands—suggested that the management of emotions moves in concert with external makeovers. The formalization of delinquency demanded emotional, bodily, and aesthetic comportment; the market economy would accept nothing less.

SURPRISE ENDINGS

Clothing, cuisine, and confession—these are the delicate, Christian-inflected techniques that *Desafío 10* (as reality television) made gangly for the sake of regional security, preparing ex–gang members for the formal economy through the cultivation of a formal self. Sit up straight. Be on time. Iron your slacks. This is the formalization of delinquency, an effort at governance that promotes a set of ideas, images, and institutions about security by way of self-transformation. Through the promise of good Christian living, *Desafío 10* mapped public concern onto private spaces (namely, body and soul) to engineer a world in which ex–gang members might be able to avoid recidivism and to embrace an honest wage. That this effort took the form of reality programming could, with good reason, lead many to dismiss *Desafío 10* as fantastic— fantastic in the sense of being antic, in the sense of being ludicrously odd. Yet the medium as the message proves instructive on at least two counts: exaggerating the practical limits of both reality and self-transformation while also reminding those critical of development programs that increased streams of international monies carry with them a range of unintended consequences.

The first consequence addresses the question of life and death through the show's surprise ending. It is a conclusion that any reasonable person could have anticipated but one that is still rather difficult to accept. In late 2007, once the sets had been broken down and the episodes aired, Panadero, a former member of Barrio 18 and the contestant who arguably changed the most during the five episodes, walked down a busy Guatemala City street toward his shoe repair station. With his wife at his side and a remarkable biography in tow, a life story that placed a gun in his hand at ten years of age and then a Bible in that same hand nine years later, Panadero's conversion from gang life to church life had inspired *Desafío 10*'s producers. With talk of college in his future and with a sustainable business running in Guatemala City, USAID had even flown Panadero to Washington, DC, as real life evidence—as someone who had weathered the storm and had come out the other side stronger, more capable, more grateful of aid than anyone could have possibly expected. At some point along the way, however, as Panadero strode optimistically into the formal economy for Christ and country, for himself and his family, a rival gang member—one who either did not know or did not care that Panadero had converted out of gang life—shot him in the back of the head. Panadero died immediately, on a street corner, with his wife weeping over him. Virgilio Cordón, one of *Desafío 10*'s two team mentors and the CEO of the boutique business coaching firm Virus Institute, later reflected, "He didn't die with a knife in his hand. He wasn't killed by the police. He died working, buying things for his shoe shine shop. He died well. He didn't die as a bad person. He died as a good person. That makes me proud." His comments are not surprising. They are lined with piety. Cordón's own company announces that "a unity between God, our family and work must exist, which is the foundation to our own fulfillment, as persons as well as professionals."[47] Cordón then climbed into his vintage sports car and headed home.[48] Mission accomplished.

Carpintero, two years later, reflected aloud to me about Panadero's murder as well as the violent death of another contestant, Mexican Boy. Carpintero, after lifting his shirt to show me two bullet holes and a thick scar that began below his belly button and that snaked up his abdomen, after tracing the flight of another bullet that entered his chin and exited his cheek, after explaining his crippled hand as the result of an unexpected prison riot, commented, "That's the risk we all ran with this reality show. Everyone knows our faces. All I do now is wake up, come wash cars here, and then go home. I can't walk around my neighborhood freely. I can't do anything. Since the show, people have tried to kill me. Sometimes I sneak out to see my mother-in-law. But that's the risk we all took with this show." And risky it was. Only one year after this interview, Carpintero died at the hands of a neighborhood gang. He was shot dead. So were most of this show's participants. At the time of publication, six of the original ten have been murdered and one is in permanent hiding for his life. Sitting with one of the few surviving members, ripping through the names, the effects of this experiment come crashing into relief: "Panadero? Dead. Bibliotecario? Dead. Mexican Boy? Dead. Seco? Dead. Carpintero? Dead. Pintor? Dead. Chejo? Hiding for his life." Their deaths, juxtaposed alongside the show's commitment to personal transformations and conspicuous consumption, reminds not only the viewer but also the security official and the aid worker that before-and-after shots do not always bend toward productivity. Happily-ever-after is a cruel contrast to the violent fate that these participants have met.

The second unintended consequence addresses the fact that *Desafío 10* set out to transform ten ex–gang members into small business owners but in the end rendered each of them poor. "Poor" does not mean that these men were ever rich. Before receiving not one but two free pairs of shoes, Promotor had remarked that he had not eaten a proper meal for days. Gang life, again, is not lucrative. Yet, rather than poor, at the beginning of the show these men were by all standards (from the folk to the criminological) delinquents. The distinction is important. Unlike delinquency, poverty has long been understood within the liberal tradition as natural. There will always be poor people. In fact, there need to be poor people. Wealth depends upon poverty. The two categories exist within the same field of relations, indexing one's relative success within a market economy. Without the risk of poverty, without the fear of becoming poor, there would be no incentive to work hard. Alternatively, without the possibility of wealth, without the chance of becoming rich, there would be no reason to take financial risks. This is one reason why the free market has come to be understood as a competitive field that some play better than others. The wealthy have done well; the poor have not. To the victor go the spoils. *Desafío 10* as reality programming—as explicit contest—tried to turn this fiction into reality.

For centuries liberalism has made political economy inseparable from social economy; material well-being has long been entangled with moral well-being. This has meant, among other things, a palpable concern for those men and women who refuse to play the game—for those who care not whether they are rich or poor, success or failure. These material and, in turn, moral misfits include the pauper, the insane, the savage, and the delinquent. These figures are men and women incapable of properly governing themselves; they are social dangers in need of an intervention. They live between buildings—in alleyways and rail yards, street corners and front stoops. This is how and why "a disparate band of administrators, economists, philanthropists, doctors, and others" took up the moral problem of delinquency under the guise of material concerns.[49] If the delinquent are not a part of the game, if they are unconcerned about whether they win or lose, then who would work? Who would consume? Who would dare to change their life?

Inculcating poverty, disciplining the supposed delinquent, however, is not a smooth process. The history of the institution tells us as much; *Desafío 10* as an effort at regional security concedes this fact. This is why so much of *Desafío 10* involved pedagogical interventions as obvious as scenes shot in a classroom setting and as subtle as footage taken in supermarket aisles. This is also why *Desafío 10* leaned on Christian techniques of self-transformation. What better a social force to set men straight, to put them in their place, than Christianity? In the early nineteenth century, Antoine Cherbuliez cites *Dictionnaire historique:* "Even if we were to instill in [Brazilian natives] only enough Christianity so that they feel the need to go around dressed, this would be a great benefit to English manufacturers."[50] The social problem, driven by the material, concerns how one can incorporate the unincorporated, enlist the disinterested, shepherd the lost. Clothing, cuisine, and confession—each tinged with Christianity—worked to instill within each ex–gang member an appreciation for the game.

Yet the kind of consumption that these ex–gang members experienced through *Desafío 10* was obviously unrealistic for the jobs that they were being trained to pursue. Throughout the show, there was a false sense of expectation around how these men would experience the formal. While the show presented these men with an alternative to gang life in upper-middle-class indulgences, it is safe to say that none of these men would ever become middle class. They would, at best, become what they were trained to be: car washers and shoe shiners. This is the fundamental lie that *Desafío 10* tried to sell these men. For more likely than not, as car washers and as shoe shiners, they would wear the same knockoff sneakers that they wore as gang members but would work even harder to buy eggs for their family. Or, as Robert Kiyosaki, the author of *Rich Dad, Poor Dad,* the book that each of these contestants received, writes, "Broke is temporary. Poor is eternal."[51]

The question remains, of course: how well did each participant come to appreciate the formal economy? The answer is not easily quantified. Six of the ten have been killed, one is in hiding, and the survivors have had uneven work experiences. One was last seen heading north toward the United States—with a keener sense of punctuality but nonetheless without the proper immigration papers. Yet an interview with one of the participants, a young man who remained inspired by *Desafío 10,* suggests what the formalization of delinquency might sound like. In a modest Guatemala City eatery, one that the man chose over a more upscale restaurant because, as he told me, "I still look like a gang member," the onetime *Desafío 10* participant described the first time he cashed a paycheck. His emphasis on consumption and satisfaction, on brand names and conspicuous gratification, suggests just how much traction the formalization of delinquency can gain in a life. He waxed, "That first paycheck, man. That first paycheck felt good. I remember feeling really happy when I got my first paycheck. I went to Burger King and bought an ice-cold Coca-Cola, a big burger, and some fries. And I just relaxed. All by myself in Burger King. I just relaxed watching the television and eating my burger. And I felt happy because I wasn't eating someone else's money. I wasn't thinking to myself, 'Oh man, I just messed that guy up' or that maybe that guy was out to buy some milk or some Pampers for his kid. I just ate my burger and felt happy." Proud that he was no longer delinquent, this man relived his *Desafío 10* days by celebrating a job well done through consuming what can easily be understood as an extravagant meal. Shoe shiners and car washers rarely (if ever) eat at Burger King. The food is not too expensive. It is too rich.

Pangs

We were talking over the wind. In a taxi, with the widows open, Mateo tripped a nerve. His coworker, hitching a ride with us, shouted out something about Mateo's first day on the job. "You told us about your son. In training, that's how you introduced yourself. I was there." Mateo looked out the window. Street life whirled past as we made our way to the call center.

"Why would you do that?" I asked, "Why would you—not, like, say, 'Hey, I'm from LA.'"

The coworker jumped the question, "It was training, as a group, and you say a little bit about yourself. You introduce yourself."

I nudged Mateo. "Why didn't you say you're from LA?"

Mateo shook his head. "'Cause, basically everybody there knows I'm from the States, so why not say something else? And, you know, everybody does that shit. They say shit like, 'Yeah, I come from Nebraska.' Some come from New York. Things like that, so—of course, I'm gonna say, 'I'm from the States. I'm from LA. You know, I got deported from LA. Been out here.' So, a little short introduction, you know. Things like that. Basically everybody in the call center has been in the States, man. Everybody—different states, but they've all been in the States."

Now stuck in traffic, the air still and the taxi quiet, the coworker mumbled to himself, "'Cause my daughter was just born. I remember that meeting. She was only a month old . . . she was one month old when I started working there."

Mateo, coming back to the conversation, breaking his relative silence, said, "I just wonder how my son woulda been . . ." He trailed off again.

"So what did you say?" I asked.

"I said this." Mateo straightened himself up in the taxi: "Hello. My name is Mateo and my son died a few weeks ago."

I remember the baby shower. It had such strident aspirations to be a proper, middle-class affair. There was cake. There was punch. There were games. Colorful banners connected one corner of the room to another. A piñata hung with anticipation. And all of it was hosted on the other side of the city, across a bridge and through a canyon, in a newly incorporated section of the city. "Infrastructure-lite" would be one way to describe the area. Unpaved roads and one-story structures met infrequent bus routes and rising levels of crime. Mateo had lived out there with his girlfriend in a one-room rental before his father bought the townhouse. She taught English, and Mateo completed small contract jobs for violence prevention programs. That was how they met. "I was at this one school and went to give a speech to the kids. To stay in school and to stay out of gangs and shit. She was working there. I started seeing her more often at the school, and we fell in love, and we started talking. I started rappin' to her. And that's how we got . . . you know, like that, and things . . . things were going real good, man." Mateo flipped through some texts of hers that he had archived on his cellphone. Emoticons and exclamation points framed abbreviated gestures of absolute devotion.

The first baby shower game was a staple. With everybody in a circle, a roll of toilet paper passed from one person to another, and everyone ripped off a stretch of paper that was supposed to match the circumference of the pregnant mother's stomach. I pulled what I thought to be a comically long stretch of paper, not wanting to win this game at all. The prospect of taking home a gift basket seemed gauche; the idea of knowing the dimensions of Mateo's woman was unthinkable; and I also wanted to lean toward observation rather than participation. I tanked my chances. So I thought. Mateo's common-law sister-in-law emceed the shower, collecting the strips of toilet paper and measuring each diligently. She'd bring the group to giggles when one strip was too short. She'd bring them to outright laughter when another was really too short. Mine was the last one. With great showmanship but little expectation, she draped the paper across the belly—until it fit like a glove. I had somehow hit the jackpot. My strip matched her stomach perfectly.

The women roared. One of only two men in the circle, I had somehow won the game. Mateo shot me a glance and I feigned indignation while Mateo's girlfriend avoided eye contact. I ultimately accepted my prize: a box of fruit wrapped in pink cellophane and tied with a ribbon. It would sit on my lap for the rest of the party.

"He died before birth," Mateo remembered. Back in the taxi, still in traffic, he opened up. "The day before, or two days before the baby was gonna be born, he was choked by the cord. I guess, probably in the night, he moved, and the cord just . . ." Mateo started to talk out the window, "So the next day my woman woke up. She didn't feel the baby moving, of course, 'cause he's in a bag, inside her stomach . . . so she thought it was normal. Maybe he was asleep. But then she started feeling that 'Damn, this fool hasn't moved all day,' and she started getting worried. I was in La Paloma with some pastors. I was down there with a lot of people from the States. There were a lot of them—American women and shit. They were doing a meeting about something. They were talking about, you know, the child sponsorship project and opening a new place for the kids. And that's when I got the call, and it was my woman, and she was crying and shit, and she was in the hospital."

It was cold. They had hosted the baby shower in an open-air room, a patio of sorts, in the middle of the rainy season. Everything was damp. Everyone shivered. The kids ran about, partly to keep warm, and eventually grew restless enough to turn to the piñata. After the cake and the presents, after some songs and some games, a young child spun around, stick in hand with eyes closed, until he could barely stand. He swung and missed. He swung again and tapped the piñata. It swayed a bit. Another child had a try and then another. Some of the women took their turn. Nothing happened. I sheepishly declined, knowing that I might not do any better than any of them. And the pink cellophaned gift was emasculatization enough for one day. But with a little bit of cajoling, after just the slightest of invitations, Mateo picked up the stick. Earlier, the women at this baby shower had all questioned Mateo. They were suspicious—and maybe rightly so, of this ex–gang member with poor Spanish and tattoos. He was a criminal to them, to most of Guatemala, and they treated him as such. "My woman's sister," Mateo once told me, "we got into some mean-ass arguments. She says I was prob'ly not gonna be a good dad." In many ways the entire shower, this parade of feminized etiquette, had been a performance for Mateo, to show his new family just how affable he was, just how honorable he could be— just how good of a father he could be for his young family.

"Yo! That's the hospital where I lost my kid . . ." Mateo passed the place every time he went to work. The taxi, battling traffic, parked itself in front of the building. "Right here," Mateo said, "There's some people that have their own private clinic, right here . . ." Mateo trailed off again. "So we went and, well . . . she went and then, I dunno what happened. They checked her and everything, and then sent her to the emergency hospital. That's when I got there. And shit . . . I seen her mom, her sister. I got there and everything, and she was already goin' in. She was already in bed, towels on her, and all this shit, you know." Mateo relaxed a bit in the taxi seat, feeling a bit freer with himself, a little more comfortable about the conversation. He rarely spoke about the details. They hurt too much. "Before anything, I spoke to her. You know, I just told her that I loved her, that I was sorry for what was goin' on with her, you know what I'm sayin'. And that I was not gonna leave her, or abandon her, you know. I just told her, 'You do what you gotta do. I'll be there for you.' And that's it. That's what happened, bro."

Mateo picked up the stick, spun around three times, and then leaned into the piñata. His first hit echoed throughout the neighborhood. It sounded like a gunshot. And then he paused. He held still between his first swing and his second swing. He didn't relax. His forearms were still flexed, his eyes still trained on the piñata, but he paused—if only to size up his next swing. The piñata had already started to buckle. He swung again, with such overstated force. The piñata dangled by a string, on the verge of giving up its goods, while all the women sat in awkward silence. Mateo then let out a flurry of heaves, following the piñata to floor, pummeling it to pieces. He just kept beating the piñata. The candy went everywhere, breaking much of the tension. The kids scampered about while Mateo caught his breath.

"What the fuck was that about?" I later asked him.

"That shit just got to be too much. Too much smiling. Too much laughing. Too many woman games. And that sister doesn't take me seriously. I needed to stretch out a bit. I needed to show her what the fuck is up."

"Did she have to give birth?" I asked.

"No, they opened her up and took the baby out. The doctor was like, 'Come here, look.' I recorded it all, but I lost that memory card."

"Shit," I whispered, surprised that he would film such a moment, on a cell phone no less.

"The doctor said, 'You see. Your son died . . . so you can know what happened.' And so, he showed me—it was the cord. And ah, her sister got to see too. He held my son out, so we could see what happened." The taxi driver honked. Other cars honked. Nobody budged. "But . . . it was something. It was hard, man. And I was, like, trying to be tough for my woman, and listening to her. But it was hurtin' me also." The death brought Mateo closer to the sister. "Yeah, homes—but after the baby died, and everything . . . like, she apologized to me and I also apologized to her. I told her that I'm sorry for the . . . you know . . . for the words and the way that I treated her." Mateo hated to apologize, but it was the Christian thing to do. "And she recognized her own fault, too. So, every time I see her now . . . and I see her a lot. She works in the infirmary. She's the one that takes the tattoos off the ex–gang members. She's the one that burns my tattoos off. Anyway, when I see her she's real attentive. I give her a hug. She gives me a hug."

We arrived at the call center, finally. However long that taxi ride proved to be, however thick capital city traffic can be, it was a fraction of the time it would have taken by public bus. On top of his ten-hour workday, it takes more than an hour for Mateo to commute to work each way by public transportation. Mateo turned to me as we walked to the front gate. "That's why I started working at this place, you know? My son." Mateo meant his son that died but also another son he had soon after arriving in Guatemala. He has responsibilities. "But it was also the stress, dawg. I didn't wanna be at home—with my woman's family all day, and shit . . . And 'cause I . . . I needed to help her out, too. She was still in, you know, bad conditions—the medicine. I needed to help her out at that time, 'cause she was not working. And I was helping out with the medication, food, and shit like that. There's just no other place here to make this kind of money legally. And I ain't going back to the other shit. But I don't like working here. I'll do it but I don't like it. It all just fuckin' pisses me off."

We stood at the front door of the call center, with employees passing by, clocking in and clocking out. Mateo had a few extra minutes on his side because of the taxi. " 'Cause it's the people that run this place. Sometimes, man . . . there's . . . They throw pressure on the agents, and it shouldn't be like that, man. You should—whoever's account manager or bosses should make the people that are working there at ease. Not too many calls, you know. All this desperate shit. Mellow out, man. Calls, yes, but stop killing the agent, making the agent be like, 'Damn, mothafucka. Fuck this shit. I'm outta here.' Know what I'm sayin? And there's people that quit, man. People that jus'—they leave, man. 'Cause of the pressure—that's why, homie." Mateo himself also fades in and out of the call center, working for months at a time but then just throwing up his hands and yelling, "Fuck this shit."

The funeral literally plays on loop for Mateo. He filmed it on his phone. I was not prepared the first time he showed it to me. He just dropped it in my lap one day and then left the room. The production quality was weak but the audio was clear. Mateo just let the phone record as he leaned into his son's tomb. "Wassup, sweetie?" he asks, "I'll always love you. We love you so much." The video had also surprised Mateo. He had not remembered that he had filmed it. "Shit, this file had no name or nothin', and then when I played it, the next thing I know, I see the shots of my baby—'What the fuck?' I just started looking at this, and I was, like, 'Damn, I remember that. I remember that day. That was the day that we, ah . . . we had the service.'" Mateo recounted the funeral but also every day that followed. "I just found this old video, dawg, that I recorded, of my son's death, and his funeral. And when I went to bury him, right? And I found it a couple days ago, and I was watching it yesterday . . . and I was like, 'Damn, I didn't even know I had that right there. That's when I put my baby . . . my baby boy to sleep.'"

Still outside the call center, Mateo picked at his current pressures. "I had a couple of tough calls recently. I tell 'em that I understand their situation, that I'm listening. I'm trying to help them out. But there are fucked-up people out there. They say, 'Well, you're asking for too much shit. You're asking too much. Just do your damn job, and shut up.' They say shit like that to me, and I'm like 'Wha'?' And then—the good thing about this call center is like, 'You know what? You talk to me like that again, I'm gonna release this call. All right? I'm talking to you professionally. I'm not disrespecting you. You're talking with foul language. You're overtalking me. You're not allowing me to talk. You're not allowing me to explain. You know? Calm down, please. I'm just trying to help you out, man.' But then they get pissed, like, 'No. Shut up.' Then I say, 'Well, OK, you know what, sir? Definitely you don't understand what I'm saying, and I'm releasing this call.' And then we release 'em."

"My woman and I aren't together anymore." The miscarriage complicated the relationship. "She asked me in a text message if I was willing . . . if I had the will to wait for her, to hang for her, to wait, to hang tight, and . . . um . . . she was hoping I did. She said, ''Cause I still love you. I wanna make a home with you, a family. But that's if you don't have other kids with another woman, or get another hook-up with someone.' And I told her, 'Nah, if you want me to wait for you, I'll wait for you. Just keep in mind that I also . . . I'm tired of being alone, and stuff—know what I'm sayin'? I need you. So, if I'm thinking of having another baby, in my mind I'm thinking of having it with you, but if you take too long, if you're living your life, and just move on, then I have to do the same thing too.' So . . . that was the last time I heard from her. From then on, I haven't heard nothing about her. And that's prob'ly why I work in the call center. Just to keep my mind off of things. It makes the time go fast."

Back outside the call center, on a break, I ask Mateo: "Just tell me this, like ten years ago, if someone talked to you like that, if somebody disrespected you like those callers do, what would you have done?"

He thought to himself. "Shit. Ten years ago? I was in prison, man."

This was my point. "Yeah, so if someone talked to you like that?" The answer was obvious.

"Ah, man, you—I'd beat the shit outta you, eh, boy. Just like Dr. Dre says, 'I'll smack the taste out your mouth.' Shit, yeah. You know that'd be the reaction, right? But then again, prison taught me discipline. It taught me respect. It taught me all kinds of things, right? And so does the call center. The church also. It gives me the tools to control emotions. It helps me cage the rage." Just then, like a bolt of lightning, his shift started. Mateo hustled back to his desk.

CHAPTER 3

A Calling

"I need this job," a recent deportee confessed while waiting for his interview. With a rosary tattooed around his knuckles and a faded *13* peeking out from under his collar, he continued nervously, "For real. Keep me busy. Keep me fuckin' busy. I don't need to be in the streets dodgin' bullets and shit. It's crazy out there. Guy in my church just got shot. Went to his funeral yesterday. It was sad, man. Kid was pumpin' gas. Got three to the head. Pop. Pop. Pop. He was a *taxista* [taxi driver] and wasn't paying his *impuestos* [taxes] to the gang. This isn't LA. It's fuckin' crazy out there." Born in Guatemala but raised in Los Angeles, deported on gang charges but redeemed by his faith in Jesus Christ, this born-again ex–gang member set his sights on a new life in a new home: postwar Guatemala City. As he paced the front office of Transactel, he imagined a routine that would shuttle him from work to church to home and then back again. "Keep me fuckin' busy," he prayed—in near perfect English.

Transactel is Guatemala's largest and most established call center operation in what has become one of the world's fastest-growing call center industries. Armed with government-subsidized scholarships for accent training, supported by some of civil society's most critical personalities, and leveraged by the United States Agency for International Development (USAID) and the World Bank, call centers offer steady work to a growing number of deported bilinguals while participating in a rather soft approach to postwar security—one that leans on the explicitly corporate but also conspicuously Christian logic of control.[1] Or, as one security official put it, "When they land at the airport, the deported can either work legitimately or they can go to the gangs. We obviously want them to work legally. Otherwise we have absolutely no control over them." Keep them busy, the logic insists.

This busyness, this concerted effort at moral control, raises the question, How have call centers become viable spaces of control in a postwar context that can be obviously and perpetually out of control? Thick literatures offer quick solutions: Globalization. Neoliberalism. A War on Terror. Each can be good to think with. But Guatemala's recent shift in religious affiliation foregrounds Christianity as a linchpin between the political, the economic, and the subjective. Most call center employees self-identify as born-again Christian, many attend church service together, and many learned at least some of their English at a missionary school. It is also no surprise that a neo-Pentecostal church offers Sunday services for this workforce—in English and at times convenient for those working weekend shifts. Yet, more fundamental than faith, maybe even more recognizable to the scholar of Christianity, is a manifestation of Christian piety embedded within the call center industry. Be humble. Be punctual. Be patient. These corporately Christian virtues minister to the deported at every turn, inviting them to assume and become subsumed by ascetic subjectivities. These are pious dispositions that coordinate (at the level of conduct) projects of capitalist accumulation with efforts at gang prevention. They ultimately freight this for-profit effort at gang prevention with the promise of Christian piety by linking the practice of postwar security to the behavior of individual men and women. This subjective turn, this assemblage of industry and ethics, secures the soul, prompting the deported to be pious—with flexible work schedules, perpetual training, and mission statements dripping with the language of responsibility and self-fulfillment.[2]

With the practice of postwar security concerned with the inner workings of active gang members and at-risk youth, the call center provides a context in which the deported subject themselves to rigorous self-improvement programs. Bonuses linked to punctuality, micropromotions depending on customer satisfaction, and overall job security tethered to one's ability to perform empathy and hospitality across a ten-hour shift—these call center metrics invite the deported to be the product of their decisions, not their circumstances. Herein lies the call center's confessional twist. Amid record levels of postwar violence, in a millennial milieu where new forms of Christianity undergird the most secular of social imaginaries, the call center functions neither as a prison nor as a factory but rather as an ever-pious life coach.

OF CUBICLES AND CHRISTIANITY

Transactel's interest in the deported is not charitable. It is nakedly opportunistic. Cornering the global market on what has come to be known as nearshoring, Guatemalan call centers provide multinational corporations with not only competitively priced services but also a convenient time zone, what the industry calls "value-neutral" accents, and an unbeatable (and unteachable) degree of cultural affinity with North American consumers.[3] With Guatemalan call centers paying their employees more than most of the country's doctors, lawyers, and university professors, spirits are up (as is the Gross Domestic Product).[4] Guatemala's ascent follows a certain logic. Perceived postwar opportunities combined with favorable telecommunications laws, a strong technological framework, and high levels of English-language education and fluency to draw foreign investors to Guatemala at an unexpected clip. The implementation of the Central American Free Trade Agreement also helped, providing substantially lower taxes and lower hiring costs for nearshoring initiatives. The conditions were ripe for growth. Between 2004 and 2009, foreign investment in Guatemala reached an impressive US$36 million, and by October 2009 the sector employed some 12,500 bilinguals. All this surpassed analysts' initial estimates.[5]

The problem was that the industry grew too fast. As in Panama and Costa Rica, whose call center markets ballooned and then popped, Guatemala's surge outpaced its middle-class bilingual population. With its aggregate growth of over 100 percent, experts began to worry that Guatemala's call center industry would reach full saturation, providing employees with an unsustainable leverage over management. With no one else to hire, employees could pit one call center against another— for better pay, for better hours, for better benefits. Saturation, by everyone's estimation, would kill the foreign direct investment that brought the industry to life. This is what had happened in Panama and then in Costa Rica, with the widespread poaching of talent from one call center to another—for only a few extra dollars a day. This is why a range of Guatemalan stakeholders, from security officials to CEOs, from clergy to councilmen, made a desperate pitch to a desperate population. To avoid saturation, call centers needed the deported.[6]

This need, this desperation provides a window into the soul of postwar security—and not because this recruitment strategy works. The scheme's success remains debatable, with even the most ideal outcomes forever tainted by the ironic story of refugees turned deportees turned underrepresented employees of an ever-expanding global service economy. An ethnographic look at this moralizing entanglement highlights how the practice of postwar security makes the deported's soul a site of intervention. In fact, those who work the back office for Coca-Cola, United Parcel Service, and Norwegian Cruise Line; those with extensive gang experience, with tattoos up and down their arms and on their necks, faces, and fists; those who learned their English not just in LA public schools but also in the U.S. prison system or while shuttling product from Los Angeles to Las Vegas—these call center employees embody the shifting rationalities that now link the tedium of cubicle life and the poetics of workplace Christianity to emergent patterns of global governance. And while North-South relationships in the Americas have long been defined by invasion, occupation, and covert operation, the call center now posits a new social order that invokes moral control through a mix of Christian sensibilities and corporate maxims. Be humble. Be punctual. Be patient.

Contextualizing this control begins with Christianity—not with revival or revelation but with a workplace righteousness that emerged in nineteenth-century North America. In that storied era of industrial growth, amid a roaringly provocative Social Gospel movement, a school of thought known as "industrial betterment" raised the question of management.[7] While pondering how employers should treat their employees, reformers drew on an explicitly Protestant vocabulary. They leaned steadily on the Christian notion of duty while also maintaining a sustained interest in some rather missionary metrics: frugality, industriousness, and temperance. It was a faith-inflected philosophy for the Gilded Age—one that railed against improper hygiene as much as child labor, against liquor as much as weak labor unions.

Washington Gladden was one of this school's most virtuous champions. A Congregationalist minister, Gladden tethered morality to industry in seemingly intuitive ways, forging a religious vision to improve "the mental and moral qualities of the working-people."[8] Invoking the biblical fact that Christ himself was a day laborer (i.e., a carpenter), Gladden's sermons and theological reflections understood industrialism as a teachable moment. The author of such manifestos as *Applied*

Christianity (1889) and *Social Salvation* (1901), Gladden preached, "The Christian law is, that we are to do good to all men as we have the opportunity; and certainly the employer's opportunity is among his employees."[9] A pastoral mandate if there ever was one, this sentiment caught on for reasons far less divine than Gladden's. During the late nineteenth century, as a technological revolution created a spiraling demand for labor, unkempt immigrants met morally anxious industrialists. Interested in a more reliable workforce, taking a page from Gladden's own prayer book, Cornelius Vanderbilt and other railroad magnates founded Young Men's Christian Associations, or YMCAs, along trunk lines to minister to their workers' spiritual needs.[10] And as YMCAs preached a message of sobriety, one that stewarded immigrants from the bottle to the bathtub, other industrialists went so far as to build entire communities to Christianize their workers' habits and character.[11] Suddenly, swiftly, sensibly (it would seem), management's Christian duty came into focus. The employer should be to his employees as the shepherd to his flock.

Missionary networks pushed this pastoral approach to Guatemala. As nineteenth-century liberals reoriented the national economy toward the cultivation of coffee, the Guatemalan government actively recruited Protestant missionaries from the United States. Beyond providing a hospitable atmosphere for German and North American Protestants interested in business opportunities, the Guatemalan government also sought a level of control on some rather intimate scales.[12] Edward Haymaker, one of Guatemala's first Protestant missionaries, announced in 1887, "When the people of Guatemala begin to develop [the country] along modern lines, when they learn sanitation, motherhood, education, thrift ... Guatemala will be one of the greatest little countries in the world."[13] Identifying the rural poor as "the Great Unwashed," Haymaker published Christian pamphlets on health and hygiene, all for Guatemala's Christian salvation and industrial revolution.[14] These two processes were hardly distinct. Inspired by the promise of modernity, located at the intersection of social salvation and self-help, missionaries linked techniques of the self to discourses of development for a postcolonial state on the cusp of industrialization.

In the end, these reverent reformers initiated a hemispheric conversation about proper management—one that continues to pulse with the rhetoric and ritual of Protestant progress. It is a conversation that formed the soteriological foundation of Frederick Taylor's *Principles of Scientific Management* (1911) as well as its eventual countermovement,

Elton Mayo's school of human relations (1933).[15] Both approaches have defined managerial logic for the last century by providing two contrasting points of reference. Mayo's principled commitment to employee satisfaction has offered a counterpoint to Taylor's "systematized sweating." For all their differences, however, these two approaches share a common denominator. Both Taylor and Mayo, men of science rather than salvation, spent their days (much like Gladden, much like Haymaker) asking how they could make labor *more*—not simply more wealthy or more productive but also more efficient, more punctual, more satisfied.[16] While many things have changed about the economy since the Social Gospel movement, the most obvious being the systematic restructuring of what was once known as the social, this quasi-theological interest in *more* is why the *Harvard Business Review* can oftentimes read like the *Harvard Theological Review*—why Peter Drucker and Rick Warren are the twenty-first century's most likely of bedfellows.[17] Modern management, like modern missionaries, yearns for Protestant subjects capable of self-control—of setting their pious sights on *more*.

MORE

The purpose-driven life has made the call center an ideal place to control the deported.[18] A corporate vocabulary puts into practice what a Christian faith makes intuitive: that the body is a temple to honor ("Exercising 30 minutes a day relieves stress," proclaims call center signage), that the self is a wilderness to conquer ("Attitude . . . that's the hardest thing to control here," sighs a floor supervisor), and that the soul is a terrain to control ("You cannot buy the devotion of hearts, minds, and souls. You must earn these," reads *The Successful Contact Center Manager's Bag of Tricks*).[19] Calls to self-improvement stud recruitment efforts. Buzzwords like *integrity* and *tenacity* as well as *passion* and *fulfillment* drive full-page advertisements in the daily newspapers. One even quotes William Arthur Ward, a self-identified inspirationalist and the author of *Fountains of Faith*: "If you can imagine it, you can achieve it; if you can dream it, you can become it."[20] Often framed by fluffy white clouds or with images of stairways to heaven, these advertisements present coiffed employees who deliver stilted testimonials that are overwhelmingly interested in *more*. One reads, "In Transactel, I get the necessary tools and motivation to become *more*."[21] Another explains, "Helping young people on my team is my true passion. I am pleased to be a part of their personal and professional improvement. With time, seeing someone become *more* is quite reward-ing."[22] Each profession ends with an echoing evangelical mandate: *Bring out the power in you.*

This interest in *you*—this repeated concern for *you* to become *more*—evidences how the practice of security (much like today's corporation, much like today's church) has become both flat and flexible.[23] While the nineteenth-century prison constituted individuals as a single body to the advantage of the prison guard, and while the twentieth-century factory presumed labor's natural inability to self-discipline, the call center invites the deported to recognize themselves as a "bundle of skills" in need of management.[24] "We invest in our people," announces Transactel material, "by providing a development program which includes techni-cal and soft skills training."[25] Punctuality is one such skill. Humility is one more. Empathy is yet another. To manage these unruly skill sets, the deported undergo perpetual training. They cultivate their American accent, biting their lower lip for the letter *v* and popping their mouth for the letter *b*. They memorize long lists of so-called power words, such as *awesome* and *incredible*. They master sympathetic tones. "I understand that reliable Internet service is important to you," each repeats with affected conviction. Rooted in allegories of industrial religion, colored by the making of Christian free enterprise, today's Guatemalan call centers splinter the deported into an array of skills that only the deported can manage—that only *you* can make *more*.[26] No longer is the employer to his employees as the shepherd is to his flock. Instead, the deported has become his own shepherd; his skills have become his flock.[27]

This integration of self and power tends to make control "continuous and without limit."[28] Nowhere is this more obvious, ethnographically speaking, than in those moments when the deported describe the con-trol to which they have become subject—the very freedom that controls them.[29] "You know what the call center reminds me of?" Carlos asked the question while zigzagging through traffic. Cruising some of Guate-mala City's sketchier *zonas*, he eventually answered his own query—just after explaining how his newfound faith in Christ had kept him from killing the man who had shot him in the neck just one year ago. "'Cause I see that mothafucka every day," Carlos said, "and he knows what I'm capable of. He fuckin' knows what I was like." Leaning back in his seat, taking the wheel with one hand, he waxed, "For real, you know what it feels like when I'm hustlin' throughout my day? Answer-ing phones and gettin' my shit done? It feels like prison. For real. It feels like prison 'cause I know what I got to do when I got to do it. And if I fuck up, they're gonna put me in the hole. For real. It feels like I'm back upstate, hustlin'." A former member of Mara Salvatrucha (MS-13), Carlos spoke from experience. Born in Guatemala but raised in Los Angeles, in and out of correctional facilities for the last fifteen years, Carlos knows the hum of solitary confinement in a place like San Quentin as well as the blur of a Guatemalan prison riot in a hole like Pavoncito. "I was in Pavoncito for the riot [of 2002]," he waxed, "People choppin' bodies up. Flushin' that shit down the drain. Fuckin' nuts."[30]

Carlos is no stranger to containment. He is no stranger to violence. This is why I felt comfortable calling his bluff. "But you're free," I said.

"*Por favor*," he huffed. "I ain't free. They fuckin' watch me all the time."

To Carlos's credit, they do watch him all the time. Digital security cameras observe and record every square inch of call center turf. Quality assurance managers also listen to and assess (in real time) an unspecified number of calls each day while Automatic Call Distribution technology (ACD) keeps the pace of work humming—with industry-specific software generating, in the words of Ian Hacking, "an avalanche of numbers."[31] How many minutes does it take to resolve a customer complaint before lunch as opposed to after lunch? How many seconds does an employee spend in the bathroom every day? How many minutes, on average, are employees late during the rainy season? Supervisors chart this information with ease. "See, you just press this button right here," a floor manager explains, "And all this data comes up, in a second. Everything you'd ever want to know." Even the workstations themselves function as ergonomically complete punch clocks. Employees click in and click out of their computers for forty-five-minute lunches, fifteen-minute breaks, and five minutes for the bathroom—not five minutes per trip but rather five minutes of "bathroom time" across a ten-hour shift. And an intricate swipe-card system grants certain employees access to certain spaces while restricting other employees from other spaces. This is ultimately why a dense literature assessing the call center commonly invokes the Roman slave ship and the nineteenth-century prison.[32] "Visibility," Michel Foucault reminds us, "is a trap."[33]

Critical interest in the panoptic underscores the ethnographic fact that call centers do not watch the deported nearly as much as the deported come to watch themselves. This is the soul of security. This is postwar security's subjective turn. As call centers promote a near-compulsive commitment to continuous self-improvement, as the practice of postwar security becomes increasingly concerned with the deported's moral constitution, an assemblage of Christian techniques and corporate consciousness encourages a kind of introspective selfhood that is, in the words of Jean Comaroff, "capable of searching inner dialogue and free to commit itself to a moral career in the name of truth."[34] Perpetual training, promotion schemes, and call center competitions, with winners receiving anything from iPods to buckets of Red Bull, constantly direct the deported to turn inward toward the self—until he or she stands face to face with the pious subject.

Few themes capture the ambivalent moral tenor of this inward turn better than the promotion and practice of punctuality and emotional self-control. Both skills dominate the everyday lives of call center employees; both punctuality and professionalism provide "an effective means of working on the self and a fitting medium for signaling its interior improvements."[35] As management mobilizes missionary idioms to elevate speed, efficiency, and economy well past the practical and on to the theological, the deported come to watch themselves with a Benedictine appreciation for the clock as well as a pious commitment to humility. "As a company, we want to advance Guatemala. It's our mission," a recruitment manager explains. "We want to make Guatemalans better. We want to make them *more*. Time is a big part of this. People come here, and they learn about time. They learn what it means to be on time. They learn what it means to respect time. Respecting time means respecting yourself and your neighbor." Time as a moral imperative structures the call center context—in advertisements, on signage, in the middle of American accent training. One industry newsletter encouraged the employee to complement workplace management through personal initiative: "Get your clothes ready the night before, give yourself an extra thirty minutes to get ready, leave earlier than you absolutely have to. These are all things that can help you get ready and out the door so you can face the world—in the punctual way."[36] At other times, management speaks on its own. One student overstayed his lunch break. His instructor scolded, "We are not just learning English here but also how to stay on a schedule. You get an hour for lunch right now. That's a pretty sweet deal. On the floor, you only get forty-five minutes. Time is money and you need to take care of it." Prudence, punctuality, and persistence—these pious virtues tether the political to the economic to the subjective.

These corporately Christian values also yield observable practices. Excusing themselves from interviews because they have *six minutes* (rather than a more general, much softer five minutes) left in their lunch break, the deported cut their days into hours and then their hours into minutes. A onetime member of Barrio 18 offered a representative riff. Now a born-again Christian, Andrés left Guatemala for Los Angeles when he was seven years old. Deported some twenty years later, after fighting his way through the United States prison system, Andrés now tames what he understands as his "divided self" with a Christian appreciation for punctuality. "What time you got?" Andrés asks, "I left my machine at 2:30. It's 2:31. Is it 2:31 or 2:32? 2:31? OK. I got forty-five minutes for lunch. So I got forty-four minutes left. It'll take four minutes to get to Burger King and four minutes to get back. I need to use the bathroom. That's like five minutes. What does that leave me? Shit. Like twenty-five minutes to eat. Right? Awright. Let's go." His impulses echo in uncanny ways the very values that Transactel espouses. "We are open and honest," announces the company, "We keep our promises. We make a difference."[37]

Andrés's compulsive attention to time could be linked to an intricate compensation package, one that docks a percentage of his paycheck with every second of work missed. But there is something more here than money. At the end of each month, as call centers print bonus checks by the thousands, an e-mail circulates—one that lists the full name of each employee as well as his or her rate of attendance. The names of those below 97 percent appear in bright red. This e-mail produces a controlling dose of shame for those already marked by a hypermasculine hip-hop swagger that clashes with corporate culture. As if adapted from Nathanial Hawthorne's *Scarlet Letter,* these e-mails animate why church elders did not put Hester Prynne inside a prison but rather put the prison inside of Hester Prynne. Helpful, in fact, is the juxtaposition of Hawthorne's stylized prose with Andrés's altogether raw assessment of these e-mails. Their visceral reactions correlate at a fundamental level, one that scholars of affect rightly understand as prediscursive but not presocial.[38] As Hester Prynne places the letter A to her chest, she recounts how she "experienced a sensation not altogether physical, yet almost so, as of a burning heat . . . as if the letter were not of red cloth, but red-hot iron."[39] Andrés, on his name appearing in red for all to see, sighed, "It's fuckin' cold when they do that. For real. It makes me feel like shit. Makes me feel like I need to be better. I hate when they fuckin' do that." Instead of the foreman and his steam whistle lording over labor, instead of the prison guard gazing from afar, red ink and an avalanche of numbers prompt Andrés to manage his soul for something *more.*

RESPECT

The problem, of course, is that becoming more is not easy. It never has been. Its complexity emerges in routine workplace conflicts, ones that demonstrate how an ascent of any height, any pious plod upward, can be a challenge—and especially when it can be so obviously emasculating. Humility, patience, a commitment to please—each soft skill unsteadies a cohort of men who have shifted, sometimes in a matter of months, from the streets or the prison to the cubicle. Workplace piety quiets some of this noise, making even the practice of punctuality feel like a heroic accomplishment, but observable tensions mount as these men trudge through an effeminate post-Fordist workplace. Respect sits at the very core of this corporate experiment, with authority and upward mobility challenging long-embodied notions of what it means to be a man. "I mean, you always have people who are going to hate on you," explained Fernando, a newly appointed floor supervisor and deported ex–gang member from Los Angeles. "Some people always hate it when you succeed." Fernando's ambitions were as clear as they were brash: "I'm just trying to develop, you know? I'm not trying to be stuck on the phone, taking calls forever." Fernando adjusted his shirt, smoothing it out, "You've got to think about it, the lowest position in the call center is taking calls. And that is technically a good job here in Guatemala. So your goal should be up." And so upward he strove, as encouraged by management. Transactel made some 320 promotions in 2011 alone.[40] "But there are some people who simply do not want to grow," Fernando said. "They don't want the responsibility. They don't want the pressure, but I like competition. I like to challenge myself, and I like to work hard. So I deserve to succeed, and if you were my competition [and you didn't succeed], then I'm obviously better than you." Fernando swaggered across a battlefield lined by the challenges of servitude. "The guy who sits next to me," Fernando mentioned, "I tell him every day that I'm going to fucking crush him like a cockroach."

The immediate battle is over the number of sales one makes, one's rate of customer retention, and that elusive index of customer satisfaction. The larger war is over maintaining some level of self-respect. All of it takes place in the shadows of subservience. One call center script reads, "After your difficult customer has ranted and raved, you can regain control of the conversation by interjecting—but not interrupting!—to thank them for taking the time to give you feedback."[41] All the while, whiteboards dot call center walls, with scores scribbled on each. "Look," Fernando sniffed,

FIGURE 10. Call center signage. Photo by Benjamin Fogarty-Valenzuela.

"If you have 1 [sale] on the board and I have 10 [sales], I'm going to say that you're a onetime fucking fling. And that I'm a consistent performer. I let it be known, you know? I work hard for this shit." But they oftentimes work hard for this shit.

"I won an umbrella," shrugged Jorge, an ex–gang member from Chicago who was deported on concealed weapon charges, "because I won a call. I was expecting a little one. But they hooked me up with a big-ass one. I told my mom I got an umbrella, and she was like, 'This ain't no umbrella. This is a *paragua* (a large umbrella).'"

Jorge takes calls ten hours a day, and Fernando supervises him. This hierarchal distinction creates workplace tensions, upending the semiotics of streetwise masculinity. "It's a matter of respect," Fernando explained, "of people skills, and it's a matter of understanding." But becoming *more* (at Transactel) often means becoming less (of a man).[42]

"I'm a fair person," Jorge explained, "and if you need to get something off your chest, you got to do that." And so they did.

Fernando tells the story without much detail. "I had on a Ralph Lauren sweater, and Jorge told me that I looked like one of those Orange County girls from [the television show] *The O.C.* or some shit like that."[43] With his new position, higher income, and elevated status, Jorge bought new clothes, stretching himself toward an image that reflected his status as a supervisor. It was all part of his evolving makeover. "If I am an agent," he explained, "My next step is that I have to get promoted. I have to. I need to develop myself into a supervisor. From there into an operations manager and then, from there, who knows what next." He paused, focusing his thoughts as well as his ambitions: "You need to have motivation. You need to have a great attitude. You need to embrace change." But change can be clumsy. The distinctions can be awkward. Piety has no dress code. "You know, I never knew any of that shit," Fernando admitted. "My call center job is like my first real job. Before that I worked at Dunkin' Donuts [in Los Angeles]. I worked at Del Taco [in Los Angeles]. I worked at Kohl's [in Los Angeles], like in the warehouse. What the fuck do I know what I'm supposed to wear?"

Standing (as a supervisor) while Jorge sat (as an operator), exposed to the floor, to the snickers, Fernando responded to Jorge's tease: "This sweater costs more than you would ever be able to afford."

And then Jorge replied, "Oh yeah, I bet I could afford you an ass whooping."

The story runs from there: "And I was like 'Oh yeah, is that right?' So then I told Jorge, 'Let's go to the bathroom.'" Fernando made an aside: "And, look, I used to go to the gym back then, so I had my gym clothes with me. So I changed into my gym clothes because I was all formal and shit." Not wanting to fight in his sweater, not wanting to bloody his white slacks, he changed into shorts and a T-shirt. A street fight suddenly became gym class. "We then went to the bathroom, we got into a fight, and we shook hands afterwards. That's it."

Jorge tells the same story, but with more swagger. "Oh yeah, I beat him down," Jorge said. "Basically we always used to joke around. And that day he wore some . . . You ever see them rich people walking on Miami Beach with them white pants and shit, with the sandals?" Jorge struck a pose, posing with a limp wrist to his side. "That's how he was dressed, right? So I told him, 'Hey, man, you look like one of them females walking down the beach. And then he goes, like, 'At least I can afford it, nigga.' I'm like, 'Man, I don't wear those gay-ass clothes anyway.' And then he walked past." The damage was already done. "I was just playing with him," insisted Jorge, "because I thought he was fucking around with me too. I told him 'Hey, yo, Fernando, you know what you could afford?' He's like, 'What?' I was like, 'An ass whoopin', nigga.' I guess he felt like I disrespected him." Fernando did.

Punctuality and workplace responsibilities made the fight near impossible. The call center's disciplinary structures frustrated the actualization of their masculinity at every turn. "Fernando came up to me when I was taking a call," Jorge said, "and I look out the corner of my eye and he's standing right next to me. 'So what you trying to say to me?' he asks me. 'You wanna to get down with me?' I was like, 'I'm not saying nothin', nigga. I come from the 'hood. Do what you want to do.'" The entire time he told the story, Jorge adjusted an imaginary headset—removing the earpieces, covering the microphone, even setting it to one side.

"I got break in fifteen minutes," Fernando told Jorge. "Wait for me outside. We can go box it out at the gas station. Keep this shit out of work." But schedules got complicated. "My fifteen-minute break came up," Jorge said, "and that nigga ended up having to go to a supervisor meeting. But I went down and I waited for that mothafucka at the gas station. Because I didn't know about his meeting. And when I came back up, he's over there monitoring some mothafuckin' calls. And I was like, 'What happened?' And he holds his fuckin' finger up, like 'Hold on, one second.'" In his white pants, with his sweater, Fernando placated Jorge, with his oversized umbrella, as if he was an impatient customer. "I understand that reliable service is important to you," Fernando's finger seemed to suggest, with affected conviction.

Jorge walked away. "I was like, fuck this, I'm going to go log in," remembered Jorge, "'cause your bonus gets all fucked up if you clock in late. I'm like, 'You come get me when you're ready.' So I logged in and started taking a call. And then I put myself off the call because he's now in front of me."

Fernando stepped to Jorge. "Wassup, dawg," Fernando asked, "you ready?"

Jorge did not flinch. "I been ready," he said, "You know what I mean?" With waning minutes working against them and their bonuses on the line, they decided on a more convenient place than the gas station. "So I tell him, 'Wassup, nigga, where we going to go?' And Fernando's like, 'Meet me in the bathroom.' 'So fuck it,' I say, and I went upstairs in the bathroom. But he wasn't there!" Jorge was indignant. "He was downstairs changing into his workout clothes. What the fuck?!" The idea of preserving the very clothes that got Fernando into this fight in the first place struck Jorge as unbelievable. Fernando's masculinity flagged at every turn.

"But I was all formal and shit," Fernando insisted.

Fernando eventually returned. And they fought, with the door held shut by a mutual friend and with employees standing in the stalls, on the toilets, taking bets. "I gave that nigga a bloody nose," Jorge beamed, "a bloody lip. I gave him my napkin that I had taken my sweat off with so he could clean his nose and shit. He was upstairs like this (holding his nose). After that we were cool and shit. I told him, 'Hey, if you didn't like the way we did it right now, we could do this shit again, nigga.' I told him, 'I ain't scared. So if you wanna get down again, we could do it again.'"

Back on top, even if he was still at the bottom, fielding calls while Fernando controlled his schedule, Jorge regained respect: "But [Fernando] was like, 'No, it's cool. I'm straight.' I gave it to him pretty good though. I gave him a bloody nose and a fat lip. I think he learned his lesson." And the lesson was simple. Jorge stated it clearly: "Don't fuck with me. Don't play with me." An amalgamation of street honor and office culture emerged as Jorge pressed for more respect through the language of professionalism: "I never played jokes with him, but he started opening gates like that. And he approached me in a bullshit manner in front of everybody. *That shit ain't professional.* That shit offended me. I felt disrespected in front of everybody." Jorge's resilience, his attention to respect, and his willingness to risk his own well-being provided a release, an obvious escape, from the often demeaning demands of call center work while also reestablishing just how perilous an upward climb can be.

Yet Fernando held perspective. His lip healed, his eye better, he reflected, "Five years ago, I would've never saw myself working at a call center. Never. I would have never seen myself even going to Paiz [an upscale supermarket]. Now that I have a job, now that I have a great future ahead of me, I don't do any crimes." His pride still bruised from the fight, Fernando weighed his options, concluding that success is his only bet: "I don't have anything to worry about. I won't go to Paiz to steal. Why would I? I have money to pay for shit. Before I would've done anything for money. And now it's like my life has completely changed because, thank god, I have an opportunity to work at a call center." Fernando reflected, "The call center just literally saved a lot of people's lives who are in the same situation that I am. Because if there wasn't a call center, where else would we be?" And this is why men like Fernando, in spite of their own masculinity, at the expense of their own respect, strive toward something *more*.

HUMILITY

But, again, becoming *more* is not easy. It never has been. Augustine of
Hippo narrates as much in his *Confessions*, with the bounded will con-
stituting Christianity's most spectacular moral drama.[44] Yet the difficulty of it all has strengthened, it would seem. While Augustine wrestled
with pear trees, these deported men and women, Fernando and Jorge
included, struggle with histories of sexual abuse, drug addiction, and
extended periods of incarceration. Salvation has since steadied the lives
of many, with big falls yielding even bigger redemptions. Nevertheless,
the call center is a somewhat surreal stage on which society expects the
deported to perform Christian respectability. Wrenching cultural con-
frontations complicate the effort at every turn.[45] The call center, to reference a pair of television shows, pulls these deported men and women
from the set of *The Wire* and plants them (without a wardrobe change,
without a new set of lines) onto the set of *The Office*.[46] Instructed by
minister and manager alike to embody the Christian virtues of service
and humility, public subordination still chafes for those ordered to act
like—at times to lie that—they live and work in Nashville, Tennessee, or
in Tacoma, Washington. In some effort to assuage a culturally conservative clientele, one committed (at least in theory) to buying American,
the deported must swallow the fact that they were of absolutely no
use to the United States until the United States deported them. Now
repatriated, they play the part of an American while getting paid like a
Guatemalan—an irony that the deported do not miss. "They pay us
shit," a former member of Barrio 18 explains, "It's shit money. [The call
center] pays us $2.50 [USD] an hour. In Tacoma, I got paid $37.50
[USD] an hour working construction. $2.50/hour! It's good for here—
[but] that's shit money, man."

Frustration turns to insult as the deported realize that their middle-
class lives in Guatemala look absolutely nothing like middle-class lives
in Los Angeles, California. "I used to have my own place in LA," explains
one employee. "It was nice. Big bedroom. I was making money. Running
crystal [meth] between Vegas and LA. I miss it." Another used to sell
crack in Los Angeles. He lived in what he considered to be the lap of
luxury. "I lived at the Holiday Inn," he said. "I used to pay $80 a night.
One time I stayed there for a whole month. That's a lot of Holiday Inn.
But it's crazy, because it wasn't a lot of money to me. I mean, I wouldn't
look at it like a lot of money." The tables turned after being deported.
Guatemala City's Holiday Inn, located in the city's most exclusive *zona*,

charges almost twice as much as its Los Angeles counterpart. With deportation came the visceral experience of downward mobility. Cinderblock houses, corrugated metal roofs, and chickens underfoot—this is Guatemala's professional class. And as their pirated cable television reminds them of what they are missing, from where they came, insult becomes injury as the work itself gets out of control—as the customers themselves get aggressive.

The very nature of customer service, as one might expect, invites a certain amount of customer abuse. "No one calls to say thank you," a floor manager admitted. But more than simple complaints, calls quickly and constantly escalate to outlandishly violent events. During heated disputes over credit card statements and primary billing addresses, over misplaced parcels and delayed deliveries, bigoted customers often ask the deported if they are monkeys, if they live in trees. Baited by Spanish accents, by soft *j*'s and rolled *r*'s, customers invite the deported to go fuck themselves; they call the deported "niggers" and "spics," "wetbacks" and "fuckfaces." All the while, management coaches the deported to respond with empathy, compassion, and emotional self-discipline. "Humility." This is how Andrés answered my question about how he weathers such storms. "I'm not perfect," he added. "No one is. I just try to be humble. To be faithful and humble. It's hard, man. For real. I make mistakes. They make mistakes. I'm no robot. You know? It's hard. It hurts me. Real bad. But I try to be humble and just serve the person."

This language of selfless service braids the material demands of a post-Fordist economy with the new-age rhetoric of Christian servitude.[47] Customer service manuals, quality assurance supervisors, and a seemingly endless cycle of training sessions now frame humility as a heroic venture against the darker side of humanity. All invite the deported to corral their unwieldy instincts for something *more*. A representative call center handbook pleads with the employee to avoid ("at all costs") the four Fs: *fretting, flailing, fuming,* and *freaking out*. In their stead, the handbook asks them to choose—to recognize that they have the power to choose—an "optimal lifestyle." Seven daily practices define this vision of optimal living, one that links the cultivation of the body with the moral maintenance of the soul. These seven daily practices are (1) do not smoke, (2) do not consume caffeine, (3) do not drink alcohol, (4) relax fifteen minutes a day, (5) exercise twenty minutes a day, (6) consume no more than 30 percent of daily calories in the form of fat, and (7) consume twenty to thirty grams of fiber a day.[48] This optimal lifestyle, the handbook insists, generates an optimal attitude, which in turn fosters optimal service. It is this very logic that organized the development of managerial discourse, of industrial betterment itself, allowing a range of Protestant reformers from Gladden to Haymaker to link rituals of consumption and moral posture with the demands of industrial labor. Eat right, drink less, walk more, they preached. *Bring out the power in you,* they insisted.

These same themes of service and humility structured a sermon that Andrés and I had witnessed just a few days before our conversation about humility. In fact, moments before the pastor invited Andrés to tell his own story of salvation, to deliver an hour-long testimony about persistence and progress, he lauded the Christian duty to serve, to understand (with humility) that no one is perfect, that no one is a robot. Shuttling between the themes of crack and cubicles as well as redemption and renewal, Andrés pitched his testimony broadly to everyone in the church that night. But his real target, he would later admit, was a young man named Mario. Raised in the United States but deported from Los Angeles in 2002, this former gang member had spent the last five years on the streets of Guatemala City, where he slept, stole, and smoked—be it crack, PCP, or marijuana. One month sober, in and out of Pentecostal rehabilitation centers for more than a year, Mario twitched from withdrawals as his language skills landed him a back-office job for a major multinational corporation, one that promised upward mobility, expendable income, and self-fulfillment. Hope swelled. This is why, soon after the service, with the aftertaste of revelry still shifting his weight from foot to foot, Mario explained:

> I'm gonna be at this job for five years. Minimum. Five years. I'm gonna work every day, man. [He puts an imaginary phone to his ear.] "Hello, can I have your tracking number, please? Oh, you are experiencing a problem with your delivery? Let me see, how I may help you?" I'm gonna work this. Five years, man. At least. I mean, I'm gonna work and then be manager or supervisor or whatever. This is a good job. This is good money. I'm not gonna go back to the streets. No fuckin' way, man. No fuckin' way. And I know Jesus will help me.

Later into the night, after having attended not one but two services with Mario, his confidence began to wane. Emotionally exhausted, driving along a poorly lit highway, his spirits drooped as his thoughts turned to his first paycheck:

> I'm kinda nervous about having all that money, man. I mean, I'm not the kind of guy who does well with all that kind of money. I mean, take that guy right there. You give him some money and he's gonna buy a burger and go to the movies. That guy over there? He's gonna buy some donuts or something.

But that [other] guy? He's gonna get lost. He gonna get some crack and just get lost. I'm that guy, man. That's why I'm at church. I'm making a fresh start. I'm gonna go to church. I'm gonna go to work. I'm gonna go home. That's what I'm gonna do. And I need to do it all [at once]. None of this step-by-step stuff. This *poco a poco* bullshit. If I don't change totally, I'll be back into it again. I'll be back on the streets smokin' crack and jackin' people for cell phones.

One week later, Mario handed his entire paycheck over to his brother for safekeeping. Also a deported ex–gang member who found Jesus at about the same time that he found work at a call center, Mario's brother promised to dole out the money at a responsible clip while also setting some money aside to pay for Mario's rent, activate his cell phone, and buy Mario a kitchen stove. This effort, planned weeks in advance, reso-nated with the kind of individual responsibilities advocated by not just church elders and faithful coworkers but also onsite sales representatives who spend their days peddling credit cards to call center employees.

The problem is that Mario's plan did not work. Mario cashed his paycheck late one Friday afternoon and delivered, as planned, the money to his brother—but not before taking a bigger cut than he had originally intended. Mario burned through that money in a matter of hours, asked his brother for more money, and then burned through that money as well. Within twenty-four hours, Mario had smoked his entire paycheck, stretching a late night into a weeklong bender. Having never returned to work, having for all intents and purposes disappeared, Mario next spoke to me by phone. He was working on a coffee plantation just outside of Guatemala City, where it sounded like he was living hard and drinking harder. His plan, he told me, was to return to the city to find work at a different call center. Having sold his own phone for crack, I then lost contact with him. His father told me that he left the plantation shortly after we last spoke, but his brother, at that time still employed by a call center, had no idea where he was. His former roommate, a fellow ex–gang member and close friend from Los Angeles, said the same.

To be fair, Mario could have been anywhere. He could have been working at a different plantation, holed up in another rehabilitation center, or hustling crack in the capital. He could also have made another break for the United States. But each of these scenarios seemed unlikely at the time, given how small the country can feel and how violent it had become. Someone would have heard from him by now, I thought. Some-one would have seen him. This is why family and friends, until proven otherwise, assumed that Mario was dead. Until he wasn't.

One year later, I found Mario, by total chance. He was being held captive in a Pentecostal rehabilitation center well beyond the city limits. His face had been beaten beyond recognition. His eye was an enflamed, deep purple. "Kevin," he whispered to me.

"Do I know you?" I asked.

"It's me, Mario," he mumbled.

"What the fuck!" I blurted. Once lost, Mario was now found. Soon after, Mario tried his hand at another call center, but soon disappeared. A pattern emerged, with absolutely no resources available to keep Mario off drugs, out of a rehab, and on the job.

Another year passed, and again I found Mario by total chance. He was passed out in front of a different Pentecostal rehabilitation center in a different part of the city. He had come to visit his brother, the very one who had held (but did not hold) Mario's call center paycheck. Now the brother was being held captive inside the center, for both drugs and alcohol. Mario stumbled to his feet. After a meal and a long conversation, after making a plan for his life and passing me his crack pipe, Mario checked himself into a different Pentecostal rehabilitation center—"for a miracle," he said.

One more year later, after he had tried yet another stint at a call center, with his brother in yet another Pentecostal rehabilitation center, I visited Mario in prison. He had shaved his head, making prominent a tattoo etched across the back of his neck. It read, "Me against the World." Mario scribbled in a notebook while we spoke about his future. At the top of the page, he had written: "Act like a man. This is a man's world." At the bottom of the page he had traced, with meticulous detail, a computer keyboard, upon which he practiced his typing.

As I handed Mario 200 quetzales (US $25) to get him on his feet once he got out, he passed me a letter to mail to a girlfriend. She lives in the United States. Written with care, and without knowing whether this woman would ever (could ever) reciprocate with her own note, Mario wrote with a mix of presumption and intimacy. The letter read, in part:

> I'm locked down in jail right now. I went wild the other day. These two women tried to hit [me and my brother] with sticks. I had done nothing. For real. I didn't do shit. I didn't let them hit me. I've had enough. Fuck that. I have been thru [sic] too much shit. Been in too many fights. They hit my brother though in the forehead. He was all bleeding. Had to take him to the hospital to get stiches. I almost smashed one of [those] bitches with a glass. I'm glad I didn't. I would have gotten into all kinds of shit and troubles and I don't need that. [But] that's not the reason I'm in jail. The reason is that I was drinking, and I got into an argument with my dad and the police said

something and I didn't like it so I argued. They got me in here for drinking. Sorry baby. I had stopped. I'm not drinking in here. Not even smoking. They got cigarettes. But if I don't smoke, I don't drink. So I don't smoke no more. I pray to God to help me stop drinking. I trust in God. And I pray. [Because] drinking every day is fucked up.

LIFE ITSELF

Inconceivable as it is indicative, painful as it is predictable, Mario's disappearance, his perpetual displacement, is tragic. Yet, sadly, it is not unusual. While an increasing number of deported ex–gang members find their professional groove within this rapidly growing industry, their Christianity syncing smoothly with the moral demands of corporate culture, many more do not make it. They return to gang life, fall back into addiction, or simply lose faith—in Jesus, in themselves, in life. Here one day, many are gone the next. Management, in response, does not blink. They are not paid to blink, they insist. Instead they troll the airports looking for more talent. "The ones that we fight for are the *mojados* [wetbacks]," the director of human resources admitted. "They are the most valuable here. Because they have perfect English. Perfect. We can place them in any account. We find them in the airport."

The call center's laissez-faire approach to human capital would seem to demand a righteous response, one that relies on the power of critique.[49] Much could be said along these lines, of course. Mario and Andrés, Jorge and Fernando have all been jerked around by powerful economies for far too long. Yet it is important to note that the strength of critique tends to evade the less comfortable possibility of implication—of not simply the idea that we all participate in global capitalism but also the ethnographic fact that deported ex–gang members tend to want (at times, desperately need) call center jobs. Critiquing call centers for their practices flattens the fact that these positions provide calm ports amid unthinkably turbulent storms as well as some much-needed dignity. "I remember I was on the eighth floor of Transactel," explained a born-again Christian and onetime member of Barrio 18. "That's near the airport. And I was on the eighth floor [looking out the windows]. And I remember I had a mug, right, a coffee mug. And I was on the eighth floor with the mug, and I could see all the garbage trucks, right, and I start crying. 'Cause it was raining. I start crying because I remember I was working, under the rain, the year before [as a garbage collector]. And I could see the trash truck pass by . . .

I could see myself, sitting, inside the truck, behind there. Just like, wondering what God was going to do with my life." Pushed to Los Angeles at three years of age, deported on gang charges seventeen years later, he flailed in Guatemala. McDonald's rejected him. "When I landed in Guatemala, I decided to do something I would never do in LA . . . Work at McDonald's. 'Cause McDonald's *sucks* in LA, right? It's the worst job you can get. To work at a fast food restaurant? But when I got there, what do you think they told me? They said, 'You got tattoos, pal. We are not accepting people with tattoos.'" Years later, after gathering Guatemala's garbage, he found himself overlooking the city—from the eighth floor, in a pressed shirt and with a warm cup of coffee. Emotions grabbed him. "And I would just see myself right there [in the garbage truck], and like, I just broke down. And . . . and people [at Transactel] would be like, 'Hey, are you OK?' I just . . . and I would be like, I just . . . I can't believe how good, how good God is. God has been wonderful, man." It is this wonder, this potential for dignity, that makes the work of the call center more complicated than some crass distinction between right and wrong.[50] To quote Fernando again, "The call center just literally saved a lot of people's lives. Because if there wasn't a call center, where else would we be?" This is why radical critique (at least for now) gives way to what Fiona Terry has called a "second best world."[51] This is a world in which call centers crave the same self-regulating subjectivities that postwar security officials covet and that new forms of Christianity help cultivate.

In critique's stead, in the spirit of a conclusion, a nuanced observation comes into focus about Christianity, corporatism, and control in the practice of postwar security. It is an observation that shifts this analysis from the ethnographic to the political. To what effect have call centers become viable spaces of control in a postwar context that can be obviously and perpetually out of control? The answer pursued here begins with the fact that the soul of security provides a softer approach to the deported than ever before. Again, jobs, not jails; control, not containment—this is the move. But by turning toward the subjective, by availing the soul to the practice of security, a growing number of men and women come to be understood not as a menace to society but rather as unsound and unproductive—as expendable. The call center (as a supremely soft security scheme) has come to define life itself along some rather Christian coordinates. If they are humble, punctual, and patient, then the call center rewards the deported—with bonuses, corporate swag, and training programs that *bring out the power in you*. Yet, if

prideful or undisciplined, if reckless or rough, the deported disappear—
and are allowed to disappear, to vanish without a trace. Their divided
souls—the very souls that the call center makes legible through a corporately Christian register—end up justifying their disappearance as well
as a socially acceptable lack of concern for those never seen again. The
soul of security, in the end, advances a set of criteria by which a range
of social actors assesses the deported as either out of control or in control, as either lost or found.

Take the lead-up to Mario's first paycheck. In between church services, on his day off, Mario found himself the subject of an intervention.
Organized by coworkers and fellow churchgoers, riddled with shouting
matches and long bouts of weeping, the meeting eventually ended in
frustration. Mario ultimately left the room to clear his head while
Andrés talked to me about preparing Mario for payday. He explained,
"You gotta know how to talk to these cats. You can't just get up in their
face and talk down to them. You see how he was gettin' all frustrated
and angry? I just calmed 'im down. I was like, 'Check yourself, bro.' And
then I was like, *pow!* You can't talk to them when they are all frustrated.
They aren't gonna listen. You gotta wait until their heart is open." That
Andrés participated (along with Mario) in the governance of Mario
well beyond the reach of not just the call center but also the nation-state
evidences an ever-expanding security apparatus, one that extends into
the everyday lives of the deported.[52] The soul of security shoulders an
increasing number of individuals with not simply new responsibilities
(e.g., Mario) but also new domains of control (e.g., Mario's heart).

Yet, the constitution of the soul as the terrain upon which individuals
practice security also reframes the criteria by which these individuals
assess these new responsibilities and these new domains of control.
Again, the case of Mario proves instructive. One month after the intervention, catching Mario's floor manager on his break, I asked what had
happened. "To Mario?" he asked. "He didn't come to work—it happens
all the time. It's not my problem. Why [did he leave]? No idea. I guess
his heart wasn't into it." To the manager's credit, he quickly substanti-
ated this otherwise flippant comment with rows of numbers, each making legible the quality of Mario's heart. On a scale from 1 to 100,
Mario's heart had been mapped along the lines of rudeness, politeness,
customer rapport, professionalism, personal responsibility, tone, and
accent. That each metric seemed to confirm the manager's suspicion is
not the issue, which, rather, is the simple fact that we sat there together
reading Mario's heart across a morass of numbers.

These moral metrics, the very ones by which management controls employees, bring the deported's soul into being; they make the deported (by way of the soul) both governable and self-governing.[53] These numbers also frame not just the deported but also security more generally as a matter of having a heart that is either open or not, that is either into it or not. This is a significant development for a postwar context long defined by a strong-fisted approach to delinquency. The wrath of the sovereign now competes against much softer efforts at control. From informal death squads to the politics of self-improvement, from overcrowded prisons to *bringing out the power in you,* the call center allows the practice of security to nest on the surface of the heart—to bury itself deep inside the soul. Whether this approach proves effective, in some kind of criminological sense, is not yet clear. It may never be clear. Obvious, though, is that the Christian underpinnings of this corporate construction provide a moral mechanism by which to determine the value of life itself. Mario's heart, for example, "wasn't into it." The numbers say as much. This is why management did not blink when he disappeared. They just counted him as lost and then headed back to the airport.

Service

I wasn't sure he had heard me. I yelled again. This time a little louder: "Mateo, get the fuck off of him!" Mateo was in his front yard, on top of some teenager, throwing punches. It had all happened so fast that I didn't know how to react. One moment, we were watching a movie in Mateo's living room. Then an older woman walked through the door. She was looking for her son. Mateo got upset, raised his voice at the woman, and said that her son was not in his house. And maybe she should keep a better eye on her son, he huffed. To add insult to injury, Mateo had been on the phone when the woman barged into his house, disrespecting his airtime as well as his home.

"Get the fuck out of here," he screamed. "Get the fuck out of my house."

She left, throwing out a rather common religious reference with a rather sarcastic tone: *"Dios le bendiga"* (God bless you).

"Fuck that bitch," Mateo mumbled. "Talking about God and bringing in my faith in the Lord. How the fuck do I know where her son is?"

The thing is, Mateo usually knew where her son was. He tended to be in Mateo's house getting high most every afternoon. Mateo's house, over the years, had become a kind of safe space for wayward teenagers who could not smoke in their parents' house. They would come over, watch movies, and get high, splitting their stash with the house. This kept Mateo in proximity to a steady stream of low-quality marijuana while also providing him a chance to do what he loves the most: work with youth. "These young guys come here to learn shit, to learn how to come up. It keeps them off the streets and in my house, where they learn about everything. Girls. Drugs. Gangs." Sometimes twice the age of these young men, with life experiences that radically outpace theirs, Mateo models himself as a mentor. It is what he has always wanted to be.

"That was my dream," he once told me while standing at a bus stop, "I could have a little office. Right? 'Come into my office,' I'd say. 'Hey, how's it going, man?' You know—talking to the kids. That was—that was my dream. Being a gang counselor." Now kids sit on his couch to smoke a joint. "I wanna be working in prevention," he would tell me, "That's what I wanna do, man. You got all these little young kids out here—imagine me, putting myself straight." Part of the fantasy of helping always included Mateo setting himself straight. Mateo would save the youth and the youth would save him. "And next thing you know, they're coming out here, looking for me, maybe all high, but they wanna hear something about life. And, little by little, I start throwing the good things at them, like 'Dawg, you know, you're better than this, you're better than that,' and next thing you know, I'm hanging out with these young kids right here, they're coming here, asking for advice—that's something that I would love."

The problem was that not everyone appreciated his guidance. The kid—that is, the son of the woman Mateo had cursed out—stormed into Mateo's house not long after his mother had left. She had told him the things that Mateo had said to her, the way he had treated her, the disrespect he had extended to her—in front of everybody, in front of strangers. Standing inside Mateo's front door, interrupting the movie, this young man screamed at Mateo, marshaling as low a voice as his eighteen years could muster. Mateo told him to get the fuck out of his house. The young man did not. Mateo told him to back the fuck up. The young man inched forward. Mateo took a step toward him while the young man stood his ground. That's when Mateo rushed him, pushing this skinny teenager out his front door and onto the ground. On top of the kid, Mateo threw punch after punch, landing only a few. A fifteen-year-old kid from the neighborhood quickly separated the two. The young man then stood up, told Mateo to fuck off, and walked home. Mateo followed him, slowly, clicking his index finger on his thumb on both hands. It is a common Guatemalan gesture that means "You're fucked. Just wait for what's coming." He did this until the young man turned a corner. "I went easy on him," Mateo said, still out of breath, "I didn't want to hurt him. The fucker just came into my property speaking all loud and shit—at me during my visit and disrespecting me. He can't disrespect my home during a visit. Mothafucka gotta learn."

Mateo tried, several times, to connect with funding streams. Billions of dollars have entered Guatemala in the name of gang prevention, but the work is surprisingly difficult to secure. The U.S. Congress allocates money to USAID, which generates overhead; USAID subcontracts its gang prevention programs to the Research Triangle Institute (RTI), which creates overhead; RTI connects with local non-governmental organizations to steward programs, which builds overhead. By the end, when the money has been allocated, very little is left for those working on the ground—for men like Mateo, who have the experience and the passion but need a sustainable income. I once watched Mateo pitch his services to USAID program officers, inside their eleventh floor offices, masterfully shuttling between the organization's own talking points and his life experience. The program officers were impressed but had no role for Mateo. They were in the middle of an expensive advertising campaign to keep children in school. Their flyers dotted the capital city with catchy phrases. "Preventing violence is everybody's work," one read. "Shoot goals, not bullets," a more popular one stated. "Hands up!" read yet another, with a picture of arms extended upward, "Let's unite against the violence." "Send me to school," the last one pleaded, with the face of a child, "not to the streets." These flyers ate up their budget. So Mateo left the meeting with no leads and a deep frustration.

Only a few minutes after the fight, on his way to the mall in the hopes of buying a new phone card, Mateo's imagination expanded. "It felt like I was back in LA, getting into fights with guys every day, guys from different neighborhoods. You'd fight and never know when the next one would be. Maybe it would be an hour later or that night." His nostalgia sounded tinny. It was the kind of homesickness that replays the past onto a flagging present, with no hope of the future. "He's 18. I'm 34. And I have a hurt wrist, and he couldn't even drop me. The drugs must be making him weak and hurting his health." Still sparked with emotion, on edge with adrenaline, Mateo channeled his energy into life lessons. "That's why people get robbed, 'cause they walk around all pussy, looking scared of everyone, afraid of everything. You gotta show that you're not afraid. You gotta show how tough you are. People will see you and be like, that mothafucka is tough. I'm not gonna rob him." Taking a deep breath, collecting himself, Mateo started to calm down. Laughing a little, he turned to me and said, "At least I'm real with you, bro. I don't try to hide shit."

Mateo's dream once dragged him to La Paloma—to work with youth, to make a difference. Soon after his deportation, while working as a prison chaplain, he connected with a gang prevention program in La Paloma. To paint a quick picture, La Paloma is in the middle of the city but sits at the bottom of a canyon. These canyons, or *barrancos,* cut the capital, with cliffs appearing throughout the city. At the bottom of these dramatic gorges sit squatter communities that formed in the late 1970s, after a massive earthquake jump-started rural-to-urban migration, forcing poor, indigenous families to claim seemingly unclaimable land. Their location, in the middle of the city but at the bottom of it, places them close to the capital but absolutely beyond the reach of state services. Or as Mateo said, "Shit, dawg, yeah—it smells. [La Paloma] is dangerous. It's fucking dangerous, dawg. La Paloma is not a place to play around. You got those little young kids, homie, but they will not hesitate to rob you or kill you day or night." Unsurprisingly, La Paloma has a gang problem. "They shoot each other," Mateo explained, "'cause there's like four gangs in La Paloma. There's 18th, Sureños, MS. And there's the Sicarios as well. And they shoot each other. So some parts of La Paloma, not even regular people can go to them. And the ones on top, on the north side, northeast, cannot go down, and the ones on southeast can't go down either. So they fight—basically, they fight each other all the time. It's like a war zone." Mateo was not exaggerating.

The logistics of La Paloma have always been challenging. "They're really stuck," Mateo said, "These people in La Paloma, they have to come out at a certain hour, at a certain time." With multiple gangs controlling limited entry points into the community, Mateo had to adjust to a schedule that was beyond his control. "So, when people leave, when they climb up to the city, they always go during the gap, 'cause they know . . . the other side already knows what time they get out. So it's just a risk for them. For everybody. They don't know if they're gonna come back out, or if they're gonna go up, prob'ly stay down . . . You can't go out anytime. They shoot you, man. It could be this time. It could be the next time. Like when I wanted to get out—shit, it took me like two hours to get outta there sometimes, 'cause you gotta find a way, you gotta see who's there, you know—things like that. Shit is complicated."

Complicated as it was, Mateo found himself called to help, largely because a North American nonprofit organization started a child sponsorship program in La Paloma, in the hope that an influx of material and moral resources might help change the situation. Mateo, fluent in

English and with street swagger to spare, proved the perfect ambassador for North Americans interested in visiting their sponsored child. "Yeah, I would take 'em around. But sometimes it was just bullshit. Sometimes they ask a lot of questions, and it's like, 'You just gotta relax, man—like, you can't know everything in one pop.' I mean, sometimes they ask questions like what kind of robberies the youngsters do, if they use guns, where they get the guns—things like that." Much of the work turned into keeping North Americans safe. It was not the kind of prevention that stoked Mateo's flames.

"I'd tell 'em it's dangerous here, that you guys can't be walking out here by yourselves—you guys can't even come out with the amount of things you have with you, like cameras. One time they tried to jack this guy named John. One of the kids from the neighborhood tried to jack him. The dude from the States thought he had trust with the neighborhood already. But these gangsters there, they were about to rob him, his cameras, everything. But we were able to talk to the North Americans. We said, 'Nah, let's just get outta here. If you were with more people, you guys could be walking like that, but without us, you guys cannot be walking around like that. People will rob you.' They went too deep into the neighborhood. They went past the part of the neighborhood where the sponsorship program works. They stopped—they tried to go visit a family. And the guys were like, 'Hey, wassup. Gimme some dollars, and shit. Gimme some money.' And they were like, 'No, we don't have none.' And they said, 'What you got right there?' you know. They had some cameras and stuff. We all got upset. These people from the States, they don't listen, man."

Mateo spent most of his time decoding his unfamiliar world to unfamiliar people. "It's not like we have that kinda stuff in LA. La Paloma surprised me, man. Some people living there in their own homes with Pampers with shit right there—fuckin' no cleanup. Even the kids were all rusty and shit—all ashed on their skin." But he did the work of an ambassador. "I told the North Americans, 'They're gonna think that you guys are recording, or taking something, you know, and they're not gonna like that, 'cause you're gonna be exposing their neighborhood.' There's certain rules here. There's certain politics. There's certain things that you cannot do. And they were like, 'Yeah, we're sorry. We just, you know, we just thought it'd be OK.' Nah, man, it's not cool. It's not safe. These kids, man, they . . . they . . . they come from broken homes, man. They have to see how they're gonna come up for their bread, man. You know what I'm sayin'? Some of these kids have kids. Those guys are young, but they got babies, man. They gotta see how their kids gonna eat, man. They need something. They'll rob you. They don't care. You know what I'm saying?"

But the work excited Mateo. "I had it nice, man," Mateo mentioned, still at the bus stop, "I didn't have to go the call center and log myself in, be inside. I'd go to a rehab and preach a little. Give a little word to the men, there. And then I'd take off, to La Paloma, get down there around 10:00, 10:30—I'd stay there 'til like, 5:00, 6:00. I'd go visit people, and there was church services, too. And I'd go to the church service, for like an hour or two—sing a little bit. Sometimes I'd preach the Word. I would speak up, like, you know, read Psalm 25 and give an explanation or whatever. I'd be, 'OK, brother, just read this and that—OK, brothers.' Now try to give them explanation of what that verse is talking about, you know?" Mateo looked down the road, in search of the bus. He didn't want to be late for his call center shift. "Maybe I preach about tribulations," he continued, "and maybe I'd tell 'em, 'Listen, tribulations is necessary for us to go through, because that makes us stronger, makes us see other perspectives, point of views, that some of us are living blessed, and some other people are living, you know, messed up, you know. Tribulations can mold us. So, you know, when the big giants stand up against us, you know, we'll be able to . . . we'll know how to resist them, how to deal with them. And yeah, sometimes we do fail. We fall. But that doesn't mean that you have to quit, you know. Where there's life, you can do it, so . . . if you don't have no more life, well, you're cashed out.' That's the kind of shit I'd say." The bus was late. He was going to be late.

And people responded to Mateo. "They even hug you. They even cry with me—they open their hearts to me. They talk about, like, secret things, like damn . . . like, oh, shit. 'Cause we did it together. We prayed together, we played together. You know, we went out there with the kids, you know—do like, soccer activities. Just play with them and stuff. And they'd be like, 'Damn, this guy's here with us.' They would ask questions about my tattoos, certain drugs, and my life. It's deep. But that's what we need here in Guatemala. We need prevention. There's people that are able to do it, but others can't. They don't, dawg. They haven't lived that life. They haven't lived in prisons. They never been in gangs, and stuff like that—because if you have, you have a better way to communicate with these youngsters, with these young cats, man. You know . . . the pastor . . . the pastor is good—I'm not saying pastors are not good—but in this situation, it's better, because people like me are able to answer questions about the lifestyle, you know."

Mateo always considered himself an answer, an untapped resource. "If I had the opportunity to do prevention work again, I would, you know. I've got the skills. I got the talent. I got the patience. I love it. I love doing that—I'd rather be working outside than inside. I'm more of an outside dude . . . But all that I know I put it to work in these call centers, man. But believe me, dawg, sometimes I feel like quitting the call center, man, you know. I told my dad about it, 'Hey, Dad, I'm tired of working in these call centers. I wanna work somewhere else. I wish I could. I used to go fishing for souls. That's what I call it. You know what I mean? With the little hook—next thing you know, we got the fish. We got a good handful. So that's how I did it, you know? I came in there, like, 'Yeah, homies, how many you guys like gangbanging? How many guys here like cars and drugs, and the money, the guns, and the power . . . the respect?'—you know? And everybody would be like, 'Oh, yeah! I do, man. Yeah, yeah! And the kids are already all into it, and then you start, talking a little bit about your lifestyle, and then the consequences.' You know, living on the streets, being homeless, being a drug addict, going to rehab—things like that." He said all of this right before hopping on the bus to make his call center shift. As he leapt aboard, Mateo conceded, "I guess it's all service." He meant gang prevention, whether in La Paloma or in the office of USAID, but he also meant his work at the call center. The boundaries between these sites seemed to bleed into one another, if only by way of piety. He might have also meant his free time spent with the kids in his neighborhood. "It's all service, you know."

CHAPTER 4

Left Behind

"It's not so much that they need me and that they need us, but we need them. We need the people of La Paloma." An evangelical Christian from Barey, North Carolina, with hipster hair and a tasteful tattoo, clarified his commitment to the child sponsorship program that his faith-based 501(c)(3) facilitates. Pitched in the name of gang prevention, the program connects North American evangelical Christians with at-risk children in one of Guatemala City's most structurally violent neighborhoods: La Paloma. Along with US$35 a month, sponsors shower the sponsored with handwritten letters, birthday presents, and even the occasional site visit—all to create a context in which these kids might choose God over gangs. The effort is an uphill battle, to be sure. Bullet holes pock La Paloma's narrow streets as perpetually unemployed men huff paint thinner. Petty theft, extortion, and close-range shootouts have also encouraged a variety of institutions to disengage with this so-called red zone (*zona roja*).[1] Located in the very center of the city, at the very bottom of a canyon, La Paloma, by all accounts, is off the grid.[2] With an estimated 60,000 residents, the neighborhood has no formal economy, no public schools, and no basic infrastructure. Often described as the largest urban slum in Central America, the Guatemalan National Police rarely enters the area, nor does the United States Agency for International Development (USAID). Even with tens of millions of dollars earmarked for gang prevention, USAID program directors insist (without the slightest bit of irony) that La Paloma is too thick with gang activity for them to pursue gang prevention.

FIGURE 11. La Paloma. Photo by Benjamin Fogarty-Valenzuela.

A different sensibility places this child sponsorship program directly in the streets of La Paloma as well as on the front lines of postwar security. Following the talk of prevention rather than the penitentiary, evangelical programs from across the Americas have answered a growing call to engage neighborhoods that no other program would enter and experiment with approaches that no other project would entertain. This is why child sponsorship now coordinates comfortably with an ever-expanding network of house churches, faith-based youth groups, and "play and pray" afterschool programs. Each targets at-risk youth. Each focuses on gang prevention. And each plays it pretty close to the Bible.

Stretched between North Carolina and Guatemala, between child sponsors and sponsored children, an evangelical imperative to sponsor at-risk youth locates the question of postwar security at the level of the subject more than the neighborhood, the population, or even society. The net result is what I understand as the *subject* of prevention: the individual imagined and acted upon by the imperative to prevent.[3] This "subject of prevention" includes not only the at-risk youth in all his racialized otherness, but also, and increasingly so, evangelical Christians who piously craft their subjectivities through their participation in gang prevention—as ministers, missionaries, and mentors. Consider the sense of self that child sponsorship affords this Carolinian. "Yes," he continued, "[the people of La Paloma] need to be liberated from the oppression of poverty, drug abuse, sexual abuse, a lack of education, and opportunity. But I (and we) need to be liberated from materialism, consumerism, narcissism, entitlement, meaningless distractions, and so much more. And our liberation from these things is bound up with the people of La Paloma." For the sake of security, in the spirit of salvation, child sponsorship makes the work of gang prevention dependent upon the practice of self-cultivation.

Inspired techniques with long Christian histories assemble the subject of prevention one uneven exchange at a time: site visits, letter exchanges, and gifts sent from afar. This chapter assesses all three, not only to detail their productive qualities but also to theorize their effects.[4] A properly assembled subject behaves well. The sponsored child asks the right questions. He writes the perfect letter. She recites a beautiful prayer. This pious behavior tends to mobilize the compassionate Carolinian, motivating a transfer of resources and opportunities.[5] Those children who misbehave, those assembled otherwise, oftentimes get left behind. This radical disparity—between those sponsored and those not, between those "needed" and those not—illuminates the surgically selective nature of postwar security. For antigang efforts across the Americas do not just dominate or manipulate subjects, but they also mobilize them by linking certain passions and anxieties to the possibility of an alternate future. Again, listen to this Carolinian: "Our relationships with [the people of La Paloma] will liberate them and will liberate us. They need us and we need them." It is this need, this liberation, that not only constitutes the sponsored child as a privileged site for ethical self-formation but also cuts a place like La Paloma into hundreds of little enclaves of privilege.

"FOR $21 A MONTH"

The evangelical impetus to secure is, of course, nothing new. Faith-based initiatives have long trafficked in missional intimacies that inspire, in the spirit of Gayatri Spivak, white Christians to save brown children from red zones.[6] U.S. foreign policy, by the mid-twentieth century, had also made fashionable an emphasis on winning hearts and minds.[7] Yet, this specific story of security qua sponsorship starts largely in North America. There, in the early 1980s, middle-class men and women framed their lives as distinct projects of self-cultivation.[8] As the liberal gave way to the neoliberal, as Phil Donahue lost out to Oprah Winfrey, cable and late-night television programming offered new occasions for subjective work, with a host of personalities equipping a new class of consumer to meet the demands of flexible accumulation.[9] Sally Struthers proved iconic. She endorsed VHS tapes that extolled the virtues of power walking; she promoted diet books that lowered cholesterol one kefir shake at a time. She also pioneered distance education, framing retraining as affordable, fun, and risk-free: "Would you like to make more money? Sure, we all would."[10] But beyond certificates in child day care, gun repair, and interior decorating, Struthers's most recognizable work coupled middle-class North Americans with desperately poor children throughout the so-called Third World. Amid rubbish and rubble, always within arm's reach of starving children, Struthers pitched child sponsorship as an intuitive answer to everyone's suffering—to the child's (for lack of food) but also to the sponsor's (for lack of love). "For about $21," her commercials for the Christian Children's Fund explained, "you can buy an all-day ticket to an amusement park. In Guatemala, for $21 a month, you can help a child like Wilma get the clothes she needs to attend school."[11] Often straining the ethics of representation, with images of mosquitoes buzzing from lip to nose and then back to lip, Struthers offered charitable outlets that not only paid for eyeglasses and bags of rice but that also presented middle-class North Americans with a distinct set of practices that could cultivate moral consciousness, empathy, and self-worth. Writing to, praying for, and thinking about poor children such as Wilma allowed sponsors to exchange vice for virtue, to replace conspicuous consumption with "conspicuous compassion."[12]

A new era of evangelical Christianity celebrated this asceticism, framing faith not so much as a religion as a relationship—between you and God, between you and your neighbor, and (most importantly) between you and yourself.[13] From the Pentecostal to the Presbyterian, from the layman to the life coach, a denominationally diverse set of "morally ambitious Christians" raised their level of expectancy; they "got up on the inside" and they reprogrammed their "mental computers."[14] As a "purpose driven life" slowly came into focus, as millions of Christians committed themselves to becoming a better *you*, charity grew alongside chastity as a way to increase in God's favor.[15] "If you want to live your best life now," megachurch mogul Joel Osteen writes, "you must develop a lifestyle of giving: living to give instead of living to get."[16] This evangelical imperative ultimately put a premium on those charitable organizations that could deliver bite-sized bits of *caritas* to the masses. To its credit, child sponsorship programs delivered these "ordinary affects" in spades.[17] Grainy Polaroids, handwritten notes, and annual report cards brokered hypermediated relationships while at the same time generating significant amounts of money. By 2012, the top five child sponsorship programs managed over US$5 billion in global revenue.[18] These deep pockets have ultimately allowed the industry not only to take up "the spirit of development" but also to set its sights on security.[19] Because the problems are real and the answers are relational. World Vision sponsors at-risk children in the *favelas* of São Paulo; Compassion International does the same in the slums of San Salvador; and this Carolinian directs his 501(c)(3) toward the children of La Paloma.[20] Each effort provides youth with a purportedly viable alternative to the streets. And so for US$35 a month, the logic now goes, you can create a context in which Wilma might choose God over gangs. It is a technique, a mode of governing, that tethers security to salvation to subjectivity—that assembles the subject of prevention one transnational exchange at a time.

ON THE OUTSKIRTS OF EDEN

In La Paloma for a week, with corrugated metal overhead and chickens underfoot, a half-dozen child sponsors sat at the bed of a recent gunshot victim. A gang member had attacked her taxi a week earlier, the woman explained, shooting her in the leg and killing her mother, her sister, and the *taxista*. Although the motive was not (and may never be) clear, what was obvious, at least to the missionary translating this exchange, was that this act of gang violence orphaned children, it tore apart already unstable families, and it perpetuated cycles upon cycles of violence. Also obvious was that this shooting was entirely preventable. "If someone would have been by their side," this missionary insisted, "if someone would have been there defending these gang members, being supportive while they were little children suffering traumas, if only someone had loved them and helped them, then they would not be who they are today." She paused, to punctuate her next point. "A lack of love causes them to become like monsters that extort, kill, rob, and rape. And only the love of God can heal and prevent." Presence, not absence; love, not hate; affection, not aggression—these practices assemble the subject of prevention.

So too do moments of righteousness: as these child sponsors sat awkwardly on the edge of this bed, with each Carolinian wanting to fade as quietly as possible into the background, this young lady, this gunshot victim, began to cry. She cried for her sister. She cried for her mother. She wept until a middle-aged man from North Carolina spoke up. Called by the Holy Spirit to testify, to announce the saving grace of Jesus Christ, he proclaimed God's eternal wisdom, describing Him as an omniscient gardener who tends to His flowers from a vantage we can never completely understand. Ultimately making an awkward parallel between pruning and perishing, between the trimming of rose bushes and the murder of this young woman's family, he invited everyone, this woman included, to read her tragedy as an invitation to become stronger Christians. Tears are fine, he conceded, but her future, everyone's future, holds the promise of real happiness—of real salvation. He then prayed aloud for this woman's pain as well as her children. They are the real victims, he stressed, yet they also hold the promise of real happiness—of real salvation.

This sermon, whether timely or tactless, resonates with the history of North American evangelical Christianity. The virtuous have been staging morality plays in the homes of poor folk for centuries now, offering the unfortunate not so much leading roles in these fictions as opportunities to play "the human scenery before which the melodrama of middle-class redemption [can] be enacted."[21] Antebellum literature drips with these kinds of digressions. Henry David Thoreau, Nathaniel Hawthorne, and Herman Melville each place upright men and women in disheveled spaces so that they can lecture to the poor on comparative poverties and spiritual wealth.[22] Louisa May Alcott's *Little Women* even opens with a so-called poor visit: "'It's so dreadful to be poor,' sighed Meg, looking down at her old dress."[23] For centuries, throughout the Americas, an evangelical thematic has synchronized material abundance with ritualized piety as well as poverty's material culture with the trappings of delinquency. To control one's urges, to wear that old dress for just one more season, has long distinguished civilization from savagery, deservedness from delinquency.[24]

New here is that a pilgrim's progress now gets coded as security.[25] This not only elevates the reformation of subjectivity over the restoration of society but also prioritizes revelation over results. "It's not really our job or responsibility to get results," reasons one child sponsor. "We just need to go out there and live in obedience to what Jesus wants us to do." This faithfulness is one reason why the existential fallout of these short-term mission trips is not just a financial recommitment to La Paloma but also a moral reordering of child sponsors. "There's just as much darkness in Barey," confessed Susan, a mother of two and sponsor

FIGURE 12. Barey, North Carolina. Photo by Tomas Matza.

of one. "Maybe more in Barey than in Guatemala." Sitting at her formal dining table, already late for her daughter's tae kwon do class, Susan continued, "They have poverty and oppression in Guatemala, but here we're blind to the fact that we need God. So our affluence here keeps us from God. It keeps us from knowing our identity in Christ." Susan sipped tea, adding, "I came back [from La Paloma] a completely different person. I sold my car. I got a little thing, you know. And actually I had a lot of trouble with the house. I came back and I was like 'I hate my house. I hate it.'" Fidgeting with her tablecloth, fingering a loose end, she confessed, "I did [hate the house] because his face, and seeing where he lived, it just . . . I have thought about him every single day. Every single day since I left." Susan trailed off.

Brought back by idle small talk, by memories of past mission trips, nostalgia mixed with observable anxieties about her own security: "A former police officer talked to my women's [bible] group about gangs and what a gang problem there is in Barey." She sat up in her chair. "And he was saying, 'You gotta be careful because the people doing your lawns are in gangs. There are gangs all over. You just don't know it.'"

If this was the case, I asked, why did she not sponsor a child in Barey instead of Guatemala?

Susan answered. "We have stereotypes in America, and they are mountains to get over. It's sad because Christ says there will always be the poor among us . . . but it's hard to help here. But with Guatemala, you don't have any of those [stereotypes]. There's no presumption over why that person is there. And even though this might sound selfish, like I go to help and I get helped, I think child sponsorship can also be the catalyst for a different mindset." Sponsorship displaces sponsors just enough to keep them on track. Yet, this displacement disturbs them. Susan whispered, "I went in one house, and it was just a dirt floor. [It was a] dirt floor with a dog chained to the wall, bloodied because he had all these bugs. I mean, it was nasty. It was oozing. And the toilet was sitting on the dirt, in the back, over a pipe. [The whole house] smelled like dirt, you know?" This filth, this danger, this difference—it stirs Susan.

And stir it should. Susan's memories are visceral. "I was the organizer for the last trip," Susan remembered with a shiver. "I get chills on my arms just thinking about it." She took a sip of tea, steadied herself, and continued, "It was a scary situation. We went into this person's house, and we're just singing music but at the same time you heard gunshots going off and . . . like . . . just lots of noise outside." Susan flipped through some photos from the trip as she spoke, pointing out the ravines and the unstable houses, the winding alleyways and the abject poverty. "I guess at night . . . you know . . . in that community everybody comes out at night, right? Not like here where everybody goes in their houses at night. So it was . . . you know . . . it was just such an intense moment for us to be in that house, singing Spanish songs." The experience for Susan had nothing to do with content and more to do with context. Susan does not speak Spanish: "I had no idea what people are saying. We're listening to the pastor give a message, and it was just really, really powerful—something that I've never experienced before, and it really felt like we were in such a dark place and this little house was like a light." Christian idiom provided Susan with some moral coordinates. Light versus dark, good versus evil, here as opposed to there—these divisions allowed Susan to comport her experience of alterity. "It was like . . . you know, God was just coming out of this house. And . . . uh . . . in a positive way but also in a way that was attracting evil at the same time." Susan's eyes lingered on the photos. An experience, an unforgettable evening, a story to be retold dozens of times over.

The output of it all is a feeling. "You go around and you do home visits, right? So that's pretty powerful. When you start going around [La

Paloma] and you go into people's homes—and I wouldn't even call them homes. I call them caves, some of them." Susan pushed a few more photos my way: windowless structures made of sheet metal, pushed up against a canyon wall. "But we saw one girl in the alleyway, smiling, hugging, and then . . . you know—it wasn't twenty minutes later we had wound our way back to a house where she was, and we went in there, and she's just bawling." In what seemed like a moment, between caves, maybe even inside of one, everything changed—not just for that little girl but also for Susan: "We find out that she pretty much had been sexually molested right then. From the time we saw her to the time we got to her house, and you know just . . . just the power of thinking . . . man . . . this little girl . . . I have little girls. I just couldn't imagine the life they live." Susan broke story, looping back onto something she said earlier: "I mean, I really did hate my house. When I got back from La Paloma, I just hated my house. I did."[26] Cast aside by privilege, left pushing a camel through the eye of a needle, the practice of child sponsorship delivers to sponsors, to Susan herself, a clear sense of their place in this world. It is rarely in Barey, North Carolina, or even in Guatemala City, but rather on the outskirts of Eden.

NOT EVEN A BLOT

The prospect of clawing their way back into the Kingdom prompts many to travel to La Paloma, to pray with their sponsored children amid the smell of weed and the crack of gunfire, but it also mobilizes many more to put pen to paper—to write to their sponsored children in the hope of saving a soul perched on the edge of a moral precipice. It is an epistolary engagement, iconic to the industry, driven by an evangelical interest in proper etiquette. "The letter you write," explained Emily Post in 1922, that mistress of middle-class American morals, "is always a mirror which reflects your appearance, taste and character." "A sloppy letter," she continues, "with the writing all pouring into one corner of the page, badly worded, badly spelled, and with unmatched paper and envelope—even possibly a blot—proclaims the sort of person who would have unkempt hair, unclean linen and broken shoe laces."[27] What Post knew intuitively, a half century after Protestant missionaries first set foot in Guatemala, a half century before the publication of Pierre Bourdieu's *Distinction,* was that the terrain of cultural production communicates the quality and character of one's self.[28] Delinquency is in the details. And an attention to these details has come to manage the practice of gang prevention in La Paloma. From correct grammar to suitable stationery, from appropriate topics of conversation to just the right question, letters exchanged between sponsors and the sponsored discipline the at-risk child.

"It was ridiculous," the director of child sponsorship complained. "Sponsors would write these wonderful letters. They'd write about their life and their hobbies. And then they'd get a letter back from a fourteen-year-old kid who should know how to write, and all it says is, 'Dear sponsor. I love you. Love, your sponsor child.'" These scrawny efforts suggested ungracious subjects. "I like the color blue," rambles one letter, "I weigh 110 pounds. I don't know how tall I am. That's how I am. I am fourteen-years-old. I love you a lot." So too did misinterpretations. "I sent a picture of myself, my son, and my daughter some time ago," a sponsor writes, "You wrote back that I had a beautiful house. We were not in my house in that picture. We were in a conference hall at a wedding." Lined with gaffes, providing clouded windows into complicated lives, these letters assemble the subject of prevention one missive at a time.

To the director's credit, child sponsors do write wonderful letters. They are clear, creative, and intimate (without being intrusive). They perform the very sense and sensibility—the very self-restraint—that sponsors want for the children of La Paloma. "Please know," writes one sponsor, "that even though we can't see you in person, you are in our hearts and thoughts every day. We love you very much and want to continue to be a part of your life." Driving these letters, in fact, is a vision of domestic bliss motivated by the pleasures of Protestant self-mastery. "On the weekends we usually go for a run," writes one sponsor. "Tate and Logan ride in a stroller and I push. Mason and I both love to run. It's one of our favorite things to do. My job right now is to be mommy to Tate and Logan. I feed them and take them places. I also clean a lot of boys' clothes." Running as recreation, motherhood as a profession, children with places to go—these letters present the children of La Paloma with a distant vision of domesticity. Yet, this is the air that these Carolinians breathe. Professional degrees and six-figure salaries mix with the rise of intentional parenting as well as a new generation of stay-at-home mothers, all to make Barey, North Carolina, revolve around the life of children. A list of child-centered enterprises that border this sponsorship program's evangelical church includes Uptown Kids Toy Store, Children's Academy Daycare, Youthologie, The Little Gym, Klaystation Crafts Studio, Lil' Chef Cooking Studio, and Junior Judo for Jesus, which provides a "God-centered resource for training your children 3 ½ years and older in godliness, Christ-like character, physical fitness and self-defense." Palpable expectations abound.

The children of La Paloma struggle to keep pace. It is simply not obvious how they are supposed to maintain a correspondence with middle-class North Americans. The two contexts can be so radically different. "I understand the fear you have for Diego walking from school [because of gangs]," writes one sponsor. "[Our daughter] Molly walks to and from school on one of our busiest streets." A painfully brief letter sums up this disconnect. "Send me a Wii," one child writes—without a please, without a thank-you, without any written concern or consideration for his sponsor's family or well-being.[29] This request, and letters that revolve around similar requests, upset not simply the sponsor but also program directors who want these letters to be as relational as the evangelical Christianity that now helps structure postwar security. Expected, in fact, is not a Wii wish list but rather a Christian conversation between child and adult—one that couples childhood awe with a mature spirituality. "Your encouraging letter," explains one video, "can give your child an emotional, social, and spiritual boost. So it is important for their development. It can inspire them to study harder, be more confident, and draw closer to God."[30] Yet, brief and brash letters routinely reduce the practice of gang prevention to producing the proper letter and, in turn, the proper subject.

"A lot of it," admits the director, "is just looking over their shoulder and making sure that they're doing it right." And look over their shoulder they do. In the office, the sponsored child reads the translated letter out loud and then replies immediately. With the letter fresh in the child's mind, program officers coach the child in proper penmanship, correct grammar, and appropriate word choice. They also prompt the child to pose some questions of his or her own. One effort at a correspondence revolved around the seemingly innocuous topic of household pets. The children of La Paloma, coached by program officers, described their own pets, and then asked their sponsors to describe theirs. Dog or cat, male or female, young or old—sponsored children navigated a series of binaries to script a recognizable narrative for an almost unrelatable audience. "I like animals," writes one child, "like dogs and rabbits. Which animals do you like? I like the ones I just told you. The dog. I like the dog the best." Sponsors proved more than happy to engage. "My family is doing very well," writes one sponsor. "We've been busy trying to keep our dog clean because it has been raining a lot here, and he is very white." The problem is that the vast majority of children in La Paloma do not usually have pets. Some have guard dogs, but the custom of domesticating a cat or dog for companionship has not yet made its way to La Paloma. It is a hiccup that ultimately makes strange a letter that reads: "Dear Sponsor, I tell you that I have a cat and a dog. They're very caring, and I like to play with them. My dog's name is Wilson and my cat's name is Chucho. I like your dog and cat. I say goodbye with many hugs and kisses. Love, Your Sponsored Child." In what spirit is such a fiction scripted?

Much of the imagination here has to do with the mechanics of the industry. Standards of practice keep this supposedly personable ritual rather impersonal. Sponsors, for example, are prohibited from revealing their full names, home addresses, and contact information to their sponsored children. This is for everyone's security, the literature insists.[31] "A lot of these kids have cousins or older brothers in the United States," explains one program officer. "We don't want any of our sponsors in North Carolina to be approached by a family member." The officer then squared her shoulders a bit, "And it's not like the children here don't have access to the Internet. How awkward would it be for a [sponsored] kid to go on Google Maps, type in the address, and then see their sponsor's huge house?" Google Street View could even put the sponsor child at the sponsor's front door. So the exchanges are light. "Keep your letters simple and not long," advises one organization, "Don't go into too much detail. Avoid topics of religion or politics. Do you have a garden? Many children are involved in growing some form of crops."[32] The impersonal can even mutate into the anonymous: "Letter writing not your thing?" asks another organization. "Let us know. We can arrange for someone to write on your behalf."[33] And so in light of it all, the topic of pets—even if they do not exist, even if they are not a recognizable category for the children of La Paloma—can seem like a pretty safe topic of conversation. "If you have pets," prompts yet another organization, "let your child know. They may have an animal too."

The children of La Paloma tend not to have animals. Yet this fiction's intent, one might venture, is to assemble a subject amenable to the practice of prevention—one that is conveniently distant but appropriately intimate, reassuringly familiar but timelessly foreign, uncomfortably gauche but ultimately responsive. The myth of pets, of domesticated animals, helps to configure the alterity that sits at the very center of sponsorship itself. Driven by domestic expectations, this vision of the at-risk youth also contorts the sponsored child, fusing the production of a letter to the production of subjectivity. For the practice bends the

sponsored child to understand how unmatched paper and envelope—
even possibly a blot—evidences the sort of person who has unkempt
hair, unclean linen, and broken shoelaces. "Just as a neat, precise, evenly
written note," adds Post, "portrays a person of like characteristics."
Again, delinquency is in the details. Or, as Post concludes, "One may
read the future of a person by [the] study of his handwriting."[34] Faith-
based gang prevention and, in turn, an integrated approach to security
follows this adage as well as the morality upon which it rests. And it
does so compulsively—as do the subjectivities subsumed by the practice
of child sponsorship.

HE LOOKS LOST

"There's a story behind Ronald," admitted Mary over dinner. Eighteen
years old, Mary's sponsored child, Ronald, is alive, not in a gang, and
gainfully employed in Guatemala's formal economy. He stocks shelves
thirty hours a week for a Walmart subsidiary, punching his clock and
paying his taxes. Child sponsorship made all the difference, Ronald
insists. Those thirty-five dollars a month kept him in school, off the
streets, and within earshot of ministers, missionaries, and mentors. But
so too did an anxiety disorder. "He's obsessive-compulsive [or OCD],"
Mary admitted. "It's a real predicament because it's so filthy [in La Pal-
oma]. I don't know how he does it. There's actually a high suicide rate
in children with OCD, especially in areas where cleanliness . . . where
being . . . you know . . . being in . . . The ghetto is kind of tough." Tough
it is—for everyone involved. Ronald's grandmother, who works at an
area elementary school, cried on my shoulder, explaining that Ronald's
compulsiveness keeps him indoors for long stretches of time; it sparks
seemingly irrational bouts of anger while also sliding him in and out of
depression. He irons his shirts for hours, she explained.
    "But we've helped him with his OCD," continued Mary. "We always
send him soap, rubber gloves, cleaning stuff, and the . . . uh . . . whadya
call it . . . hand sanitizers." Ronald's compulsiveness even connected the
two. "I didn't know [he has OCD] when I picked him," explained Mary.
"I just saw his picture [online], and you know—and no offense—when
you see the cute little girly faces, the little boy faces . . . and you know,
you say, 'Oh, he's so sweet, she's so sweet.' But I felt God . . . I felt God
pulling me, because I thought, 'Well, all the little children are getting
[sponsored], but what about these older kids?" Mary ultimately took
the road less traveled by selecting a decidedly uncute kid. "Anyway,

when we picked him, we didn't know. 'Cause when you pick a child, you just pick one, and then you get a bio on them, and when they did . . ." Mary paused, eventually adding, "When they did, I understood God's plan. I am a perfectionist, cleanliness kind of freak in a way, so I knew God led me to him, and not only . . . not only because I felt . . . I looked at his picture and felt a connection. He needed somebody. Look at his face in that picture. He just looks . . . he just looks . . . lost. He looks lost." She raised Ronald's sponsorship photo up to my face, as if the image would mirror back to me the very existential displacement that Ronald reflects onto her. I admitted to seeing a young man. "But he looks so lost," Mary insisted.

However lost Ronald looked, finding him proved relatively easy. At first aloof, even distant, Ronald eventually engaged Mary and her husband, providing the two with the emotional means to cultivate their own Christianity while at the same time allowing Ronald to garner some resources. "I wouldn't have finished school without them," Ronald confessed. "I just wouldn't have finished." We spoke in a Burger King restaurant near his place of work. "I was awarded a scholarship to go to school because of them. They paid for me to study." Throughout the meal, and during every meeting afterward, he exuded appreciation—for his sponsors, for the program, and for the not-so-simple fact that he never joined a gang. "There are these thugs in the neighborhood," Ronald explained. "They steal stuff and the gang of them just keeps getting bigger. The gang keeps growing bigger with evil thoughts." He was right on track, with clearly articulated aspirations to attend college and eventually work at a bank. Yet he also ate with fresh napkins, never letting his bare skin touch his own food; he would also excuse himself midmeal, even midconversation, for the washroom. With the smell of antibacterial soap often framing our time together, with nervous energy shifting his weight from side to side, Ronald's ability to embody the subject of prevention often seemed less a heroic accomplishment than some kind of pathological inevitability. The proof was always in his production. His sponsorship letters were immaculate. The writing never poured into one corner of the page. There was never a blot—not even a smudge. His penmanship and spelling proved as tirelessly obedient as the pleats in his pants. Easily coded as moral rectitude, as man over mania, Ronald punches his clock and pays his taxes amid unprecedented gang violence. He is a true success by all accounts. "But he paces," his grandmother wept. "At home he sometimes paces all night."

The singularity of Ronald's pacing, his commitment to pleating, helps shed light on the shifting forces that allocate the recognizability of certain persons as amenable to evangelical prevention. Looking lost, for example, as opposed to looking delinquent, is a delicate cultural accomplishment. So too is the ability to *feel* that someone, like Ronald, looks lost. All of it depends upon a certain field of perceptible reality already established, at least here, by a faith-based 501(c)(3) devoted to making legible the intimate contours of both the sponsor and the sponsored through the language of being either lost or found. The blogs, the photos, the letters, the trips, the gifts, the money—especially the money—mediate this exchange, framing young men and women in Guatemala as well as well-intentioned evangelical Christians in North Carolina as interrelated projects of self-cultivation.

One observable effect of this mediation is that a certain kind of subject, a subject not unlike Ronald, connects (at times compulsively) with class to embody personal transformation. Polite letters, ironed slacks, and a punctual lifestyle keep young men like Ronald on the grid. It cements the sponsorship. "He didn't have clothes to go interview," explained Mary, "so we sent him $100 for him to go out and get clothes for his job interviews." Ronald happily complied. "I bought pants, a sweater and a button-down, formal shirt," Ronald beamed. "I was with him that day," mentioned one program director. "He was so excited about picking out new clothes in the store, you just wouldn't believe it." Shopping in a solidly middle-class mall, Ronald bought the kind of clothes that made him look as if he lived somewhere other than La Paloma. And this was the point. "Because the way I understand it," Mary explained, "if you've got an address in La Paloma, it's hard to get a job down there." This is true. With less than one-third of the country working within Guatemala's formal economy, with so-called legitimate work difficult to secure even for university graduates, the people of La Paloma often lie about where they live. No one would hire them otherwise. This is why Mary's gift proved so productive. It allowed Ronald to double down on the act with a new pair of slacks and a crisp oxford shirt while at the same time confirming the rejuvenating power of wearing one's Sunday best. A refined appearance, missionaries have long argued, delivers a new sense of self. Makeovers are not only material but also moral. New clothes make the man.[35]

"I'm trying to think of the word," Mary murmured. "[The program director] used a word [to describe Ronald's shopping trip], and she said it was, um, a holy moment. She literally used that word, she said it was a 'holy moment.'" Commenting on her goose bumps, tearing up, Mary continued, "To see him, knowing that he went in that store and picked out anything he wanted. And he got new clothes, and now he has a job!" Mary took a moment. Collecting herself, she continued, "I mean, [La Paloma] is just a group of people like anybody else, just in a condition where we as Americans, or whoever in the world, just say . . . you know . . . you're worthless . . . you know . . . you're not worth anything. Gangs are all it's about, and people breeding children, and children turning into gang members." Mary shook her head in disgust—because her gift, her US$100, this holy moment, it all argued otherwise: it all placed Ronald, or better yet allowed Ronald to place himself, within a certain field of representability. Sponsorship framed Ronald faithfully; it made him legible to those who needed him the most: North American evangelical Christians. For without Mary, Ronald probably would have joined a gang. But without Ronald, without a story like Ronald's, Mary would never have liberated herself from materialism, consumerism, narcissism, entitlement, meaningless distractions, and so much more. She would never have come to hate her own house. "Sometimes I wish he had never come across my path," Mary admitted, flinching at how harsh her words sounded, "because I have so much love and compassion and worry for him, and I feel so helpless that sometimes it causes me so much heartbreak." But heartbreak is what Mary is after. And it is what child sponsorship delivers.

The practice of evangelical gang prevention permits Mary to change Mary by way of Ronald and, in doing so, provides Ronald with the means to change himself. This security scheme is, to borrow the language of philanthrocapitalism, "a win-win."[36] Luckily for Ronald, Mary's desire piques with every short-term mission trip. The texture teases her every time. "Until you are walking in there," Mary insisted, "and you are smelling and hearing and seeing, you don't get it at all. Your brain changes. You change gears once you've witnessed all of this." Yet, not everyone is as attentive as Mary, and not everyone proves as supple a subject as Ronald. This Barey-based 501(c)(3) manages some four hundred sponsorships in La Paloma while another twenty thousand children from the same community go without a connection. An understandably small organization, one committed to the quality rather than to the quantity of sponsorships maintained, this faith-based approach to gang prevention nonetheless cuts a place like La Paloma into hundreds of little enclaves of privilege, the spatial contours of which say something about postwar security today. Some children make connections; they fulfill a need. Others do not. They get left behind.

LEFT BEHIND

"She started dating one of the new gang members," explained the director of child sponsorship. "He recently got out of prison. Anyway, they asked her to do a couple of errands and she came back without a sufficient amount of money. So her boyfriend's gang did that awful thing to her." She, the victim, was fifteen years old. The sister of two sponsored children, the cousin of seven more, she lived a life proximate to prevention. Presents peppered the spaces she crossed—but never her space; letters lined the lives of her loved ones—but never her life. Without a sponsor, without a Mary, this young woman had few holy moments. Instead, like so many others in La Paloma, she lived (and died) completely off the grid. Rarely a minister or a missionary or a mentor wrote to, prayed for, or thought about this young woman. This may be one reason why it came as a shock but not as a surprise when, on October 15, 2011, residents of La Paloma found this young woman at the bottom of a sewer—as well as in an alleyway and in a trash dump. Killed, quartered, and then cast aside, this fifteen-year-old woman quickly entered a field of representability radically different from that of sponsorship. After death, at the point of discovery, she became a number. Sixty-two. Her death marked the sixty-second time in 2011 that a Guatemalan woman had been murdered, mutilated, and then found in multiple locations.[37]

The Guatemalan National Police made an appearance. They took some pictures and asked some questions, but they never initiated a full investigation. "No one from the community wanted to talk," a homicide detective explained to me more than a year after the murder. "And with every day that passes, more cases come in." So no arrests have been made. And none are expected. It is an unbelievably brutal, depressingly quotidian fact that tells a number of different stories—of feminicide, of postwar impunity, even of structural effacement.[38] "The young man who killed this young woman," the detective added, "he cut her up into pieces. It was terrible. But we think he was also killed. We think." His conclusions stayed in the subjunctive tense, confirming neither an assumption nor a lead. His ambiguity affronted any sense of justice while highlighting the manufactured distance between those sponsored and those not, between those "needed" and those not. These sharp realities underscore a central claim here: that the practice of evangelical gang prevention produces its subject through a series of confessional images and imperatives, generating an extractive geography of salvation, of security, that saves some while leaving many more behind. This observable fact is best understood in light of not just Gilles Deleuze's insights on postindustrial cartographies of control but also the faith-based fiction of Tim LaHaye and Jerry B. Jenkins. Their *New York Times*–bestselling book series sheds some light on the extractive dimensions of being Left Behind.[39]

The young woman, to explain, lived alongside (literally beside) dozens of sponsored boys and girls. She was related to no less than nine of them. She even knew Ronald. They brushed shoulders, shared acquaintances, and even spoke from time to time. Yet, on October 15, 2011, Ronald could be found stocking the shelves of a Walmart subsidiary while neighbors found this young woman in pieces. "It was a terrible murder," the detective stressed. "She was mutilated very, very badly." He shuffled papers on his desk. "We just can't do anything," he said, "if we don't know anything." It is a contrast that could provoke the predictable critique that Christian charity is either imperfect or individualistic. Helping can hurt—but social scientists know this.[40] Christians know this.[41] Instead, the distance between these two life stories betrays a spatially significant kind of disparity that the practice of evangelical gang prevention makes possible. Given that ministers, missionaries, and mentors throughout the Americas have long coupled prevention with proximity—by placing young men and women shoulder to shoulder inside churches, schools, factories, prisons, rehabilitation centers, and so on—it is astounding how irrelevant brute proximity (standing shoulder to shoulder) has become to the practice of gang prevention today. "I hadn't even seen a picture of Mary and her husband before I met them [in La Paloma]," mentioned Ronald. "I had no idea what they looked like." Not only does Mary not need to live next to Ronald to save Ronald, but Ronald's onetime proximity to the murdered woman also said nothing about either's relationship to an ever-expanding postwar security apparatus. Providence plucked one out of obscurity, dusted him off, and bought him a fresh pair of slacks; the other got left behind.

Gilles Deleuze, a quarter century ago, forecast the fall of the built-form: the astounding irrelevance of brute proximity. "Man is no longer man enclosed, but man in debt," he wrote.[42] The prison, hospital, factory—environments of enclosure—are in crisis, he insisted. In their stead, fields of perceptibility make individuals legible (or not); they make certain people needed (or not). This shift is part of postwar security. For child sponsorship today mobilizes individuals one life story at a time—praying that the at-risk youth as well as the North American evangelical Christian will recognize himself or herself in the very subject imagined and acted upon by the imperative to prevent. "Because my kids," Mary reasoned, "they go to bed, and really, there's no worries. There's food. They have what they need, and they have a good school. But this one family I know [in La Paloma]—the husband's in jail, because he attacked the wife with a machete. Now the wife is functioning with only one arm but still needs to care for her kids." Mary sighed, "It just weighs so heavy on me." This exhaustion, directed toward control rather than containment, marks the subjectification of security.[43]

One observable effect of this effort is an extractive geography, as captured by LaHaye and Jenkins's book series. To recap, the Left Behind series begins in an airborne Boeing 747. In flight to London, without any warning, select passengers suddenly disappear from their seats. Millions more disappear around the world. Their bodies vanish. "Harold's clothes," the opening chapter narrates, "were in a neat pile on his seat, his glasses and hearing aid on top. The pant legs still hung over the edge and led to his shoes and socks." As the story unfolds, it becomes clear that those who disappeared have met their maker; they are safe with God. It is a narrative that ultimately explores the emotional texture of the sudden selection of one life over another—of one saved and one not. To their credit, the authors start slowly, with a closed, contained environment. The person in seat 15C disappears, but the person in 15B remains. Harold vanishes, but his wife stays—to rock and to whimper in her seat, to bury her face in her hands. When the plane lands, however, the authors push their trope to its logical conclusion. An unborn baby disappears from the womb of a pregnant woman; a groom vanishes while slipping the ring onto his bride's finger. Panic erupts: "She lifted a blazer," the novel continues, "shirt and tie still intact. Trousers lay at her feet. Hattie [the stewardess] frantically turned the blazer to the low light and read the name tag. 'Tony!' she wailed. 'Tony's gone!' "[44]

What connects this fiction to the fact of La Paloma is the dramatic distinction between those sponsored and those not, between those saved and those not. These distinctions typify the spatial contours of postwar security today, revealing a salvific kind of segregation that looks less like a city of walls or a planet of slums than a city of the saved (and not).[45] Certain individuals assume and become subsumed by the subject of gang prevention (and others not). This willingness, as explained above, has much to do with coding compulsiveness as Christian. Yet other reasons remain. In response to my question why a young boy named Jefferson does not have a sponsor, the program director explained, "Well, it turns out that Jefferson's dad beats his mom. But when Jefferson is [home], he [beats his mom] less often because the dad is embarrassed to do it in front of Jefferson. So that's why he stays home [instead of participating in the program], because he doesn't want his mom to get beaten." And so Jefferson stays home, in a windowless house that can be as dark as night even in the middle of the day. He sometimes stays there all day, oftentimes all alone. The sacrifice is real. And it is desperately heroic. But it does not improve Jefferson's life trajectory. Willing or not, able or not, the effect of Jefferson's isolation is the same. Jefferson has been left behind. But Ronald, by way of Mary, has not. He is connected. It is an extractive kind of outcome. For when evangelical gang prevention programs drill down, "all the way down," to quote Clifford Geertz,[46] into the life of the subject, to imbricate the subjectification of security into mutually constitutive projects of self-cultivation, what tends to emerge is a bright line between those on the grid and those not—between Ronald and number sixty-two, between seat 15B and seat 15C. This selection can seem serendipitous ("I knew God led me to him," Mary insisted), but it can also seem sudden, surgical, and senseless ("Why did God let this tragedy happen to my poor little girl?" the aunt of number sixty-two wailed). The ultimate effect leaves many (far too many) to rock and to whimper, to bury their faces in their hands. In the end, what emerges on the ground, ethnographically speaking, is not just a clear sense that the subject of prevention saves a select few, but also that for those left behind, for young boys like Jefferson, the apocalypse has only just begun.

AFTERLIVES

Christianity Today, the evangelical magazine founded by Billy Graham in the 1950s, published a cover story in June 2013 that asked, in all earnestness, "Want to change the world?" Its answer was simple: sponsor a child. Economist Bruce Wydick of the University of San Francisco wrote the lead article, which complemented his peer-reviewed article in the University of Chicago Press's *Journal of Political Economy.*[47] Both pieces use firsthand survey data from a study of Compassion International to examine the adult life outcomes of a group of 10,144 individuals in Bolivia, Guatemala, India, Kenya, the Philippines, and Uganda. The conclusions were clear: Child sponsorship increased the probability of a child completing secondary school by 27 to 40 percent, completing a university education by 50 to 80 percent, and obtaining a white-collar job as an adult by almost 35 percent.[48] "This is amazing,' was all I could mumble," recounted Wydick. "We tried slicing the data different ways, but each showed significant educational improvements. You could beat this data senseless, and it was incapable of showing anything other than extremely large and statistically significant impacts on educational outcomes for sponsored children." Inspired deductions followed. Wydick lingered on the power of hope. In *Christianity Today*, Wydick quotes Compassion International's director of research, whose own work noticed "a big difference between the sponsored kids and the other kids." He clarified his point. "You see," he explained, "poverty causes children to have very low self-esteem, low aspirations. The big difference that sponsorship makes is that it expands children's views about their own possibilities. Many of these children don't think they are capable of much. We help them realize that they are each given special gifts from God to benefit their communities, and we try to help them develop aspirations for their future."[49] Wydick dubbed this unquantifiable, affective charge "the hope hypothesis."

The practice of child sponsorship traffics in hope. This is clear. Ronald is an early success for a relatively young organization, but others exist. In Guatemala, a young man named Hugo Castellanos also embodies the promise of sponsorship. He is a bit of a celebrity within sponsorship circles, but I came to know him by way of a friend at the U.S. Embassy. In Guatemala for a three-year tour, having heard about my research on child sponsorship, this State Department worker told me the story of his wife's aunt. She lived in Ohio, never married, and largely kept to herself. She was a quiet woman. When she passed away, the family learned that she had sponsored a young boy in Guatemala. The letters they found were intimate. The young boy called her mother. The aunt referred to the child as her son. The relationship "worked," as Wydick might say. Years later, as a grown man, Hugo explained to me that her financial support had changed everything, as did her emotional outpouring. "I knew somebody cared," Hugo said. "I knew I was important to her." The story ends with Hugo graduating from medical school, marrying, and becoming a father himself. Compassion International, the organization that facilitated this relationship, publishes Hugo's story as often as possible.[50] Nearly every sponsorship brochure they print includes this first person letter: "I became a sponsored child," writes Hugo, "when I was just 5 years old. Being sponsored changed the course of my life. Most important was the educational assistance I received, which helped me earn my high school diploma. With hard work, a small scholarship and help from my mother, I achieved my dream at age 25, when I graduated from medical school. Sponsorship made me realize poverty did not have to be an obstacle to my success." He signs his letter with lofty, hopeful script, beginning with the title Doctor.

Child sponsorship works, quantitative research claims. It creates "a big difference between the sponsored kids and the other kids." Qualitative research argues the same. There is an undeniable difference between sponsored children and unsponsored children. The distance between Ronald and number sixty-two is evidence enough. Yet as sponsorship reconfigures to meet the demands of postwar security, as the industry stretches its assumptions to meet the threat of gang violence, the stakes of this difference also reconfigure in ways that can empty the future and eviscerate the present. At the age of 16, to explain, Hugo aged out of his sponsorship program. Still living in relative poverty, his single mother, a medical doctor, stewarded her son through high school and on to university, even in the absence of Hugo's father, who also is a medical doctor. Church scholarships helped along the way. It was not easy. Hugo tells a story of bumping into his father at a grocery store, essentially meeting him for the first time. They shook hands and then went on their way. There was no connection, no apologies, and no long awaited reunion. There was nothing. It was a traumatic event for Hugo, confirming that his father did not care about him, that Hugo was not important to him. In light of all this, it is somewhat intuitive how a child sponsorship program could change the course of Hugo's life. A little money and a little attention put him on the path of the straight and narrow.

But beating back precarity and achieving security are two very different things. Ronald also aged out of his child sponsorship program—to meet the realities of abject (rather than relative) poverty, a chronically disabled (rather than a professional) single mother, and entrenched (rather than nonexistent) gang violence. The effects of this disconnection, the effect of sponsorship's afterlife, proved disastrous. Still working for Walmart, still hustling toward his goal of one day attending university, Ronald walked through the winding streets of La Paloma. Two years after the death of number sixty-two and no longer a part of the sponsorship program, he rounded a corner only a few blocks from his house. Two young boys, not much younger than Ronald, also turned the corner with masks over their faces. The memory of it all moves fast for Ronald. The details are distant, but he knows that his feet felt frozen. He remembers not knowing where to run, if only because there is often nowhere to run in the unplanned slums of La Paloma. Every alleyway can seem narrower than the next. He knows that the boys raised their pistols. And he knows that they shot at him. Everything else is a blur.

Ronald suffered three gunshot wounds. One bullet pierced his thigh. One bullet punctured his back. The third hit his stomach. Ronald collapsed and blacked out while neighbors carried him up the canyon—to catch a cab to the nearest public hospital. No major organs had been hit, thankfully. Ronald's spinal cord had also been spared. He lost significant but not mortal amounts of blood. But the gunshots severely limited his mobility. With his legs unable to bend properly, with chronic back pain now limiting even the simplest movements, Ronald found himself confined to his one-room home, sharing space with his mother, who is also confined to a bed. Their respective mattresses form an L and take up the vast majority of the home. Most days Ronald sits in his bed, or on a chair, and watches pirated DVDs, leaving his home only for the occasional session with a government-provided physical therapist. The effort is a tremendous challenge, both because of the ascent from the bottom to the top of the canyon and because he often sees the two boys who shot him. He has to swallow so much anger and so much pride each time they run into each other. These meetings serve as violent extension of that terrible day.

So too does Ronald's immobility. Accustomed to traveling across the city most every day for his job, used to snaking through the alleyways of La Paloma, he is now, in his own words, "confined to these four walls." Several months after the incident, with his scars slowly healing, Ronald still could not sleep comfortably. His nightmares only added to his back pain. He did not have an appetite. His stomach, now lined with a thick scar, had shrunk in size and so too had Ronald's hope.

Mary, after hearing about the shooting, sent money for groceries, paid for most of Ronald's medication, and then passed along a letter. It is a sincere missive that struggles for answers, that wants to help but does not know how. It is also a letter that signals (even if unintentionally) the structural limitations of sponsorship itself. Groceries, some medicine, even a letter: they are the right response, for sure, but they also seem to flag the challenges that postwar security presents not just for Ronald and Mary but for all of Guatemala. For if child sponsorship delivers to postwar Guatemala a surgically selective solution, with an extractive geography that saves some while leaving many more behind, it also delivers a kind of temporality that saves some—but only for some time. The sponsorship's afterlife exposes security's shelf life. It is a theme, maybe even a thesis, that seems to organize Mary's letter. She writes, in part,

Ronald, we are still praying for your recovery and I know it will be hard to get back to where you were prior to the shooting. We think about you and your situation daily, as well as praying for you and your family during this time. I understand the many frustrating days you must be having trying to understand why this has happened to you. You're a wonderful young man who is striving to do your best to support your life and family. I wish I had the answer for you, but I don't. All I know is that God will use this time for his Good either for you and your family or for another person whom you come in contact with. We don't know why now, but one day down the road, it will be shown to you. Just know we are thinking about you and wish we could be there to physically help you out. You are a great person and you will bounce back and be a stronger person and I am sure your faith in God has grown during this time because He is the only person we can truly depend upon. So, please take good care of yourself, know that we still love and pray for you every day and that you are a part of our family.

Captivity

A house sits atop a hill, just beyond the reach of Guatemala City. The capital's skyline frames its northern vista. Rolling hills and jutting volcanoes sit to the south of it. A former military man and now Pentecostal pastor owns the house. He lives there with his wife and two children on the first floor. They enjoy a quiet, middle-class existence, with a full kitchen, tiled floors, and an above-average television. A steady stream of income keeps them afloat amid an otherwise downwardly mobile neighborhood. "Drug addicts are all around," the pastor complained. "This area used to be nice. It used to be quiet, but now it's changed. Drugs and alcohol have changed this neighborhood into a place for delinquents. And the gangs . . . the gangs extort. They have ruined this neighborhood." His ministry, this man argues, combats this crime by rehabilitating criminals into Christians. "I do the work of God here. I heal these men. I make them whole." He does his work in the very same house in which he lives.

Mateo is prone to bouts of what might be called depression. He can slip into long stretches of melancholy, of true sadness, for what he has lost in his life. From his father to his son, from his home to his health, these memories have a kind of momentum that can push him to drinking and to drugs, to disappearing for several days at a time. On more than one occasion, after having some beers, my wanting to call it a night and Mateo wanting to push on, he would cajole just a little more money from me for just a few more drinks—only to slip into a weeklong bender.

"Don't you trust me, Kev?" he asked, at the corner of a whirling intersection. He was already slurring his speech, holding my shoulder in a way that confirmed intimacy while bracing his swaying self. The way he held my arm also made it clear that he could take me down with one punch. He asked me this question only a few blocks from this pastor's house.

The second floor, above the pastor's apartment, is a relatively open space. There are bunk beds. There is a bathroom. There is a simple kitchen as well as a room big enough to hold a church service. A feeble lectern stands in the corner. Iron bars obscure the windows, and a heavy steel gate seals the front door. A mix of cement and chicken wire plugs up every other inch of opening. And the door locks with a key, from the outside. On one of the walls, in the room where the pastor holds services, is a long list of rules. They are the house's "rules of procedure" and they enumerate the law of the land. They also explain the price of infraction. "We bring men here," the pastor explained, "and we discipline them. We discipline their hearts. We discipline their will. We discipline their bodies. If they break a rule, then they need to pay the price. They need to learn a lesson." The house holds as many as fifty men at a time. It should probably only hold twenty. At one point, sometime after his deportation, a few months after his stint on the reality television show, this house held Mateo.

"I did like three months there, man. That place was real messed up." *Rule #1—No respect for religion, worship, prayer or the Bible. Penalty—3,500 squats, 1 non-stop security shift, and bathroom duty for 8 days.* "They snatched me up," Mateo said, explaining how he ended up in the house, "'cause that's what this pastor guy does. He comes out at night, around ten, eleven at night time, and what he does is he comes with a pickup truck, like one of those right there with those tubes." Mateo pointed to a pickup truck. We spoke in the parking lot of a grocery store, a little past noon. The sun was straight above us. "Some other guys from the rehab that work for him, that probably been there for maybe a year or ten months, they become workers. They go out hunting for guys." *Rule #2—Attempted escape. Penalty—3,000 squats every day for 8 days, 1 non-stop security shift, bathroom duty for 8 days.* Mateo continued, "They go out hunting and shit for people who are really high or running the streets, or things like that, and they just get out the car and . . . and the guy tries to . . . you know . . . the guy starts saying, 'I don't wanna go there,' and then they hit you—the guys. The same guys that are in the rehab, they hit these guys and put them in the truck." *Rule #3—Bad words. Penalty—100 squats per letter, including spaces.*

"Why'd they take you?" I asked Mateo as we found some shade.

"I was drinking with some other guys, so when they came and did that hunting thing, they snatched me up." Unbeknownst to Mateo, he is the perfect catch. A sociable guy, his benders tend to take him to the streets, where he often finds himself sitting down or even lying down to catch his breath. Sometimes too drunk or too high to really resist, he is not the hardest guy to pick up. It is also obvious—by his dress, his tattoos, even his way of standing and sitting—that he has been deported. This means, at least for pastors, that he might have family in the United States willing to pay above market rate to fund Mateo's time in a Pentecostal rehabilitation center. *Rule #4—Immoral jokes. Penalty—3,000 squats and bathroom duty for 8 days.*

"Nobody paid for me," Mateo remembered. While a family member will often pay a pastor to pick up a brother, a cousin, or a father, to lock them up until they sober up, sometimes pastors get proactive. They stir up a bit of business by picking up guys from the streets. *Rule #5—Inciting group factions. Penalty—3,000 squats for 8 days and bathroom duty for 3 days.* "They're stupid. My family didn't pay. This pastor is just stupid. He just snatched me up and then I had to live there. And that's it. That's this pastor's mentality. It's to bring delinquents into his rehab. His mentality is to clean up the street, but it's not right. Because all he does is beat up people." *Rule #6—Homosexuality. Penalty—5,000 squats for 8 days, non-stop shifts for 3 days, and bathroom duty for 8 days.*

"I was there for three months. And that place, like I said, it was real messed up. The beds . . . when it's nighttime . . . the beds—they bring out these mattresses and you sleep on the floor." *Rule #7—Masturbation. Penalty—2,500 squats.* "Some sleep in the bathroom, and you only take a shower maybe once or maybe twice every week. They got two big buckets. I don't know how it is now, but that time when I was there, they had buckets filled with water, and they give you one cup full of water. You get to soap up and then one more cup full of water. You just have to do your best to get all the soap off." *Rule #8—Burglary and theft. Penalty—Repay what you stole, 2,300 squats, and bathroom duty for 8 days.* "And the food was real crappy. They gave us the same food for breakfast, lunch, and dinner. It was like a *caldo*. They call it a *caldo de Rosario*. It's just water and a little bit of vegetables." *Rule #9—Fighting. Penalty—Solitary confinement, eat from the same plate [with the person whom you fought] for 8 days and do everything [with the person whom you fought].* "They add a little bit of vegetables and a little bones and shit like that—you know, bones. People call that shit 'dinosaur soup' because it's just bones and a little vegetables. Three times a fuckin' day." *Rule #10—Psychological violence. Penalty— Solitary confinement for 10 days and 1,500 squats daily.*

"There were all these fuckin' levels of trust—like, if you behaved well, you'd earn a higher level. And with a higher level, you'd get more responsibilities. But if you misbehaved, then you fell. You could really fall down levels in the house. And you know, they had kids there—like, young guys—and they'd lower their pants and beat 'em with a wooden stick. And other guys would get the same. Hit them in the ass. The pastor would leave 'em purple—but like, purple-purple." *Rule #11—Bribery. Penalty—3,500 squats daily, non-stop security shift for 5 days, and bathroom duty for 8 days.* "I seen it. I seen it with my own eyes. I seen these guys cry. And those kids, those young kids, would cry. They were young kids, like 17, 18, 19 years old." *Rule #12—Tattling. Penalty—4,000 squats, 2 non-stop shifts, and bathroom shifts for 8 days.*

Rule #13—Humming. Penalty—2,000 squats. "I mean, these kids probably were not even gang members, but they were into drugs and shit . . . and alcohol. But this pastor would treat them bad." *Rule #14— Lack of respect for the prayer group. Penalty—5,000 squats, 3 non-stop shifts, and 10 bathroom shifts.* "There was even faggots in that rehab that he would supposedly make them suck his privates—things like that." *Rule #15—Spitting on the floor. Penalty—1,000 squats.* "And that time when I was there, there was some kid, he was almost . . . he was like, 20, 21. He had a plastic bag where he shitted and pissed. This guy was an ex–gang member from MS, from Mara Salvatrucha. And this pastor one day beat him up 'cause he don't wanna take a shower or something like that." *Rule #16—Saying "I can't," "I don't want to," or "I don't like it." Penalty—1,000 squats.* "So this pastor hung him up. He hung up this MS guy on a post, with the bag hanging, and he was whacking him, smacking him. The pastor would then sit down and have the guys from the rehab do the work; he had these guys hit this MS guy. They beat the shit out of him." *Rule #17—Buying, selling, or giving objects. Penalty—1,000 squats.*

I stopped Mateo, just to clarify: "He was hanging with his hands over his head?"

Mateo nodded. "Yeah, like there was like a post there, and he would tie up the guys like this." Mateo stretched upwards, his hands held together above his head, his stomach stretched to capacity. "And he'd turn you around and he would hit you." *Rule #18—Keeping trash. Penalty—500 squats.*

"I mean, it's fucked up. This guy from MS, he was involved in gangs. When he was in the streets gangbanging, right?—he got hurt. He got shot. So they had to give him one of those bags." *Rule #19—Making fun of speakers. Penalty—5,000 squats, 3 non-stop security shifts, and 10 bathroom shifts.* "But I'm saying . . . I mean, to hurt a guy with a bag that shits out the side of his rib, and tie him up and hit him because he didn't want to take a shower or because he was not following the procedures of the rehabs . . . I mean, there was other ways, other norms to . . . ah . . . to discipline somebody. Not that way. That's animal discipline, man." *Rule #20—Speaking bad about the food. Penalty—1,000 squats.*

Inside this rehab, at the whim of this pastor, Mateo had slipped out of sight. "The pastor would tell the family, 'Look, we have your son at a rehab. You have to pay so we can accept him. It's a nice place. He gets three meals a day, he gets church.' But all that shit's a lie, man. It's a lie, man." *Rule #21—Mumbling about the authorities. Penalty—2,000 squats.* "There's people from churches who could go and donate tamales or bread to this fuckin' rehab, and he wouldn't even pass that food. He would maybe give the old bread that was there for like a day before or two days before, and he would keep the fresh bread for him and his family. And then the other trustees that were his bodyguards, they would eat the good stuff. And us, we'd always get the shitty shit." *Rule #22—Not being hygienic. Penalty—350 squats.* "Every two days, they'd always take a bag of sweet bread from the bakery—some of it would come with mold, shit like that—and he would give it out. And people in there would eat it, because, God, you're in a rehab, man, and you're fuckin' hungry, man." *Rule #23—Writing signs or symbols on the wall. Penalty—1,500 squats, 5 bathroom turns.*

Mateo's voice grew tense. The absence of something to do while inside these centers competed with the torture that he both experienced and witnessed. It all seemed so violent. "You'd just sit around, sit around, sit around all day long, sit around, sit around, and maybe one day some people from another church would come. They'd preach real quick for about an hour or two and that's it, and everybody else was just sitting down and fuckin' doin' nothing.'" *Rule #24—Making vulgar gestures. Penalty—500 squats.* "Shit, I was really like, damn, there's no . . . There's no food here. There's no rehabilitation. There's no counseling. There's no studies. There's no TV. There's no recreation. There's no yard time. There's nothing. Just punishment." *Rule #25—Inciting protest. Penalty—3,000 squats and 1 long shift.* "The logic of this fuckin' pastor is to hit you, lock you up, and make you kick your addiction cold turkey. That's it. Clean yourself up and realize that you can do it—shit like that." *Rule #26—Passing gas in a group. Penalty—250 squats.*

We were still sitting in the parking lot. "I'm surprised nobody comes back to take revenge," I mentioned. "Why wouldn't people come back and torch the place?"

"They did," Mateo said, "They did. That's when they burned his house, before Christmas night—on Christmas Eve. They burned his house—the same people in the rehab, they got tired of him." *Rule #27— Provoking divisions. Penalty—1,500 squats and 2 non-stop shifts.* "This pastor was doing a lot of damage. He was hurting people. He was basically extorting the families. He was not giving the food that was being donated by churches. He was keeping all that shit. People got tired of it man, and they burned that fucking house." *Rule #28—Walking around half-naked. Penalty—3,000 squats.* "But he rebuilt it the next year."

"So how'd you get out?" I asked.

"One day somebody visited me," Mateo said. "And what they do is . . . like, when you sit down with your family, one of the guys that are locked up in the rehab, one that has privileges, will sit there with you. He's there to hear what you're speaking about." *Rule #29—Not practicing personal prayer. Penalty—800 squats.* "And if you say anything or even give a clue that you're getting hurt or that you're getting mistreated or trying to get out of that rehab, he'll automatically go snitch on you." *Rule #30—Not obeying requests. Penalty—3,000 squats.* "And the pastor, he'll hit you. After your visit is done, he will come back for you and pull you down. He'll hit you on the floor and take you to the other rooms he has in his house. And he will let the other guys hit you up. He'll hit you for that shit." *Rule #31—Abandoning your post. Penalty—3 non-stop shifts from 1 A.M. onward.*

"But this guy who visited me helped me get out. It was a dude from USAID. He had been searching for me, 'cause nobody knew where I was. The pastor would not even let me call anyone. They just fuckin' snatched me from the streets, locked me up, and didn't tell anyone." *Rule #32—Clothes not properly ironed. Penalty—Non-stop shift for 3 days from 1 A.M. onward.* "But this pastor wanted me 'cause he knew that my family was in the States, so he thought, 'Oh, he's got money.' But fuck that asshole—this fuckin' thief—that's why he wanted to keep me there. That's his game. 'Hey, we got your son here. Look, he's pretty bad, I found him, he came for help, but you know what, there's a price, send him money, and shit like that.'" Mateo's voice grew louder, "He tried to do it to me, man. He tried to do it to me but thank God he didn't. He almost made me give him my number, man, but I didn't give him shit. 'Cause then I'd be in there forever. But luckily this guy from USAID started investigating where I was at. I don't know how he found me. I have no idea how he found me. But he got there and he was like, 'If you don't release Mateo, I'm gonna call the police because you got a fuckin' prison in your attic, man.'" *Rule #33—Sleeping during the day. Penalty—2,000 squats.* "And he let me out. He didn't wanna let me out, but he let me out."

Still outside the grocery store, under some shade, Mateo was obviously pissed. And I was pissed, too. The target of salvation, the subject of slavery, Mateo had been held hostage in the name of rehabilitation. "I was mad. I was heated. I wanted to go back and hurt that pastor, man, because not only for what he did but what he did to other people." *Rule #34—Wandering from room to room. Penalty—1,000 squats.* "The way he hurt them and the way he treated their families—I mean, fuck, man, you can't even sit with your family. He would send some other guy there to listen to your conversations. He had us all locked up in that place, man." *Rule #35—Speaking out of turn (while in line, at the dinner table, or during service). Penalty—5,000 squats.* "I'm surprised that mothafucka is still alive." *The general administrator will resolve cases not anticipated by these statutes.*

Forsaken

He was completely tied up. Wrapped in a thin mattress, then trussed with twine, a young man lay on the floor of a Pentecostal rehabilitation center. Straight from the streets of Guatemala City, on a mix of crack and *química,* he struggled to free himself as the echoes of an uncanny interview returned to me.[1] Earlier in the week, from the same window-less rehab, a different young man had confessed, "I feel tied up. Crack ties me up. I see my life slipping away but I can't do anything about it. I know that the blood of Jesus has the power to break any chains. But crack has got me around the neck. These chains, they've got me. But that's why I'm here. For liberation." Breaking the memory, pulling me back into the moment, the man in the mattress moaned, seemingly to himself, *"Me quiero ir a la mierda"* (Get me the fuck out of here).[2]

The politics of Christian liberation grow particularly acute from the perspective of captivity. In Guatemala City, amid rising levels of drug use and gang violence, informal, unregulated, and oftentimes for-profit Pentecostal rehabilitation centers keep pace with this country's growing consumption of crack cocaine. They warehouse users (against their will) in the name of liberation, for the sake of security. "If these guys were on the streets," reasoned one police chief, "they'd drug themselves. They'd rob. They would kill." He continued, leaning back in his oversized office chair. "And, really, the state has no capacity. So instead of having two hundred delinquents committing crimes in the streets, they're locked up inside one of these houses. It's a prevention thing. None of those guys

FIGURE 13. Captive. Photo by Benjamin Fogarty-Valenzuela.

inside [any one of these houses] is going to be fucking with citizen security. They can't go anywhere." It is a clean, contagious logic with at least
one clear consequence: today more Guatemalans find themselves tied
up in Pentecostal rehabilitation centers than locked up in maximum
security prisons.[3]

As gang violence becomes synonymous with drug use, with Guatemala's gang problem enveloping its drug problem, these Pentecostal
structures prove critically important. They not only rearticulate Christian liberation's political coordinates but also reorganize the spatial
contours of Guatemala City—proposing a key question along the way:
How does the practice of liberation in all of its piety bind crack and
Christianity to captivity? Or, posed in a slightly more philosophical key,
how do openings become enclosures? How do lines of flight become
absolute dead ends?

The context for these questions is clear. Anthropologists, political
scientists, and theologians tend to speak about Latin American Christian liberation in the past tense, often with deep nostalgia. They
announce, along with cultural theorists and historians of religion, that
globalization, neoliberalism, and Pentecostalism have unwound, if not
dissolved, its promise.[4] Yet from the vantage of the Pentecostal rehabilitation center, Latin American Christian liberation has never been so

relevant to so many people. It just looks different now than it once did. Roman Catholic theologians, only a few decades ago, made Christian liberation a matter of time. They prophesied (with Hegelian flair) about social progress, economic development, and the long arc of history. "The praxis of liberation," theologian Gustavo Gutiérrez once wrote, "is pregnant with the future."[5] Yet in postwar Guatemala, with Christian piety pressed into the service of security, Christian liberation is no longer primarily about time (or progress or even the future). It is about space.[6] It is about getting the fuck out of here.

From temporality to spatiality, from progress to egress, an ethics of escape organizes the practice of Christian liberation.[7] Locked up, tied up, and told to shape up, users come to confess, at times plead, that they want out and they want it now. Pentecostal rehabilitation centers, in response, assure these users that captivity is itself liberation—that slavery is salvation.[8] The effects of this ethics are twofold. The first is political. The practice of Christian liberation disembeds (effectively, disappears) thousands of users from the city. It helps render a new genre of captivity. The second effect is analytical. The Pentecostal rehabilitation center flips the study of political theology. While this subfield tends to either evaluate the theological origins of political concepts or provide theological reflections on political questions, the Pentecostal rehabilitation center inspires neither.[9] Instead, these dark, dank structures, with their ropes and razor wire, provide a window onto Christian liberation as a technique of rule, as a mode of governance.[10] Christian liberation may liberate Christians, in some kind of soteriological sense, but it also contains them in ways that now organize Guatemala City's carceral landscape.

CRACK AND CHRISTIANITY

To appreciate this confluence of crack, Christianity, and captivity—this ethics of escape—one must begin neither in the streets of Guatemala City nor its Pentecostal rehabilitation centers but rather in the nostrils of North Americans. It is a history that runs parallel to that of the gangs. A gourmet soft drug in the 1960s, cocaine found its clientele courtesy of President Richard Nixon. His 1969 Operation Intercept, with its aerial sprays of Mexican hemp fields and its crackdown on Mexican marijuana smugglers, prompted the American middle class to seek out alternative thrills. As demand soared, cocaine corridors connected Medellín to Miami and Cali to Northern Mexico—all by way of the Caribbean. The

United States responded with hugely militarized antidrug policies. "America's public enemy number one in the United States is drug abuse," Nixon declared in a June 17, 1971, press conference. "In order to fight and defeat this enemy, it is necessary to wage a new, all-out offensive."[11] Yet U.S. Navy and Coast Guard patrols ultimately accomplished very little. By the early 1990s, the Andean region produced an estimated 1,000 metric tons of cocaine every year. Twenty years and one trillion U.S. tax dollars later, the region still does, making the War on Drugs, by accounts across the political spectrum, a complete and unwavering failure.[12]

Yet this failure has not been without effect. Increasingly expensive, progressively effective maritime blockades have prompted traffickers to shift their transport operations from sea to land, making Central America their principal transit hub. Today planes, boats, and submarines ferry cocaine along the Pacific coast to northern Guatemala. There, in the jungles of Petén, beyond the reach of U.S. interdiction efforts, traffickers prep their product for its eventual trip north. "When it comes to Central American cocaine trafficking," says a United Nations report, "all roads lead to Guatemala . . . making the border area [between Guatemala and Honduras] one of the most violent areas in the world."[13] Yet, the real challenge, at least for traffickers, has not been the violence but rather the demand. In 2004, an estimated 10 percent of the cocaine produced for the United States passed through Guatemala.[14] This number jumped to 23 percent in 2006 and then 44 percent in 2008.[15] In 2011, in the shadows of Plan Mexico, a U.S.-led $1.6-billion security initiative, 84 percent of the cocaine produced for the United States moved through Guatemala.[16] This means that more than $100 billion worth of narcotics now touches Guatemalan soil every year.[17] This is three times Guatemala's legitimate gross domestic product.

The mass movement of all this cocaine comes with considerable logistics. Equipment, labor, infrastructure—traffickers need all of these but pay for none of them in cash. Instead, they pay with cocaine, which holds very little value in Guatemala. There are simply not enough Guatemalans who can afford the drug. To monetize this material, to turn cocaine into cash, laboratories mix the drug with baking soda to make crack cocaine. Now sold throughout Guatemala City, crack cocaine is a far more affordable, far more addictive version of powder cocaine. Crack cocaine is the substance that hit Los Angeles, New York, and Miami in the mid-1980s.[18] Smoked through a pipe one rock at a time, it is as intense as it is cheap as it is fleeting. Crack leaves the user hungry for more. In the United States, this desperation met growing urban violence and decidedly racist antidrug policies in ways that tripled the country's prison population.[19] But in Guatemala, with a homicide rate nearly ten times the U.S. average, crack cocaine has not only been criminalized.[20] It has been Pentecostalized.

The Pentecostalization of crack begins and ends with captivity, with the felt reality of being locked up and tied down. "They can be freed from this slavery," reasons one pastor, "but they are slaves. They do not want to be free. These guys are people with problems. They come from the streets. They come from gangs. They are all tied up and are completely lost." Much of this captivity has to do with the built form. An entrepreneurial network of semifortified, quasi-clandestine houses holds men for months, sometimes for years. Their fortified walls and razor wire, their steel doors and barred windows punctuate Guatemala City—to little critique. Neither unlawful nor illegitimate, although inhumane and illiberal, these Pentecostal rehabilitation centers provide a practical solution to a concrete problem. Drug use is up. State resources are down. And Pentecostalism is *the* discourse of change in Guatemala. Jesus saves. "Do you want to die in the streets or be locked up in a rehab?" asked that same pastor. The answer seemed obvious, at least to him.

But captivity here is not just about architecture. It is also about affect. It is about feeling tied up, narrating this captivity, and then struggling to free oneself from oneself. Augustine of Hippo confesses this story with such clarity, describing the human condition as literally bounded by sin. "I was bound by the iron chain of my own will," he writes. "The enemy held my will and of it he made a chain and bound me. Because my will was perverse it changed to lust, and lust yielded to become habit, and habit not resisted became necessity. These were like links hanging one on another—which is which is why I have called it a chain—and their hard bondage held me bound hand and foot."[21] Hand and foot, bound tightly, with a chain—this is the Pentecostal predicament. This is crack cocaine. The experience is brute, Augustine insists. His chains are made of iron. He drags them. They chafe him. Their clanging drowns out the voice of God.[22] "Thus my two wills—the old and the new, the carnal and the spiritual—were in conflict within me; and by their discord they tore my soul apart."[23] Rolling and writhing in the fetters he forged for himself, Augustine's temptations began with a pear tree but might as well have started with the crack house. Each nails the sinner to the floor. Images of such incarceration literally litter the Pentecostal rehabilitation center. Pinned to walls, tucked under pillows, and folded into Bibles—Pentecostal print media mashes together abolitionist iconography with cheeky references to *Gulliver's Travels*.[24] These flyers depict, with real Christian clarity, grown men wrapped up and tied down by a thicket of sin. How to be free?

Escape, Augustine answers. Turn inward toward the soul and upward toward God.[25] Monastic, ascetic, and contemplative—this approach is absolute. And so too are the stakes, at least for Pentecostals. For the end is not near. It is now. So escape. Escape for your life. The ultimate effect of this effort, this ethics, is a double bind, of sorts.[26] Crack ties the user up, metaphorically, which is why pastors tie the user up, literally, with every effort at literal escape confirming the necessity of literal captivity. It is only when the user "becomes a sinner," when he takes on the logic of liberation, that he begins to plod toward eschatological escape, toward Judgment Day.[27] Yet even this monkish effort tends to take place inside a Pentecostal rehabilitation center. The streets prove too seductive, too sinful. So for many, for far too many, liberation becomes a life sentence.

WHERE DO YOU WANT TO GO?

Take Javier. Twenty-two years old, he sat quietly on the second floor of an abandoned factory building. Repurposed for rehabilitation, beyond the reach of natural light, the space smelled of urine and feces, of mildew and rotting vegetables. His chair, made for a child, pushed his knees up to his ears. Resting his hands around his ankles, his shoulders atop his thighs, he mumbled just loud enough for me to hear him, "I have no idea why I'm here. No fucking idea." Javier fiddled with his shoelaces. As I turned toward him for a follow-up, the pastor kicked at the front door. With a steel lock rattling against a steel chain, banging against a steel gate, the pastor entered his house of liberation. Fifty users made their way toward him for the daily sermon, gathering around a pulpit with a mix of duty and anticipation. With no television, radio, or newspaper at hand, the pastor's daily instructions proved popular even if they were compulsory. Javier, fresh from the streets, still a little high, listened from afar. It was only his first day.

"Every man has three enemies," the pastor preached. "Three enemies," he repeated. Taken by the power of enumeration, with the simplicity of it all, the pastor counted each enemy off with his fingers. "There's Satan. That's the first enemy. The devil is strong. Then there's the world. That's the second. The world of pleasures. The world of drugs." The pastor tapped a Bible against his thigh. He let the group think a bit about their last enemy, wonder aloud who it could possibly be. "And then there's you . . . That's the third. You are your own enemy." He paused, allowing each man to try on the accusation for size. Javier stirred. Lifting his chin from his knees, his eyes from the floor, Javier muttered, "I mean, I have no idea why I'm here." Someone shushed him, but Javier honestly did not know. He would learn, of course, that his mother had called the pastor. Earlier that month, on the outskirts of town, she had bumped into the pastor's hunting party (*grupo de cacería*). This is what the industry calls the four or five men tapped to collect users from the streets. More often than not these men are themselves in rehab, also under lock and key, but they are bigger, stronger, and sometimes smarter than the average user. Hunting (*cacería*) is a privilege, and the rewards are immediate: status, adventure, and a bit of sunlight. The work pays for itself.

The pastor's hunting party had been in the area—to pick up a neighbor's kid but also to drum up some business. Abducting those too high or too drunk to resist keeps the rehabilitation center at capacity, with the abducted paying their way through a mix of unpaid labor and family offerings. "The simple fact is that financial support is necessary," the pastor later mentioned to me, "and families pay what they can pay to keep their sons, brothers, or husbands here. Some pay something. Others pay nothing. Because there are so many spiritual prisons out there in the world. There are so many. And it's either here or the cemetery for these guys." The pastor, seeming to complete some kind of calculation in his head, then added, "There are so many more people incarcerated spiritually than physically. So many more." Amid all this, during some lull in the hunt, one of the men handed Javier's mother a business card. Liberation, it promised, from drugs, alcohol, and that ever-capacious category of delinquency (*delincuencia*). So she called the number when things got bad.

"The apostle Paul," the pastor continued, "describes a great battle raging inside each of us. Did you know that? But this isn't a battle that beats your body or that marks your flesh. It is a battle over what your body wants. What does your body want? Does your body want drugs? Does it want crack?" Not a single man answered. Javier stared blankly. "Because," the pastor added, "we can see that Satan is in our hearts. And we know where bad thoughts come from, where all fights, wars, murders, drugs, adultery come from. It all comes from the heart. The problem is *here*." He pointed to his chest, fingering his sternum with some force, naming the place of weakness but also the site of intervention. "It's here in the heart. It is inside of me." A young man, on the floor, quietly touched his own chest. "It's inside each of us," the pastor announced.

Things did get bad, for Javier and his mother. A year earlier, Javier had started smoking crack. He had smoked weed for years, but crack was different. He didn't like it at first. "It tasted like shit," he told me. "*Piedra* made me feel weak. It made me feel really shitty." But then Javier started smoking *primos*. A combination of marijuana and crack, *primos* cut the rush by mixing the effects. Javier liked *primos*. "It would just make me laugh and laugh," he remembered. "There was such a tremendous laughter. I just couldn't stop laughing." But eventually, at least for Javier, the weed made for a muddled composition, a literal buzz kill. So he started picking out the bits of crack from the weed to smoke it straight from the pipe. "That's when it began to destroy me," Javier explained. That's when the laughter died. "The crack killed it," Javier said. "And so that's when I started stealing, when I started selling stuff to smoke." Javier simply could not smoke enough crack. There was no end to it. "You want to smoke it all the time and every time," he said. "And so I started robbing. With a gun. We'd wait, with a gun, for cars to pass and then pull them over for money. But mostly, I'd find stuff to sell. I'd sell anything I could." The last thing Javier sold, before his mother called the pastor, was the door off her hinges. "He sold it for like 150 quetzales [US$20]," his mother winced. "And to someone in our neighborhood," she blushed. "I had to buy it back." Open, exposed, and absolutely humiliated, Javier's mother had no other choice. "Javier just started to get really abusive," she told me, "hitting me and saying that he was going to kill me. I tried to lock him up myself, in the back room, but he got out." Under lock and key, in a modest bedroom turned private cell, Javier would pull back the tin roof, hoist himself up, and crawl out. An open-air drug market was just around the corner. So Javier's mother called the pastor. "I'd do it again," she said.

"The thing is," the pastor preached, "the thing is, you just don't have the confidence to tell yourself that you can leave, to tell yourself that 'I want to get out of here,' that 'I can escape my desires.'" He shuffled his feet. "Liberation can be yours," he promised, "It can. But you keep telling yourself, 'I can't leave. I can't leave. I just can't leave.'" Shaking his head, tucking his shirt into his pants, he added, "Well, that kind of thinking is going to kill you. Because if you keep saying 'I can't leave,' then you'll never get out of here. Never." The pastor then caught the eye of a young man. He took a step toward him, proclaiming, "Because we know that there is a heaven and that there is a hell. God said to choose between blessings and a life of sin. Which do you choose? There is eternal life, and there is eternal death. Where do you want to go?" Holding the young man's attention, locking eyes, the pastor persisted, "I asked you, where do *you* want to go?" Javier, arrested by the question, his interest piqued by the performance, answered for himself, to himself: *"Me quiero salir"* (I want out).

THE ETHICS OF ESCAPE

The pastor, to be fair, also wants Javier to get out. So too does Javier's mother, and the police as well. "Their method is not the greatest," observed one officer, "and the inmates complain that they get hit, abused, and tied down, but many times it's the family that brings them there, and it's the family that wants them out. We all want them out." The hiccup here is a signifier that will not stop floating. Empty as it is undetermined, with its impasses and imbrications, the word in constant question here is *out*—*out* of the rehab, *out* of drug use, even *out* of this world (and into the next). "Baptism, truth, and redemption can get them out," promised the pastor—in a way that suggested both *out* of addiction and *out* of the rehab. Operating through the contradictions inherent to its signification, this *out* proves productive. "Getting out," even within the context of the Pentecostal rehabilitation center, can mean so many different things. Its significance shifts with every part of speech—adverb ("moving or appearing to move away from a particular place, especially one that is enclosed or hidden"), adjective ("revealed or made public"), and noun ("a way of escaping from a problem or dilemma").[28] The pastor's question, his vision of liberation, shot to the eschaton. It posed a fundamental (if familiar) question to those locked up: Where do you want to go?

Many users, at least at first, take the question literally. Javier did. Soon after his abduction, Javier kicked against a third-floor window. He pulled at its bars. Twenty feet above traffic, he tried to push himself out of the building. "I told myself I was going to escape. So I went to the window, pulled hard, and opened one of the bars. Then I just stared out. I didn't know if I could survive the jump." The pastor had him tied up. Javier fought back until he threw up—on himself as well as the rope and the mattress that held him down. "They punished me. An ugly punishment. They held me down. They tied my hands and my legs behind my back. I cried out. Lost my food. Afterward my wrists were purple. They were hot to the touch." But this is just one story. There are so many more—of men rushing the door or peeling back the roof in the dead of night. "We were in the middle of worship and praise," an eighteen-year-old user once recounted to me, "and we all knew that we were going to storm the door. And all at once, we went for it. Somebody pushed the pastor to the side. Others grabbed chairs. A few grabbed a bench. We just rammed that door until it buckled." But what kind of freedom does such courage yield? *Animalitos,* little animals, this is what the workers at a conjoined factory call the users who make it out of one rehab only to end up scampering around their building looking for a way out. *"¡Corre, animalito, corre!"* (Run, you little animal, run!), the workers whistle. These hoots, these hollers, echo all too well Giorgio Agamben's observations about the progressive animalization of man, what Michel Foucault takes to be the bestialization of biopolitics.[29] But to linger on this kind of escape, to make these immediate efforts the sole evidence, distracts from a deep, dark existential struggle over self-governance as well as the disciplinary techniques that link apocalypticism and asceticism to the privatization of security. The escape of broader interest here is not literal but rather ethical. It is ethical in something of a Foucauldian sense—as the aestheticization of the subject, as the self working on the self.[30]

"You, me, everyone—we all need to think," the pastor explained. "We all need to examine our lives." We sat around a secondhand card table. Users milled about. Some slept. Some read. Some eavesdropped on our conversation. "We need to ask ourselves what we are doing with ourselves. And then we need to get up. And this is an important point. Who tells us to get up? God doesn't tell us. You need to tell yourself to get up, to rise up. You need to figure out for yourself what you are going to do with your life."

A man suddenly screamed. Somewhere, behind some wall, under some shadow, he screamed. "They're ripping out my eyes," he shrieked, "Oh, God, they're ripping out my eyes!"

The pastor did not pause. "And you can't do this exam when you are drunk or on drugs. You need to be sober. You need to be healthy. You need to be able to see around you, to understand your circumstances. And this is why these men are here. To examine themselves. To say that they want out." The man yelled again. The pastor checked his cell phone. "Because, look," he reasoned, "these guys are enslaved in a kind of prison for the soul. And we brought them here, to this house, for liberation. We brought them here to meet God. [We brought them here] to liberate themselves from slavery." Picking up his phone, plugging his free ear with his free hand, the pastor fielded a call.

"Oh, my eyes," the man cried. "They're burning my eyes!"

Slouching toward Bethlehem, descending into bedlam, the Pentecostal rehabilitation center offers few tools for self-discovery, for self-mastery.[31] There are no twelve steps or group sessions. There is no occupational therapy. None of the users have caseworkers or even files. Progress is not measured. It is rarely mentioned. One is neither better nor worse, only liberated or not. "A lot people say it's a process," mentioned the pastor, "but it's not a process. Liberation is a miracle."[32] Like a switch that flips on and off, with nothing in between, the practice of Christian liberation delivers to users a sense of being either in or out, here or there, enslaved or free.

Moral manuals written by Pentecostals dot the rehabilitation center. Strewn about like life preservers, each ready for the Flood, they instruct the inflicted to empower themselves.[33] Alone before God, these manuals encourage men, in the words of one user, to become "their own therapist." The titles tell all. One extols *The Unlimited Power Inside of Me.*[34] Another speaks of *Autoliberación Interior* (Interior Self-Liberation).[35] A third promises to *Turn Your Heart in 40 Days.*[36] Each invokes what Augustine once called and Lauren Berlant reads as "cruel optimism"— "a kind of relation in which one depends on objects that block the very thriving that motivates our attachment in the first place."[37] None of these texts does so more than the manual titled *I Can and Should Have Success.*[38] With an upwardly mobile businessman on the cover, a suit literally climbing the ladder of success, this image of corporate Christianity contrasts ever so cruelly with the makeshift mattress upon which it so often rests. One of these manuals asks its subject to complete an X-ray (*una radiografía*) of the heart.[39] It quotes scripture: "The Spirit of the Lord has sent me to proclaim freedom for the prisoners and recovery of sight for the blind, to set the oppressed free" (Luke 4:18–19).[40] The instructions ask the Christian to pray quietly and then to ask God two questions: "Oh Lord, what parts of my heart need to be restored?" and "In what part of my heart do you, oh Lord, want to begin this process of restoration?"[41] The assignment continues with a quiz: "Yes or No, I feel that pain holds me captive. Yes or No, I feel that the past has a hold on me. Yes or No, I am mourning a loss. Yes or No, I am languishing without hope."[42] These questions and their answers frame Christian liberation, this ethics of escape, as an "inner dialogue" between self and self.[43]

THE SLAVERY OF SALVATION

This inner dialogue is site specific. Christian liberation happens *inside,* rather than *outside,* the Pentecostal rehabilitation center. This crystallized for me never more so than in the middle of a sermon. "Let's talk about having a positive attitude," the pastor preached. "If you think you can do something, you can do something. And when people change their attitude, they change their life. Jesus Christ came to change our lives, and he wants to help us change our lives. Jesus came to set the captives free, to give freedom to the prisoners and to the oppressed." Muffled by the brick and the mortar, by the boarded-up windows and the locked-down doors, gunshots punctuated the sermon. Pop. Pop. Pop. Some of the men looked up. One shook his head. The pastor impassively continued, "And the biggest discovery of this generation is that human beings can change their lives by changing their mindset. In other words, all people can change, but what do you need to have?" He held silent, waiting for an answer. None came. "You need to have a positive attitude. We all have problems in life in one or another way, and God has the solution for us. Jesus is the way. He is the truth. He is life, and no one comes to the Father except through the Son." He held up his Bible. "Jesus has something special for you today. I want you to tell the person next you something. Tell him 'Jesus has something special for you.'" Men turned to each other, repeating the phrase. "Tell him 'He wants to change your life.' Tell him 'God has miracles for you. God will do extraordinary things in your life.' And tell him 'God will change your attitude.'" The group repeated every word.

The gunfire sparked some reflection. "Out there I'd get killed," confessed one user. Spooked by the noises, having not seen the light of day for three months, he continued, "I was behaving well out there. I had a job, I smoked. But I smoked after work. I didn't smoke on the job. I never smoked on the job. It was just the people I was hanging out with. That was the problem." Building on the sermon, taking apart his own attitude, he said, "We smoked a lot. And when my cousins smoked, they'd start shooting. Pop. Pop. Pop. Then some guys would shoot back. Pop. Pop. Pop. I was hanging out with the wrong people." He shook his head, "For real, I'd get killed out there." *Out there* as opposed to *right here, inside* as opposed to *outside*—these distinctions organize this ethics of escape. *Here,* inside the rehab, is where you get *out.* "Because basically," he explained, "when you come to this place, the first thing [you realize] is that you're not free. You can't leave. But your spirit is free. Your soul is free. Your spirit is free from doing bad things." Leaning back, trying to gain some perspective, he continued, "This house lets me escape this world. I am free here. Spiritually free. I can strengthen my spirit here. I can dominate (*dominar*) my flesh here."

So much of liberation is about domination. Having once been tied down, thrown inside a room, left to scream for help, this user went on to narrate his own inside as if it were his outside.[44] "Crack is like . . ." He searched for the right words. "It's like your spirit is telling you not to smoke. But what do you do? You smoke. And this ties you up. You tie up your spirit. And you don't listen to your spirit. You just tie it up. And you put it in a room and shut the door. It's still there. And you can still hear it. It's screaming for you. You can still hear your spirit screaming for you." Making the metaphor material, he continued, "I just need to break the chains. I need to break the chains that haunt me. The chains of hatred, the chains of adultery and witchcraft, the chains of drugs. I need to have a direct line with God. That's the release; that's how you break the chains. That is the battle, the decision." He then pointed his finger at himself. "Last night," he whispered, "while I was lying in bed, I realized that maybe I'm the one who put this chain on me. I mean, this could be a chain I put on myself. And maybe I need to be the one to take it off." He paused and then came to some kind of conclusion. "Maybe I tied myself up."

The haunting image of this man abducting himself, of locking himself up, is compounded by the fact that those cracks of air, the ones that kicked up so much conversation, were actually not gunshots. They were fireworks. Leaving the rehab later that day, standing just outside the front door, I waited for my eyes to adjust to the midday sun. As I stood there, it slowly occurred to me that a procession had passed in front of the rehab. Signs of a celebration were everywhere, and someone must have lit some fireworks. Burnt casings littered the street. And the neighbors confirmed this. Duped. We had all been duped, as the anthropologist Diane Nelson might say.[45] But how?

One answer races to the difficulty of distinguishing the sound of a firecracker from that of a firearm when inside a Pentecostal rehabilitation center. Pop pop pop. The materiality involved makes it near impossible. Makeshift spaces, cobbled together with secondhand materials, produce cavernous enclosures that are completely walled off from the outside. Inescapable sensoriums, these echo chambers completely distort the senses. From the inside, a warped noise from outside could be anything. And given how these spaces systematically disaggregate the signifier from the signified, it comes as no surprise that pastors can bend users (so effectively, so efficiently) toward a cataclysmic reading of the world. "We love the pleasures of the flesh, of this world," explained the pastor, "but we need to fight. We need to conquer death. Christ overcame the cross of Calvary, so now I have to overcome my sin. Let me read you a passage." The pastor turned to Apocalypse 2:16: "Repent therefore! Otherwise, I will soon come to you and will fight against them with the sword of my mouth." These are places of great eschatological tension.

"There is fear in the streets," the pastor continued, almost in passing. "These are the end of days. We are living in the time of the apocalypse. These are very, very dangerous times." He squared himself to me, "I'm not totally sure if you've seen the movies. With the zombies. They're out there, you know? Zombies are in the streets. They don't want to be free. But that's why we bring them here. *Here,* brother. We bring them here to be free." Possibly putting too fine a point on it all, the pastor then gestured to a cache of pirated DVDs. He plays them for the occasional movie night. Titles include *Escape from Hell* (2000), *Doomsday* (2008), *The Lazarus Project* (2008), *The Devil's Mercy* (2008), and *The Haunting in Connecticut* (2009). This last one, "based on a true story," features a family forced to relocate for their son's health. They end up moving into a former mortuary. The rest is fairly predictable, but one scene stands out. It depicts the teenage son with hundreds of satanic words carved into his flesh. His body is pink with sin. The demons did it to him, but his mother, shaking with panic, shrieks, "What have you done to yourself?" This scene is uncanny for most. The question, with its concern, forever folds back onto the user, naked and ashamed, marked by possession: What have you done to yourself?

DISEMBEDDING THE SINNER

The answer to this question is not always obvious, but its effects are observable. Christian liberation, with its ethics of escape, ensnares the user. It holds him captive. "The battle is against yourself," explained one user, "it holds you captive. They say like after twenty days of doing something, it becomes a habit. Be it drinking or drugs or some other addiction. Once that happens, it becomes a battle against yourself. It's a battle to get out." But this captivity happens at more than one scale. The soul is only one site. Christian liberation stewards the individual person, to be sure, but it also governs entire populations. "These centers," one police chief admitted, "are critical to security. If these guys aren't on the streets, then the sale of drugs goes down, which means the sellers go out of business or to another part of the city, because there's a lack of demand. In the same way, aggravated assaults diminish." This police chief's perspective propels this analysis toward the broader question of the city as a whole. Before returning to the individual, to Javier's abduction in particular, it is important to consider, if only briefly, a perspective that holds the entirety of Guatemala City in a single frame. For it is only at this scale where one can ask a familiar and daunting question, one that pokes at the righteous at every turn: Liberation for whom?

There is, to answer, no single Pentecostal rehabilitation center. There are Pentecostal rehabilitation centers, in the plural. There are, in fact, as many as two hundred Pentecostal rehabilitation centers in the metropolitan area. A quick mapping of some of these structures calls to mind Michel Foucault's notion of the carceral archipelago.[46] A cluster huddles close to the presidential palace, at the very center of the city, and another in the unplanned suburbs. Dozens line the city's already congested mainways. Some are completely anonymous. They look like any old storefront. Others advertise, hanging a shingle or hosting a sign. But they spread throughout the metropolitan area, dotting the region with sites of subjectiviation. "So many cages, so many small theatres," writes Foucault, "in which each actor is alone, perfectly individualized and constantly visible."[47] Posts and lintels; towers and angles; modest houses and dilapidated factories—a carceral city, constructed block by block, house by house, by way of the Pentecostal rehabilitation center. In Foucault's words, these are "institutions of repression, rejection, exclusion, marginalization."[48] And this is true. These centers house heaping levels of torment. "My heart is damaged," one man confessed. "Permanently," he stressed. Yet Foucault's metaphor is static, while this formation in Guatemala City is no archipelago. These centers are not islands. They close. They relocate. They reopen. Users also graduate, so to speak, and start their own outfits. Others escape but then return (and return and return). Recidivism is common. This assemblage, put simply, is in constant motion. "We used to be in a smaller space, across town," explained the pastor, "but then this space opened up. It's darker here but there's more room for more people."

This movement is productive. This is because Guatemala City is not a particularly large metropolis. With approximately three million residents, the city cannot support what a growing literature describes as "fortified enclaves." Those are internally complete spaces of privilege where the wealthy live in peaceful solidarity. Gated communities and closed condo-miniums, with security guards and surveillance technology—this is forti-fication with schools, stores, and even office space inside (as opposed to outside) their walls. There is little reason for any resident to leave. Mexico City, Bogotá, and São Paulo—each of these mega-cities typifies what Ter-esa Caldeira understands as a "city of walls."[49] "As spaces are enclosed and turned inside," she writes, "the outside space is left for those who cannot afford to go in."[50] But this is not the case with Guatemala City.[51] There are simply not enough wealthy Guatemalans to wall themselves off from the world. The quick fix, however, has been to invert private secu-rity's infrastructure—its steel bars, razor wire, and reinforced concrete—to keep users in rather than out, to wall them off from the rest of the world. "At least this place is safe," I mentioned to one user, in an off-handed kind of way. Facing a security wall, one topped with shards of broken glass, he corrected me. "That doesn't keep people out," he said. "It keeps us in."

This *in*, as opposed to that *out*, is how the practice of Christian lib-eration reorganizes the spatial contours of Guatemala City, enacting not just a new genre of captivity but also a distinct kind of segregation. Rather than an archipelago of isolated enclaves, rather than fortresses of privilege, rising levels of drug use and street crime prompt the faithful to "disembed" an entire population from the city.[52] They rip users from city life, disconnecting them from the general fabric of society. "I don't have any contact with my wife, with anyone," a man explained. "I just sit here, waiting to get out." Javier can relate. He was ripped out of his own home. He too was left to himself. "I was just watching a movie with my girlfriend," he told me. "I was smoking some weed and watch-ing a movie, when these guys rushed in. They rushed in and grabbed me. They were screaming at me. They were loud. And they just totally freaked me out (*me friquearon*). They told me not to fight. Not to resist. So I was like, 'All right! Calm down!' I stood up. They tied me up and drove me here." Others involved in Javier's abduction report more of a struggle. "He had a knife," the pastor said, "He pulled the knife on my guys and they had to tackle him." As he was dragged kicking and screaming out of his bedroom and into the van, neighbors watched in passive silence. The same hunting party had just taken another kid from the same neighborhood a few days earlier. In the end, it is this ripping apart that makes possible the practice of Christian liberation. This rip-ping motion pulls people *inside* as opposed to *outside*. "This place is a refuge," explained one user. "I am free here. I can strengthen my spirit here. This [rehab] is where I can heal." When asked if he thought he was ready to leave, the answer was decisive: "No." But then when, I pushed. "Maybe never," he answered.

Disembedded from the city, users rarely return to city life. Instead they move from one Pentecostal rehabilitation center to another. Some enter dozens of centers, which can create a bit of a disconcerting return, if only for me. Years would have passed between interviews—I would not recognize the face—when a user would hand me a wrinkled business card from an institution I had long since left. Where had he been all this time, I would wonder? Yet, the rhythm of their return is somewhat predictable. Pentecostal rehabilitation centers, laced with liberationist techniques, practice an abstinence-only approach to sobriety. Inside the rehab, the men are drug free. Outside the center, they find themselves bombarded by temptation, without any new skills to corral their desires. Initially picked up or dragged in by hunting parties or family members, they often leave these centers only to fall back into drug use after a few days, at times a few months. Then the cycle begins again, but rarely do these men return to the same center—if only because their former center may no longer be open. Yet the overall effect is the same. Through a shifting network of Pentecostal rehabilitation centers, the practice of Christian liberation lifts thousands of users from city life. It rips them off the streets and then warehouses them. The net effect is what some critics would call "worlds of inequality, alienation, and injustice."[53] But this logic comes with Marxist language. In a Christian key, in light of Latin American Christian liberation's genealogy, the more theologically accurate, more ethnographically appropriate word for this predicament would be *forsaken*.

FORSAKEN

Latin American liberation theologians often wrote about "the forsaken." Always a collective tethered to a teleology, they argued, the people, the poor, the masses had been forsaken—but not for long. Liberation would come.[54] Their optimism, theologically speaking, was hard fought. Liberation theologians, from Leonardo Boff to Ignacio Ellacuría, from Jürgen Moltmann to Jon Sobrino, upended the idea that human history was simply a trial through which the faithful must pass. Together, in community, these theologians forged real continuity between temporal progress and ultimate transcendence.[55] A preferential option for the poor made this possible. So too did practical interventions. These included co-ops, teach-ins, and literacy programs. Each trafficked in Western ideas of modernization and economic development. Social progress, they argued, enacted the biblical story of Exodus.[56] Mixing the metanarratives of Marxism and modernity with a strong dose of temporal distancing, the faithful read papal ruminations over integral development as a reason to see God working in human history.[57] Key to this theology was not just an ascending order of human development but also a temporal framework that maintained a stable relationship between history and hierarchy. Given enough time, enough effort, Third Worlds would become First Worlds. The poor would inherit the earth.[58]

Fifty years later, however, the practice of Christian liberation is no longer about development.[59] It is about deliverance. "There is only one way out of here," the pastor explained. "It's to stand up, to stand up in front of the Father and tell him, 'Father, I have sinned against heaven and against you.' This is liberation. It is to be humble, to have a humble attitude. Because the biggest problem today is pride. Pride is buried in our life. No one wants to humble themselves to anyone. No one wants to say they are sorry."

Take Javier, once again. One month into captivity, he confided, "I want to kill myself." He avoided eye contact but kept on talking, "No one listens to me. No one wants to help me. No one understands me. They say that I'm a disgrace and that I'm self-destructive. But I want my freedom. I want liberation. I want to get out of here. To look for my family. To look for a job. I have all these dreams, but here I'm treated like trash." He shook his head, adding, "I've been discarded (*deshechado*) like a piece of trash." Javier etched in a notebook he kept by his bed, drawing circles with a pen. He continued, "I'm in a tomb. I can't move. I can't talk to anyone because no one listens to me. I can't express myself. Because everyone here thinks I'm stupid or foolish. And no one speaks about life. No one speaks about recovery. This is total bullshit, and I'm slowly dying . . . I want to die."

Javier's intentions are not without precedent. Earlier in the month, another man from the same rehab stole a DVD from the pastor's collection of apocalyptic films. He cracked it in two and then tried to cut himself free. He tried to dig his way out of captivity through his wrists. The pastor had him stopped, of course. The man healed, eventually. But this desperate effort to take his life presented the practice of Christian liberation in the starkest possible terms. Out—he wanted out, and he wanted it now. So does Javier. With suicide still on his mind, he wrote a letter to his mother. It read, in part,

Dear Mom, This is Javier. I'm sending you this letter to ask a favor. I want you to get me out of here. They don't treat me right, and they hit me. I don't want to suffer anymore. Help me. Only you can help me. . . . Come soon. I promise I will change everything. I'll change my way of life. Don't leave me here. I can't stand it here. If you leave me here I'm going to kill myself. Please come and get me out. I want to keep on living. Help me to get out of here. I beg you. Mom, come once you get this letter. I love you. I am waiting here for you. Javier.

Javier's mother received the letter. It terrified her. "What am I supposed to think?" she said. Sitting in her two-room house, on her bed, she continued, "I put him in this rehab to heal, to get better, and I get this letter that he wants to kill himself. He's not getting better. I worry so much. My heart hurts so much. I do not know what to do." Miles away from the rehabilitation center, which is accessible only by an infrequent bus, Javier's mother began to lose confidence in this promise of liberation. But the pastor insisted that Javier's letter only proved just how much Javier needed to be *inside* as opposed to *outside*, *there* as opposed to *here*. "He's in a prison," explained the pastor. "This world is a prison. Javier is enslaved. He's full of spirits. He's hearing voices. He wants to kill himself. The Lord will allow him to leave this prison [of drugs] but he needs to be here. He needs to be here now." Javier's mother conceded, not knowing what else to do. "I mean, really," this aging woman asked, "what am I supposed to do?" And so Javier stayed, waiting for Godot as much as for God.[60] And in his staying, in his failed effort at escape, the practice of Christian liberation shifted. The idea of the forsaken changed.

For decades, liberation theologians linked Christ's passion to the people's passion. Each progressively plodded past every station of the cross, with Good Friday giving way to Easter Sunday. "With a great cry," writes theologian Jon Sobrino, "there is also resurrection, a word continues to resound and the crucified endure through history."[61] For a time, for a rather long time, Christian liberation was about a progressive notion of time.[62] But this no longer holds. Christian liberation's invocation of Christ's passion still fits, and maybe more now than ever before. Yet it is more ethnographically convincing to shift focus away from the stations of the cross—the progression from one moment in time to another—and toward Jesus's last words, which seem to have everything to do with space and not time, with egress and not progress, with immediacies and not eventualities. Decidedly nonprogressive, absolutely desperate, these last words seem the most biblically proximate to the user who just wants to get the fuck out: "My God, My God, why have you forsaken me?" (Matthew 27:45–46).

THE STATE OF LIBERATION

Javier escaped, eventually. Six months after his initial abduction, half a year beyond the reach of natural light, he finally pulled the bars clear off that third floor window. He then squirreled his way out of the opening and shimmied down the side of the building until he could safely free-fall to the street. The young man from Javier's neighborhood, the one who had been picked up a few days before him, also escaped—at the same time, through the same opening. Free at last, it would seem. But not so, it turned out. Javier returned home immediately. So too did the other young man. And both fell back into drugs. "He'd get stubborn, really foolish, until I would give him money," Javier's mother explained, "I know it was for drugs. I'd give him 50 quetzales and then he'd say he lost it. So I'd have to give him more. I told him that I needed to stop giving him money or I'd be left with nothing. That I wouldn't be able to eat." Javier's mother eventually took action, dragging her son to the national mental health hospital, but the doctors there deemed him of sane mind, or at least not unstable enough to justify holding him there against his will. "And how could they?" she asked me, "The front gate isn't even locked. The doors are wide open. He'd run away." And he would have. I visited the state institution not long after speaking with Javier's mother. The gate was open. Patients wandered aimlessly. Many were obviously sedated. One lay face down on the ground, his pants around his knees. This place could obviously not handle Javier.

The situation grew dire, however, with Javier's mom reading a tragic event as an obvious warning shot. The young man who escaped with Javier, the one who had turned back to crack as soon as he had returned back to the neighborhood, walked the streets one day. Louder than Javier, less stable than Javier, and far more prone to outbursts than Javier, this young man upset the wrong people for the last time. Echoes of this kind of attitude often lined the rehabilitation center. This young man would yell at the pastor. He would fight with other users and throw his food at the walls. He was often a gentle, fun-loving person but would then break composure. I often thought that this mercurial disposition, these manic impulses, is how he escaped. If pressed, I often think that the pastor let this young man escape—and that he let Javier "escape" as well. Liberation or not, both proved too much for this radically underfunded and hopelessly understaffed rehabilitation center. So they let them go.

This is why it came with great sadness but little surprise to learn that in the middle of the day, in the middle of the street, a group of equally young men put a gun to this young man's head and shot him dead. He died in the streets. With no investigation pending and no arrests made, the murderers still walk around the same neighborhood selling the same product. Nothing changed, which frightened Javier's mom. "He's going to die in the streets," she insisted, fearing for her son's life. "But I am also really afraid," she added, "because there are these stories of sons killing their mothers. I've heard about it in the news. There was some story of a boy killing his mother with a stone. He said that he had to kill her." The problem was that Javier was growing more violent by the day. He would spend hours in his room and then erupt in anger, throwing his clothes around the room, further breaking his bed, and destroying (bit by bit) a mirror that once hung there. His room and his life, by all accounts, were a mess—observably unlivable. "I get nervous and sick to my stomach," Javier's mother said, still sitting in her room on her bed, bracing herself for (but also hoping against) Javier's return from his latest binge.

Javier and his mother ultimately found refuge at the price of embarrassment. Javier, high on crack, climbed onto the tin roof of his house. It was the middle of the night. Sharing not just walls but also roofs with neighbors, he woke up the block with his yelling and stomping. His mother begged for Javier to calm down and come down, but he did not, until the police came, pulled him from the roof and then beat him with a baton. Javier landed in jail while his mother finally got a good night's sleep. She knew that her son was safe. The next morning, after some confusion as to where he actually was, in which prison he sat, Javier's mother waited for a dozen hours outside the prison for the judge to hear her son's case. The entire time Javier's mother used his cell phone to secure a space in a different Pentecostal rehabilitation center that was secure enough to hold him but not so firm as to beat him. At some point during the course of the day, sitting on a curb, Javier's mother passed me Javier's cell phone to note the "reminders" that he had programmed for himself. Pinging nearly every hour, they glimpsed the contours of his troubled soul: "11am—Please avoid thinking of Ana. 12pm—Be careful of Ana. Remember how she made you feel humiliated. 3pm—Think about your time in Mexico. 4pm—Head up [the hill] to buy some [crack] from Letty. 7:30pm—Be careful with those women from the capital. 9:00pm—Loser. Loser. Loser. 9:10pm—Seek out your freedom (*libertad*) from your mom. She annoys you. 11:00pm—Be careful of those dudes in the streets. 11:45pm—Thinking of Ana hurts you. Think of something else. Try to distract yourself." As I read through Javier's notes, another woman, waiting for her own son and sitting on the same curb, turned to say, "Children are like avocados. You just don't know if they are rotten on the inside." Her son was also confounded by crack. She continued, waxing theological, "We're human and we're really small. We can't do anything. We can try [to help our sons]. We can bring them to church. We can hit them, but our efforts are nothing. Only God is the one who can break them, only God. And they have to be willing."

The judge ultimately presented Javier with a choice. He offered Javier thirty days in prison or two months in a Pentecostal rehabilitation center, but the rehab came with a catch. If he escaped, he would have to pay either 50,000 quetzales and/or spend five years in prison. Although the offer did not strike anyone as constitutional, not even vaguely legal, suggesting the extreme informality of not just the rehabilitation centers but also the judicial system, the answer was easy enough for Javier. He chose the Pentecostal rehabilitation center, which is exactly what the judge wanted. The police even transferred Javier in handcuffs, driving him through the streets of Guatemala City, with its emergency lights flooding the streets as well as my eyes, as I sat in the back. With the city asleep and the occasional street light casting the odd shadow— with the speed of the ride making me hold the truck's roll bar tighter and tighter—we toured the city in ways that connected Guatemala's formal carceral system to its informal carceral system. For as the police handed Javier over to a pastor, as Javier retreated past an iron door and into a darkened room, spending his first evening in the rehab, it became obvious how much the state draws on Christian liberation, on the power of political theology. It is a material resource, for sure. The state contributes not a cent to these centers. But the resource is also moral, locking these men inside a subjectivity that quarantines their problems to the confines of the self. The conclusion became clear: liberation is no longer some endgame, some goal to be achieved, in either the near or distant future, but rather the principal means through which thousands of poor, unemployable men, like Javier, come to be governed here and now.

FIGURE 14. Forsaken. Photo by Benjamin Fogarty-Valenzuela.

AGAIN, WHERE DO YOU WANT TO GO?

"I'm always trying to find the way out," Javier told to me. It was his first full day in the new Pentecostal rehabilitation center. We sat together for the afternoon service. An itinerant pastor had come to preach the word.

"Out of the center? You're always trying to find a way out of the center." I replied.

"No," he said, "I'm always trying to find a way out of my problems."

The pastor then quieted the group. He opened his Bible and preached for more than an hour, winding his way through a number of eerily familiar talking points. "There are two ways out of here," he said. His arms spread wide, as if he himself had been crucified: "Two ways. There is the straight path and there is the winding path; there is Jesus and there is the devil; there is eternal life and there is hell. Which do you choose?" An unbelievable return to an unnervingly familiar narrative, Javier sat in his chair, with more interest and concern for this pastor's words than he'd had for the last one. "If you start walking with Christ," the pastor continued, "your life will be different. Your thoughts will be different. If you liked drugs, you will no longer get high. If you liked prostitution, you will no longer buy sex. If you liked to rob people, you will no longer rob people. If you liked to kill people, you will no longer kill people. God will guide your steps. Because it's about controlling ourselves."

"Amen," Javier mumbled.

Adrift

We walked. Nearly seven years after we first met in a church parking lot, Mateo and I strolled through his neighborhood. I was over for a visit and Mateo wanted to get some fresh air. Out of work and absolutely bored, with much of the day ahead of him, Mateo was going a little stir crazy. He had nothing to do—that afternoon, or that week. So we walked.

Mateo's neighborhood is not huge. A main drag divides three streets, with twenty townhouses on each side. The houses themselves are nearly identical. Distinctions have emerged over the years, of course, but they are subtle. Covered garages now embellish some of the structures, thanks to remittances, and a few have fallen into disrepair, because of overextended efforts at upward mobility. But the aesthetics are incredibly consistent—so much so, in fact, that one day I absentmindedly turned onto a street just south of Mateo's. Not recognizing my mistake, I even knocked on what I thought to be Mateo's front door. The confused homeowner set me straight. "Mateo lives one block north," she told me. "Of course he does," I blushed.

As we walked, we took turns noticing ever more refined distinctions— a new terrace, a fresh coat of paint, some potted plants. And we shook our heads at the abandoned houses, even peeking into their windows to see what was inside. Most were empty, with piles of debris collecting in the corners. "It's a nice place," Mateo reassured me about the neighborhood, "Security. Maintenance. A bit of grass." We walked and I nodded

FIGURE 15. Walking. Photo by Benjamin Fogarty-Valenzuela.

while Mateo talked out his immediate future. "I'll have some cash by Friday," he said. Mateo had recently completed some contract work at a call center. It was a small center. It was also a small contract. "Nothing fancy," he said. And this was too bad. Years earlier, at the top of his game, Mateo had mapped out the city's call centers. "Everybody knows that Atento is kind of one of those last options," he had once said. A friend had been fired from Transactel for smoking weed on the job and had found himself working at a lesser place. "If you want to get a career and start big," Mateo had told me with a bit of pride, "Transactel, 24/7, NCO, and ACS. That's it. Anything else is second rate." He then pressed his point, perhaps too much, picking himself up while pushing his buddy down: "I mean, third rate. The rest are third rate call centers." But after years of bouncing around the industry, coming and going almost at whim, Mateo had burned too many bridges. Now he could only scrape together part-time work from some rather ragtag operations. The shop in question moonlighted for bigger operations when they found them-selves momentarily needing more manpower. So Mateo worked the Fourth of July, Thanksgiving Day, even Christmas Day. He was living on scraps of work.

"The call center pays us on Friday," he told me as we walked past another set of townhouses. It was midmorning and the neighborhood was nearly empty. People either stayed inside, in an effort to beat the heat, or they had gone to work. "I'm already all paid up," Mateo reported. "I already paid my services here for two months, for May and June." By "services," Mateo meant his neighborhood association fees for upkeep and security. These were some of the only monthly expenses he had. Mateo's father owned the townhouse outright, and so Mateo did not pay rent. "I just have to pay my light," he said without much fanfare. "Once you have water and light in your home," he explained, "you're cool. You don't need nothin' else. You can always survive."

Mateo's last comment struck me. So much of his life had been about survival, rather dramatic efforts at survival. Borders. Prisons. Riots. "In the streets of Los Angeles," Mateo once said, "I learned respect. I learned how to be a survivor. I learned how to protect myself. That's what they teach you in the gangs: how to be a soldier." Mateo even tells a rather harrowing story of being shot at in Los Angeles while police helicopters circled overhead. But now, as he entered his late thirties, the stakes of his survival seemed to slow down. They were real, of course. He was living from paycheck to paycheck for light and water, but they didn't pop like they used to. No shootings. No helicopters. Just bills and boredom.

This pace of survival has everything to do with some relatively modest resources. "You know we're not all like Mateo," one call center worker had explained, years earlier. Having learned his English on Rikers Island and then having hustled his way to the position of floor supervisor after his deportation, in spite of his tattoos, this young man was jealous: "Mateo's got a place to stay. He's got his dad to fall back on. He just don't have to work like the rest of us." All of this is true. The rest of them, as this young man put it, have to work. They have no other option. "I got nothing else here," he told me, "no family. There's no other job here for me. There's no other way for me to survive." So he worked not just tirelessly but also piously. This young man is punctual, respectful, and ever striving—because he has to be.

The message is clear. And it is one of necessity. Those who do not perform piety in postwar Guatemala often end up dead. This is no exaggeration. My own notes and personal records, over nearly a decade of research, are littered with the names and phone numbers of men who tried but then failed not just to exit gang life and street violence but also to perform piety—to get a job, stay sober, and maintain some sense of self. But piety is not easy to perform, at least not every day. Early in my fieldwork, one young gang member, hiding out in a rehab, admitted to being addicted to murder. "My problem is not with drugs or liquor," he told me, "but with blood. I love to watch it fall." With the word of God on his lips, citing scripture every chance he got, he worked piously toward radical change. "I want to have a heart of flesh and not of stone," he confessed. And so he sought out forgiveness and salvation—until he didn't. Three days later, before I could follow up with him, this young man escaped from the rehab and then died in the streets. A rival gang member shot him in the face.

Piety in the absence of personal resources has become a precondition for life itself. Billions of dollars have been directed toward prevention programs, with each scheme contributing to a surprisingly Christian, decidedly uneven security assemblage that actively intervenes in the lives of Guatemalans. At the heart of these interventions sits an affective infrastructure that distinguishes between those with a heart of flesh and those with a heart of stone. And this distinction has consequences. Those with a heart of flesh are allowed to leap from one fleeting security scheme to another. They are, in fact, encouraged to do so. From the pastoral care of the prison chaplain (chapter 1) to the ruthless captivity of the rehab (chapter 5), from the possibility of a work program (chapter 2) to the moral demands of a call center job (chapter 3), the pious tap the promise of prevention for the sake of survival. Some projects even prime children to be pious (chapter 4). The ultimate effect of this security assemblage is rather precarious, even for the pious. Those with a heart of flesh navigate not so much a safety net (however poorly knit) as a series of randomly inflating and suddenly deflating life rafts. Completely uncoordinated and absolutely unpredictable, these rafts serve only the pious. The impious, in contrast, have been left to sink or swim—with hearts of stone, no less.

For Mateo, piety has always been an unsteady affair. It hiccups and stalls but then restarts. "I've suffered," Mateo explained as we walked through his neighborhood, "and maybe that's why I'm the way I am. Defensive, serious—but only God has helped me break these chains and still I ask a lot of God, you know." Mateo slid his hands into his pockets. "I'm not going to church either," he admitted, "but I'm praying. I'm praying every once in a while. I try to go to church—like, trying to be involved. But I don't know, man. I just don't know." Unlike those addicted to murder, or even those surviving through the call center, Mateo has been able to strive and then fail, and then strive again and fail again. His father's townhouse has made all the difference. It has been his life raft. So too has the occasional remittance. Without either, it is clear—painfully obvious, in fact, for those who sit with his story, even if only for a moment—that Mateo would be dead by now. This too is no exaggeration. "When I go to the city, I'm in the mothafuckin' jungle," Mateo explained. "It's the jungle. That's what they call Guatemala City. So when I leave my neighborhood, I'm careful. I strap my shoes on. I secure my wallet, and I am gone. Because you just never know if you comin' back home." And so when Mateo reflects aloud, as he often does, over "the shit I got into," when he exhales a punctuated *fuck* or *damn,* adding with no small amount of disbelief that "I'm still alive to tell you this story," it is important to take him at his word—to be just as surprised as he is. Against all odds, Mateo is alive. And this is a blessing.

Mateo's survival, his relatively long life, also opens a rare window onto the longitudinal effects of soft security. If this book had been researched across a single year rather than nine years, it would have been about death—about men shot in the face and then left to die. Or it would have been about the rare soul who makes it out of gang life—to live a punctual, respectful, and ever-striving life. But Mateo upends both these stories. Strolling through his neighborhood, settling into precarity, Mateo makes visible how efforts at prevention, when laced with piety, distinguish between those with a heart of flesh and those with a heart of stone, justifying (in the end) a politics of making the pious live and letting the rest die.

. . .

Hard security is about death. It is about deducting, suppressing, and punishing life. Hemispheric upticks in the practices of deportation, incarceration, and extrajuridical executions signal the supremacy of hard security across the Americas. Soft security, on the other hand, is about life. It is about administering, optimizing, and multiplying life.[1] Conceding that society must be defended, soft security works diligently to enhance the health and well-being of postwar Guatemala. More life. Better life. These are its intentions. And young, unemployable men are its subjects.

But there are limitations. Most everyone admits it. A member of MS-13 once named them with surprising clarity. Inside prison, completely high, he mentioned something he had seen on television. "I saw a commercial," he told me, "just the other day." He stepped a little closer. "There was this little kid in a desert. He was just sitting there. Dirty and thirsty. And not too far away from this kid, this little baby, was a vulture." He spread out his arms as if they were wings. "The vulture was just waiting for the baby to die." He pulled from his joint. As he smoked, I told him that I had seen the same commercial just the other day. It was for a child sponsorship program. They can sometimes appear on Guatemalan channels in the middle of U.S. programming. Mistaking me for a missionary, even though I insisted that I am an anthropologist, he then pressed, "You need to save that kid. Save him, not us. Don't come here. We need you. But we don't deserve you."

Soft security is about making live. But it is often (too often) about deciding who should live. And this is what this young man knew so well. To help *here* often means not helping *there*. Bettering his life came at the expense of losing that baby's life. And while principled arguments can be made against the idea that some people must die to make others live, while examples abound of societies that organize social forces wholly to make live, the experience of soft security in postwar Guatemala makes absolutely clear that life has become a zero-sum game.[2] Decisions must be made. This means administering to some populations (and not others), optimizing certain lives (but not all lives), and multiplying specific populations (at the expense of other populations). Most everyone needs life, but not everyone deserves life.

Piety structures this sense of deservedness. It allows program officers and project managers to distinguish between the ineligible and the eligible, the lost and the found. It also allows the supposedly lost, such as this member of MS-13, to see himself as such. And a particular vision of the human person drives this piety. Familiar to most every Guatemalan, its basic plot points traffic toward the promise of an intimate, decidedly individual need for change. Again, Augustine of Hippo puts it best. Writing in the fourth century, uttering his *Confessions*, he narrates Christian piety as implanted on the viscera. His meditations on the problem of evil and on salvation, on the body and the soul, are as felt as they are thought. Sin, for Augustine, is gratuitous. It is irrational, provoking waves of regret and sorrow. Remember the pears?

In the vineyard, as a young boy, Augustine stole pears for no other reason than to steal pears. He was simply bored. So too were his friends. They shook the trees, scooped them up, and fed them to the pigs. They didn't even eat them. Years later, after his conversion, Augustine wonders what possibly could have animated him. His answer to his own question is the pleasure of sin. "The pleasure I got," Augustine writes, "was not from the pears. It was in the crime itself, enhanced by the companionship of my fellow sinners."[3] His appetite for sin, compounded by the crowd, unsettled everything. He was, he recalls, "a depraved soul, falling away from security in thee to destruction in itself, seeking nothing from the shameful deed but shame itself."[4] Captivated by crime, overruled by recklessness, Augustine fell away from security.

But then he changed. Years later, in a garden at Milan, he transformed his life. It was a struggle. He understood Scripture. It all made sense to him, but he did not yet feel the word of God. It did not own his body. So Augustine grew impatient. Thrashing about on the ground, with tears in his eyes, he cried, "How long? Tomorrow? Why not now? Why not this very hour make an end to my uncleanness?" A child's voice then sang out. He or she—Augustine could not tell—invited him to "pick it up; read it. Pick it up; read it."[5] Augustine did. Grabbing his Bible, opening it at random, his eyes fell on Romans 13:13: "Let us walk honestly, as in the day; not in rioting and drunkenness, not in chambering and wantonness, not in strife and envying." His heart swelled with certainty. "Devotion overflowed, and my tears ran down, and I was happy in all these things."[6] His conversion to Christianity propelled him toward a life of piety, one devoted to conquering his desires, mastering his will, and extending himself toward God. "Observe how my life," he writes, "is but a stretching out."[7] This extension ultimately delivered to Augustine the gift of free will, which empowered him to assume moral responsibility for the existence of evil. He was to blame, and no one else.

Soft security, in its Christian piety, places a pear in the hand of every Guatemalan, and then asks him to lay down in a garden, to thrash about with tears in his eyes. If he does, then there is the possibility that he might become a subject of prevention. Authorities will do their best to make him live. They will minister to him, educate him, and connect him with the formal economy. But if he does not lay down, if he does not thrash about with tears in his eyes, or if he does so only intermittently, then he is allowed to die. This book pivots atop this process to make ethnographically clear what is so omnipresent: the violence of piety is not its inability to extend prevention to everyone but its tendency to distinguish between the deserved and the disposable, the men worthy of intervention and those not.[8] To let die is not piety's limitation: it is Christian piety's most basic function.

Take but one example. Halfway through my own fieldwork, the United States Agency for International Development (USAID) changed course. USAID had long supported a range of antigang initiatives that included gang prevention programs as well as gang intervention and reinsertion programs. Gang intervention programs target active gang members, while gang reinsertion programs often connect ex–gang members with legitimate work. Neither intervention nor reinsertion proved especially productive. Both are time-intensive strategies with no immediate payoff. They often target troubled adults who have long histories of poverty, substance abuse, and social exclusion. Success stories are hard to find and even harder to maintain. Augustine himself would probably have been impatient with both approaches. How to get these men to submit, to lie down in the garden? Obvious answers never emerged. And so USAID made a decision. With the signing of the Central American Regional Security Initiative and its influx of money, policy makers and program officers cancelled their intervention and reinsertion programs to focus entirely on gang prevention. Prevention is a better investment, many argued, one that would more efficiently administer, optimize, and multiply life. The statistics said as much. With two-thirds of its population of almost fifteen million people under the age of 25, authorities argued that Guatemala is a young country. More importantly, at least when it comes to issues of security, 89 percent of assailants are between the ages of 18 and 35 years old. Start young, the logic crowed.[9]

Eliminating intervention and reinsertion programs for the sake of prevention programs proved tragic. In a matter of months, hundreds of active and former gang members found themselves without programming. They lost access to counselors and community initiatives. Support networks crumbled. And the men were let go, allowed to sink or swim. Most sank. "The tall skinny guy?" Mateo asked. "He's dead already. They killed him in La Paloma. He used to shine shoes as part of some reinsertion program. But then programmers dropped it." Without a job, courting the idea of returning to the gang, this man did not last long on the streets. He used to shine shoes in an upscale office complex, making just enough money to support his family. Part of the program included interactions with elite *capitalinos*. Every time one of them wanted their shoes cleaned or repaired, they would have to interact with this former gang member. I would sit with him, often for hours, observing his work and these interactions. They never paid off as intended, but at least he got paid. And then he didn't. "His own gang members, his own friends, spotted him," Mateo said, "They found him, waited for him, followed him, and then pulled up on a motorbike. Pah. Pah. Pah. Left him laying right there in front of his house."

Not only USAID but also the entire postwar security industry shifted focus in a way that administered life for thousands of at-risk youth while letting die a generation of criminalized and utterly unemployable men. At the core of this decision sits an assumption about the pious subject and his ability to change—not just for the better but for good.

Again, intervention and reinsertion are time intensive, with no immediate payoff. They are also expensive. And while one could argue that this murdered man had already changed, that, in Mateo's words, he was "responsible and always there for his kids," any such argument in his moral defense concedes the terms of the argument itself. It upholds piety. The more righteous task, the one that this book pursues, is to problematize piety until prevention is seen as a historical construction with rather tragic consequences. "It's sad," Mateo added. "It's sad that they killed him. They killed a lot of kids, a lot of young kids from that reinsertion program. A lot of those guys are dead."

. . .

Letting die is a slow, steady accomplishment. The work of letting die lines most every page of this book. Piety renders visible the willing subject—to prison chaplains (chapter 1), small business owners (chapter 2), even call center supervisors (chapter 3). The unwilling subject disappears, or is more often allowed to disappear. Piety also segregates the lost from the found—with the soul disaggregated from the body (chapter 1) and the sponsored child living next to (but somehow not alongside) the unsponsored child (chapter 4). And piety holds captive the willing for the sake of liberation while eventually setting loose the absolutely unwilling (chapter 5). The effects are observably moral and material, but they are also existential.

We were still walking. "You ask me these questions," Mateo said, "and . . . like, sometimes when you leave and I'm here by myself, I think about the conversations that we had, you know? I think about the things you're doing. I think about the book that you're writing down. I think about . . . I mean, I'm smart too, Kevin." We held silent for a bit. The comment did not appear out of thin air, of course, but after years of reflection between the two of us about his immediate life and the larger history that defines so much of it. Mateo broke our silence. "I know what's going on," he sighed, "I know what's up. I know everybody gots their point of view. Everybody has their own head on their shoulder and everybody has a different world. And I think it's good what you're doing, man, 'cause you're allowing people to know that I'm just . . . I'm out here in the ghetto, man. That this violence do exist, that the corruption is real high up here." Mateo had always been supportive of our exchanges, appreciating the attention and the reflection it provided, but things had suddenly turned melancholic. As we circled the neighborhood yet again, Mateo insisted: "I mean, I'm smart too, Kev."

Mateo's emphasis on his intelligence emerged through our extended conversations but also through his conversion to Christianity, his work experience in prevention programs, and his success in the call center industry. Mateo knows he is smart. Mateo also has a critical awareness as to why he never proved to be a stand-out student. Preaching, as he often does, about his childhood, he returns constantly to that fateful day when he showed his father a B+—an event recounted at the beginning of this book, and haunting much thereafter. Mateo routinely admits, "I could have done better in school. I know I could have done better if I had been raised in an environment with love, and attention, and an environment of humbleness, but my environment wasn't like that. It just wasn't like that." Seemingly innumerable forces made it so. A genocidal civil war, undocumented immigration, the LA race riots, the War on Drugs, and mass incarceration mixed with the War on Terror, new regimes of deportation, uneven efforts at democratization, and neoliberal economic reforms. From a certain perspective, Mateo never had a chance. And this is what he meant, what he continues to mean, when he spots his own intelligence. His comments in those moments are meant to question why I wrote this book and not he—or, even more broadly, why I tend to have a sense of purpose most every time we meet and he often does not. The abbreviated list above, the one that starts with genocide and ends with neoliberalism, names the most obvious reasons. But the one missing, the one that is absolutely crucial to the politics of letting die, is Christian piety.

Mateo has been left to die. He has his own life raft, meaning a roof over his head and few monthly expenses, and this allows him to float— but often in the same place and in ways that suggest little to no progress. So he walks his neighborhood as if it were some kind of medieval labyrinth. In lieu of a pilgrimage, possibly on his own path to Jerusalem, Mateo's meditative meanderings keep him out of trouble. But they do not, nor cannot, reverse the fact that the Guatemalan and United States governments, as well as their respective economies, often have had absolutely no use for Mateo. They do not, or cannot, upend the idea that a multibillion dollar gang prevention industry has no place for him. And they do not, or cannot, overturn the assumptions that this prevention industry employs. Mateo is no longer a deserving subject. He qualifies for nothing. For he is no longer, and may never have been, a properly pious subject. He is not the repentant prisoner (chapter 1), the upright entrepreneur (chapter 2), the eager agent (chapter 3), the smiling youth (chapter 4), or the liberated addict (chapter 5). He is none of these—at least not consistently. And so he floats atop a raft not of his own making. And he will do so until it sinks.

And sink it might. Mateo's stepmother once started a rumor. She mentioned to Mateo that she was going to sell the house within a matter of months. He should pack his things, she said, and move out as soon as possible. Neither the fear and the confusion that followed nor the relief that cascaded over him when the rumor was revealed jump-started Mateo into seeking out new opportunities to remake himself as a punctual, respectful, and ever-striving person. Instead it starkly reminded him that few, if any, noncriminal avenues exist by which he and men like him can swim on their own. And so the threat of losing his only means of survival underscored his relative disposability. It is a disposability shared by the young prisoner who, having seen the child sponsorship commercial, insisted that I save the baby, not him. It is a disposability familiar to the other young gang member who escaped from the rehab only to end up shot in the face. And it is a disposability familiar to the shoe shiner who died at his front door, at the hands of his former gang. Mateo's disposability is simply actualizing more slowly than theirs. But it is no less real.

So Mateo floats. Soft security intervenes in some lives and abandons others. It does so by way of a moral compass, one that draws deeply and decidedly from Christianity. Augustine and his *Confessions* prove a shared vernacular to articulate the idioms and affects that converge in ways that make some live and let others die. Abandonment and disposability are not passive constructs. They do not appear in the absence of activity but emerge in the shadows of otherwise concentrated efforts at making live. Christianity, in this milieu, is also not passive nor is it necessarily limited. Piety's central role, its seemingly eternal uptake, is to judge between the sinner and the saved and then justify the former's life at the expense of the latter's life. Make no mistake: hard security, the strong fist, is alive and well. Deportation, incarceration, and execution still stack bodies atop bodies—on tarmacs, in jails, and at morgues. Yet it is piety and prevention that reorders the city as well as its souls, in ways that connect the pious to programs while letting the impious swim for their lives. In this sense, this rather sad sense, Mateo is not an accident but an intended outcome. Prevention efforts mixed with some modest resources instill in Mateo enough piety to walk in circles rather than walk the streets, to accept disposability rather than embody delinquency. "Fuck, Kevin," Mateo said as we walked his neighborhood one more time, "I don't know where I'm going."

Epilogue

I pulled the manuscript from my bag. It was just a stack of papers, hundreds of pages of paper, but it piqued Mateo's interest. "'Bout fuckin' time," he smiled.

"It's just a draft," I insisted, suddenly nervous. We hadn't spoken in months. Mateo's cell phone had stopped working. "We were drinking," explained a recent deportee from Miami. "And you know Mateo. He passed out in the streets and someone took his phone." But I had caught Mateo on a better day, on his way home from a church service. He looked fit.

"Well, what's it say?" Mateo asked. So I started to read, with Mateo checking me on the facts. "Bro," he said, "I got a B+ [not a C+] on that test."

I smiled. And as I bumped up his grade, I asked Mateo what was next, or better yet, how we would want his story to end.

"Whatever," Mateo said, "Whatever, dawg. I just want to get this finished, and I want to see the book, man. Bring me a copy." Of course, I said. "This book is something I want to—when my son grows up . . . when he grows up, I'm gonna tell him, 'Look, this book talks about me, your dad, about my life in prison.' I'm gonna give it to my son as a gift when he's 18 years old—God willing I see him that age. I'm gonna give him this book. I'm gonna tell him, 'Take care of this book, son. It's about me. It talks about my life. How I grew up. How I was, and how you can be now.'" Mateo's piety never ceased to amaze me.

Acknowledgments

I want to thank Mateo. We met years ago, and this book is, in part, a tribute to his life and the lessons it tells. I also want to thank so many other men and women for allowing me into their lives, with a sad note of condolence for those who died along the way. There were moments over the years when I did not think this book would ever come to fruition—given how many of my informants (who so often became my friends) died. Beyond the mechanical concerns of research continuity, an almost impossible goal in such a setting, their murders placed a toll on me. This was oftentimes brutal research. But Mateo pushed on with his life, encouraging me to push on with my research. "If you leave," he once told me, "then you're punkin' out, instead of being there and facing that shit. I know it hurts. It does hurt. But I'm toughin' it out, brother." He then started to preach, "Is it hard? Yes. Does it hurt? Yes. Does it make you cry? Yes. Does it make you angry, frustrated? Yes, it does. But if you're man enough and can deal with that, then that's what makes you a man." And so I pushed on. Thank you, Mateo.

I couldn't have done any of this the fieldwork without access. My deepest gratitude to those who let me in—the prison chaplains and the gang ministers that allowed me to shadow them in the prison setting; the cast and crew of *Desafío 10* as well as the program officers that kept the show going long after the cameras were turned off; the department of human resources at Transactel who granted me a clearance badge and office space; the sponsorship program that allowed me into the lives of so many inspiring people; and the pastors who unlocked their rehab gates just long enough to let me in and then opened those same gates just long enough to let me out. To these men, I will most certainly return. My work with the rehabs is far from over.

I received support for research and writing from the American Council of Learned Societies, the Harry Frank Guggenheim Foundation, the Open Society Foundations, the Social Science Research Council, the Social Sciences and Humanities Research Council of Canada, and the Wenner Gren Foundation as well as Stanford University, Indiana University Bloomington, and the University of Toronto. The money not only let me travel but it also allowed me to hire an outstanding team of research assistants. Over the years, my assistants have included Liggia Samayoa, Margarita Rivera, Luna Sofía Oliva Alfaro, Monica Pelaez, Mandy Lucía Ortega Lemus, Lucía Jiménez, Sloka Krishnan, Joan Sullivan, Jodie Boyer Hatlem, Victoria Nguyen, Rebecca Bartel, Benjamin Fogarty-Valenzuela, and Basit Kareem Iqbal.

The last three assistants deserve special recognition. Rebecca Bartel transcribed and provided initial translations of my more formal interviews with Mateo. Her outstanding research in Colombia also allowed for a productive point of reference for conversations about Mateo and his life. Thank you. Benjamin Fogarty-Valenzuela quickly became my most trusted research assistant. Benji worked with me in Guatemala City, allowing me to process much of this material (often in real time) at an accelerated rate. His presence in the field and intuitive feel for social relationships also put a constant check on my conclusions. The caliber of our conversations while in the field often felt like the very best of seminar settings. His photos, which line so much of this book, are the tip of an ethnographic iceberg. Thank you. Basit Kareem Iqbal knows this book better than I do. My copyeditor and Toronto-side interlocutor, Basit pored over every word choice and reference, every conclusion and narrative arc. He also fielded an absurd number of e-mails, about the smallest of details. While the mistakes are all mine, his steady voice and creative mind added incredible value at every turn. Thank you.

Parts of this book began as much shorter essays. Extended, rewritten, and oftentimes completely rethought for the purposes of this book, they assemble here under the auspices of a larger argument. A very early version of chapter 1 appeared in *Public Culture* 22, no. 1 (2010) as "The Reckless Will." Chapter 2 appeared in *American Quarterly* 63, no. 2 (2011) as "Delinquent Realities." Truncated versions of chapters 3 and 5 appeared in *Social Text*, as "The Soul of Security" 111 (2012) and "On

Liberation" 121 (2014). A shorter version of chapter 4 appeared in *Cultural Anthropology* 28, no. 2 (2013). These more formal efforts at review sat atop a whirl of conversations. They include invited talks at Boston University, Columbia University, Duke University, Stanford University, University of California, San Diego, University of Chicago, The University of Texas at Austin, University of Toronto, and Yale University as well as papers presented at the American Academy of Religion, the American Anthropological Association, the Latin American Studies Association, and the Society for the Anthropology of Religion. The same goes for a series of workshops: American University ("Religion and Violence in Latin America"), Cornell University ("Religion, Abolition, Mass Incarceration"), Harvard University ("The Killable Subject"), Indiana University ("Young Scholars in American Religion"), National University of Singapore ("Transnational Cities"), Universidad de los Andes ("Drugs, Security, and Democracy"), The University of Texas at Austin ("Violence at the Margins"), University of Toronto ("Politically Unwilling," "Faith in Security," "(Re)placing the City," "Whose Conviction?"), and University of Utrecht ("Postsecular Publics").

To those who read a chunk (or chunks) of this manuscript, at some point along the way, thank you: Tania Ahmad, Anne Allison, Lalaie Ameeriar, Nikhil Anand, Hannah Appel, Sarah Banet-Weiser, Peter Benson, Mun Young Cho, Simon Coleman, Bianca Dahl, Brent Hayes Edwards, Tanya Erzen, James Ferguson, William Garriott, Pamela Klassen, Brian Larkin, Kathryn Lofton, Claudio Lomnitz, Ruth Marshall, Randy Martin, Tomas Matza, Anna McCarthy, Micki McGee, Ramah McKay, Bruce O'Neill, Elaine Peña, Laurence Ralph, Daromir Rudnyckyj, Robert Samet, Aaron Shaw, Ju Hyung Shim, Harris Solomon, Archana Sridhar, Nefertí X. M. Tadiar, Kedron Thomas, Graham Denyer Willis, Mariana Valverde, Ludger Viefhues, and Austin Ziederman.

To those who engaged my thoughts, with a conversation or a question, for a moment or for years, thank you: Enrique Desmond Arias, Javier Auyero, Adam Baird, Jon Bialecki, Philippe Bourgois, Jody Boyer, Rosi Braidotti, Anne Braude, Robert Brenneman, Frank Cody, Girish Daswani, Naisargi Dave, Joshua Dubler, Matthew Engelke, Linford Fisher, Anthony Fontes, Chris Garces, Virginia Garrard-Burnett, Yanilda Gonzalez, Jennifer Graeber, Clara Han, John Hayes, Matt Hedstrom, Robert Hefner, David Holiday, Chris Krupa, Anna Lawrence, Tania Li, Vincent Lloyd, Ken MacDonald, Donald MacPherson, Dale Martin, Joseph Masco, John Marshall, William Mazzarella, Amira Mittermaier, John Lardas Modern, Andrea Muehlebach, Ethan Nadelmann, Valentina

Napolitano, Quincy Newell, Joshua Paddison, Michael Pasquier, Alejandro Paz, Ato Quayson, Lorna Rhodes, Joel Robbins, Dennis Rodgers, Nancy Scheper-Hughes, Chad Seales, Ellen Sharp, Mark Lewis Taylor, Kimberly Theidon, Arlene Beth Tickner, Thomas Tweed, Mark Valeri, Adrian Chastain Weimer, Alex Wilde, Jeff Wilson, Lauren F. Winner, Daniel Wolfe, and Sylvia Yanagisako. Special thanks to Joel Van Dyke and Erwin Luna for jump-starting so much of this. And many thanks to Jay and Rebecca Raman for so much support when our time in Guatemala overlapped.

This project started at one institution, developed at another, and came to fruition at yet another. I first pitched the idea for this book while a graduate student at Stanford University. Thanks, as always, to James Ferguson, Liisa Malkki, Carol Smith, and the late Catherine Bell. The American Studies Program at Indiana University Bloomington, directed by Matt Guterl, proved to be a laboratory of ideas. So too did Indiana University's Department of Religious Studies, chaired by David Brakke. At the University of Toronto, the Department for the Study of Religion, especially under the chair of John Kloppenborg and James Dicenso (2012–13), proved supportive. The Centre for Diaspora and Transnational Studies, directed by Ato Quayson, was limitless with its sometimes contagious aspirations for rethinking our most basic assumptions about knowledge production. The Centre's annual lecture series also provided a steady stream of inspiration. Other important sites for this book at the University of Toronto include the Centre for the Study of the United States under the direction of Elspeth Brown, the Jackman Humanities Institute under the direction of Robert Gibbs, and the Religion in the Public Sphere Initiative directed by Pamela Klassen.

Reed Malcolm at the University of California Press placed an inspiring level of trust in this book while recruiting anonymous reviewers that transformed this manuscript into something far better. My many, many thanks to Reed and to the Press. Stacy Eisenstark and Elena McAnespie of the Press also added value at every turn while Barbara Armentrout provided the most detailed, most thorough copyedit I have ever seen. Brendan George Ko of the University of Toronto made sure the photos were just right. Thank you. I repeatedly dragged my students into the act. To those who read drafts of these chapters and listened to lectures on this material—completely against their will—I am in debt to you and your insights. These classes included, at la Universidad del Valle, Métodos Cualitativos and, at the University of Toronto, Anthropology of Christianity (co-taught with Pamela Klassen); Method and Theory in the Study of Religion; North American Religions (co-taught with Pamela Klassen); Religion, Globalization, and Space; Delinquency and Citizenship; and Research Methods in Diaspora and Transnational Studies (co-taught with Ato Quayson and Ken MacDonald).

I have, in the end, two great loves: my family and my work. And it frustrates me to no end that I haven't found a better way to integrate the two. The anthropological life can seem so at odds with domestic bliss. My parents, Bruce and Mary O'Neill, have always been supportive. And my wife, Archana Sridhar, has done so much for this book; I am in her debt. The travel for this research peaked amid a new city, a new baby, and a new job. For this book, and for everything else, thank you. But it was my in-laws, Mojundar and Usha Sridhar, who so often traveled to Indiana and then to Toronto to be with my wife and my young son when I traveled. In the midst of confusing schedules and negotiated boundaries, air mattresses and muffled debates over who would do the dishes, I would often think to myself: "I'm not sure what a family is supposed to look like, but I think this is it." While this book is *for* Archana and Ignatius, it is dedicated *to* Mojundar and Usha Sridhar. Because it just wouldn't have happened without them. Thank you.

Notes on Research

I conducted twelve months of fieldwork in Guatemala City for this book in 2006–2007 and then returned annually between 2008 and 2014, completing eighteen more months of fieldwork across five sites. Fieldwork took place in Guatemala City across the following months: June through December of 2006; January through May of 2007; March and December of 2008; March, April, May, and December of 2009; April through August and December of 2010; April, May, June, August and December of 2011; February, May, July, June, and August of 2012; July of 2013; and March, June, July, and August of 2014. This effort comprised thousands of hours of participant observation, hundreds of interviews, and year-round archival work, as well as phone calls and e-mail exchanges between North America and Central America. Those I interviewed remain anonymous or are cited by pseudonym. In some cases, certain details (insignificant to the analysis) have been changed to protect the identities of certain people. These changes include the use of composite scenes that contain elements from more than one situation. They accurately reflect actual events but have been rearranged to preserve anonymity. Quotations are from recorded interviews or from detailed notes.

A portion of this research took place in English. Mateo and many of the deported men and women represented in this book preferred to speak English. The call center also proved to be an English-dominant site, as did many of the sponsorship settings. Spanish prevailed in the prisons and the rehabs as well as many of the back-to-work programs I observed. The streets of Guatemala City are also Spanish-speaking. For the sake of clarity and tone, I have chosen to synchronize interview transcriptions and translations with a version of standard American slang, one that reflects the tone and cadence of my informants. Any other approach yielded far too choppy a composition, whether Spanish translations appearing in italics or translated phrases paired with italicized Spanish words.

Another issue of representation regards girls and women. My research subjects were overwhelmingly male, so females throughout this book appear at the margins: at prison gates (chapter 1), as emotional sponsors (chapter 4), at the bottom of a ditch (chapter 4), even as mothers afraid of their own sons (chapter 5). I tried to correct for this imbalance as best as I could, but soft security targets men. The prisons, for example, are all-male institutions, except for Centro de Orientación Femenino. So too are the rehabilitation centers. At the time of research, only two of the city's approximately two hundred centers were for women. The reality television show featured ten male participants. Women appeared in the call center setting and the child sponsorship programs, but my own subject position as a relatively young North American man complicated my access to the sisters, cousins, and girlfriends of my main informants. It turned out to be improper to engage any of them individually for any extended amount of time, putting their reputation as well as my personal safety at risk.

There is another issue to note. My place inside this ethnography runs the risk of presenting a more coherent and competent anthropologist than the years of fieldwork evidenced. When I do appear in the text, I tend to be charitable, compassionate, and reasonable rather than confused, scared, or incompetent—although I was (at times) all of these. One explanation is that this book is not about me. It is about soft security. I appear as an ethnographic character when needed to move the narrative and the analysis along. Mateo is neither speaking to himself nor into a digital recorder. He is speaking to me. My place in the text intends to highlight this fact. I should also remind the reader that the anthropological trope of the confused ethnographer is itself a kind of performance, one that should not mark some kind of epistemological high ground. I have intentionally written a decentered ethnography to approximate the shifting contours of soft security. But I have also written relatively tight narratives—to suggest, at the very least, that I take this material very seriously, that I have thought about it for years, and that I have come to some kind of decision about how I understand what I have observed, felt, and learned. Foregrounding the mishaps too much or too often does a disservice, I argue, to the nine years of research that I have completed and the people that I have engaged.

The work proved near constant. The first stage of fieldwork took place in 2006 and 2007 while I completed research for my first book, *City of God: Christian Citizenship in Postwar Guatemala*. However, not a single informant appears in both *City of God* and *Secure the Soul*. There is no overlap. Each book represents a distinct line of research, albeit with interrelated concerns about Christianity and governance. *Secure the Soul* is in many ways the flip side of *City of God*, with the present book concerned with delinquency and biopolitics and the earlier one interested in citizenship and governmentality.

In-depth interviews and participant observation for *Secure the Soul* began in 2006 with prison chaplains as well as with pastors that run rehabilitation centers. This fieldwork anchors the book. I completed prison chaplaincy fieldwork within Pavón, Pavoncito, Boqueron, Preventivo, and Centro de Orientación Femenino prisons, interviewing and shadowing the work of nearly three dozen prison chaplains. This took place within the prison setting and outside it, with complementary fieldwork taking place with prison officials from the Dirección

General del Sistema Penitenciaro. In the prison setting, I observed one-on-one counseling sessions, group therapy meetings, bible study, church services, and church-organized social events. I also accompanied these chaplains on their weekly visits. Although these visits were relatively short (two to five hours), I complemented them with in-depth interviews. I reviewed with each chaplain the events of each visit while also asking open-ended questions. These chaplains included Pentecostal and Charismatic pastors as well as Roman Catholics. Because this fieldwork extended over some nine years, initial insights and observations as well as contacts and relationships matured. The majority of this prison research took place in 2006, 2007, 2008, and 2013.

Fieldwork with Pentecostal rehabilitation centers also began in 2006, with an interest in the relationship between theology and psychology. This interest faded as it became clear that these sites were intimately related to the city's security infrastructure. Initially, in 2006, these centers were places where active gang members hid from threats or sought a Christian conversion that might allow them to leave gang life, or both. This was still true by 2013, but to a much lesser extent. The central function of these centers had changed dramatically, as did the size and scope of this network. As the focus of these centers turned to drug use, so too did my fieldwork, with a survey interest in some fifty Pentecostal rehabilitation centers and a deeper ethnographic commitment to five centers. In these centers, as in the prisons, I observed one-on-one counseling sessions, group therapy meetings, and social events, such as movie nights and special meals. I also interviewed pastors to understand how certain theological assumptions affect the Christian production and practice of rehabilitation. To complement this perspective, I visited the families of men held inside these centers while also documenting the print media that appeared inside these centers. Much of this fieldwork could be characterized as deep hanging out, for stretches of up to twelve hours. The majority of this research took place in 2006, 2007, 2011, 2012, and 2013. It is research that I expect to continue in the following years for the sake of a different book.

Three other kinds of sites emerged. *Desafío 10* was a reinsertion program for ex–gang members looking for work. This program's flashy beachhead culminated in a reality television show, which I analyzed through in-depth interviews and participant observation with program officers and producers while also pursuing participants in the program's subsequent projects: Desafío 100 and Desafío 200. This included attending weekly support groups, church services, and shadowing participants at their place of work. Important also was understanding the lives of those men who left gang life in search of work in the formal economy. This meant meeting and speaking with the families of these participants, both those who actively work in and those who dropped out of the program. Extended (albeit guarded) interviews with the intellectual architect of this project, Harold Sibaja, filled in some of the gaps. Key to the analysis was also a close textual reading of each show, taking seriously the editorial decisions made by those behind the cameras. The majority of this research took place in 2006, 2007, and 2008, though continued interviews with surviving participants proved invaluable over the years.

Fieldwork in Guatemala's call center industry took place primarily in 2010 and 2011, with follow-up fieldwork in 2013. With formal permission and donated office space, I pursued this research in the offices of Transactel while also interviewing men and women from other call centers—namely, 24/7, NCO, and UPS. With research assistants from the Universidad del Valle, I completed more than three hundred open-ended interviews. And I complemented this baseline information with a series of key informants. Some of my time inside the call centers took place "on the floor," next to the agents while they fielded phone calls. But this line of research quickly proved redundant. More productive was sitting with agents during their thirty-minute lunch breaks, which management staggered in such a way as to never overflow the cafeteria at any one moment. The result was a constant tide of agents entering and exiting the cafeteria. Daily interviews quickly built on each other and extended beyond the call center itself, into the lives of these men and women. Observations of the office space also were important. Management was outstandingly helpful, granting me access to the company's archive of advertisements.

Research on the child sponsorship program began by chance. While walking with a pastor in the community I call La Paloma, seemingly miles away from any other North American, finally feeling like an old-fashioned anthropologist, I bumped into a group of child sponsors from North Carolina. This was in 2010. I then worked backward, shoring up a strong ethnographic sense of La Paloma and the Guatemalan side of this child sponsorship program before traveling between North Carolina and Guatemala. The bulk of this transnational research took place in 2011, with follow-up trips in 2012 and 2013. I met several times with child sponsors to contextualize as best I could their interest in intervention. This involved attending church services with child sponsors, speaking with the sponsorship program's North American leadership, and interviewing sponsors in their homes or in nearby restaurants. This also meant contrasting fieldwork in North Carolina with fieldwork in La Paloma. Although the air travel ultimately felt excessive, it provided ample time to consider the infrastructure necessary for this kind of intervention. I should also note that I have made every possible effort to maintain the anonymity of the sponsorship program, its sponsors, and the community it serves.

I met Mateo in 2006, and we hit it off. His sincerity melded well with my inquisitive nature. Our schedules also always seemed serendipitously in line. It was not until 2012 that I considered making Mateo central to this book. He had been a key informant for years, but it eventually became clear that Mateo represented the very piety that this book tries to explain. There are other men whose stories I gathered who exhibited a far more reckless will than Mateo. Many of them are now dead. There are also other men, many of them also now dead, who proved obediently pious. The decision to work with Mateo in the form of a life history stemmed from Mateo's realism—his sincere but always-frustrated effort to be better. That Mateo continually entered and reentered the world of soft security, as both subject and agent, also allows his story to connect this book's five ethnographies. To this end, we made a concerted effort to work together to record his life in a way that he felt was honest to him and to his family. Less an extended confession than informal conversation, the hours we spent together (the recorder both on and off) allowed Mateo to reflect over his life while allowing us both to consider the very conditions of that life.

Notes

All quotations of scripture come from The Holy Bible: New International Version, 2011, Colorado Springs, CO: Biblica.

INTRODUCTION

1. For the most violent noncombat zone, see "Organized Crime in Central America: The Rot Spreads" (2011) from *The Economist* and the Woodrow Wilson Center report *Organized Crime in Central America: The Northern Triangle* (Cynthia Arnson and Eric Olson 2011). Some scholars even compare Guatemala to Iraq (see David Grann 2011). For only 2 percent of homicides being brought to a conviction, see Julie Suarez and Marty Jordan (2007, 5); see also Maya Wilson (2009). Given the country's conviction rate, one international observer dubbed Guatemala a "good place to commit murder" (Philip Alston 2011). For Guatemala's homicide rate being more than twenty times the U.S. average, see Jorge A. Restrepo and Alonso Tobón García, *Guatemala en la encrucijada: Panorama de una violencia transformada* (2011), which documents that in 2010 the homicide rate per 100,000 of population in Guatemala City was 116; by comparison, the United States has a rate of about 5. In all, homicide rates vary from year to year. One statistic from 2006 announced that there had been seventeen murders a day that year (Guatemala Human Rights Commission 2006, 1). In 2006, the postwar homicide rate was at its highest. In 2009, Guatemala had 46.3 murders per 100,000 people; in 2010, the rate fell to 41.4; in 2011, it dropped to 38.5; and in 2012, it declined for a third consecutive year, to 34.4 (United Nations Office on Drugs and Crime 2013). This adds up to a reduction of more than 25 percent in three years (T. W. 2013). But 2013 reversed this trend, returning to the levels of 2006 (Michael Tatone 2013). This overall reduction owes much to the work of Attorney General Claudia Paz y Paz

(Campbell Clark 2013). For the numbers on police officers and private security agents, see Centro de Estudios de Guatemala (CEG) and European Union, *Las múltiples violencias y las juventudes* (2012).

2. Security is not a thing to be defined by the anthropologist. Instead, the ethnographic aim here is to observe how security as a signifier attaches to certain practices, performances, and discourses. What counts as security, and in what contexts? These are the questions. In Guatemala, this book argues, these practices can look very Christian. This is because Christian piety underlies the practice of soft security.

The division between hard security and soft security tends to mirror two more generalizable forms of security. The former mirrors what Stephen Collier calls "sovereign state security," or "practices oriented to the defense of territorial sovereignty against foreign enemies using military means" (2008, 36; see also Michel Foucault 2007, 65). In Guatemala, this means the policing of borders and neighborhoods. Soft security resembles what Collier defines as "population security," or the "protection of the national population against regularly occurring internal threats, such as illness, industrial accident, or infirmity" (2008, 36). Foucault puts it in a succinct (albeit guarded way) when he writes, "sovereignty is exercised within the borders of a territory, discipline is exercised on the bodies of individuals, and security is exercised over a whole population" (2007, 25). Although Foucault would go on to argue that this typology is much too simple, it does provide some basic coordinates.

Yet, both state sovereign security and population security make the state central, which is not realistic for postwar Guatemala. The state is present at times, as in the case of the prison in chapter 1, but also pointedly absent at others, as in the case of rehabilitation centers in chapter 5. This book ultimately pursues an ethnography of security without the state. Peter Redfield raises a parallel question in "Bioexpectations: Life Technologies as Humanitarian Goods": "Foucault's account of biopower famously focuses on the emergence of the modern European state. Contemporary experience, however, includes concerns about life and health that exceed this political form, involving international agencies, nongovernmental organizations (NGOs), and private corporations. What might biopolitics look like 'without the state,' so to speak? Or, more accurately, what might it look like within a terrain where the state appears through chronic inadequacy, not the exercise of certain force?" (2012, 158).

Another important text to think with is Austin Zeiderman's "Life at Risk: Governing the Future in Bogotá, Colombia" (2012). See also Paul Amar's *Security Archipelago* (2013), in which he explores the rise of what he calls "human security" and its efforts to reconcile human rights and national security agendas.

3. For Guatemala being 60 percent Charismatic and Pentecostal, see Pew Forum on Religion and Public Life (2006). However, the accuracy of such statistics is contested by many, including scholars (Corten 1997; Levine 1995; Stoll 1990) identified by Joel Robbins (2004b) in a wide-ranging review article on Christianity in Latin America. For the case of Guatemala in particular, see Andrea Althoff (2005), Manuela Cantón Delgado (1998), and Jesús García-Ruiz (2004).

4. I use the masculine pronoun throughout this book in referring to informants. This is largely because the book is about male-majority gangs as well as programs and institutions that target primarily or only men. As I mention in my research notes in the appendix, the prisons are all-male institutions, except for Centro de Orientación Femenino. Almost all the rehabilitation centers are for men as well. At the time of research, only two of the city's approximately two hundred centers were for women. Women are in the call center setting and the child sponsorship programs, but my own subject position complicated my access to the sisters, cousins, and girlfriends of my main informants.

Statistics seem to back up the idea that prevention is about men rather than women. Men, for example, were victims of 91 percent of the homicides in Guatemala in 2011: of 5,681 homicides, 5,050 victims were male and 62 percent of them were aged between 18 and 35 (Centro de Estudios de Guatemala [CEG] and European Union 2012). Explorations into the violence against women in Guatemala remain critically important (see Victoria Sanford 2008), yet the poor, unemployable young man—and not the young woman—has become the subject of prevention. Edward Orozco Flores pursues this question in *God's Gangs: Barrio Ministry, Masculinity, and Gang Recovery* (2013).

5. For more on the term *assemble*, see Aihwa Ong and Stephen J. Collier, *Global Assemblages: Technology, Politics, and Ethics as Anthropological Problems* (2005).

6. Literature that views religion as a threat to security includes *Dying to Kill* (Mia Bloom 2005), *Holy Terror* (Terry Eagleton 2005), *Belief and Bloodshed* (James K. Wellman, Jr. 2007), *The Destructive Power of Religion* (J. Harold Ellens 2004), and *Freedom from Religion* (Amos Guiora 2009). Literature that views religion as a solution to insecurity includes *More God, Less Crime* (Byron Johnson 2011), *World of Faith* (Thomas Farr 2008), *Holy War, Holy Peace* (Marc Gopin 2002), *The Price of Freedom Denied* (Brian Grim and Roger Finke 2010), and *Religion, the Missing Dimension of Statecraft* (Douglas Johnston and Cynthia Sampson 1994). For a look at the corrective influences of religion on gang affiliation, see David Brotherton and Luis Barrios, *The Almighty Latin King and Queen Nation: Street Politics and the Transformation of a New York City Gang* (2013) and Edward Orozco Flores, *God's Gangs: Barrio Ministry, Masculinity, and Gang Recovery* (2013). One should also note William Cavanaugh's *The Myth of Religious Violence* (2009), which focuses on the tendency for scholars to understand religion as violent. Of interest also is Hent de Vries's *Religion and Violence: Philosophical Perspectives from Kant to Derrida* (2002), which productively reconfigures the relationship between religion and violence.

7. It is important to emphasize, as I am reminded by Ruth Marshall (e.g., 2009), that philosophers of modernity also relate religion to security. Hegel's phenomenology ([1807] 2009), Marx's messianic proletarian revolution (Marx and Engels [1848] 2002), William James's psychologized religious experience ([1902] 2007), and Freud's illusion ([1927] 2012) were all ways to rethink human coexistence in a conflicted world. The consequent political organization of human coexistence has as its premise the emancipation from religion; see variously Talal Asad (2007), Jacques Derrida (1990, 1998), and Jean-Luc Nancy (2008).

8. I follow the work of Michel Foucault to see the soul as not only the effect of power but something that has become a site of intervention. Foucault writes, "[The soul] exists, it has a reality ... A 'soul' inhabits [man] and brings him to existence" (1995, 29–30). See also Foucault (1988); Peter Miller and Nikolas Rose (1988); Nikolas Rose (1990, 1992, 366); and Colin Gordon (1987). I should also note that I treat the terms *soul* and *subject* as interchangeable, and my interest in both, as with Foucault, is with forms of control.

A particularly clear articulation of this interest in the soul and, in turn, subjectivity appears in Foucault's *Use of Pleasure* (1990, 26–28). Here Foucault notes that any ethics, or ethos of the self's relationship to itself, has four components. The first is ethical substance. This is the ethical field or its theory of being. An aspect of the soul's ethical substance for this book, for example, is Christianity. Other parts include, in the broadest of strokes, neoliberalism, humanitarianism, development, and so on. The second component is the mode of subjection, which largely relates to the practices one employs to establish the soul's relationship to oneself. For this book, Christian practices emerge across each of the sites explored: bodily comportment (as with the attention paid to proper dress in chapters 3, 4, and 5); the control of one's emotions (as seen in chapter 1 with self-esteem, chapter 3 with customer service, and chapter 5 with sobriety); or even proper etiquette (as explored in chapter 2 with formal dining and chapter 4 with letter writing). The third component is the ethical work that one performs on oneself. Christian piety is central here, as a particular attitude accompanies Christian piety: steadfastness in the face of ever-frustrated success. Mateo's resilience is a clear example of this attitude as is Transactel's concern for its workers to become more (see chapter 3). The final component is a teleology, a direction to which all this effort flows. This teleology works on many different scales, with the security of postwar Guatemala as one end and the success of individuals as another. Ultimately the subject that emerges through these interrelated components can be both a governed and self-governing subject. A focus on the subject, or the soul, does not mean that Christian piety should not be understood as a path toward security, freedom, or even liberation, but rather as the principal means by which a growing number of Guatemalans have come to be governed at some of the most intimate scales.

9. By *aspiration*, I mean something akin to an affect, or a raw, reactive sensation that takes place before consciousness and before discourse (Kevin Lewis O'Neill 2013). Hair standing on the back of a neck, the warm glow of holiday festivities, the rush of enthusiasm at a political rally—this is affect. From the standpoint of affect, writes William Mazzarella, "society is inscribed on our nervous system and in our flesh before it appears in our consciousness" (2009, 291). Affect theory has taken an important step toward augmenting anthropology's longstanding commitment to discourse theory and the body. Brian Massumi (2002, 3) finds frustration with how discursive analyses render the body limp. Foucault, Massumi notes, tends to treat the body like a big lump of clay. "Society has an immediate hold on the body," Foucault writes. "Society invests it, marks it, trains it, tortures it, forces it to carry out tasks, to perform ceremonies, to emit signs" (1995: 23). This does not satisfy Massumi—if only because bodies are not always docile (2002, 25). From the perspective of affect, the body is excitable.

One approach to affect theory pivots atop Deleuze's reading of Spinoza. Affect here is ontological (Gilles Deleuze 1988b; William Connolly 2008). Another approach, one that shifts away from questions of becoming, homes in on what Donovan Schaefer calls "the phenomenology of the political" (2013). Here the work of Sara Ahmed (2010), Kathleen Stewart (2007), Lauren Berlant (2011), and Eve Kosofsky Sedgwick (2003) form a second kind of lineage.

This book's sense of Christian piety as an affect is very much in line with the former's attention to the fact that so much struggle and contestation over improving and becoming better (in the context of soft security) takes place through the body, in its flesh, and at the pit of the stomach. Mateo's will to be better is Christian piety. Mateo's cringe when he messes up is Christian piety. His elation when he succeeds and his deflated sense of self when he fails contribute to a political terrain of struggle that this book makes its ethnographic object of analysis.

Affect as a religiously managed and politically manipulated sensation makes legible a series of spaces that are not necessarily territorial but that are nonetheless deeply political. These include, for example, the felt distance that exists between the pious and the impious. It is a divide that mirrors the disjuncture between reason and affect that Elizabeth Povinelli documents in multicultural Australia: "I should be tolerant, but you make me sick" (2002, 4). The move toward affect is important when it comes to the study of piety, which is more than just a discourse (Michel Foucault 1988), a mentality (Foucault 1991), or even ethical formation through bodily practices (Saba Mahmood 2004). Scholars working in the anthropology of Islam have begun to move "beyond the trope of self-cultivation" (Amira Mittermaier 2012) by, at the very least, emphasizing how piety as an aspirational affect competes with other modes of being (see, for example, Samuli Schielke 2008). My ethnography follows suit.

10. The intent here is to draw in some broad themes common to conservative Christianities while also acknowledging that not just Christianity is at play. It is Christianity in assemblage with humanitarianism, state security, neoliberalism, international development, and so on. Underlying my approach to Christian piety is the coordination of several strands of thought.

The first is Perry Miller's sense of an "Augustinian strain of piety" (1982, 3–34). I am attracted to his idea that "when the wave of religious assertion which we call Puritanism is considered in the broad perspective of Christian history, it appears no longer as a unique phenomenon, peculiar to England of the seventeenth century, but as one more instance of a recurrent spiritual answer to interrogations eternally posed by human existence" (1982, 4). The sentiment of this statement, for me, suggests an approach to Christianity that extends beyond church history and nestles atop some sense of affect, as understood in note 9.

The second strand of thought is Michel Foucault's (1991) understanding of governmentality. This book is committed to understanding how "governing people is not a way to force people to do what the governor wants" (Foucault 1999, 162). Rather, governing involves getting citizens to "evaluate and act upon [themselves] so that the police, the guards and the doctors do not have to" (Cruikshank 1996, 234). Christian piety governs. This is one of my most basic working assumptions.

The third strand of thought is Gilles Deleuze's notion of control and his sense that "we are in a generalized crisis in relation to all the environments of enclosure—prison, hospital, factory, school, family" (1992, 4). My interest is in the shifting nature of governance and how, much like Deleuze, we can spot a waning centrality to disciplinary institutions. This does not mean less governance but new modes of governance. Christian piety, this book argues, is one such mode.

And the fourth strand of thought gathers insights from the so-called affective turn (Sara Ahmed 2010; Lauren Berlant 2011; Eve Kosofsky Sedgwick 2003; Kathleen Stewart 2007). Berlant's sense of cruel optimism captures a great deal about what this book means by *Christian piety*: "I define 'cruel optimism' as a kind of relation in which one depends on objects that block the very thriving that motivates our attachment in the first place" (2012). Augustine, it is said, first coined the term "cruel optimism" during his debates with Pelagius on the importance of grace and salvation. Pelagius insisted that one could simply will oneself back into God's proximity. Augustine stressed the role of divine intervention, of grace itself, and suggested that this heroic asceticism was a kind of cruel optimism. No one can do it on his own, Augustine suggested. Much of the ethnographic material that I collected for this book parallels this debate over whether one can set oneself right or whether one requires at least some help (from the sovereign).

The ultimate yield of these four strands is an understanding of Christian piety as an impulse qua imperative to improve, one structured by a redemptive narrative that Augustine writes so well in his *Confessions* (1955).

11. "Denomination" is an ethnographically unhelpful category in postwar Guatemala. It holds great analytical value for scholars of North American religion, largely because this subfield's object of study has long been mainline Protestantism, a manifestation of Christianity that relies heavily on classification. But denomination proves unhelpful when thinking about Christianities that are not mainline. As Charles Long writes, "The category [of denomination] must suffer from too many qualifications to be adequate to the religious experience and expression of such diverse groups" (1994, 104); see also Louis Benjamin Rolsky (2012). One move has been to articulate so-called popular expressions of Christianity (Kathryn Lofton 2011; Leigh Schmidt 2002; Grant Wacker 2001), building from American religion's notion of lived religion (Marie Griffith 2004; David D. Hall 1997; Pamela Klassen 2011; Robert A. Orsi 1982; Elaine Peña 2011; Thomas Tweed 1997; Manuel Vásquez 2011). But Christian piety, for the purposes of this book, is more observable than popularism, more ethnographically sensible than lived religion, and far more embodied than denominationalism. This book, in a sense, makes a call for the study of American Christianity as undenominated (Kevin Lewis O'Neill 2013).

12. This book's ethnographic commitment to Christian piety in postwar Guatemala is in many ways an effort to engage Gil Anidjar's (2009) notion of an idea of Christianity. While more cognitive than my notion of Christian piety, more discursive in its genealogical approach, Anidjar's notion builds from the work of Talal Asad (1986) to argue that "what we need is less a definition of Christianity, than an 'idea' of it. What we need, in other words, is a concept of Christianity and of 'the acts that perform its civilization'—its *religion* (in the

most expansive, and specifically local, sense of the term)" (2009, 392). Important here is Anidjar's urging to look at the differences that make a difference, which for scholars of Christianity could very well include mapping the dialogical distinctions (cutting across denominations) between the good Christian and the bad Christian (William Garriott and Kevin Lewis O'Neill 2008).

13. Important ethnographies are organized around the life of one person. For a thoughtful look at this subgenre, see Michael Fischer (1991). My own approach follows the work of Philippe Bourgois, who intended a certain kind of experience for his reader: "I frequently selected and edited personal narrative [when writing *In Search of Respect* (1996)] so as to evoke sympathy from readers, so that they would recognize emotionally as well as intellectually their common humanity with the crack dealers" (2002, 227). Other powerful examples include Ruth Behar (2003); João Biehl (2005); Karen McCarthy Brown (2001); Vincent Crapanzano (1985); Robert Desjarlais (2003); Angela Garcia (2010); Neni Panourgiá (1995); and Marjorie Shostak (1981). More broadly, it is important to remember, as Mary Louise Pratt states in "Fieldwork in Common Places," the "practice of combining personal narrative and objectified description is hardly the invention of modern ethnography" (1986, 33).

14. This brief account provides a schematic background to a generally agreed-upon history. Its presentation builds from a number of histories and ethnographies. They include Richard Adams, *Crucifixion by Power: Essays on Guatemalan National Social Structure, 1944–1966* (1970); Comisión para el Esclarecimiento Histórico (CEH), *Guatemala, memoria del silencio* (1999), 5 vols.; Edward F. Fischer and R. McKenna Brown, *Maya Cultural Activism in Guatemala* (1996); Greg Grandin, *The Blood of Guatemala: A History of Race and Nation* (2000); Greg Grandin, *The Last Colonial Massacre: Latin America in the Cold War* (2004); Linda Green, *Fear as a Way of Life: Mayan Widows in Rural Guatemala* (1999); Charles R. Hale, *Más que un indio: Racial Ambivalence and Neoliberal Multiculturalism in Guatemala* (2006); Beatriz Manz, *Refugees of a Hidden War: The Aftermath of Counterinsurgency in Guatemala* (1988); David McCreery, *Rural Guatemala, 1760–1940* (1994); Proyecto Interdiocesano de Recuperación de la Memoria Histórica (REMHI), *Guatemala, nunca más*, 4 vols. (1998); Victoria Sanford, *Buried Secrets: Truth and Human Rights in Guatemala* (2003); Jennifer Schirmer, *The Guatemalan Military Project: A Violence Called Democracy* (1998); Stephen Schlesinger and Stephen Kinzer, *Bitter Fruit: The Story of the American Coup in Guatemala* (1999); Carol A. Smith, "El desarollo de la primacia urbana en Guatemala" (1984); Carol A. Smith, *Guatemalan Indians and the State, 1540 to 1988* (1990); David Stoll, *Between Two Armies in the Ixil Towns of Guatemala* (1993); and Kay Warren, *Indigenous Movements and their Critics: Pan-Maya Activism in Guatemala* (1998).

15. Stephen Kinzer, *The Brothers: John Foster Dulles, Allen Dulles, and Their Secret World War* (2013).

16. Edward Bernays, the author of *Propaganda*, writes, "But clearly it is the intelligent minorities which need to make use of propaganda continuously and systematically. . . . Only through the active energy of the intelligent few can the public at large become aware of and act upon new ideas" (1928, 57). See also Piero Gleijeses (1992) and Larry Tye (1998).

17. For more on Montt's remarkable career, see Virginia Garrard-Burnett, *Terror in the Land of the Holy Spirit: Guatemala under General Efraín Ríos Montt, 1982–1983* (2010).

18. The Oslo Accord, signed in 1994 as part of the United Nations peace process, initiated the Historical Clarification Commission (Comisión para Esclarecimiento Histórico [CEH]). The Roman Catholic Church, motivated by the CEH, initiated its own Recovery of the Historical Memory Project (Proyecto Interdiocesano de Recuperación de la Memoria Histórica [REMHI] 1998). Although two distinct projects, both reports came to strikingly similar conclusions.

According to the United Nations, more than 200,000 people died or disappeared as a result of the armed conflict, of whom more than 80 percent were Mayan; the report also establishes that 93 percent of these human rights violations can be connected to the state (Comisión para Esclarecimiento Histórico [CEH] 1999). The Catholic Church, similarly, asserts that 150,000 civilians were killed, that another 50,000 disappeared, and that 90 percent of the perpetrators were members of Guatemala's armed forces or the army-commissioned Civil Defense Patrols (Proyecto Interdiocesano de Recuperación de la Memoria Histórica 1998). Moreover, both reports agree that roughly 1 million people were displaced during the country's civil conflict and that members of Mayan groups were "systematically killed, incurred serious bodily or mental harm, and deliberately subjected to living conditions calculated to bring about the group's physical destruction" (CEH 1999, 5:38). See also Robert Carmack (1988); Ricardo Falla (1992); Beatriz Manz (2005); Diane M. Nelson (1999, 2009); Kevin Lewis O'Neill (2005, 333–334); and Victoria Sanford (2012); and the references in note 14.

19. Concerned about the spread of communism, the United States invested heavily in El Salvador's civil war. A $7-billion, ten-year aid package was authorized during the Carter administration and paid out during the Reagan and George H. W. Bush administrations (Paul D. Almeida 2008; John H. Coatsworth 1994; Jeff Gould and Lowell Gudmunson 1997; Aldo Lauria-Santiago and Leigh Binford 2004; William Stanley 1996; Philip Williams and Walter Knut 1997; Elisabeth Jean Wood 2003).

20. A number of studies and journalistic accounts have agreed on a common history. The following describe, with great care, the expansion of the Central American gang throughout the Americas: Ana Arana, "How the Street Gangs Took Central America" (2005); Robert Brenneman, *Homies and Hermanos: God and Gangs in Central America* (2012); Thomas Bruneau, Lucía Dammert, and Elizabeth Skinner, *Maras: Gang Violence and Security in Central America* (2011); Donna DeCesare, *Unsettled/Desasosiego: Los niños en un mundo de las pandillas* (2013); Fen Montaigne, "Deporting America's Gang Culture" (1999); Thomas Diaz, *No Boundaries: Transnational Latino Gangs and American Law Enforcement* (2009); Matthew Quirk, "How to Grow a Gang" (2008); Wim Savenije, "La Mara Salvatrucha y el Barrio 18 St.: Fenómenos sociales transnacionales, respuestas represivas nacionales" (2004); and Scott Wallace, "You Must Go Home Again: Deported LA Gangbangers Take Over El Salvador" (2000). See the work of Deborah Levenson for prescient and precise research on this topic: *Por sí mismos: Un estudio preliminar de las "maras" en la Ciudad de*

Guatemala (1988) and *Adiós Niño: The Gangs of Guatemala City and the Politics of Death* (2013).

21. The first offensive expanded the California Street Terrorism Enforcement and Prevention Act of 1988, allowing prosecutors to charge minors as adults. Police hunted down hundreds of Central American gang members, as detailed in "Juvenile Curfews and Gang Violence: Exiled on Main Street" (1994) from *Harvard Law Review*; Matthew Werdegar, "Enjoining the Constitution: The Use of Public Nuisance Abatement Injunctions against Urban Street Gangs" (1999); and John Worrall, "California Street Terrorism Enforcement and Prevention Act" (2003). The second attack was Proposition 184. This allowed the state of California to sentence repeat offenders with a mandatory minimum of twenty-five years in prison. See Campus Coalitions for Human Rights and Social Justice, "California at a Crossroads: Social Strife or Social Unity?" (1995); Erwin Chemerinsky, "Life in Prison for Shoplifting: Cruel and Unusual Punishment" (2004); and Franklin E. Zimring, Gordon Hawkins, and Sam Kamin, *Punishment and Democracy: Three Strikes and You're Out in California* (2001). The death knell came with the federal Illegal Immigration Reform and Immigrant Responsibility Act, which had far-reaching consequences for Central American gangs. See, for example, Susan Bibler Coutin, "Falling Outside: Excavating the History of Central American Asylum Seekers" (2011); Bernard Headley, "Giving Critical Context to the Deportee Phenomenon" (2006); and Daniel Kanstroom, "Deportation, Social Control, and Punishment: Some Thoughts about Why Hard Laws Make Bad Cases" (2000).

22. For the full text of this speech, see Patrick Buchanan (1992).

23. For statistics, see figure 1 in Mary Helen Johnson (2006), whose information is drawn from Office of Immigration Statistics (2004). For discussion of deportation, see Susan Bibler Coutin, "Suspension of Deportation Hearings: Racialization, Immigration, and 'Americanness'" (2003a); Susan Bibler Coutin, "Cultural Logics of Belonging and Movement: Transnationalism, Naturalization, and U.S. Immigration Politics" (2003b); and Elana Zilberg, *Space of Detention: The Making of a Transnational Gang Crisis between Los Angeles and San Salvador* (2011).

24. See Clare Ribando Seelke, "Gangs in Central America" (2011, 9). Also consider that between 2001 and 2010, the United States deported 129,726 convicted criminals to Central America, over 90 percent of whom were sent to Guatemala, El Salvador, and Honduras (Steven Dudley 2012, 8). The percentage of Central Americans deported on criminal grounds has increased significantly. In 2008, 18 percent of deportees were returned to Guatemala on criminal charges. In 2011, this number jumped to 38 percent. El Salvador and Honduras fared even worse. In 2011, 47 percent of deportees returned to El Salvador and Honduras on criminal charges (Clare Ribando Seelke 2013, 8).

25. For the full quote, see U.S. Senate Judiciary Committee (2005).

26. Peter Slevin, "Deportation of Illegal Immigrants Increases under Obama Administration" (2010).

27. Estimates of the number of gang members in Central America vary widely, with a top U.S. State Department official estimating that there may be 85,000 members of MS-13 and Barrio 18 in the northern triangle countries—namely, El

Salvador, Guatemala, and Honduras (released remarks by William R. Brownfield, Assistant Secretary, Bureau of International Narcotics and Law Enforcement Affairs, at the Institute of the Americas, October 1, 2012, "Gangs, Youth, and Drugs: Breaking the Cycle of Violence," as cited in Clare Ribando Seelke 2013). Guatemala's interior minister offered similar numbers, estimating there to be 20,000 gang members operating in Guatemala, 40,000 in El Salvador, and 35,000 in Honduras (Mariela Castañon 2012). The United Nations Office on Drugs and Crime (UNODC) estimated total MS-13 and Barrio 18 membership in the northern triangle countries at a more modest 54,000 (2012, 29).

28. As explored in chapter 5, "When it comes to Central American cocaine trafficking, all roads lead to Guatemala" (United Nations Office on Drugs and Crime 2012, 39). See also the reports of the Beckley Foundation (Amanda Feilding and Corina Giacomello, *Illicit Drug Markets and Dimensions of Violence in Guatemala* [2013a]; Feilding and Giacomello, *Paths for Reform: Proposed Options for Alternative Drug Policies in Guatemala* [2013b]); June S. Beittel, *Mexico's Drug Trafficking Organizations: Source and Scope of the Violence* (2013); Organization of American States, The Drug Problem in the Americas (2013); and Clare Ribando Seelke, Liana Wyler, and June Beittel, *Latin America and the Caribbean: Illicit Drug Trafficking and U.S. Counterdrug Programs* (2010).

29. On Alaska, see Kevin Johnson, "FBI: Burgeoning Gangs Rival Foreign Drug Cartels" (2009) and Chris Hawley, "On the Border, A Crisis Escalates" (2009). On Argentina, see Douglas Farah and Pamela Phillips Lum, *Central American Gangs and Transnational Criminal Organizations* (2013, 20).

30. Figures from 2012 report that El Salvador's prisons were at 324% capacity (as of December 31); Guatemala's prisons were at 230.9% capacity (as of December 31); and Honduras's were at 143.8% capacity (as of September 30) (International Centre for Prison Studies 2013).

31. See Dennis Rodgers, Robert Muggah, and Chris Stevenson, *Gangs of Central America: Causes, Costs, and Interventions* (2009) as well as Nielan Barnes, "Pandillas juveniles transnacionales en Centroamérica, México y Los Estados Unidos: Resumen ejecutivo" (2007); Celinda Franco, *The MS-13 and 18th Street Gangs: Emerging Transnational Gang Threats?* (2008); and Elin Cecilie Ranum, "Pandillas juveniles transnacionales en Centroamérica, México y Estados Unidos: Diagnóstico nacional Guatemala" (2006). For studies of gangs in Central America, see José Luis Rocha, *Lanzando piedras, fumando "piedras": Evolución de las pandillas en Nicaragua 1997–2006* (2007); Wim Savenije, *Maras y barras: Pandillas y violencia juvenil en los barrios marginales de Centroamérica* (2009); and Clare Ribando Seelke, *Gangs in Central America* (2013); and see the four-volume series *Maras y pandillas en Centroamérica*: ERIC, IDESO, et al. 2001, 2004; ERIC, IDIES, et al. 2004; and José Miguel Cruz 2006. For discussion of Mano Dura, see Jeanette Aguilar, "Los efectos contraproducentes de los Planes Mano Dura" (2006); Ley Antimaras, Decreto Legislativo No. 158, Diario Oficial (October 10, 2003); Sentencia de inconstitucionalidad de la Ley Antimaras, Sentencia Definitiva n° 52–2003 Ac de Sala de lo Constitucional (April 1, 2004); Mo Hume, "Mano Dura: El Salvador Responds to Gangs" (2007); and Alejandro Rodríguez Barillas and Gerardo Pérez Castillo, "Transparentando el Plan Escoba" (2005).

32. For a discussion of state-sponsored extrajudicial killings in Guatemala, see USAID, *Central America and Mexico Gang Assessment* (2006, 79) and Washington Office on Latin America, *Youth Gangs in Central America: Issues in Human Rights, Effective Policing, and Prevention* (2006, 12).

33. One such program is the Gang Resistance Education and Training (G.R.E.A.T.) program. See its website at www.great-online.org. For a detailed assessment of U.S. Congressional money supporting programs such as G.R.E.A.T., see Clare Ribando Seelke, *Gangs in Central America* (2013) and Peter Meyer and Clare Seelke, *Central America Regional Security Initiative: Background and Policy Issues for Congress* (2013); also see U.S. Department of State Bureau of Western Hemisphere Affairs, "U.S. Strategy to Combat the Threat of Criminal Gangs from Central America and Mexico" (2007).

34. On October 22, 2007, the United States and Mexico announced the Mérida Initiative. This is a multiyear initiative, dedicating more than $1 billion in U.S. counterdrug and anticrime assistance to Mexico and Central America. For more, see Clare Ribando Seelke, *Mérida Initiative for Mexico and Central America: Funding and Policy Issues* (2009). The initiative proved complicated. Although the violence in Mexico has declined since late 2011, analysts estimate that it may have claimed more than 60,000 lives between December 2006 and November 2012. For effects of the Mérida Initiative, see Clare Ribando Seelke and Kristin M. Finklea, *U.S.-Mexican Security Cooperation: The Mérida Initiative and Beyond* (2013). See also Vanda Felbab-Brown, "*Peña Nieto's Piñata: The Promise and Pitfalls of Mexico's New Security Policy against Organized Crime* (2013).

35. A total of 527 international security programs have been implemented in Central America, for which US$1.728 billion have been authorized. Of the 475 projects running, the majority (72 percent) are nonrefundable. The rest of the resources (28 percent) are investment loans that need to be repaid by the Central American countries. Of all of this money, 32 percent goes toward prevention, 22 percent fights organized crime, 4 percent funds rehabilitation programs, and 42 percent contributes to institution building. The United States accounts for 36 percent of all this money. For more on money, see Inter-American Development Bank (IDB) and Washington Office on Latin America (WOLA), "Mapeo de las intervenciones de seguridad ciudadana en Centroamérica financiadas por la cooperación internacional" (2011).

36. One analogue to this kind of development can be seen in Johanna Tayloe Crane, *Scrambling for Africa: AIDS, Expertise, and the Rise of American Global Health Science* (2013).

37. The mission statement also lists core values. They are responsibility, perseverance, reliability, generosity, honesty, diligence, honesty, bravery, respect, loyalty, dedication, and love.

38. See Hussein Ali Agrama, "Secularism, Sovereignty, Indeterminacy: Is Egypt a Secular or a Religious State?" (2010). Also see, among the growing literature on secularism, Tracy Fessenden, *Culture and Redemption: Religion, the Secular, and American Literature* (2007) and John Lardas Modern, *Secularism in Antebellum America* (2011).

39. By abandonment, I follow Elizabeth Povinelli, *Economies of Abandonment: Social Belonging and Endurance in Late Liberalism* (2011). Her interest

is in how late liberal imaginaries make the distribution of life and death just. This book rightly considers Ursula Le Guin's "The Ones Who Walk Away From Omelas" (1975), a short story about an imagined city's happiness depending on a child's confinement to a broom closet. Another work of importance is João Biehl, *Vita: Life in a Zone of Social Abandonment* (2005, 372). His approach to abandonment follows the work of Hannah Arendt and Michel Foucault by way of Giorgio Agamben. In Western democracies, Agamben writes and Biehl quotes, sovereign power is "not simple natural life, but life exposed to death" (Agamben 1998, 24).

40. For more detailed work on Christianity in Guatemala, see Andrea Althoff, "Religion im Wandel: Einflüsse von Ethnizität auf die Religiöse Ordnung am Beispiel Guatemalas" (2005); Manuela Cantón Delgado, "*Bautizados en fuego: Protestantes, discursos de conversión y política en Guatemala (1989–1993)* (1998); Jesús García-Ruiz, "Le néopentecôtisme au Guatemala: Entre privatisation, marché et réseaux" (2004); Virginia Garrard-Burnett, *Protestantism in Guatemala: Living in the New Jerusalem* (1998); Garrard-Burnett, *Terror in the Land of the Holy Spirit: Guatemala under General Efraín Ríos Montt, 1982–1983* (2010); Kevin Lewis O'Neill, *City of God: Christian Citizenship in Postwar Guatemala* (2010a); Tim Steigenga, *Politics of the Spirit: The Political Implications of Pentecostalized Religion in Costa Rica and Guatemala* (2001); and David Stoll, *Is Latin America Turning Protestant? The Politics of Evangelical Growth* (1990).

41. The term *affective infrastructure* builds from Raymond Williams's "Structures of Feeling" (1977), where he writes, "We are talking about characteristic elements of impulse, restraint, and tone; specifically affective elements of consciousness and relationships: not feeling against thought, but thought as felt and feeling as thought: practical consciousness of a present kind, in a living and inter-relating continuity" (132). Yet Williams's formulation remains deeply wedded to both Marxism and semiotics. His structure of feeling is about linking the signifier to the signified. Affective infrastructure draws upon a different literature (Sara Ahmed 2010; Lauren Berlant 2011; Kathleen Stewart 2007; Eve Kosofsky Sedgwick 2003) to articulate how feelings and emotions underlie and organize bodies—here in lieu of the prison, factory, and asylum. This is not to make a claim that infrastructure cannot be affective but rather that affect provides order and direction for life itself. Christian piety as an assemblage of affect and idiom is one such moral infrastructure that helps to distinguish between, for example, the pious and the impious.

42. Frederic Thrasher, *The Gang* (1927); Clifford Shaw and Henry McKay, *Juvenile Delinquency and Urban Areas* (1942); and William Foote Whyte, *Street Corner Society: The Social Structure of an Italian Slum* (1943).

43. Irving Spergel, *The Youth Gang Problem: A Community Approach* (1995).

44. Malcolm Klein, *The American Street Gang: Its Nature, Prevalence, and Control* (1995); see also Eva Rosen and Sudhir Venkatesh, "Legal Innovation and the Control of Gang Behavior" (2007).

45. Mary Helen Johnson, "National Policies and the Rise of Transnational Gangs" (2006) and Sudhir Venkatesh and Steven Levitt, "Are We a Family or a Business? History and Disjuncture in the Urban American Street Gang" (2000).

46. For a more critical engagement with the literature on gangs in and outside of the United States, see Ellen Moodie, *El Salvador in the Aftermath of Peace: Crime, Uncertainty, and the Transition to Democracy* (2010); Dennis Rodgers, "Living in the Shadow of Death: Gangs, Violence, and Social Order in Urban Nicaragua, 1996–2002" (2006); Wim Savenije, "Las pandillas transnacionales o 'maras': Violencia urbana en Centroamérica" (2007); and Jon Wolseth, "Safety and Sanctuary: Pentecostalism and Youth Gang Violence in Honduras" (2008).

47. Michel Foucault, *Discipline and Punish: The Birth of the Prison* (1995, 147).

48. In *A Thousand Plateaus,* Gilles Deleuze and Félix Guattari write, "The line of flight marks: the reality of a finite number of dimensions that the multiplicity effectively fills; the impossibility of a supplementary dimension, unless the multiplicity is transformed by the line of flight; the possibility and necessity of flattening all of the multiplicities on a single plane of consistency or exteriority, regardless of their number of dimensions" (2001, 9).

49. Tania Li, *The Will to Improve: Governmentality, Development, and the Practice of Politics* (2007, 7). This is rooted in work by James Ferguson, for which see *The Anti-Politics Machine: "Development," Depoliticization, and Bureaucratic Power in Lesotho* (1994). Both offer extended reflections on the relationship between problems and their answers and how problems are themselves culturally constructed.

50. Surely the literature on Augustine notes that his *Confessions* straddle the divide of fiction and nonfiction. My point here has less to do with fiction/nonfiction than with the standards of narrative. While Augustine animates the plot points of Christian piety and gang prevention, men like Mateo need not adopt Augustine's standards. For reflections on Augustine, conversion, and narrative, see, for example, Sara Byers, "Augustine on the 'Divided Self:' Platonist or Stoic?" (2007); Leo C. Ferrari, "Paul at the Conversion of Augustine" (1980); Leo Ferrari, *The Conversions of St. Augustine* (1984); Jean-Luc Marion, *In the Self's Place: The Approach of St. Augustine* (2012), especially chapter 4; and Paul Ricoeur, *Time and Narrative,* vol. 1 (1984), especially chapter 1.

51. For the politics of letting die, see the concluding chapter of this book, and see Tania Li, "To Make Live or Let Die? Rural Dispossession and the Protection of Surplus Populations" (2010). She writes, "While Foucault highlighted the general historical conditions for the emergence of biopolitics, that is, an orientation to intervene in populations to enhance their health and wellbeing, he had little to say about when or how this orientation would be activated. Nor did he say much about the politics of let die scenarios: why governing authorities would elect not to intervene when they could, or select one subset of the population for life enhancement while abandoning another" (66). Also see Anne Allison's *Precarious Japan* (2013).

CHAPTER 1

1. "'Paisas' están transformándose en organización criminal, dice MP" (2012).

2. Regarding the riot, prison spokesperson Rudy Esquivel said, "This is a dispute between prisoners belonging to different gangs, who bring their conflicts with them when they are locked up" (Claudia Acuña 2008; see also "Beheadings in Guatemala Jail Fight" 2008; Rosy Carroll 2008; Rosemery González and Mervin del Cid 2008; "Seven Killed in Prison Gang Fight" 2008). My initial analysis of the event followed this assumption, linking the violence against MS-13 to Barrio 18 (Kevin Lewis O'Neill 2010a). After additional research, with several years of hindsight, it still seems accurate to link these riots to gang violence but to stress two points. The first is that the rival was the Paisas, not Barrio 18. The second is that Pavoncito's general prison population, led by the Paisas, murdered these men to send a message to prison officials. They did not target active gang members in the general prison population. They wanted the ones cordoned off in other prisons or in specific holding cells. Put another way, this was a struggle over prison territory.

3. This quote appears in several newspaper articles (e.g., Claudia Acuña 2008). A working definition of *cholo* is a Latino gang member in the United States, whose common caricature wears khaki pants, a white T-shirt, and a flannel shirt. Tattoos, bandanas, and hairnets also mark this derogatory sketch (Angie Chabram-Dernersesian 2006). Many of the connotations of cholo, at least within the Central American context, connect to issues of deportation and gang membership (for more work on the term, see Elana Zilberg 2004).

4. Prison capacity in Guatemala is 6,492 as of August 13, 2013. As of that same date, there were 16,336 prisoners (International Centre for Prison Studies 2013).

5. Insecurity is a common trope for the study of postwar Central America, especially postwar Guatemala. Scholars and activists commonly pair the term with *crime* and *violence*. The term *insecurity* organizes events. See, for example, the Wilson Center webcast "Crime, Violence, and Insecurity in Central America" (Elizabeth J. Zechmeister, José Miguel Cruz, Susan Berk-Seligson, and Rodrigo Serrano-Berthet 2013). The term *insecurity* also underlies policy initiatives. See, for example, the Brookings Institute paper *The Merida Initiative and Central America: The Challenges of Containing Public Insecurity and Criminal Violence* (Diana Villiers Negroponte 2009) and the Migration Policy Institute paper *Paying for Crime: A Review of the Relationships between Insecurity and Development in Mexico and Central America* (Eleanor Sohnen 2012). For a parallel use of the term *insecurity* and its double valence, see Erica James, *Democratic Insecurities: Violence, Trauma, and Intervention in Haiti* (2010).

6. The Latinobarometer, an annual survey conducted in eighteen Latin American countries, has long connected rising levels of insecurity with emotional states of being. Daniel Zovatto, a member of the Latino Barometer's International Consulting Council, argued in 2011 that "pessimism increases hand in hand with the economic crisis and insecurity." Zovatto continues, "When we compare Central America to Latin America, we see more marked pessimism currently pervading Central America."

7. For the practice of bibliotherapy, see Esther Angela Hartman, *Imaginative Literature as a Projective Technique: A Study of Bibliotherapy* (1951). Much of this chapter relies on evidence in the form of print media self-esteem manuals. I use the term *manual* loosely, as most amount to printed pages from

the World Wide Web held together by paper clips. It is, thus, impossible to cite them properly or credit an author. This should not distract from the analysis, since this chapter is less about the genealogies of self-esteem in the prison setting than the actual practice of self-esteem in the prison setting.

8. This chapter works against critics who argue that self-esteem prompts subjects to withdraw into themselves and, thus, escape from the public sphere and citizenship responsibilities. The work of Barbara Cruikshank (1996) and Eva Illouz (2008) inspire a different argument, suggesting that the personal is in fact political and that the work of self-esteem avails the self to a range of social interventions and political projects.

9. Mark Fleisher, *Warehousing Violence* (1989); Erving Goffman, *Asylums: Essays on the Social Situation of Mental Patients and Other Inmates* (1961); and Lorna A. Rhodes, *Total Confinement: Madness and Reason in the Maximum Security Prison* (2004).

10. Barbara Cruikshank, "Revolution Within: Self-Government and Self-Esteem" (1996). Cruikshank's work builds from that of Michel Foucault, who sees the problem of government as not only tied to state politics but also linked to the formation of the modern subject, especially the citizen, in a variety of ways and through certain modes of thought (Foucault 1991). Neo-Pentecostalism, the present book argues at length, is one such "mode of thought" that provides a range of cultural practices through which citizens are both constituted and governed: "Governing people is not a way to force people to do what the governor wants" (Foucault 1999, 162). If Foucault's work on the concept of governmentality, alongside that of Patrick Joyce (2003) and Nikolas Rose (1999), teaches us anything, it is that one can never be simply a subject or a citizen—disempowered or empowered. Rather, freedom and agency are themselves techniques of control through which citizens willingly become subject to themselves.

11. Andrew Skotnicki, *Religion and the Development of the American Penal System* (2000, 2); also see Joshua Dubler, *Down in the Chapel: Religious Life in an American Prison* (2013); Jennifer Graber, *The Furnace of Affliction: Prisons and Religion in Antebellum America* (2011); Adam J. Hirsch, *The Rise of the Penitentiary: Prisons and Punishment in Early America* (1992); Dario Melossi and Massimo Pavarini, *The Prison and the Factory: Origins of the Penitentiary System* (1981); Norval Morris and David Rothman, *The Oxford History of the Prison: The Practice of Punishment in Western Society* (1998); Alexander Pisciotta, *Benevolent Repression: Social Control and the American Reformatory-Prison Movement* (1994); and Caleb Smith, *The Prison and the American Imagination* (2009).

12. E. Shaskan Bumas, "Fictions of the Panopticon: Prison, Utopia, and the Out-Penitent in the Works of Nathaniel Hawthorne" (2001, 131).

13. Michael Ignatieff, *A Just Measure of Pain: The Penitentiary in the Industrial Revolution, 1750–1850* (1978, 9).

14. Jonathan Franzen, *How to Be Alone: Essays* (2003, 210).

15. David Rothman, *The Discovery of the Asylum: Social Order and Disorder in the New Republic* (1971, 83); see also John Bender, *Imagining the Penitentiary: Fiction and the Architecture of Mind in Eighteenth-Century England* (1987).

16. Gustave de Beaumont and Alexis de Tocqueville, *On the Penitentiary System in the United States and its Application in France* ([1833] 1964, 87), as quoted in John Lardas Modern, "Ghosts of Sing Sing, or the Metaphysics of Secularism" (2007, 639).

17. Ricardo Donato Salvatore and Carlos Aguirre, *The Birth of the Penitentiary in Latin America: Essays on Criminology, Prison Reform, and Social Control, 1830–1940* (1996).

18. Matthew W. Meskell, "An American Resolution: The History of Prisons in the United States from 1777 to 1877" (1999, 852).

19. See "Guatemala Jail Riot Leaves 17 Dead" (2002).

20. For a discussion of state-sponsored extrajudicial killings in Guatemala, see USAID Bureau for Latin America and the Caribbean (2006, 79) and Washington Office on Latin America (2006, 12). For discussion of the charges against Alejandro Giammattei, see "Guatemala Acts on Extra-Judicial Prison Killings" (2010), and about his trial and ultimate acquittal, see Comisión Internacional contra la Impunidad en Guatemala (2013).

21. Gangs murdered four policemen. The policemen were being held in connection with the killing of three visiting politicians from El Salvador's ruling Arena Party. Key evidence about those assassinations was lost with the deaths of the policemen ("Arrests in Guatemala Jail Killing" 2007).

22. The killing of the four police officers in Boqueron sparked a twelve-hour riot among inmates. It ended only after the prisoners—mostly members of street gangs—were allowed to tell a TV crew that they had not been behind the killings of the police officers ("Arrests in Guatemala Jail Killing" 2007).

23. Giorgio Agamben, *State of Exception* (2005). See also his "Security and Terror" (2001), where he writes, "The search for security leads to a world civil war which makes all civil coexistence impossible. In the new situation created by the end of the classical form of war between sovereign states it becomes clear that security finds its end in globalization: it implies the idea of a new planetary order which is in truth the worst of all disorders. But there is another danger. Because they require constant reference to a state of exception, measure of security work towards a growing depoliticization of society."

24. Romans 12:19 reads, "Do not take revenge, my dear friends, but leave room for God's wrath, for it is written: 'It is mine to avenge; I will repay,' says the Lord."

25. A comparative perspective is possible. Reporting from the Ecuadorian context, Chris Garces writes, "Unlike high modern constructs of the prison as a zone of inmate reclusion, discipline, and rehabilitation, Guayaquil's Penitenciaría serves, rather, as a local state mechanism for the concentration and indefinite warehousing of suspected criminals with minimal discipline and no formal rehabilitation per se. Cellblock mafias rule quite indiscriminately within the complex, in collusion with guards who openly wield firearms and coercive power across the prison grounds and buildings" (2010, 492). He adds in a footnote, consistent with the themes of this chapter and this book, "Although hard to imagine a less panoptical structure than Guayaquil's Peni, I might add that the prisoners' gesture of crucifixion appealed to Christian notions of piety as an index of interior religious identity—only to denounce the penal regime to which they were subjected."

26. Roger Deacon, "Theory as Practice: Foucault's Concept of Problematization" (2000, 127).

27. The Guatemalan government regulates prison chaplains, with annual meetings and rules of engagement. Roughly one hundred prison chaplains participate in this loose association. An unknown number of men, however, do not participate in it. They gain daily access to prisons by registering each day as a visitor. Many pursue their chaplaincy this way, which allows them to sidestep any government oversight and the micropolitics of this association. The chaplains followed in this chapter are among those who are independent of the government.

28. Michel Foucault, "Polemics, Politics, and Problematizations" (1997b, 117).

29. Most self-esteem manuals are produced in the United States. They include titles such as *The Biblical View of Self-Esteem, Self-Love, and Self-Image* (Adams 1986); *Christ Esteem: Where the Search for Self-Esteem Ends* (Matzat 1990); *Christ-Centered Self-Esteem: Seeing Ourselves Through God's Eyes* (Gerber 1996); *Self-Esteem: The Cross and Christian Confidence* (McGrath and McGrath 2002); and *Christians, Beware!: The Dangers of Secular Psychology* (Parks 2007).

30. The quotations are from self-esteem "manuals" printed from the World Wide Web, as described in note 7. These manuals are often derived from U.S.-published self-esteem manuals such as those listed in note 29.

31. The "manual" here is another of the informal documents described in note 7.

32. For a critical look at the concept of unintended consequences from an anthropological perspective, see James Ferguson, *The Anti-Politics Machine: "Development," Depoliticization, and Bureaucratic Power in Lesotho* (1994); Tania Li, *The Will to Improve: Governmentality, Development, and the Practice of Politics* (2007); and Miriam Ticktin, *Casualties of Care: Immigration and the Politics of Humanitarianism in France* (2011).

33. Mariana Valverde, *Diseases of the Will: Alcohol and the Dilemmas of Freedom* (1998, 2).

34. Jodie Boyer, "Sin and Sanity in Nineteenth-Century America" (2013); see also German E. Berrios and Margaret Gili, "The Will and its Disorders" (1995); Vernon Bourke, *Will in Western Thought* (1964).

35. Catherine Albanese, *A Republic of Mind and Spirit: A Cultural History of American Metaphysical Religion* (2007, 510).

36. Phillip Cary, *Augustine's Invention of the Inner Self: The Legacy of a Christian Platonist* (2000, 64).

37. The believer's rapprochement with God, Augustine insists, involves turning *inward* toward the self and then *upward* toward the glory of God (Phillip Cary 2000). Original sin, however, complicates this double movement, this seemingly straightforward negotiation of inner space. Michel Foucault, commenting on Augustine's characterization of the sexual act, begins to estimate the kinds of difficulties that emerge for believers as they try to will themselves to see God. Foucault notes:

> Before the Fall, Adam's body, every part of it, was perfectly obedient to the soul and the will. If Adam wanted to procreate in Paradise, he could do it in the same way and

with the same control as he could, for instance, sow seeds in the earth. Every part of his body was like the fingers, which one can control in all their gestures. But what happened with the Fall? Adam lost control of himself. His body, and parts of his body, stopped obeying his commands, revolted against him, and the sexual parts of his body were the first to rise up in this disobedience. The famous gesture of Adam covering his genitals with a fig leaf is, according to Augustine, due not to the simple fact that Adam was ashamed of their presence but to the fact that his sexual organs were moving by themselves without his consent. (1997c, 181)

38. For securing the city, see Kevin Lewis O'Neill and Kedron Thomas, *Securing the City: Neoliberalism, Space, and Insecurity in Postwar Guatemala* (2011); for disembedding the city, see Dennis Rodgers, "Disembedding the City: Crime, Insecurity and Spatial Organisation in Managua, Nicaragua" (2004); for neoliberal privatization of the city, see Saskia Sassen, *The Global City: New York, London, Tokyo* (2001); James Ferguson, *Global Shadows: Africa in the Neoliberal World Order* (2006a); and Teresa Caldeira, *City of Walls: Crime, Segregation, and Citizenship in São Paulo* (2000).

39. Phillip Cary, *Augustine's Invention of the Inner Self* (2000, 63–76); Charles Taylor, *Sources of the Self: The Making of the Modern Identity* (1989, 127–142).

40. Barbara Cruikshank, "Revolutions Within: Self-Government and Self-Esteem" (1996, 236).

41. Michel Foucault, *Discipline and Punish: The Birth of the Prison* (1995, 3).

42. Michel Foucault, *Discipline and Punish: The Birth of the Prison* (1995, 6).

43. Michel Foucault, *The Order of Things: An Archaeology of Human Sciences* (1994a).

44. Donald S. Moore, *Suffering for Territory: Race, Place, and Power in Zimbabwe* (2005, 29).

45. The United States prison-industrial complex has always been an export product to Latin America. The privatization model continues to become more popular. See, for example, "Private Jails: Locking in the Best Price"(2007); Carey L. Biron, "More Countries Turn to Faltering U.S. Prison Privatisation Model" (2013); and Anjani Trivedi, "How the American Privatized Prison Is Spreading Overseas" (2013).

46. See "Four Severed Heads Found in Guatemala City" (2010).

47. Vivien Stern, *A Sin against the Future: Imprisonment in the World* (1998).

CHAPTER 2

1. Unless otherwise noted, all quotations from contestants have been transcribed from one of five *Desafío 10* episodes (Creative Associates International 2006). Translations throughout are my own.

2. USAID provided a grant for US$15,000 to Creative Associates International. Guatemala's private sector invested more than US$50,000 in cash, equipment, and time (Marcela Sanchez 2006).

3. *Desafío 10* stars ten ex–gang members. Early in the first episode, the narrator provides the audience with a helpful summary:

Chejo, 24 years old, has been a member of Mara Salvatrucha since he was 13 years old. Fish, 26 years old, entered Mara Salvatrucha at the age of 12 and left when he was 21 years old. Bibliotecario, 23 years old, joined White Fence at the age of 11 and fathered a child when he was 14 years old. Mexican Boy, 24 years old, entered White Fence when he was 9 years old and left when he was 21 years old. He never knew his father. Panadero, 22 years old, entered Barrio 18 when he was 13 years old and left when he was 19 years old. He suffered a great deal of violent abuse as a child. California, 26 years old, entered North Hollywood when he was 10 years old, was raised in the California penal system, and was deported back to Guatemala in 2005. Seco, 22 years old, entered Mara Salvatrucha when he was 11 years old. He was looking for friends only to become a gang member. Promotor, 22 years old, joined White Fence when he was 9 years old and stayed a member of the gang until he was 16. He has not been back home for more than a year because he fears for his life. Carpintero, 27 years old, entered Mara Salvatrucha when he was 10 but left after 6 years. New York, 23 years old, was a member of Mara Salvatrucha for 11 years. Fourteen days after he was born, his mother left for the United States.

4. For some rather optimistic reports, see articles in the *Washington Post* (Marcela Sanchez 2006) and *Guardian* (Juan Carlos Llorca 2006). Sanchez writes, "Scheduled to air in March, 'Desafío 10' (Challenge 10) should already be considered significant just for bringing very disparate elements together." Quotations from USAID personnel, such as Harold Sibaja and José Garzón, build on extended interviews; they also come from the show's promotional materials (Creative Associates International 2006).

5. This quote comes from the show's promotional materials (Creative Associates International 2006) and has been corroborated with extensive interviews.

6. References abound when considering the citizen-worker and the consumer-citizen. I note just two. William Galston's *Liberal Purposes* (1991) argues that work shapes the citizen; a proper citizen is a citizen who works. For consumer-citizens, see Lizabeth Cohen's *A Consumer's Republic* (2003), which smartly explores the rise of a consumer society in twentieth-century America, one in which citizens built an economy and a nationalism around the practice of consumption.

7. This and all subsequent values are calculated as of May 1, 2013.

8. The idea here is that soft security must include legitimate, or mainstream, opportunities to earn a living. This comes out clearly in the review essay by Eva Rosen and Sudhir Venkatesh (2007, 266). See also the work of Felix Padilla (1992), Philippe Bourgois (1996), and Sudhir Venkatesh (2000). Much attention has been given to this idea within policy circles. See, for example, the *Strategy to Combat the Threat of Criminal Gangs from Central America and Mexico* (U.S. Department of State, Bureau of Western Hemisphere Affairs 2007).

9. Jean Comaroff and John Comaroff (1997, 223) note that "a tension between inner and outer verities, between the enterprise of spirit and things of the sensuous world, lay at the core of the civilizing mission from the start. It would never be fully resolved. Clothes epitomized this conflict."

10. The phrase "moral fitness" comes from scripture. "Do you not know that in a race all the runners run, but only one gets the prize? Run in such a way as to get the prize. Everyone who competes in the games goes into strict training."

They do it to get a crown that will not last, but we do it to get a crown that will last forever" (1 Corinthians 9:24–25). "Brothers and sisters, I do not consider myself yet to have taken hold of it. But one thing I do: Forgetting what is behind and straining toward what is ahead, I press on toward the goal to win the prize for which God has called me heavenward in Christ Jesus" (Philippians 3:13).

11. This sentence carries three quick references. The first, "the will to improve," is a gesture toward Tania Li's 2007 work of that title. The second reference is to Christian citizenship, a term I develop in *City of God* (Kevin Lewis O'Neill 2010a). The third, to a "sign bearing, sign-wearing body," is the phrasing of Pierre Bourdieu (1984, 192), who artfully reminds the scholar about the embodied semiotics of class.

12. The show's promotional materials (Creative Associates International 2006) mention that most of these former gang members came recommended by a Pentecostal church. The credits at the end of each show also give thanks to the Pentecostal churches that recommended these men to participate in the program.

13. Laurie Ouellette and James Hay, in *Better Living through Reality TV* (2008, 12), draw on the work of Michel Foucault and Nikolas Rose to frame reality television as a strategy of liberal governance. These shows empower their viewers to become enterprising citizens (Mark Andrejevic 2007; Brenda Weber 2009; Bernadette Wegenstein 2007).

14. For an extended look at this dynamic between inner and outer, see Virginia Blum, "Objects of Love: I Want a Famous Face and the Illusions of Star Culture" (2007, 36); Richard Brodhead, "Sparing the Rod: Discipline and Fiction in Antebellum America" (1988); and Jon Dovey, *Freakshow: First Person Media and Factual Television* (2000).

15. Brenda Weber continues, "This reliance on all-powerful experts is consistent throughout the makeover canon: doctors are glorified, powerful, and full discursive agents; patients (a disproportionate number of them women) are passive and yielding, even grateful for their transformations, creating a culture of docile bodies eager for discipline" (2007, 91). For more on the notion of makeover as takeover, see Rachel Moseley, *Makeover Takeover on British Television* (2002).

16. Anna McCarthy writes in "Reality Television: A Neoliberal Theater of Suffering" that personal triumph as a competition is a way to transform the format's opportunistic narrative techniques into a pedagogy of the soul" (2007, 22).

17. Andrew Shanken, in "Better Living: Toward a Cultural History of a Business Slogan" (2006), sheds light on the relationships that can exist between brandings and wartime efforts.

18. Annette Hill, in *Reality TV: Factual Entertainment and Television Audiences* (2005), makes the important observation that the audience is oftentimes absent during debates about reality television.

19. Joanna Zylinska writes that "radical makeover shows such as *The Swan*, produced in the United States and the United Kingdom and aired on satellite TV stations across the world, constitute yet another instance of such exemplary places of modern biopolitics" (2007, 130).

20. Kimberly Jackson notes, on reality television's ritual, "The makers of *The Swan* have pushed the editing process to the point of parody. The content of each episode is so minimal, one wonders if there exist more than five minutes of actual footage from the narrative of each woman's journey through the program" (2007, 62).

21. Jean Comaroff and John Comaroff write, in full,

> Of course, "civilized" homes were made of "proper" materials, "fitted up," as one contemporary observer put it, "in European style," and implying a new order of "needs" that hitched these communities irrevocably to the commodity market. Such standards of Christian decency also applied to dress, and converts had to ensure that their distinction from their fellows was shown in their attire [cf. Beidelman 1982, 20]. "Traditional" body coverings were tantamount to nakedness in missionary eyes, and expressed a flagrant lack of physical containment. (1986, 14)

See also Birgit Meyer (1999).

22. Jean Comaroff and John Comaroff write, "We begin, now, with the effort of the Protestant mission to cover African 'nakedness': to re-dress the savagery of Tswana by dressing them in European fashions, by making them receptive to the ethics and aesthetics of refined attire, and by insinuating in them a newly embodied sense of self, taste and personhood" (1997, 220).

23. For the politics of brand piracy in postwar Guatemala, see the work of Kedron Thomas (2012; 2013).

24. Kathryn Lofton writes, "[Oprah] presents her presumptively peculiar features (her segregated suffering, her nouveau riche tastes, and her monetary excess) to convert her viewers from their provincial limits to her cosmopolitan expanse" (2011, 125). For parallel arguments, if in different contexts, see Tanya Erzen (2006) and Daromir Rudnyckyj (2010).

25. For the economics behind reality television and product placement, see June Deery's "Reality TV as Advertisement" (2004, 1).

26. Jean Comaroff and John Comaroff write, "Proper, propertied, prosperous agriculture and self-possessed labor might seed the Christian spirit. But prosperity was itself the reward of a pious heart and disciplined body. Both—prosperity and piety—were therefore to be enjoyed, and to be measured, in sober, not too conspicuous consumption" (1997, 218).

27. For more on gospels of prosperity, see Simon Coleman, *The Globalisation of Charismatic Christianity: Spreading the Gospel of Prosperity* (2000); Bethany Moreton, *To Serve God and Wal-Mart: The Making of Christian Free Enterprise* (2009); and Jeremy Walton, *Watch This! The Ethics and Aesthetics of Black Televangelism* (2009).

28. By "economy of appearance," I mean something more than simple editing or sleights of hand. I mean something closer to what Ana Tsing describes in her essay "Inside the Economy of Appearances" (2000). Of course, attention should also be paid to the fact that a morality template frames *Desafío 10* (Roland Barthes 1974).

29. The Chicago School of Urban Thought pioneered what has come to be known as the ecological approach to understanding the social and demographic development of cities. This group produced a series of notable ethnographies.

See, for example, those that addressed gangs, including Frederic Thrasher, *The Gang* (1927); Clifford Shaw and Henry McKay, *Juvenile Delinquency and Urban Areas* (1942); and William Foote Whyte, *Street Corner Society: The Social Structure of an Italian Slum* (1943). For a vivid rethinking of the Chicago School, see Laurence Ralph, *Renegade Dreams* (2014).

30. Key ethnographies of this kind, coming from this cohort, include William I. Thomas and Florian Znaniecki, *The Polish Peasant in Europe and America* (1918); Nels Anderson, *The Hobo: The Sociology of the Homeless Man* (1923); Frederic Thrasher, *The Gang* (1927); Harvey Warren Zorbaugh, *The Gold Coast and the Slum: A Sociological Study of Chicago's Near North Side* (1929); and Clifford Shaw, *The Jack Roller: A Delinquent Boy's Own Story* (1930).

31. Robert Park writes, "There are areas infested by boy gangs and the athletic and political clubs into which the members of these gangs or the gangs themselves frequently graduate. There are regions in which the suicide rate is excessive; regions in which there is, as recorded by statistics, an excessive amount of juvenile delinquency, and other regions in which there is almost none" (1926, 9).

32. The "social work" approach to fighting gangs connects with the assumptions of the ecological paradigm of the Chicago School of Urban Thought. "Mainstream social institutions would control their behavior and transmit proper values to the youth," elaborate Eva Rosen and Sudhir Venkatesh (2007, 256; see also Irving Spergel 1995). As for "sitting up straight," Pierre Bourdieu lends great insight into the relationship between bodily comportment and the embodied principles that exist beyond consciousness. He writes, "An implicit pedagogy, capable of instilling a whole cosmology, an ethic, a metaphysic, a political philosophy, [can be communicated] through injunctions as insignificant as 'stand up straight' or 'don't hold your knife in your left hand'" (1977, 94–95).

33. It is important to note the pedagogical dimensions of embodied etiquette, which Pierre Bourdieu articulates so clearly. His work rejects a traditional notion of "taste" (as either good or bad) and "culture" (as either high or low). For Bourdieu (1977, 87–92), taste defines good from bad and high from low, especially in matters of food and drink. See also John Kasson (1990); Margaret Visser (1991, 194).

34. Mary Douglas writes, "A code affords a general set of possibilities for sending particular messages. If food is treated as a code, the message it encodes will be found in the pattern of social relations being expressed. The message is about different degrees of hierarchy, inclusion and exclusion, boundaries and transactions across the boundaries . . . Food categories therefore encode social events" (1972, 61).

35. Pierre Bourdieu writes, "The body is the most indisputable materialization of class taste" (1984, 190). He continues, "The legitimate use of the body is spontaneously perceived as an index of moral uprightness, so that its opposite, a 'natural' body, is seen as an index of *laisser-aller* ('letting oneself go'), a culpable surrender to facility" (193). See also Ron Scapp and Brian Seitz (2006).

36. John Bunyan, *Pilgrim's Progress* (1998, 71); and see Webb Keane's *Christian Moderns* (2007, 51) for a productive invocation of Bunyan.

37. Jerome Branche, *Colonialism and Race in Luso-Hispanic Literature* (2006, 42). See also Benjamin Keen and Keith Haynes, *The Hispanic Background* (2000); Bartolomé de las Casas, *A Short Account of the Destruction of the Indies* (1992); Kenneth Mills and William Taylor, *Colonial Spanish America: A Documentary History* (1998); and Anthony Pagden, *Spanish Imperialism and Political Imagination* (1990).

38. Robert Kiyosaki and Sharon Lechter, *Rich Dad, Poor Dad: What the Rich Teach Their Kids about Money That the Poor and Middle Class Do Not!* (2000, 129).

39. See David Fischman, *El camino del líder* (2003), as cited in Alan la Rue, "Interview with David Fischman" (2006).

40. Ann Cameron, *The Most Beautiful Place in the World* (2011, 23).

41. Stacy Gillis and Joanne Hollows, *Feminism, Domesticity and Popular Culture* (2008).

42. It is the idea of the self as the terrain or site of governance that I find compelling. Tomas Matza argues this well, connecting Erving Goffman (1971, 29–32, 60–61) to the literature on governmentality and suggesting that in liberal societies personhood is at issue in contestations around personal space. That is, personal space marks "'the role the individual is allowed in determining what happens to his claim [for it].' This and other preserves comprising the 'territories of the self' are actually sites for the performance of rituals for demonstrating self-determination, which he [Goffman] says are crucial to what it means to be a 'full-fledged person')" (2009, 506). Matza also writes, "As Cruikshank has noted in her study of the self-esteem movement in the United States, 'By isolating a self to act upon, to appreciate and to esteem, we avail ourselves of a terrain of action, we exercise power upon ourselves' (1996, 234). The exercise of power on oneself, even a liberatory power, is a form of subjectivation situated in relations of power" (2009, 500).

43. Guatemala has consistently had the hemisphere's second-lowest tax revenue next to Haiti and routinely has the lowest public investment in social services and the lowest tax collection base in Central America (USAID Bureau for Latin America and the Caribbean 2006, 73). In the year 2000, for example, only 600 taxpayers represented 60 to 70 percent of all of Guatemala's income tax revenue, and the wealthiest class of "special taxpayers," as of 1999, represented 38 to 40 percent of the total revenue collected from all taxes. At the same time, government spending in Guatemala in 2003 was lower in terms of GDP than in any other country in all of the Americas. A cluster of very smart Guatemalan tax pamphlets and books provide the statistical backbone for this paragraph. These include the work of Rolando Escobar Menaldo and Ana Maritza Morales (2000) and Pablo Rodas Martini (2000). Further statistical support was provided by "Guatemala Tax Protests Turn Violent" (2001) and the USAID document *Guatemala Tax and Investment Policy Reform Program* (2001). See also Archana Sridhar (2007).

44. For extensive reporting and implications on the role of drug traffickers in the governance of Guatemala, see United Nations Office on Drugs and Crime, *Transnational Organized Crime in Central America and the Caribbean: A Threat Assessment* (2012).

45. Nikolas Rose, *Governing the Soul: The Shaping of the Private Self* (1990).

46. Aaron Doyle, *Arresting Images: Crime and Policing in Front of the Camera* (2003).

47. See the "Culture and Values" page at the Virtus Institute Business Coaching website, http://www.virtusinstitute.com/?page_id=806&lang = en.

48. The quote comes from an interview recorded and edited by Countercamera. See the full report at Countercamera 2009.

49. Giovanna Procacci, *Social Economy and the Government of Poverty* (1991, 156).

50. See Giovanna Procacci (1991, 160). Antoine Cherbuliez (1797–1869) was a Swiss liberal thinker who lived in Geneva and Paris, and worked in both economics and theology. See, for example, his *Précis de la science économique* (1862).

51. Robert Kiyosaki and Sharon Lechter, *Rich Dad, Poor Dad* (2000, 7).

CHAPTER 3

1. The Guatemalan government subsidized some 2,000 scholarships for advanced English language skills and training for call center work, according to Government of Guatemala, "Beca de perfeccionamiento intensivo de idioma inglés para Contact Center" (2010). The World Bank supported Invest in Guatemala, a not-for-profit organization that supports the call center industry (Agencia de Atracción de Inversiones and Invest in Guatemala 2009). USAID runs rehabilitation programs that prepares ex–gang members for the formal economy, including call centers (Creative Associates International 2009).

2. Michael Hardt, "The Global Society of Control": "Where the production of soul is concerned, as Musil might say, we should no longer look to the soil and organic development, nor to the factory and mechanical development, but rather to today's dominant economic forms, that is, to production defined by a combination of cybernetics and affect" (1998, 97).

3. For background on Guatemala's call center industry, see Philip Peters, "Zagada Selects Transactel as Premier Guatemala BPO Member for Its Sphaero Alliance" (2007) and a number of newspaper articles ("Empresa Allied inaugura centro de atención telefónica en Guatemala" 2009; Urías Moisés Gamarro 2008a, 2008b, 2009; Byron Dardón Garzaro 2009).

4. According to the publication *The Banker*, "Guatemala's economy has been humming along nicely, if not spectacularly, for the past few years of its post-civil war recovery, with gross domestic product (GDP) accelerating from 2.6% in 2005 to an expected 5.6% this year" (Rumsey 2008).

5. See a number of articles that appeared in *Siglo Veintiuno* (Edgar López 2008a, 2008b, 2008c; Roxana Larios 2009) and a report prepared for the Zagada Institute (Philip Peters 2009), which says:

> Zagada has validated the Central America Nearshore agent and Business Process Outsourcing (BPO) worker density at 45,095—a net growth of 24,083 workers from the 21,012 figures reported in our 2007 reports. This represents an aggregate growth of

115% over the last 24 months. This growth momentum exceeding 50% per annum is anticipated to be sustained and will drive contact center and BPOs worker density to 66,700 by the end of 2010. . . . While the Central American Nearshore region registered a 32% growth rate in our 2007 report and was projects to improve just under 40% per annum over the next 24 months, the region far exceeded those numbers by registering a 57% average annual rate over the last two years. Underpinning this growth in the Central American Nearshore market have been the strategic decisions by large U.S. firms and outsourcing service suppliers to expand and establish scalable captive operations as well as secure the services of a growing number of small to mid-size regional firms keen at delivering competitive bilingual customer care BPO services. (6)

6. Byron Dardón Garzaro, "Call Centers demandan más guatemaltecos que hablen ingles" (2009).

7. William Howe Tolman, *Industrial Betterment* (1900); Tolman, *Hygiene for the Worker* (1912).

8. Washington Gladden, *Working People and Their Employers* (1876, 44–50).

9. Washington Gladden, *Working People and Their Employers* (1876, 181); see also Gladden, *Applied Christianity: Moral Aspects of Social Questions* (1889) and Gladden, *Social Salvation* (1901).

10. Samuel W. Latta, *Rest Houses for Railroad Men: How the Railroad Men Regard Such Conveniences* (1906); C. Howard Hopkins, *History of the Y.M.C.A. in North America* (1951); and Stuart D. Brandes, *American Welfare Capitalism, 1880–1940* (1984).

11. Stephen R. Barley and Gideon Kunda, "Design and Devotion: Surges of Rational and Normative Ideologies of Control in Managerial Discourse" (1992, 366).

12. Washington Gladden's *Working People and Their Employers* (1876) shared a readership with Samuel Smiles's wildly popular *Self-Help* (1866). "Heaven helps those who help themselves," Smiles writes ([1866] 2002, 13). Distributed throughout Latin America, Smiles's other three volumes painted an equally Protestant profile, one with pious impulses: *Character* (1859), *Thrift* (1878), and *Duty* (1880).

13. Virginia Garrard-Burnett, "Liberalism, Protestantism, and Indigenous Resistance in Guatemala, 1870–1920" (1997).

14. Marilyn T. Williams, *Washing "The Great Unwashed": Public Baths in Urban America, 1840–1920* (1991).

15. Frederick Winslow Taylor, *The Principles of Scientific Management* (1911); Elton Mayo, *The Human Problems of an Industrial Civilization* (1933).

16. Kim McQuaid, "The Businessman as Reformer: Nelson O. Nelson and Late 19th Century Social Movements in America" (1974).

17. Rick Warren quotes Peter Drucker liberally. In *Management Challenges for the 21st Century*, Drucker, in turn, declared the megachurch "surely the most important social phenomenon in American society in the last thirty years" (1999, 29).

18. Rick Warren, *The Purpose Driven Life: What on Earth Am I Here For?* (2002).

19. Malcolm Carlaw et al., *Managing and Motivating Contact Center Employees: Tools and Techniques for Inspiring Outstanding Performance from Your Frontline Staff* (2002, 209).

20. See the advertisements as posted at the "Career Inspiration" Transactel Pinterest site, http://www.pinterest.com/pin/227009637439187173/; accessed September 20, 2013.

21. Transactel, "Bring Out the Power in You" advertisement in *Prensa Libre* (2010).

22. Transactel, "Bring Out the Power in You" advertisement in *Prensa Libre* (2009).

23. Emily Martin, *Flexible Bodies: Tracking Immunity in American Culture From the Days of Polio to the Age of AIDS* (1994). See also Edward F. Fischer and Peter Benson, *Broccoli and Desire: Global Connections and Maya Struggles in Postwar Guatemala* (2006).

24. In "Skills and Selves in the New Workplace," Bonnie Urciuoli writes, "The notion of 'worker-self-as-skills-bundle' (not only is the worker's labor power a commodity but the worker's very person is also defined by the summation of commodifiable bits) is a social construction cumulatively produced by years of skills discourses in business and education. These skills discourses operate in and index (indicate the existence of) the history and conditions of capitalist production, particularly since the 1970s, variously called 'post-Fordism,' 'late capitalism,' 'flexible accumulation,' and, most relevant to this study, 'neoliberalism,' in which all possible forms of sociality and being are treated as market exchanges (Harvey 2005)" (2008, 211–212).

25. The full quote reads

> Part of Transactel's philosophy is to hire from the base and promote from within. This has allowed us to provide a clear and structured career path to our employees. Over 320 promotions in 2011 and a forecast of 500 promotions in 2012 demonstrate that Transactel is the place to build a career in. Along with growth opportunities, we invest in our people by providing a development program which includes technical and soft skills training. As part of this philosophy we also have an alliance with top universities to deliver both Bachelor's and Master's degrees programs in our own sites at a much lower cost. Our career path plan is based in policies of equity, skills development, performance improvement and constant growth. (Transactel 2012a)

26. For allegories of industrial religion, see Richard J. Callahan, Jr., Kathryn Lofton, and Chad E. Seales, "Allegories of Progress: Industrial Religion in the United States" (2010). For the making of Christian free enterprise, see Bethany Moreton, *To Serve God and Wal-Mart: The Making of Christian Free Enterprise* (2009).

27. See, for example, Emily Martin, "Managing Americans: Policy and Changes in the Meanings of Work and the Self" (1997).

28. I follow Michael Hardt and Antonio Negri to argue that Michel Foucault's notion of biopolitics must connect with Gilles Deleuze's notion of "control societies" to capture the new postindustrial cartography of productive relations. See Gilles Deleuze, "Post-scriptum sur les sociétés de contrôle" (1990); Michael Hardt and Antonio Negri, *Empire* (2000); and Michael

Hardt and Antonio Negri, *Multitude: War and Democracy in the Age of Empire* (2004).

29. Patrick Joyce, *The Rule of Freedom: Liberalism and the Modern City* (2003). Critical to the work of Joyce is the idea that liberal governance of the nineteenth century ruled through freedom. This meant that freedom was not the end game. It was not the goal but rather the discourse, at times affect, through which the state and city governed its citizens, producing (in the end) certain patterns of social life. This included the material form of the city (its layout, architecture, infrastructure) as well as the way people lived the city.

30. Pavoncito is a maximum security prison in Guatemala that has been the site of prison riots. On December 25, 2002, Guatemalan authorities lost control of this prison after a violent uprising left eighteen prisoners dead and more than thirty injured. Many of the bodies were mutilated or badly burned. One person was decapitated in the fighting ("Guatemala Jail Riot Leaves 17 Dead" 2002).

31. Ian Hacking, *The Taming of Chance* (1990, vii). The work of Ian Hacking looks at the eighteenth-century developments in statistical theory to the end of the nineteenth century. One of his central points is that we think statistically so often that we rarely, if ever, notice it. Yet we are most often defined and governed by numbers. And the call center is no exception. The process that Hacking details produced a sea change in culture writ large.

32. David Sims, "The Right Balance for the Call Center: Somewhere between Prison and an Encounter Group" (2006).

33. Michel Foucault, *Discipline and Punish: The Birth of the Prison* (1995, 200).

34. Jean Comaroff, "Missionaries and Mechanical Clocks: An Essay on Religion and History in South Africa" (1991, 10).

35. Jean Comaroff and John Comaroff, *Of Revelation and Revolution,* Vol. 2: *The Dialectics of Modernity on a South African Frontier* (1997, 223).

36. The full advice reads

Organize Your Pre-Work Routine: Get your clothes ready the night before, give yourself an extra thirty minutes to get ready, leave earlier than you absolutely have to. These are all things that can help you get ready and out the door so you can face the world—in the punctual way.

Know the importance of rest: Being well rested is another key to having your day go on schedule. If you are tired and fatigued you are less likely to be prepared for the next day. Just like having a set time to get up in the morning, you should also have a set time to go to bed.

Make a Record of Your Attendance: If your boss isn't doing it for you and sending you reminders, make a record of when you come in to work late and when you get there on time. This may give you a clearer picture of how often you are tardy.

Work on Time Management: You are not going to get things done if you don't make the time for that to happen. Most people can't make up success as they go along. (Executive Boutique 2011)

37. The full list of principles reads

Integrity: We are open and honest. Proud to do things right.

Commitment: We keep our promises.

Respect: We embrace diversity.

Passionate About Our People: As a team we make a difference.

Drive, Innovation & Embrace Change: We do extraordinary things everyday. (Transactel 2012b)

38. In "Affect: What Is It Good For?" William Mazzarella writes, "society is inscribed on our nervous system and in our flesh before it appears in our consciousness" (2009, 291). See also Brian Massumi, *Parables for the Virtual: Movement, Affect, Sensation* (2002, 30).

39. Nathaniel Hawthorne, *The Scarlet Letter* (1850, 35).

40. See the Transactel "Career Path" webpage for more (Transactel 2012a).

41. This quote comes from the training video "Top 6 Ways to Get An Angry Customer to Back Down" (Myra Golden 2007).

42. For a powerful analysis of the relationships that exist between masculinity and post-Fordism, see Bethany Moreton, *To Serve God and Wal-Mart* (2009). She writes, "The least industrialized sections of the country might see their sons fall prey to the same dehumanizing factory discipline as the immigrant masses of the North and East. These Americans weren't supposed to be working for the Man. They *were* the man" (52).

43. *The O.C.* is an American teen drama television series that originally aired on the Fox network in the United States from August 5, 2003, to February 22, 2007. It ran for four seasons, portraying the fictional lives of teenagers from an affluent community in Orange County, California.

44. Augustine, *Confessions and Enchiridion* (1955).

45. See Philippe Bourgois, *In Search of Respect: Selling Crack in El Barrio* (1996, 114–174).

46. *The Wire* is an HBO drama series dealing with the complexities of Baltimore city police efforts at infiltrating an inner-city drug syndicate. *The Office* is an NBC "mockumentary" that pokes fun at the idiosyncrasies of a dysfunctional branch office of the Dunder Mifflin Paper Company.

47. See Bethany Moreton, "The Soul of Neoliberalism" (2007).

48. Rosanne D'Ausilio, *Wake Up Your Call Center: Humanizing Your Interaction Hub* (1998, 80).

49. This approach and paragraph owes full credit to Peter Redfield, "Doctors, Borders, and Life in Crisis" (2005). I quote Redfield at length:

> The ambition of this work is not simply to produce a general critique of humanitarian action or an elaboration of its political limitations . . . The rhetorical force of critique stems from a promise to unveil and denounce untruths and violations. As such, it structurally evades the less comfortable possibilities of implication within the process in question and the problem of approaching what is already represented or already familiar (Latour 2004; Riles 2000). Along with much recent anthropological writing on topics like torture and human rights (Asad 2003; Wilson 1997), I wish to move away from treating humanitarianism as an absolute value by approaching it as an array of particular embodied, situated practices emanating from the humanitarian desire to alleviate the suffering of others. In so doing, I hope to reintroduce a measure of anthropological distance to a familiar set of contemporary phenomena, while

simultaneously accepting the premise that action occurs in an untidy, thoroughly implicating, "second best world" (Terry 2002). (330)

50. Scholars have long observed that unemployment brings people to work, but here employment provides a certain harbor from a world of violent disappearance. While beyond the scope of this article, there is reason to think more closely about the question of gang violence as it bears on the spirit of labor formation.

51. Fiona Terry, *Condemned to Repeat? The Paradox of Humanitarian Action* (2002).

52. This is what Mariana Valverde has called "the democratization of the pastoral." See Valverde, *Diseases of the Will: Alcohol and the Dilemmas of Freedom* (1998, 19).

53. Nikolas Rose, *Governing the Soul: The Shaping of the Private Self* (1990).

CHAPTER 4

1. "Red Zone," or *zona roja*, describes areas most affected by violence. The term is used throughout Latin America. In the case of Guatemala City, *zona roja* is a term often associated with areas troubled by gang-related violence and extreme poverty. They are routinely mapped by local media. See, for example, Mariela Castañon, "Las diez zonas más peligrosas de Guatemala" (2011). In Guatemala City, unlike similar cities such as San Salvador, El Salvador, Tegucigalpa, Honduras, and Managua, Nicaragua, violence is fairly evenly distributed throughout the city. The most dangerous zones include not only very poor areas (zones 5 and 18) but also the city's most exclusive locales (zones 10 and 13).

2. Approximately one-fourth of the nearly two and a half million people residing in Guatemala City live in "precarious settlements" (Instituto Nacional de Estadística Guatemala 2004). These are "neighborhoods built with fragile materials such as cardboard, tin, or, in the best of cases, cement blocks" (Edward Murphy 2004, 64). These settlements tend to exist not just beyond the most basic of social services but also beneath the city itself, at the bottom of *barrancos,* or canyons. See Kevin Lewis O'Neill and Benjamin Fogarty-Valenzuela, "Verticality" (2013).

3. This approach draws heavily upon the work of Peter Miller and Nikolas Rose (1988, 2), especially their work on mobilizing the consumer, or making the subject of consumption. They argue that making, or assembling, the subject of consumption has been "a complex technical process." So too has been assembling the subject of prevention. The image of assemblage links Miller and Rose's work to that of Gilles Deleuze, for this process of subjectiviation involves what Deleuze would call a fold. He writes, "the relations of an outside [get] folded back upon themselves to create a doubling, to allow a relation to oneself to emerge, and to constitute an inside which is hollowed out and develops its own unique dimension" (1988a, 100). The point that this chapter develops is that child sponsorship is not simply a relationship between sponsor and child but also a relationship between sponsor and sponsor as well as child and child.

4. With regard to effects, this chapter is most keen on what Ramah McKay understands as humanitarian afterlives. She writes that in "Morrumbala, where humanitarian projects have unfolded over decades, district residents incorporate the resources of humanitarian governmentality into diverse life projects, often beyond the aims of the interventions themselves" (2012, 288). Humanitarian intervention thus has both immediate effects and afterlives. This chapter seeks out both.

5. An essay by Bianca Dahl (n.d.) examines the meaning and effects of singing and dancing in the context of death, comparing Tswana funeral practices with Bathusi Orphan Day Care Centre's music therapy intervention. Much of the essay revolves around the performativity of child grief. In a telling exchange, a moment of fantastic ethnography, she describes an exchange between an aid worker and orphans about how to sing a particular song. She writes

> This performance style looked rather incongruous to the foreign aid-workers at Bathusi (and, for that matter, to the resident anthropologist). The music was slow, written in a minor key, with a tragic subject matter, and yet the children were performing the song in exactly the same way that they sang "I'm Special." They were bright-eyed, animated, smiling and happy, wriggling their bodies in lively movements, not at all fitting the stereotype of children who had watched their parents die and were trying to express their heartache about their loss. Piet was not satisfied. One practice session in August 2003, he stopped the song midway through and said, "No, this is all wrong. This is a *sad* song. You need to perform it with *sad faces*. Can we practice doing sad faces?" (19)

See also Bianca Dahl, "Left Behind? Orphaned Children, Humanitarian Aid, and the Politics of Kinship, Culture, and Caregiving during Botswana's AIDS Crisis" (2009).

6. The original turn of phrase comes famously from Gayatri Chakravorty Spivak (1988), who writes on the abolition of the Indian rite of *sati* by the British, noting that the abolition is an example of "white men saving brown women from brown men." Diane Nelson, writing on the Guatemalan context, finds this turn of phrase productive, using some variation of it some fifteen times in *Finger in the Wound* (1999). At the core of both invocations sits the politics of intervention, of protecting someone from themselves or their community.

7. In her essay "A Bright Shining Slogan," Elizabeth Dickinson (2009) writes,

> The phrase "winning hearts and minds" has, in recent years, become indelibly associated with the challenges of an interventionist U.S. foreign policy. But the concept has had a long and circuitous life. It was first associated with democracy in the 19th century, later served as a call to national solidarity during the Great Depression, and finally became a slogan for a policy the U.S. military never quite implemented in Vietnam. As U.S. President Barack Obama fights two inherited wars and continues the daunting task of reaching out to Muslims, the concept has never been more relevant, even if the words themselves have begun to lose all meaning.

Dickinson lays out a timeline, with the first U.S. reference coming February 13, 1818: "In writing to a Baltimore newspaper editor, U.S. founding father John Adams describes the American Revolution as being 'in the minds and hearts of the people, a change in their religious sentiments of their duties and obligations.'"

8. In *Saving the Modern Soul: Therapy, Emotions, and the Culture of Self-Help*, Eva Illouz writes, "The therapeutic emotional style emerged in the relatively short period from World War I to World War II and became both solidified and widely available after the 1960s. To be sure, this style drew on residues of nineteenth-century notions of selfhood, but it also presented a new lexicon to conceptualize and discuss emotions and self in the realm of ordinary life and new ways of handling emotional life" (2008, 15). Of interest also is the work of Matthew Hedstrom, whose *The Rise of Liberal Religion* (2012) rightly details how liberal Christianity brought psychological, mystical, and cosmopolitan forms of spirituality to the American middle class.

9. Kathryn Lofton's *Oprah: The Gospel of an Icon* (2011) makes the observation that the difference between liberal and neoliberal is the difference between Donahue and Oprah. The observation is strengthened by a passage from Philippe Bourgois's *In Search of Respect,* which comments on "a photograph of me [Bourgois] on page 4 of the *New York Post* standing next to Phil Donahue following a prime time television debate on violent crime in East Harlem" (1996, 20). While Bourgois and the issue of violent crime in East Harlem fit neatly into Phil Donahue's liberal programming, with its attention to social issues and the public sphere, it is somewhat unthinkable to imagine Philippe Bourgois on the *Oprah Winfrey Show,* whose commitment to change, Lofton makes clear, "is care not of politics, not of other people, but of *you.* Care of nation will radiate from that self-nursing" (2011, 217). For a sense of how neoliberalism comes to be written, see Claudio Lomnitz, "Narrating the Neoliberal Moment: History, Journalism, Historicity" (2008).

10. Sally Struthers (Struthers and Balboa 1989) endorsed power walking; she promoted diet books that lowered cholesterol one kefir shake at a time (Struthers and Virtue 1979). She also pioneered distance education, framing retraining as affordable, fun, and risk-free: "Would you like to make more money? Sure, we all would" (Struthers 1991).

11. See her Christian Children's Fund commercial (Struthers 1987).

12. Patrick West is fierce, if not overly cynical. In his book *Conspicuous Compassion: Why Sometimes it Really Is Cruel to Be Kind,* he lingers on what he sees as hollow expressions of public caring. He argues, in a rather nostalgic way, that this lack of sincerity is linked to the decline of the family, the church, the nation, and the neighborhood. In the absence of real emotions, people manufacture conspicuous emotions. He writes, "Mourning sickness is a religion for the lonely crowd that no longer subscribes to orthodox churches. Its flowers and teddies are its rites, its collective minutes' silences its liturgy and mass. But these new bonds are phony, ephemeral and cynical" (2004, 65–66). Of interest for this chapter is not the question of sincerity so much as the performance of compassion, the effort to make this compassion outwardly evident—to make compassion conspicuous.

13. "Christianity is not a religion; it's a relationship"—the pull is also to believe in Christ, not religion. This slogan has been a rallying cry of 1970s and 1980s evangelicalism, with an emphasis placed on a personal relationship with Jesus Christ (as opposed to doctrine and ritual). Tanya Luhrmann's *When God Talks Back: Understanding the American Evangelical Relationship with God*

(2012) is premised on this historical shift, on the idea that God does talk to individual people, that God does, in fact, talk back. See also Matthew Engelke, *A Problem of Presence* (2007).

14. Moral ambition, as defined by Omri Elisha, emerges when "aspirations pertain not only to what [people] desire for themselves but also what they have come to expect of others" (2011, 2). There are other components to the definition, but this is its most generalizable form. This definition sits, at least by my reading, at the core of moral ambition. Elisha mobilizes this term ethnographically, with a close study of two Tennessee megachurches. In many ways it is a study of activism. Elisha pushes past the battered lightning rods of evangelical political debate (such as abortion, same-sex marriage, and public prayer) to explore both honestly and intimately how conservative Christians work to improve society. The important contribution here, especially for the ever-growing anthropology of Christianity, is a close look at how new forms of Protestant Christianity are not simply individualistic—that there is a rich sense of the social and a concern for how to think and act upon society. Poverty, racial justice, and urban revivalism—these are evangelical concerns.

"Reprogram Your Mental Computer" is the title of the thirteenth chapter of Joel Osteen's *Your Best Life Now: 7 Steps to Living at Your Full Potential* (2004), and "Getting Up on the Inside" is the title of the twenty-first chapter of his book.

15. Rick Warren, *The Purpose Driven Life: What on Earth Am I Here For?* (2002).

16. Joel Osteen, *Your Best Life Now* (2004, 227).

17. Kathleen Stewart, *Ordinary Affects* (2007).

18. The 2009–2010 global operating budgets of the five largest child sponsorship programs totaled over $4 billion. The 2009–2010 global operating budget of World Vision Inc. and Affiliates was $2.58 billion (KPMG 2010c); of Save the Children, $1.3 billion (KPMG 2010d); of ChildFund International, $8.3 million (KPMG 2010a); of Plan International, $7.25 million (Plan International 2010); and of Compassion International, $5.07 million (KPMG 2010b).

19. For "the spirit of development," see Erica Bornstein's book of that title (2005). In *Development, Security and Unending War: Governing the World of Peoples,* Mark Duffield (2007, viii, 216–217) rightly reads development as a technology of security that is central to liberal forms of governance. For a very fine review of Duffield's book, see David Chandler, "Review Article: Theorising the Shift from Security to Insecurity—Kaldor, Duffield and Furedi" (2008).

20. In an article in one publication (Heidi Isaza 2012), World Vision articulates its use of sponsorship to prevent gang violence:

> When the flames of gang violence reached El Salvador, they found a generation of young people who were more than willing to fuel the fire—kids who were essentially abandoned during and after the war when their parents immigrated or worked long hours to survive. . . . World Vision is providing youth with alternatives to gang activities by addressing poverty and identity issues. Culture of Peace, a new World Vision curriculum, empowers young people to express themselves and solve their problems with words instead of weapons. Culture of Peace also challenges young people to dream about their future and make plans to achieve those dreams. The lessons are

based on biblical concepts and speak to children's true identity—that in Christ they are loved, protected, and made new, no matter what their daily life is like. World Vision also provides teens with vocational skills to earn income instead of taking the gangs' easy way out of poverty. . . . Just as in fighting wildfires, the work has to focus on preventing flames from raging out of control. World Vision is addressing the issue of the "fuel" by empowering teens to reach out to their peers through youth-led clubs—providing young people with a viable alternative to joining gangs.

21. Laura Wexler, *Tender Violence: Literary Eavesdropping, Domestic Fiction, and Educational Reform* (1992, 15).

22. See, for example, Henry David Thoreau, *Walden* (1997, 184, 188); Nathaniel Hawthorne, *The Scarlet Letter* (1850, 71); Herman Melville, *Great Short Works* (1969, 165–172). Paul Lewis writes, "The poor visit offered antebellum writers a motif for exploring a wide range of ideas: from celebrations of middle-class benevolence to practical suggestions for individual, institutional, political, and social reform; from Christian and transcendental repudiations of material wealth to materialist and socialist attacks on the cruelties of a competitive market system and skeptical and irreligious critiques of pious optimism. Just as poor visit reports frequently reveal more about the judgmental middle-class visitors than about the impoverished hosts, so fictional re-creations of such visits starkly define the value systems at work in essays and stories about the poor" (2000, 246–47).

23. Louisa May Alcott, *Little Women* (1872, 7).

24. For more on the (often racialized) notion that a principle of parsimony distinguishes the civilized from the savage, from Adam Smith through Nietzsche and Bataille and including much anthropological thought, see Christopher Bracken, *Magical Criticism: The Recourse of Savage Philosophy* (2007).

25. John Bunyan, *Pilgrim's Progress* ([1837] 1998).

26. Gayatri Spivak prefaces some interview comments by saying, "All of this comes accompanied by large doses of liberal guilt about which I do not know what to begin to say, but I'm sure you understand what the problem is" (Terry Threadgold and Frances Bartkowski, "The *Intervention* Interview," 1990, 115). Spivak's uncertainty, however, has given way to a thick literature on the topic, for which see, among others, Shelby Steele, "White Guilt" (1990); Homi K. Bhabha, "Post-Colonial Authority and Postmodern Guilt" (1992); Lauren Berlant, "'68, or Something" (1994); Julie Ellison, "A Short History of Liberal Guilt" (1996); John Crowley, "Liberal Values, Liberal Guilt, and the Distaste for Politics" (2000); and Karyn Ball, "A Democracy is Being Beaten" (2006).

27. Emily Post, *Etiquette in Society, in Business, in Politics, and at Home* (1922, 448).

28. Virginia Garrard-Burnett, "Liberalism, Protestantism, and Indigenous Resistance in Guatemala, 1870–1920" (1997) and Pierre Bourdieu, *Distinction: A Social Critique of the Judgment of Taste* (1984).

29. Wii is a seventh-generation video game console released by Nintendo on November 19, 2006.

30. Compassion International, "Value of Letter Writing" (2011).

31. "Our child protection policy requires that all correspondence be handled through Compassion, both for your protection and your sponsored child's. Do

not accept a request to connect and do not attempt to connect with your sponsored child on any social network. Let us know right away if you receive a friend request from anyone claiming to be your sponsored child. Also, do not include any personal information such as your email or mailing address in your letters and cards. Thanks for understanding!" (Compassion International, "Write to Your Sponsored Child: Show How Much You Care," 2012).

32. The full text (Compassion International, "I Find It Difficult to Write Letters to My Sponsored Child," 2009) reads

- Keep your letters simple and not too long. Don't go into too much detail.
- Talk about your family and ask about theirs.
- You could share about your interests or hobbies.
- If you have pets, let your child know. They may have an animal too.
- Do you have a garden? Many children are involved in growing some form of crops.
- Share favorite Bible verses. Your faith is something you have in common.
- Ask clear questions. This helps you get to know your child and helps them know what to write to you.
- Occasional photographs and postcards add interest, and give something else to talk about in the letters.
- Remind your child that you are praying for them.
- Your letters are your personal, emotional giving to your child. Let them know that you love and value them.

Here are some resources to give you more ideas: (1) 73 Questions to Ask about Your Child, (2) 69 Questions about Country/Culture/Community, (3) 35 Questions to Ask about Family & Friends, (4) 55 Questions to Ask about School.

Want more? Check out these articles on the Compassion Blog! You Can Copy These Sample Letters!

See also World Vision Australia, "What Will I Write to My Sponsored Child?" (2013).

33. See the video at Compassion International, "Write to Your Sponsored Child" (2012).

34. Emily Post, *Etiquette in Society, in Business, in Politics, and at Home* (1922, 448).

35. Kathryn Lofton, *Oprah: The Gospel of an Icon* (2011, 86).

36. "In a narrow sense, philanthrocapitalism describes the way that a new generation of individuals and organizations are bringing the techniques of business to their giving and social investing," said Michael Green, co-author with Matthew Bishop of *Philanthrocapitalism: How Giving Can Save The World* (Bishop and Green 2008). "In a broader sense," he continued, "philanthrocapitalism is about the way that the leaders of capitalism are recognizing that our economic system is not going to be sustainable if it screws up the planet or causes social unrest by leaving millions of people behind."

37. The local news reported this event as did the child sponsorship organization's blog, but, for the sake of anonymity, those references are not cited here. It can be said, though, that the journalistic coverage proved extremely thin.

38. For feminicide, see Central American Human Rights Council Ombudsman, *Regional Report: Situation and Analysis of Femicide in Central American Region* (2006) and Victoria Sanford, "From Genocide to Feminicide: Impunity and Human Rights in Twenty-First Century Guatemala" (2008). For postwar impunity, see Angelina Snodgrass Godoy, "Lynchings and the Democratization of Terror in Postwar Guatemala: Implications for Human Rights" (2002) and Rachel Sieder, "Contested Sovereignties: Indigenous Law, Violence and State Effects in Postwar Guatemala" (2011). For structural effacement, see Peter Benson, Edward F. Fischer, and Kedron Thomas, "Resocializing Suffering: Neoliberalism, Accusation, and the Sociopolitical Context of Guatemala's New Violence" (2008). And for a sense of everyday violence, see Nancy Scheper-Hughes's *Death without Weeping* (1992) and Javier Auyero's *Patients of the State* (2012).

39. Tim LaHaye and Jerry B. Jenkins, *Left Behind: A Novel of the Earth's Last Days* (1995).

40. See, for example, James Ferguson, *The Anti-Politics Machine: "Development," Depoliticization, and Bureaucratic Power in Lesotho* (1994); Tania Li, *The Will to Improve: Governmentality, Development, and the Practice of Politics* (2007); and Miriam Ticktin, *Casualties of Care: Immigration and the Politics of Humanitarianism in France* (2011).

41. Steve Corbett and Brian Fikkert, *When Helping Hurts: How to Alleviate Poverty Without Hurting the Poor . . . and Yourself* (2009).

42. Gilles Deleuze, "Post-scriptum sur les sociétés de contrôle" (1990, 4).

43. By the subjectification of security, I mean those moments when the question of postwar security targets the subject more than the neighborhood, the population, or even society.

44. Tim LaHaye and Jerry B. Jenkins, *Left Behind* (1995, 22, 45, 19).

45. Teresa Caldeira, *City of Walls: Crime, Segregation, and Citizenship in São Paulo* (2000); Mike Davis, *Planet of Slums* (2007).

46. Clifford Geertz, *Available Light: Anthropological Reflections on Philosophical Topics* (2000, 18).

47. Bruce Wydick, "Want to Change the World? Sponsor a Child" (2013); Bruce Wydick, Paul Glewwe, and Laine Rutledge, "Does International Child Sponsorship Work? A Six-Country Study of Impacts on Adult Life Outcomes" (2013).

48. Bruce Wydick, "Want to Change the World?" (2013).

49. Bruce Wydick, "Want to Change the World?" (2013).

50. See Children International promotional material (2013a; 2013b; 2013c) and a public Facebook note by Richard Whosoever Burroughs (2011).

CHAPTER 5

1. *Química* is Guatemalan slang for rubbing alcohol.

2. The literal translation of *me quiero ir a la mierda* is "I want to go to shit." More idiomatic translations include "I want to die," "I want to go to hell," "Get me the hell out of here," and "Get me the fuck out of here." The last is closest to the context and, as was clear in follow-up interviews, closest to the intent of the original utterance.

3. Guatemala's prison population is fewer than six thousand inmates; see the "World Prison Brief" (International Centre for Prison Studies 2013). This number does not include pretrial detainees or remand prisoners. My own fieldwork suggests that there are as many as two hundred Pentecostal rehabilitation centers in Guatemala City. Some hold as many as one hundred and fifty people, some as few as ten. A conservative average is thirty people per center. This puts the number of people inside Pentecostal rehabilitation centers at well over six thousand.

4. By 1994, scholars could declare, with no small confidence, "Liberation theology has been reduced to an intellectual curiosity" (Edward Lynch, "The Retreat of Liberation Theology," 1994, 12). Ten years later, liberation theology's most enthusiastic supporters called for its reinvention; see Ivan Petrella, *The Future of Liberation Theology: An Argument and Manifesto* (2004, xvii).

5. Gustavo Gutiérrez, *A Theology of Liberation: History, Politics, and Salvation* (1988, 11).

6. For a compelling argument against this inversion, one that foregrounds the centrality of time, see Angela Garcia, *The Pastoral Clinic: Addiction and Dispossession along the Rio Grande* (2010).

7. Michel Foucault understands ethics as a relation of the self to itself in terms of moral agency. See Foucault, *Ethics: Subjectivity and Truth* (1997a).

8. Slavery as salvation has been an important metaphor in the Christian tradition, yielding the obvious question: If slavery is oppressive, how can slavery provide such a positive, soteriological symbol for a Christian's relationship to God? For a superb reflection over this very question, see Dale B. Martin, *Slavery as Salvation: The Metaphor of Slavery in Pauline Christianity* (1990). See also, more broadly, Grégoire Chamayou's *Manhunts: A Philosophical History*: "Freedom, impossible here, took on the aspect of an elsewhere. Liberation was conceived as a relationship to space rather than time, to geography rather than history" (2012, 40).

9. For the theological origins of political concepts, see, for example, Carl Schmitt, *Political Theology: Four Chapters on the Concept of Sovereignty* (2005); for theological reflection on political questions, see, for example, Gustavo Gutiérrez, *Theology of Liberation* (1988).

10. By technique, I follow the work of Foucault to mean a "practical rationality governed by a conscious goal." The conscious aim here is to escape. See Michel Foucault, "Space, Knowledge, and Power" (1984, 255).

11. Richard Nixon, "Remarks about an Intensified Program for Drug Abuse Prevention and Control" (1971), quoted in Conor Friedersdorf, "The War on Drugs Turns 40" (2011).

12. Thanks to a generation of scholars, the broad contours of this narrative are now widely known. See, for example, Peter Andreas and Ethan Nadelmann, *Policing the Globe: Criminalization and Crime Control in International Relations* (2006); Enrique Desmond Arias, *Drugs and Democracy in Rio de Janeiro: Trafficking, Social Networks and Public Security* (2006); Ted Galen Carpenter, *Bad Neighbor Policy: Washington's Futile War on Drugs in Latin America* (2003); Patrick L. Clawson and Rensselaer W. Lee III, *The Andean Cocaine Industry* (1998); Paul Gootenberg, *Andean Cocaine: The Making of a Global*

Drug (2009); and Brian Loveman, *Addicted to Failure: U.S. Security Policy in Latin America and the Andean Region* (2006).

13. United Nations Office on Drugs and Crime, *Transnational Organized Crime in Central America and the Caribbean: A Threat Assessment* (2012, 39).

14. Mary Jordan, "Pit Stop on the Cocaine Highway: Guatemala Becomes Favored Link for US-Bound Drugs" (2004).

15. Randal C. Archibold and Damien Cave, "Drug Wars Push Deeper into Central America" (2011).

16. "When it comes to Central American cocaine trafficking, all roads lead to Guatemala" (United Nations Office on Drugs and Crime 2012b, 39). See also June S. Beittel, *Mexico's Drug Trafficking Organizations: Source and Scope of the Violence* (2013); Organization of American States, *The Drug Problem in the Americas* (2013); and Clare Ribando Seelke, Liana Wyler, and June Beittel, *Latin America and the Caribbean: Illicit Drug Trafficking and U.S. Counterdrug Programs* (2010).

17. Frank Viviano, "A Vacation Goes South" (2012).

18. See, for example, Philippe Bourgois, *In Search of Respect: Selling Crack in El Barrio* (1996); Jeff Grogger and Michael Willis, "The Emergence of Crack Cocaine and the Rise in Urban Violence" (2000); Jimmie L. Reeves, *Cracked Coverage: Television News, the Anti-Cocaine Crusade, and the Reagan Legacy* (1994); Craig Reinarman and Harry G. Levine, *Crack in America: Demon Drugs and Social Justice* (1997); and Sudhir Venkatesh, *American Project: The Rise and Fall of a Modern Ghetto* (2000).

19. Michelle Alexander, *The New Jim Crow: Mass Incarceration in the Age of Colorblindness* (2010).

20. See 2009 statistics of the United Nations Office on Drugs and Crime (UNODC), "Intentional Homicide, Count and Rate per 100,000 Population (2000–2012)" (2012).

21. Augustine, *Confessions and Enchiridion* (1995, 135). For reflections on Augustine, conversion, and narrative, see, for example, Sara Byers, "Augustine on the 'Divided Self:' Platonist or Stoic?" (2007); Leo C. Ferrari, "Paul at the Conversion of Augustine" (1980); Leo C. Ferrari, *The Conversions of St. Augustine* (1984); Jean-Luc Marion, *In the Self's Place: The Approach of St. Augustine* (2012), especially chapter 4; and Paul Ricoeur, *Time and Narrative*, Vol. 1 (1984), especially chapter 1.

22. Augustine, *Confessions and Enchiridion* (1995, 23 [deaf from chains clanking], 101 [dragged the chains], 101 [chains chafe], 135 [chain of iron]).

23. Augustine, *Confessions and Enchiridion* (1995, 122).

24. Jonathan Swift, *Gulliver's Travels into Several Remote Regions of the World* (1880).

25. Phillip Cary, *Augustine's Invention of the Inner Self: The Legacy of a Christian Platonist* (2000).

26. A double bind is commonly defined as a contradiction that leads to no possible resolution. The concept begins with Gregory Bateson's theory of schizophrenia in *Steps to an Ecology of Mind* (1972). A more recent invocation can be seen in Jessica R. Cattelino, "The Double Bind of American Indian Need-Based Sovereignty" (2010).

27. Joel Robbins, *Becoming Sinners: Christianity and Moral Torment in a Papua New Guinea Society* (2004a).

28. *Oxford English Dictionary*, s.v. "out" (2013).

29. Agamben borrows this formulation from Foucault, who states that biopolitics produces "une animalization progressive de l'homme." This phrase, found in the third volume of Foucault's *Dits et Écrits*, appears in the introduction to *Homo Sacer*, where it is translated as "the progressive bestialization of man." See Michel Foucault, *Dits et Écrits*, vols. 3–4 (1994a, 719); Giorgio Agamben, *Homo Sacer: Sovereign Power and Bare Life* (1998, 3); Giorgio Agamben, "Non au tatouage biopolitique" (2004); Jacques Derrida, *The Beast and the Sovereign*, vol. 1 (2009, twelfth session); and Arne De Boever's presentation at a summer workshop of the Derrida Seminars Translation Project (2008).

30. Michel Foucault, *Technologies of the Self: A Seminar with Michel Foucault* (1988).

31. W.B. Yeats, "The Second Coming (Slouching Towards Bethlehem)" in *Michael Robartes and the Dancer* (1921) and Joan Didion, *Slouching towards Bethlehem: Essays* (1968). Joan Didion draws on Yeats to title her collection of essays describing her experiences in California during the 1960s. The poem by Yeats, describing postwar Europe, references the Apocalypse with Christian imagery and suggestions of the Second Coming.

32. For the ambiguously emancipatory event of miracles in another Pentecostal context, see Ruth Marshall, "The Sovereignty of Miracles: Pentecostal Political Theology in Nigeria" (2010).

33. Nikolas S. Rose, *Governing the Soul: The Shaping of the Private Self* (1990).

34. Richard Roberts, *¡El poder ilimitado dentro de ti!* (1999).

35. Anthony De Mello, *Autoliberación interior* (1988).

36. Rony Madrid, *La vuelta al corazón en 40 días* (2011).

37. Lauren Berlant, "Lauren Berlant on Her Book *Cruel Optimism*" (2012): "I define 'cruel optimism' as a kind of relation in which one depends on objects that block the very thriving that motivates our attachment in the first place.

"All attachment is optimistic. But what makes it cruel is different than what makes something merely disappointing. When your pen breaks, you don't think, 'This is the end of writing.' But if a relation in which you've invested fantasies of your own coherence and potential breaks down, the world itself feels endangered."

38. Lauren Berlant, *Cruel Optimism* (2011).

39. Rony Madrid, *La vuelta al corazón* (2011, 59).

40. Edited for style. The full passage reads: "The Spirit of the Lord is on me, because he has anointed me to proclaim good news to the poor. He has sent me to proclaim freedom for the prisoners and recovery of sight for the blind, to set the oppressed free, to proclaim the year of the Lord's favor."

41. Rony Madrid, *La vuelta al corazón* (2011, 18).

42. Rony Madrid, *La vuelta al corazón* (2011, 17).

43. Barbara Cruikshank, *The Will to Empower: Democratic Citizens and Other Subjects* (1999, 95).

44. Gilles Deleuze, *Foucault*: "The outside is not a fixed limit but a moving matter animated by peristaltic movements, folds and foldings that together make up an inside: they are not something other than the outside, but precisely the inside of the outside" (1988, 96).

45. Diane M. Nelson, *Reckoning: The Ends of War in Guatemala*:

To be duped is different from claiming ignorance, although that is also a way of remembering the war in Guatemala, as in many postwars. It is also different from being forced to do something. Duping suggests you went willingly but under false pretenses. What you assumed to be true was not. What you took for granted was wrong. Perhaps you ended up doing something or being someone you did not intend to be. Claiming to be duped is a way to admit you did something but to avoid full responsibility. It occurred, but it's not your fault. If you've been duped, the deflation felt when the con is revealed can be laughing bewilderment or red-faced embarrassment about being taken. You assumed, and it made an ass out of u and me. You're a sucker, a rube. (2009, 12)

46. Michel Foucault, *Discipline and Punish: The Birth of the Prison* (1995, 297); Paul Amar, *The Security Archipelago: Human-Security States, Sexuality Politics, and the End of Neoliberalism* (2013).

47. Michel Foucault, *Discipline and Punish* (1995, 200).

48. Michel Foucault, *Discipline and Punish* (1995, 308).

49. Teresa P. R. Caldeira, *City of Walls: Crime, Segregation, and Citizenship in São Paulo* (2000).

50. Teresa P. R. Caldeira, "Fortified Enclaves: The New Urban Segregation" (1999, 130).

51. Kevin Lewis O'Neill and Kedron Thomas, *Securing the City: Neoliberalism, Space, and Insecurity in Postwar Guatemala* (2011).

52. Dennis Rodgers, "'Disembedding' the City: Crime, Insecurity and Spatial Organization in Managua, Nicaragua": "The fortified network of the urban elites excludes others from specific locations, but also from the roads and intersections in the city that connect these locations. In doing so, it actively encroaches on the public space of the city in a much more extensive way than fortified enclaves do, 'ripping out'—to use Doña Yolanda's expression—large swathes of the metropolis for the sole use of the urban elites" (2004, 123). Note that Rodgers borrows the term from Anthony Giddens, who uses it to describe how social, cultural and economic relations can become detached from their localized contexts as a result of modernity and globalization. See Giddens's *The Consequences of Modernity* (1990), *Modernity and Self-Identity: Self and Society in the Late Modern Age* (1991), and *Runaway World: How Globalisation is Reshaping our Lives* (1999).

53. David Harvey, "The Right to the City" (2003).

54. Ignacio Ellacuría and Jon Sobrino, *Mysterium Liberationis: Fundamental Concepts of Liberation Theology* (2004). "Liberation is attainable," announces Alvaro Quiroz Magaña in chapter 9; "indeed [it] is part and parcel of God's salvific plan. It is committed praxis, which seeks to overcome, with lucidity, all forms (so often dissimulated and concealed) of slavery, exploitation, institutionalized violence, and socioeconomic marginalization" (196).

55. Ignacio Ellacuría and Jon Sobrino, *Mysterium Liberationis* (2004). "[Liberation theology] sees transcendence as something that transcends *in*," writes Ellacuría, "and not as something that transcends *away from*; as something that physically impels to *more* but not by taking *out of*; as something that pushes *forward*, but at the same time *retains*" (254).

56. Ignacio Ellacuría and Jon Sobrino, *Mysterium Liberationis* (2004). "This does not mean reducing God to history," writes Ellacuría, "on the contrary, it means elevating history to God, an elevation that becomes possible only because Yahweh has previously descended to it through Moses" (262).

57. For temporal distancing, see Johannes Fabian, *Time and the Other: How Anthropology Makes Its Object* ([1983] 2002): "All personal experience is produced under historical conditions, in historical contexts; it must be used with critical awareness and with constant attention to its authoritative claims. The hermeneutic stance presupposes a degree of distancing, an objectification of our experiences. That the anthropologist's experienced Other is necessarily part of his past may therefore not be an impediment, but a condition of an interpretive approach"(89). For integral development, see Paul VI, *Populorum Progressio* [Encyclical Letter on the Development of Peoples] (1967): "The hungry nations of the world cry out to the peoples blessed with abundance, and the Church, cut to the quick by this cry, asks each and every man to hear his brother's plea and answer it lovingly."

58. Oscar Romero, *The Violence of Love* ([1988] 2004). "There is no dichotomy between man and God's image," writes Bishop Romero. "Whoever tortures a human being, whoever abuses a human being, whoever outrages a human being abuses God's image, and the church takes as its own that cross, that martyrdom" (26).

59. James Ferguson, "Decomposing Modernity: History and Hierarchy after Development" (2006a): "De-temporalized statuses are not the only alternative to the developmentalist vision of progressive stages. Another possibility exists, in the form of nonprogressive temporalizations. That is, statuses and conditions of peoples and nations may be understood to change over time, but not in a progressive way" (190).

60. Samuel Beckett, *Waiting for Godot: A Tragicomedy in Two Acts* (1954).

61. Jon Sobrino, *The Principle of Mercy: Taking the Crucified People from the Cross* (1994, 173).

62. Ignacio Ellacuría and Jon Sobrino, *Mysterium Liberationis* (2004). "In Latin America this prophetic march towards utopia is driven by a great hope," writes Ellacuría, "Beyond all rhetoric and in spite of all the difficulties, there are rivers of hope on the continent. Christian hope thus becomes one of the most efficacious dynamisms for going out of the land of oppression and toward the land of promise" (304).

ADRIFT

1. As noted in the introduction, hard security and soft security mirror two more generalizable forms of security. The former mirrors what Stephen Collier calls sovereign state security. These are the "practices oriented to the defense of

territorial sovereignty against foreign enemies using military means" (2008, 36; see also Foucault 2007, 65). Soft security resembles what Collier defines as population security. This is the "protection of the national population against regularly occurring internal threats, such as illness, industrial accident, or infirmity" (2008, 36). Yet, both sovereign state security and population security make the state central, which is not realistic for postwar Guatemala. This book pursues the question of security without the state. Peter Redfield raises a parallel question in his "Bioexpectations: Life Technologies as Humanitarian Goods" (2012).

2. Tania Li (2010) makes a very smart, very impassioned argument otherwise: "Both letting die, and making live, have a politics, but I reject the idea that the two are in some kind of functional equilibrium—that it is necessary to select some to die, in order for others to live. No doubt such selections are made, according to a whole range of rationales (race, virtue, diligence, citizenship, location, age, gender, efficiency, affordability; see Sider 2006) but if 'the point is to change it', we cannot concede that selection is necessary. It is possible for social forces to mobilize in a wholly make live direction" (67).

3. Augustine, *Confessions and Enchiridion* (1955, 36).

4. Augustine, *Confessions and Enchiridion* (1955, 33).

5. Augustine, *Confessions and Enchiridion* (1955, 131).

6. Augustine, *Confessions and Enchiridion* (1955, 140).

7. Augustine, *Confessions and Enchiridion* (1955, 206).

8. For work on the intersection of social disposability and bare death, see Henry A. Giroux, "Reading Hurricane Katrina: Race, Class, and the Biopolitics of Disposability" (2006); Achille Mbembe, "Necropolitics" (2003); Orlando Patterson, "Authority, Alienation, and Social Death" (1982); and Eugene Thacker, "Necrologies; Or, the Death of the Body Politic" (2011).

9. Clare Ribando Seelke writes, "Tough anti-gang approaches carried out in the mid-2000s . . . failed to stave off rising crime rates in the region and had several negative unintended consequences. As a result, recent studies maintain that governments appear to be moving away from enforcement-only policies towards 'second generation' anti-gang programs. Newer programs have emphasized, among other things, prevention programs for at-risk youth, interventions to encourage youth to leave gangs, and the creation of municipal alliances against crime and violence" (2013, 9). It is this self-conscious move to the second generation, at the expense of the first generation, that should warrant some pause. For statistics on population and age, see Carlos Rosales (USAID Guatemala), "Prevention and Youth Are the Solution" (2012).

Reference List

Acuña, Claudia. 2008. "Masacre en Pavoncito; Siete reclusos muertos." *Prensa Libre*, November 23.

Adams, Jay. 1986. *The Biblical View of Self-Esteem, Self-Love, and Self-Image.* Eugene, OR Harvest House.

Adams, Richard N. 1970. *Crucifixion by Power: Essays on Guatemalan National Social Structure, 1944–1966.* Austin, TX: University of Texas Press.

Agamben, Giorgio. 1998. *Homo Sacer: Sovereignty and Bare Life.* Translated by Daniel Heller-Roazen. Stanford, CA: Stanford University Press.

———. 2001. "Security and Terror." *Theory and Event* 5, no. 4.

———. 2004. "Non au tatouage biopolitique." *Le Monde*, January 10. http://www.egs.edu/faculty/giorgio-agamben/articles/non-au-tatouage-biopolitique/.

———. 2005. *State of Exception.* Translated by Kevin Attell. Chicago: University of Chicago Press.

Agencia de Atracción de Inversiones and Invest in Guatemala. 2009. *Guía para el inversionista.* Accessed July 15, 2011. http://www.investinguatemala.org/pdf/guia_del_inversionista.pdf.

Agrama, Hussein Ali. 2010. "Secularism, Sovereignty, Indeterminacy: Is Egypt a Secular or a Religious State?" *Comparative Studies in Society and History* 52, no. 3:495–523.

Aguilar, Jeannette. 2006. "Los efectos contraproducentes de los Planes Mano Dura." *Quorum* 16:81–94.

Ahmed, Sara. 2010. *The Promise of Happiness.* Durham, NC: Duke University Press.

Albanese, Catherine. 2007. *A Republic of Mind and Spirit: A Cultural History of American Metaphysical Religion.* New Haven, CT: Yale University Press.

Alcott, Louisa May. 1872. *Little Women.* London: Spottiswoode.

Alexander, Michelle. 2010. *The New Jim Crow: Mass Incarceration in the Age of Colorblindness.* New York: New Press.

Allison, Anne. 2013. *Precarious Japan.* Durham, NC: Duke University Press.

Almeida, Paul D. 2008. *Waves of Protest: Popular Struggle in El Salvador, 1925–2005.* Minneapolis: University of Minnesota Press.

Alston, Philip. 2011. "A Good Place to Commit Murder." In *The Guatemala Reader: History, Culture, Politics,* edited by Greg Grandin, Deborah T. Levenson, and Elizabeth Oglesby, 473–79. Durham, NC: Duke University Press.

Althoff, Andrea. 2005. "Religion im Wandel: Einflüsse von Ethnizität auf die Religiöse Ordnung am Beispiel Guatemalas." PhD diss., Martin-Luther-Universität Halle-Wittenberg.

Amar, Paul. 2013. *The Security Archipelago: Human-Security States, Sexuality Politics, and the End of Neoliberalism.* Durham, NC: Duke University Press.

Amnesty International. 2003. "El Salvador: Open Letter on the Anti-Maras Act." http://www.amnesty.org/en/report/info/AMR29/009/2003.

Anderson, Nels. 1923. *The Hobo: The Sociology of the Homeless Man.* Chicago: University of Chicago Press.

Andreas, Peter, and Ethan Nadelmann. 2006. *Policing the Globe: Criminalization and Crime Control in International Relations.* New York: Oxford University Press.

Andrejevic, Mark. 2007. *iSpy: Surveillance and Power in the Interactive Era.* Lawrence, KS: University Press of Kansas.

Anidjar, Gil. 2009. "The Idea of an Anthropology of Christianity." *Interventions* 11, no. 3 (November):367–93.

Arana, Ana. 2005. "How the Street Gangs Took Central America." *Foreign Affairs* 84, no. 3:98–110. http://www.foreignaffairs.com/articles/60803/ana-arana/how-the-street-gangs-took-central-america.

Archibold, Randal C., and Damien Cave. 2011. "Drug Wars Push Deeper into Central America." *New York Times,* March 23.

Arias, Enrique Desmond. 2006. *Drugs and Democracy in Rio de Janeiro: Trafficking, Social Networks and Public Security.* Chapel Hill, NC: University of North Carolina Press.

Arnson, Cynthia J., and Eric L. Olson, eds. 2011. *Organized Crime in Central America: The Northern Triangle.* Woodrow Wilson Center Report on the Americas no. 29, November. Washington, DC: Woodrow Wilson Center International Center for Scholars, Latin America Program. http://www.wilsoncenter.org/sites/default/files/LAP_single_page.pdf.

"Arrests in Guatemala Jail Killing." 2007. BBC News, "Americas," February 27. http://news.bbc.co.uk/2/hi/americas/6399381.stm.

Asad, Talal. 1986. *The Idea of an Anthropology of Islam.* Occasional Papers Series. Washington, DC: Center for Contemporary Arab Studies, Georgetown University.

———. 2003. *Formations of the Secular: Christianity, Islam, Modernity.* Stanford, CA: Stanford University Press.

———. 2007. *On Suicide Bombing.* New York: Columbia University Press.

Augustine. 1955. *Confessions and Enchiridion.* Translated by Albert C. Outler. Philadelphia: Westminister Press.

Auyero, Javier. 2012. *Patients of the State*. Durham, NC: Duke University Press

Ball, Karyn. 2006. "A Democracy Is Being Beaten." *ESC: English Studies in Canada* 32, no. 1:45–76.

Barley, Stephen R., and Gideon Kunda. 1992. "Design and Devotion: Surges of Rational and Normative Ideologies of Control in Managerial Discourse." *Administrative Science Quarterly* 37, no. 3:363–99.

Barnes, Nielan. 2007. *Pandillas juveniles transnacionales en Centroamérica, México y los Estados Unidos: Resumen ejecutivo*. Mexico City: Centro de Estudios y Programas Interamericanos (CEPI) del Instituto Tecnológico Autónomo de México (ITAM). http://interamericanos.itam.mx/maras/docs/Resumen_Ejecutivo_Espanol.pdf.

Barthes, Roland. 1974. *S/Z: An Essay*. Translated by Richard Miller. New York: Hill and Wang.

Bateson, Gregory. 1972. *Steps to an Ecology of Mind*. New York: Ballantine.

Beaumont, Gustave de, and Alexis de Tocqueville. (1833) 1964. *On the Penitentiary System in the United States and Its Application in France*. Perspectives in Sociology. Carbondale, IL: Southern Illinois University Press.

Beckett, Samuel. 1954. *Waiting for Godot: A Tragicomedy in Two Acts*. New York: Grove Press.

Behar, Ruth. 2003. *Translated Woman: Crossing the Border with Esperanza's Story*. Tenth anniversary ed. Boston, MA: Beacon Press.

"Beheadings in Guatemala Jail Fight." 2008. Al Jazeera, November 23. http://www.aljazeera.com/news/americas/2008/11/2008112321234930644.html.

Beidelman, Thomas. 1982. *Colonial Evangelism: A Socio-Historical Study of an East African Mission at the Grassroots*. Bloomington: Indiana University Press.

Beittel, June S. 2013. *Mexico's Drug Trafficking Organizations: Source and Scope of the Violence*. CRS Report R41576, April 15. Washington, DC: Congressional Research Service. http://www.fas.org/sgp/crs/row/R41576.pdf.

Bender, John. 1987. *Imagining the Penitentiary: Fiction and the Architecture of Mind in Eighteenth-Century England*. Chicago: University of Chicago Press.

Benson, Peter, Edward F. Fischer, and Kedron Thomas. 2008. "Resocializing Suffering: Neoliberalism, Accusation, and the Sociopolitical Context of Guatemala's New Violence." *Latin American Perspectives* 35, no. 5:38–58.

Berlant, Lauren. 1994. "'68, or Something." *Critical Inquiry* 21, no. 1:124–55.

———. 2011. *Cruel Optimism*. Durham, NC: Duke University Press.

———. 2012. "Lauren Berlant on Her Book *Cruel Optimism*." *Rorotoko*, June 5. http://rorotoko.com/interview/20120605_berlant_lauren_on_cruel_optimism/.

Bernays, Edward L. 1928. *Propaganda*. New York: Routledge.

Berrios, German E., and Margaret Gili. 1995. "The Will and Its Disorders." *History of Psychiatry* 6:87–104.

Bhabha, Homi K. 1992. "Post-Colonial Authority and Postmodern Guilt." In *Cultural Studies,* edited by Lawrence Grossberg, Cary Nelson, and Paula Treichler, 56–68. New York: Routledge.

Biehl, João. 2005. *Vita: Life in a Zone of Social Abandonment*. Berkeley, CA: University of California Press.

Biron, Carey L. 2013. "More Countries Turn to Faltering U.S. Prison Privatisation Model." Inter Press Service, August 20. http://www.ipsnews.net/2013/08/more-countries-turn-to-faltering-u-s-prison-privatisation-model/.

Bishop, Matthew, and Michael Green. 2008. *Philanthrocapitalism: How Giving Can Save the World*. New York: Bloomsbury Press.

Bloom, Mia. 2005. *Dying to Kill: The Allure of Suicide Terror*. New York: Columbia University Press.

Blum, Virginia L. 2007. "Objects of Love: *I Want a Famous Face* and the Illusions of Star Culture." *Configurations* 15, no. 1. (Winter):33–53.

Bornstein, Erica. 2005. *The Spirit of Development: Protestant NGOs, Morality, and Economics in Zimbabwe*. Stanford, CA: Stanford University Press.

Bourdieu, Pierre. 1977. *Outline of a Theory of Practice*. Translated by Richard Nice. Cambridge: Cambridge University Press.

———. 1984. *Distinction: A Social Critique of the Judgement of Taste*. Translated by Richard Nice. Cambridge, MA: Harvard University Press.

Bourgois, Philippe. 1996. *In Search of Respect: Selling Crack in El Barrio*. Cambridge: Cambridge University Press.

———. 2002. "The Violence of Moral Binaries: Response to Leigh Binford." *Ethnography* 3, no. 2:221–31.

Bourke, Vernon. 1964. *Will in Western Thought*. New York: Sheed and Ward.

Boyer, Jodie. 2013. "Sin and Sanity in Nineteenth-Century America." PhD diss., University of Toronto.

Bracken, Christopher. 2007. *Magical Criticism: The Recourse of Savage Philosophy*. Chicago: University of Chicago Press.

Branche, Jerome. 2006. *Colonialism and Race in Luso-Hispanic Literature*. Columbia, MO: University of Missouri Press.

Brandes, Stuart D. 1984. *American Welfare Capitalism, 1880–1940*. Chicago: University of Chicago Press.

Brenneman, Robert. 2012. *Homies and Hermanos: God and Gangs in Central America*. Oxford: Oxford University Press.

Brodhead, Richard. 1988. "Sparing the Rod: Discipline and Fiction in Antebellum America." *Representations* 21:67–96.

Brotherton, David, and Luis Barrios. 2013. *The Almighty Latin King and Queen Nation: Street Politics and the Transformation of a New York City Gang*. New York: Columbia University Press.

Brown, Karen McCarthy. 2001. *Mama Lola: A Vodou Priestess in Brooklyn*. Rev. ed. Berkeley, CA: University of California Press.

Bruneau, Thomas, Lucía Dammert, and Elizabeth Skinner, eds. 2011. *Maras: Gang Violence and Security in Central America*. Austin, TX: University of Texas Press.

Buchanan, Patrick J. 1992. "1992 Republican National Convention Speech." Patrick J. Buchanan Official Website. http://buchanan.org/blog/1992-republican-national-convention-speech-148.

Bumas, E. Shaskan. 2001. "Fictions of the Panopticon: Prison, Utopia, and the Out-Penitent in the Works of Nathaniel Hawthorne." *American Literature* 73, no. 1:121–45.

Bunyan, John. (1837) 1998. *Pilgrim's Progress in Modern English*. Edited by L. Edward Hazelbaker. Alachua, FL: Bridge-Logos.

Burroughs, Richard Whosoever. 2011. "Children International." Facebook. Note. https://www.facebook.com/notes/richard-burroughs/children-international /10150649246885082.

Byers, Sara. 2007. "Augustine on the 'Divided Self': Platonist or Stoic?" *Augustinian Studies* 38, no. 1:105–18.

Caldeira, Teresa P.R. 1999. "Fortified Enclaves: The New Urban Segregation." In *Cities and Citizenship*, edited by James Holston, 114–38. Durham, NC: Duke University Press.

———. 2000. *City of Walls: Crime, Segregation, and Citizenship in São Paulo*. Berkeley, CA: University of California Press.

Callahan, Richard J., Kathryn Lofton, and Chad E. Seales. 2010. "Allegories of Progress: Industrial Religion in the United States." *Journal of the American Academy of Religion* 78, no. 1:1–39.

Cameron, Ann. 2011. *The Most Beautiful Place in the World*. New York: Random House.

Campus Coalitions for Human Rights and Social Justice. 1995. "California at a Crossroads: Social Strife or Social Unity?" *Social Justice* 22, no. 3: 53–63.

Cantón Delgado, Manuela. 1998. *Bautizados en fuego: Protestantes, discursos de conversión y política en Guatemala (1989–1993)*. Antigua, Guatemala: Centro de Investigaciones Regionales de Mesoamérica.

Carlaw, Malcolm, Kurt Friedmann, Vasudha Kathleen Deming, and Peggy Carlaw. 2002. *Managing and Motivating Contact Center Employees: Tools and Techniques for Inspiring Outstanding Performance from Your Frontline Staff*. New York: McGraw-Hill.

Carmack, Robert M., ed. 1988. *Harvest of Violence: The Maya Indians and the Guatemalan Crisis*. Norman, OK: University of Oklahoma Press.

Carpenter, Ted Galen. 2003. *Bad Neighbor Policy: Washington's Futile War on Drugs in Latin America*. New York: Palgrave MacMillan.

Carroll, Rosy. 2008. "Five Inmates Beheaded After Rival Jail Gangs Clash." *Guardian*, November 24.

Cary, Phillip. 2000. *Augustine's Invention of the Inner Self: The Legacy of a Christian Platonist*. New York: Oxford University Press.

Castañon, Mariela. 2011. "Las diez zonas más peligrosas de Guatemala." *La Hora*, November. http://lahora.com.gt/index.php/nacional/guatemala/reportajes-y-entrevistas/148368-las-diez-zonas-mas-peligrosas-de-guatemala.

———. 2012. "Estiman que 95 mil pandilleros operan en triángulo norte." *La Hora*, February 18. http://www.lahora.com.gt/index.php/nacional/guatemala/actualidad/153439-estiman-que-95-mil-pandilleros-operan-en-triangulo-norte.

Cattelino, Jessica R. 2010. "The Double Bind of American Indian Need-Based Sovereignty." *Cultural Anthropology* 25, no. 2:235–62.

Cavanaugh, William T. 2009. *The Myth of Religious Violence: Secular Ideology and the Roots of Modern Conflict*. New York: Oxford University Press.

Central American Human Rights Council Ombudsman. 2006. *Regional Report: Situation and Analysis of Femicide in Central American Region*. San José, Costa Rica.

Centro de Estudios de Guatemala (CEG) and European Union. 2012. *Las múltiples violencias y las juventudes*. Ciudad del Guatemala: CEG and European Union. http://issuu.com/ueprogramajuventud/docs/las_multiples_violencias_1/27?e=0.

Chabram-Dernersesian, Angie. 2006. "I Throw Punches for My Race But I Don't Want to Be a Man: Writing Us—Chica-Nos (Girl, Us)/Chicanas—into the Movement Script." In *The Chicana/o Cultural Studies Reader*, edited by Angie Chabram-Dernersesian, 165–82. New York: Routledge.

Chamayou, Grégoire. 2012. *Manhunts: A Philosophical History*. Translated by Steven Rendall. Princeton, NJ: Princeton University Press.

Chandler, David. 2008. "Review Article: Theorising the Shift from Security to Insecurity—Kaldor, Duffield and Furedi." *Conflict, Security & Development* 8, no. 2 (June):265–76.

Chemerinsky, Erwin. 2004. "Life in Prison for Shoplifting: Cruel and Unusual Punishment." *Human Rights* 31, no. 1:11–13.

Cherbuliez, Antoine. 1862. *Précis de la science économique*. 2 vols. Paris: Guillaumin. https://archive.org/details/prcisdelasciencoounkngoog.

Children International. 2013a. "Answer the Prayers of a Child in Need Brochure." Kansas City, MO. http://video.children.org/Advocate_Center/Documents/LiftOneDaySponsorshipBrochure0811.pdf.

———. 2013b. "End the Waiting for One Needy Child. Become a Sponsor Today!" Kansas City, MO. http://video.children.org/Advocate_Center/Documents/CI_Sponsorship_Brochure.pdf.

———. 2013c. "Share Your Blessings, Sponsor a Needy Child Today! Brochure." Kansas City, MO. http://video.children.org/Advocate_Center/Documents/FaithBasedSponsorshipBrochure10.pdf.

Clark, Campbell. 2013. "Attorney-General Brings Hope to Guatemala by Taking a Bite Out of Crime." *Globe and Mail*, October 16. http://www.theglobeandmail.com/news/politics/attorney-general-brings-hope-to-guatemala-by-taking-a-bite-out-of-crime/article14900071/.

Clawson, Patrick L., and Rensselaer W. Lee III. 1998. *The Andean Cocaine Industry*. New York: St. Martin's Griffin.

Coatsworth, John H. 1994. *Central America and the United States: The Clients and the Colossus*. Boston: Twayne.

Cohen, Lizabeth. 2003. *A Consumer's Republic: The Politics of Mass Consumption in Postwar America*. New York: Vintage.

Coleman, Simon. 2000. *The Globalisation of Charismatic Christianity: Spreading the Gospel of Prosperity*. Cambridge: Cambridge University Press.

Collier, Stephen J. 2008. "Enacting Catastrophe: Preparedness, Insurance, Budgetary Rationalization." *Economy and Society* 37, no. 2:224–50.

Comaroff, Jean. 1991. "Missionaries and Mechanical Clocks: An Essay on Religion and History in South Africa." *The Journal of Religion* 71, no. 1:1–17.

Comaroff, Jean, and John Comaroff. 1986. "Christianity and Colonialism in South Africa." *American Ethnologist* 13, no. 1:1–22.

———. 1997. *Of Revelation and Revolution*. Vol. 2, *The Dialectics of Modernity on a South African Frontier*. Chicago: University of Chicago Press.

Comisión Internacional contra la Impunidad en Guatemala (CICIG). 2013. "Court Sentences Perpetrators of Extra-Judicial Killings." Press release 41, August 8. Guatemala. http://cicig.org/index.php?mact = News,cntnto1,detai l,o&cntnto1articleid = 421&cntnto1returnid = 105.

Comisión para el Esclarecimiento Histórico (CEH). 1999. *Guatemala, memoria del silencio.* 5 vols. Guatemala: Oficina de Servicios para Proyectos de last Naciones Unidas (UNOPS). http://www.centrodememoriahistorica.gov.co/ descargas/guatemala-memoria-silencio/guatemala-memoria-del-silencio.pdf.

Compassion International. 2009. "I Find It Difficult to Write Letters to My Sponsored Child." http://compassionca.custhelp.com/app/answers/detail/a_ id/33/~/i-find-it-difficult-to-write-letters-to-my-sponsored-child.

———. 2011. "Value of Letter Writing." YouTube video. http://www.youtube. com/Cqx93WSk2UM.

———. 2012. "Write to Your Sponsored Child: Show How Much You Care." https://www.compassion.ca/writing-your-child/.

Connolly, William. 2008. *Capitalism and Christianity, American Style.* Durham, NC: Duke University Press.

Corbett, Steve, and Brian Fikkert. 2009. *When Helping Hurts: How to Alleviate Poverty Without Hurting the Poor . . . and Yourself.* Chicago: Moody.

Corten, André. 1997. "The Growth of the Literature on Afro-American, Latin American and African Pentecostalism." *Journal of Contemporary Religion* 12, no. 3:311–30.

Countercamera. 2009. "Reality Show *Desafío X* (2/2)." YouTube video. Uploaded December 7. http://youtu.be/9jnSNbFr6XM.

Coutin, Susan Bibler. 2003a. "Suspension of Deportation Hearings: Racialization, Immigration, and 'Americanness.'" *Journal of Latin American Anthropology* 8, no. 2:58–95.

———. 2003b. "Cultural Logics of Belonging and Movement: Transnationalism, Naturalization, and U.S. Immigration Politics." *American Ethnologist* 30, no. 4:508–26.

———. 2011. "Falling Outside: Excavating the History of Central American Asylum Seekers." *Law and Social Inquiry* 33, no. 1:569–96.

Crane, Johanna Tayloe. 2013. *Scrambling for Africa: AIDS, Expertise, and the Rise of American Global Health Science.* Ithaca, NY: Cornell University Press.

Crapanzano, Vincent. 1985. *Tuhami: Portrait of a Moroccan.* Chicago: University of Chicago Press.

Creative Associates International. 2006. "Guatemala: Reality Show Shines Bright Lights on Ex-Gang Members Trying to Do Good." http://www.creativeassociatesinternational.com/CAIIStaff/Dashboard_GIROAdminCAI-IStaff/Dashboard_CAIIAdminDatabase/CAIIAdminSupplemental.aspx?SurveyID=1932&SectionID=530.

———. 2009. "*Desafío 100.*" YouTube video. Uploaded May 26. http://www .youtube.com/pH5f5O5A2yQ.

Crowley, John. 2000. "Liberal Values, Liberal Guilt, and the Distaste for Politics." In *The Meaning of Liberalism: East and West,* edited by Zdeněk Suda and Jiří Musil, 47–72. Budapest: Central European University Press.

Cruikshank, Barbara. 1996. "Revolutions Within: Self-Government and Self-Esteem." In *Foucault and Political Reason: Liberalism, Neo-Liberalism, and Rationalities of Government*, edited by Andrew Barry, Thomas Osborne, and Nikolas Rose, 231–51. Chicago: University of Chicago Press.

———. 1999. *The Will to Empower: Democratic Citizens and Other Subjects*. Ithaca, NY: Cornell University Press.

Cruz, José Miguel, ed. 2006. *Maras y pandillas en Centroamérica*. Vol. 4, *Las respuestas de la sociedad civil organizada*. Colección Estructuras y procesos, serie mayor 23. San Salvador: UCA Editores.

D'Ausilio, Rosanne. 1998. *Wake Up Your Call Center: Humanizing Your Interaction Hub*. West Lafayette, IN: Purdue University Press.

Dahl, Bianca. 2009. "Left Behind? Orphaned Children, Humanitarian Aid, and the Politics of Kinship, Culture, and Caregiving during Botswana's AIDS Crisis." PhD diss., University of Chicago. Proquest 3369321.

———. n.d. "Singing with 'Sad Faces': Grieving Orphans and the Emotional Economy of Humanitarian Aid in Botswana." Unpublished manuscript.

Davis, Mike. 2007. *Planet of Slums*. London: Verso.

Deacon, Roger. 2000. "Theory as Practice: Foucault's Concept of Problematization." *Telos* 118:127–42.

De Boever, Arne. 2008. "Biopolitics in Deconstruction." Presentation at 2008 Workshop of the Derrida Seminars Translation Project, Caen, France, July. http://derridaseminars.org/pdfs/2008/Boever_2008_presentation.pdf.

DeCesare, Donna. 2013. *Unsettled/Desasosiego: Los niños en un mundo de las pandillas*. Austin, TX: University of Texas Press.

Deery, June. 2004. "Reality TV as Advertisement." *Popular Communication* 2, no. 1:1–20.

Deleuze, Gilles. 1988a. *Foucault*. Translated by Sean Hand. London: Athlone.

———. 1988b. *Spinoza: Practical Philosophy*. Translated by Robert Hurley. San Francisco: City Lights Books.

———. 1990. "Post-scriptum sur les sociétés de contrôle." *L'Autre Journal* 1:3–7.

———. 1992. "Postscript on the Societies of Control." *October* 59 (Winter):3–7.

Deleuze, Gilles, and Félix Guattari. 2001. *A Thousand Plateaus: Capitalism & Schizophrenia*. London: Continuum.

De Mello, Anthony. 1988. *Autoliberación interior*. Buenos Aires: Editorial Lumen.

Derrida, Jacques. 1990. "Force of Law: The Mystical Foundation of Authority." *Cardozo Law Review* 11, no. 5–6:920–1045.

———. 1998. "Faith and Knowledge: The Two Sources of 'Religion' at the Limits of Reason Alone." In *Religion*, edited by Jacques Derrida and Gianni Vattimo, 1–78. Stanford, CA: Stanford University Press.

———. 2009. *The Beast and the Sovereign*. Vol. 1. Chicago: University of Chicago Press.

Desjarlais, Robert R. 2003. *Sensory Biographies: Lives and Deaths among Nepal's Yolmo Buddhists*. Berkeley, CA: University of California Press.

De Vries, Hent. 2002. *Religion and Violence: Philosophical Perspectives from Kant to Derrida*. Baltimore, MD: Johns Hopkins University Press.

Diaz, Thomas. 2009. *No Boundaries: Transnational Latino Gangs and American Law Enforcement*. Ann Arbor, MI: University of Michigan Press.

Dickinson, Elizabeth. 2009. "A Bright Shining Slogan." *Foreign Affairs*, August 13.

Didion, Joan. 1968. *Slouching towards Bethlehem: Essays*. New York: Farrar, Straus, & Giroux.

Douglas, Mary. 1972. "Deciphering a Meal." Edited by Clifford Geertz. *Daedalus* 101, no. 1:61–81.

Dovey, Jon. 2000. *Freakshow: First Person Media and Factual Television*. London: Pluto Press.

Doyle, Aaron. 2003. *Arresting Images: Crime and Policing in Front of the Television Camera*. Toronto: University of Toronto Press.

Drucker, Peter F. 1999. *Management Challenges for the 21st Century*. New York: HarperBusiness.

Dubler, Joshua. 2013. *Down in the Chapel: Religious Life in an American Prison*. New York: Farrar, Straus, & Giroux.

Dudley, Steven. 2012. *Transnational Crime in Mexico and Central America: Its Evolution and Role in International Migration*. Washington, DC: Migration Policy Institute.

Duffield, Mark. 2007. *Development, Security and Unending War: Governing the World of Peoples*. London: Polity.

Eagleton, Terry. 2005. *Holy Terror*. New York: Oxford University Press.

Elisha, Omri. 2011. *Moral Ambition: Mobilization and Social Outreach in Evangelical Megachurches*. Berkeley, CA: University of California Press.

Ellacuría, Ignacio, and Jon Sobrino, eds. 2004. *Mysterium Liberationis: Fundamental Concepts of Liberation Theology*. New York: Orbis Books.

Ellens, J. Harold, ed. 2004. *The Destructive Power of Religion: Violence in Judaism, Christianity, and Islam*. Westport, CT: Praeger.

Ellison, Julie. 1996. "A Short History of Liberal Guilt." *Critical Inquiry* 22, no. 2:344–71.

"Empresa Allied inaugura centro de atención telefónica en Guatemala; Inauguran contact center de $3 millones." 2009. *Siglo Veintiuno*, October 30.

Engelke, Matthew. 2007. *A Problem of Presence: Beyond Scripture in an African Church*. Berkeley, CA: University of California Press.

ERIC, IDESO, IDIES, and IUDOP. 2001. *Maras y pandillas en Centroamérica*. Vol. 1. Colección Estructuras y procesos, serie mayor 23. Managua: UCA Publicaciones.

———. 2004. *Maras y pandillas en Centroamérica*. Vol. 2, *Pandillas y capital social*. Colección Estructuras y procesos, serie mayor 23. San Salvador: UCA Editores.

ERIC, IDIES, IUDOP, NITLAPAN, and DIRINPRO. 2004. *Maras y pandillas en Centroamérica*. Vol. 3, *Políticas juveniles y rehabilitación*. Colección Estructuras y procesos, serie mayor 23. Managua: UCA Publicaciones.

Erzen, Tanya. 2006. *Straight to Jesus: Sexual and Christian Conversions in the Ex-Gay Movement*. Berkeley, CA: University of California Press

Executive Boutique. 2011. "Call Center Career Tips: The Value of Punctuality." http://ebcallcenter.com/blog/call-center-career-tips-the-value-of-punctuality.

Fabian, Johannes. (1983) 2002. *Time and the Other: How Anthropology Makes Its Object*. New York: Columbia University Press.

Falla, Ricardo. 1992. *Masacres de la selva: Ixcán, Guatemala, 1975–1982*. Colección 500 años. Guatemala: Editorial Universitaria, Universidad de San Carlos de Guatemala.

Farah, Douglas, and Pamela Phillips Lum. 2013. *Central American Gangs and Transnational Criminal Organizations: The Changing Relationships in a Time of Turmoil*. Report, February. Alexandria, VA: International Assessment and Strategy Center. http://www.strategycenter.net/docLib/20130224_CenAmGangsandTCOs.pdf.

Farr, Thomas F. 2008. *World of Faith: Why Religious Freedom Is Key to American National Security in the 21st Century*. New York: Oxford University Press.

Feilding, Amanda, and Corina Giacomello. 2013a. *Illicit Drugs Markets and Dimensions of Violence in Guatemala*. Oxford, U.K.: Beckley Foundation. http://www.beckleyfoundation.org/Illicit-Drug-Markets.pdf.

———. 2013b. *Paths for Reform: Proposed Options for Alternative Drug Policies in Guatemala*. Oxford, U.K.: Beckley Foundation. http://www.beckleyfoundation.org/Paths-for-Reform.pdf.

Felbab-Brown, Vanda. 2013. *Peña Nieto's Piñata: The Promise and Pitfalls of Mexico's New Security Policy against Organized Crime*. Paper, February. Washington, DC: Brookings Institution. http://www.brookings.edu/research/papers/2013/02/mexico-new-security-policy-felbabbrown.

Ferguson, James. 1994. *The Anti-Politics Machine: "Development," Depoliticization, and Bureaucratic Power in Lesotho*. Minneapolis: University of Minnesota Press.

———. 2006a. "Decomposing Modernity: History and Hierarchy after Development." In *Global Shadows: Africa in the Neoliberal World Order*, 176–93. Durham, NC: Duke University Press.

———. 2006b. *Global Shadows: Africa in the Neoliberal World Order*. Durham, NC: Duke University Press.

Ferrari, Leo C. 1980. "Paul at the Conversion of Augustine." *Augustinian Studies* 11:5–20.

———. 1984. *The Conversions of St. Augustine*. Villanova, PA: Villanova University Press.

Fessenden, Tracy. 2007. *Culture and Redemption: Religion, the Secular, and American Literature*. Princeton, NJ: Princeton University Press.

Fischer, Edward F., and Peter Benson, eds. 2006. *Broccoli and Desire: Global Connections and Maya Struggles in Postwar Guatemala*. Stanford, CA: Stanford University Press.

Fischer, Edward F., and R. McKenna Brown, eds. 1996. *Maya Cultural Activism in Guatemala*. Austin, TX: University of Texas Press.

Fischer, Michael M.J. 1991. "The Uses of Life Histories." *Anthropology and Humanism* 16, no. 1:24–27.

Fischman, David. 2003. *El camino del líder*. Madrid: Alfaguara.

Fleisher, Mark. 1989. *Warehousing Violence*. Newbury Park, CA: Sage.

Flores, Edward Orozco. 2013. *God's Gangs: Barrio Ministry, Masculinity, and Gang Recovery*. New York: New York University Press.

Foucault, Michel. 1984. "Space, Knowledge, and Power." In *The Foucault Reader*, edited by Paul Rabinow, 239–56. New York: Pantheon.

———. 1988. *Technologies of the Self: A Seminar with Michel Foucault*. Edited by Luther H. Martin, Huck Gutman, and Patrick H. Hutton. Amherst, MA: University of Massachusetts Press.

———. 1990. *The History of Sexuality*. Vol. 2, *The Use of Pleasure*. London: Vintage.

———. 1991. "Governmentality." In *The Foucault Effect: Studies in Governmentality*, edited by Graham Burchell, Colin Gordon, and Peter Miller, 87–104. Chicago: University of Chicago Press.

———. 1994a. *Dits et Écrits*. Vols. 3–4. Paris: Gallimard.

———. 1994b. *The Order of Things: An Archaeology of Human Sciences*. New York: Vintage.

———. 1995. *Discipline and Punish: The Birth of the Prison*. Translated by Alan Sheridan. 2nd Vintage Books ed. New York: Random House.

———. 1997a. *The Essential Works of Michel Foucault, 1954–1984*. Vol. 1, *Ethics: Subjectivity and Truth*. Edited by Paul Rabinow. Translated by Robert Hurley et al. New York: New Press.

———. 1997b. "Polemics, Politics, and Problematizations." In *The Essential Works of Michel Foucault, 1954–1984*. Vol. 1, *Ethics: Subjectivity and Truth*, edited by Paul Rabinow, 111–20. New York: New Press.

———. 1997c. "Sexuality and Solitude." In *The Essential Works of Michel Foucault, 1954–1984*. Vol. 1, *Ethics: Subjectivity and Truth*, edited by Paul Rabinow, 175–84. New York: New Press.

———. 1999. *Religion and Culture*. Edited by J.R. Carrette. New York: Routledge.

———. 2007. *Security, Territory, Population: Lectures at the Collège de France, 1977–78*. Edited by Michael Senellart. Translated by Graham Burchell. New York: Palgrave MacMillan.

"Four Severed Heads Found in Guatemala City." 2010. BBC News, "Latin America & Caribbean," June 10. http://www.bbc.co.uk/news/10290246.

Franco, Celinda. 2008. *The MS-13 and 18th Street Gangs: Emerging Transnational Gang Threats?* CRS Report RL34233, January 30. Washington, DC: Congressional Research Service. http://www.fas.org/sgp/crs/row/RL34233.pdf.

Franzen, Jonathan. 2003. *How to Be Alone: Essays*. New York: MacMillan.

Freud, Sigmund. (1927) 2012. *The Future of an Illusion*. Edited by Todd Dufresne. Translated by Gregory C. Richter. Peterborough, ON: Broadview Press.

Friedersdorf, Conor. 2011. "The War on Drugs Turns 40." *Atlantic*, June 15. http://www.theatlantic.com/politics/archive/2011/06/the-war-on-drugs-turns-40/240472/.

Galston, William Arthur. 1991. *Liberal Purposes: Goods, Virtues, and Diversity in the Liberal State*. Cambridge: Cambridge University Press.

Gamarro, Urías Moisés. 2008a. "Grupo Financiero GE Money inaugura call center en Guatemala." *Noticias Financieras*, July 9.

———. 2008b. "Transactel anuncia nuevo centro de atención telefónica para 2009; Transactel se expande a Xela." *Noticias Financieras*, August 6.

———. 2009. "Centros de llamadas ven oportunidad en provincia." *Prensa Libre*, October 25. http://www.prensalibre.com/pl/2009/octubre/29/351444.html.

Garces, Chris. 2010. "The Cross Politics of Ecuador's Penal State." *Cultural Anthropology* 25, no. 3:459–96.

———. 2014. "Denuding Surveillance at the Carceral Boundary." *South Atlantic Quarterly* 114, no. 3:447–73.

Garcia, Angela. 2010. *The Pastoral Clinic: Addiction and Dispossession along the Rio Grande*. Berkeley, CA: University of California Press.

García-Ruiz, Jesús. 2004. "Le néopentecôtisme au Guatemala: Entre privatisation, marché et réseaux." *Critique Internationale* 22:81–94.

Garrard-Burnett, Virginia. 1997. "Liberalism, Protestantism, and Indigenous Resistance in Guatemala, 1870–1920." *Latin American Perspectives* 93, no. 2:35–55.

———. 1998. *Protestantism in Guatemala: Living in the New Jerusalem*. Austin, TX: University of Texas Press.

———. 2010. *Terror in the Land of the Holy Spirit: Guatemala under General Efraín Ríos Montt, 1982–1983*. New York: Oxford University Press.

Garriott, William, and Kevin Lewis O'Neill. 2008. "Who Is a Christian? Toward a Dialogical Approach in the Anthropology of Christianity." *Anthropological Theory* 8, no. 4:381–98.

Garzaro, Byron Dardón. 2009. "Call centers demandan más guatemaltecos que hablen inglés." *Prensa Libre*, April 4. http://prensalibre.com/pl/2009/abril/20/notashoy.html.

Geertz, Clifford. 2000. *Available Light: Anthropological Reflections on Philosophical Topics*. Princeton, NJ: Princeton University Press.

Gerber, Charles R. 1996. *Christ-Centered Self-Esteem: Seeing Ourselves through God's Eyes*. Joplin, MO: College Press.

Giddens, Anthony. 1990. *The Consequences of Modernity*. Cambridge, U.K.: Polity.

———. 1991. *Modernity and Self-Identity: Self and Society in the Late Modern Age*. Stanford, CA: Stanford University Press.

———. 1999. *Runaway World: How Globalisation Is Reshaping Our Lives*. London: Profile Books.

Gillis, Stacy, and Joanne Hollows, eds. 2008. *Feminism, Domesticity and Popular Culture*. London: Routledge.

Giroux, Henry A. 2006. "Reading Hurricane Katrina: Race, Class, and the Biopolitics of Disposability." *College Literature* 33, no. 3:171–96.

Gladden, Washington. 1876. *Working People and Their Employers*. Boston: Lockwood Brooks.

———. 1889. *Applied Christianity: Moral Aspects of Social Questions*. New York: Houghton Mifflin.

———. 1901. *Social Salvation*. New York: Houghton Mifflin.

Gleijeses, Piero. 1992. *Shattered Hope: The Guatemalan Revolution and the United States, 1944–1954*. Princeton, NJ: Princeton University Press.

Godoy, Angelina Snodgrass. 2002. "Lynchings and the Democratization of Terror in Postwar Guatemala: Implications for Human Rights." *Human Rights Quarterly* 24, no. 3:640–61.

Goffman, Erving. 1961. *Asylums: Essays on the Social Situation of Mental Patients and Other Inmates.* New York: Doubleday.

———. 1971. *Relations in Public.* New York: Basic Books.

Golden, Myra. 2007. "Top 6 Ways to Get An Angry Customer to Back Down." YouTube video. http://youtu.be/ACKbkmO9rLg.

González, Rosemery, and Mervin del Cid. 2008. "Siete reos mueren en Pavoncito, dos de ellos implicados en crimen de salvadoreños." *El Periódico,* November 23.

Gootenberg, Paul. 2009. *Andean Cocaine: The Making of a Global Drug.* Chapel Hill, NC: University of North Carolina Press.

Gopin, Marc. 2002. *Holy War, Holy Peace: How Religion Can Bring Peace to the Middle East.* New York: Oxford University Press.

Gordon, Colin. 1987. "The Soul of the Citizen: Max Weber and Michel Foucault on Rationality and Government." In *Max Weber, Rationality and Modernity,* edited by S. Whimster and S. Lash, 293–316. London: Allen and Unwin.

Gould, Jeff, and Lowell Gudmunson. 1997. "Central American Historiography after the Violence." *Latin American Research Review* 32, no. 1:244–56.

Government of Guatemala, Becas Solidarias. 2010. "Beca de perfeccionamiento intensivo de idioma inglés para Contact Center." http://www.becasolidaria.gob .gt/index.php?option=com_content&view=article&id=61&Itemid=69.

Graber, Jennifer. 2011. *The Furnace of Affliction: Prisons and Religion in Antebellum America.* Chapel Hill, NC: University of North Carolina Press.

Grandin, Greg. 2000. *The Blood of Guatemala: A History of Race and Nation.* Durham, NC: Duke University Press.

———. 2004. *The Last Colonial Massacre: Latin America in the Cold War.* Chicago: University of Chicago Press.

Grann, David. 2011. "A Murder Foretold." *The New Yorker,* April 4. http:// www.newyorker.com/reporting/2011/04/04/110404fa_fact_grann?current Page=all.

Green, Linda. 1999. *Fear as a Way of Life: Mayan Widows in Rural Guatemala.* New York: Columbia University Press.

Griffith, Marie. 2004. *Born Again Bodies: Flesh and Spirit in American Christianity.* Berkeley, CA: University of California Press.

Grim, Brian J., and Roger Finke. 2010. *The Price of Freedom Denied: Religous Persecution and Conflict in the Twenty-First Century.* Cambridge: Cambridge University Press.

Grogger, Jeff, and Michael Willis. 2000. "The Emergence of Crack Cocaine and the Rise in Urban Violence." *Review of Economics and Statistics* 82, no. 4:519–29.

"Guatemala Acts on Extra-Judicial Prison Killings." 2010. BBC News, "Latin America & Caribbean," August 10. http://www.bbc.co.uk/news/world-latin-america-10931471.

Guatemala Human Rights Commission. 2006. "Right to Life and Humane Treatment." *Guatemala Human Rights Update* 18, no. 20 (October 28). http://www.ghrc-usa.org/wp-content/uploads/2011/12/vol18no20.pdf.

"Guatemala Jail Riot Leaves 17 Dead." 2002. BBC News, "Americas," December 24. http://news.bbc.co.uk/2/hi/americas/2603455.stm.

"Guatemala Tax Protests Turn Violent," 2001. Reuters, August 2.

Guiora, Amos N. 2009. *Freedom from Religion: Rights and National Security.* New York: Oxford University Press.

Gutiérrez, Gustavo. 1988. *A Theology of Liberation: History, Politics, and Salvation.* 15th anniv. ed. Maryknoll, NY: Orbis Books.

Hacking, Ian. 1990. *The Taming of Chance.* Cambridge: Cambridge University Press.

Hale, Charles R. 2006. *Más que un indio: Racial Ambivalence and Neoliberal Multiculturalism in Guatemala.* Santa Fe, NM: School of American Research Press.

Hall, David D. 1997. Introduction to *Lived Religion in America: Toward a History of Practice,* edited by David D. Hall, vii–xiii. Princeton, NJ: Princeton University Press.

Hardt, Michael. 1998. "The Global Society of Control." *Discourse* 20, no. 3:139–52.

Hardt, Michael, and Antonio Negri. 2000. *Empire.* Cambridge, MA: Harvard University Press.

———. 2004. *Multitude: War and Democracy in the Age of Empire.* New York: Penguin.

Hartman, Esther Angela. 1951. *Imaginative Literature as a Projective Technique: A Study of Bibliotherapy.* Stanford, CA: Stanford University Press.

Harvey, David. 2003. "The Right to the City." *International Journal of Urban and Regional Research* 27, no. 4:939–41.

———. 2005. *A Brief History of Neoliberalism.* New York: Oxford University Press.

Hawley, Chris. 2009. "On the Border, a Crisis Escalates: Mexican Cartels Wage a War of Unprecedented Violence That's Spreading into the USA." *USA Today,* February 23.

Hawthorne, Nathaniel. 1850. *The Scarlet Letter.* Boston, MA: Ticknor, Reed, and Fields.

Headley, Bernard. 2006. "Giving Critical Context to the Deportee Phenomenon." *Social Justice* 33, no. 1:40–56.

Hedstrom, Matthew. 2012. *The Rise of Liberal Religion: Book Culture and American Spirituality in the Twentieth Century.* New York: Oxford University Press.

Hegel, Georg W. F. (1807) 2009. *Phenomenology of Spirit.* Translated by Arnold Vincent Miller. Oxford: Oxford University Press.

Hill, Annette. 2005. *Reality TV: Factual Entertainment and Television Audiences.* New York: Routledge.

Hirsch, Adam J. 1992. *The Rise of the Penitentiary: Prisons and Punishment in Early America.* New Haven, CT: Yale University Press.

Hopkins, C. Howard. 1951. *History of the Y.M.C.A. in North America.* New York: Association Press.

Hume, Mo. 2007. "Mano Dura: El Salvador Responds to Gangs." *Development in Practice* 17, no. 6:739–51.

Ignatieff, Michael. 1978. *A Just Measure of Pain: The Penitentiary in the Industrial Revolution, 1750–1850.* New York: Pantheon.

Illouz, Eva. 2008. *Saving the Modern Soul: Therapy, Emotions, and the Culture of Self-Help*. Berkeley, CA: University of California Press.

Inter-American Development Bank (IDB) and Washington Office on Latin America (WOLA). 2011. "Mapeo de las intervenciones de seguridad ciudadana en Centroamérica financiadas por la cooperación internacional." http://www.ideaspaz.org/tools/download/58323.

International Centre for Prison Studies. 2013. "World Prison Brief." http://www.prisonstudies.org/info/worldbrief/.

Isaza, Heidi. 2012. "Fighting Gangs' Consuming Fire." *World Vision Magazine.* http://www.worldvision.org/sites/default/files/pdf/WV_Aut12_final.pdf.

Jackson, Kimberley. 2007. "Editing as Plastic Surgery: The Swan and the Violence of Image-Creation." *Configurations* 15, no. 1:55–76.

James, Erica. 2010. *Democratic Insecurities: Violence, Trauma, and Intervention in Haiti*. Berkeley, CA: University of California Press.

James, William. (1902) 2007. *The Varieties of Religious Experience*. New York: Cosimo Classics.

Johnson, Byron R. 2011. *More God, Less Crime: Why Faith Matters and How It Could Matter More*. West Conshohocken, PA: Templeton Press.

Johnson, Kevin. 2009. "FBI: Burgeoning Gangs Rival Foreign Drug Cartels; Up to 1 Million Members Now behind 80% of Street Crime, Despite Police Crackdown." *USA Today*, January 29.

Johnson, Mary Helen. 2006. "National Policies and the Rise of Transnational Gangs." *Migration Information Source: The Online Journal of the Migration Policy Institute.* http://www.migrationpolicy.org/article/national-policies-and-rise-transnational-gangs.

Johnston, Douglas, and Cynthia Sampson, eds. 1994. *Religion, the Missing Dimension of Statecraft*. New York: Oxford University Press.

Jordan, Mary. 2004. "Pit Stop on the Cocaine Highway: Guatemala Becomes Favored Link for US-Bound Drugs." *The Washington Post*, October 6.

Joyce, Patrick. 2003. *The Rule of Freedom: Liberalism and the Modern City*. London: Verso.

"Juvenile Curfews and Gang Violence: Exiled on Main Street." 1994. *Harvard Law Review* 107, no. 7:1693–710.

Kanstroom, Daniel. 2000. "Deportation, Social Control, and Punishment: Some Thoughts about Why Hard Laws Make Bad Cases." *Harvard Law Review* 113, no. 8:1890–935.

Kasson, John F. 1990. *Rudeness & Civility: Manners in Nineteenth-Century Urban America*. New York: Hill and Wang.

Keane, Webb. 2007. *Christian Moderns: Freedom and Fetish in the Mission Encounter*. Berkeley, CA: University of California Press.

Keen, Benjamin, and Keith Haynes. 2000. "The Hispanic Background." In *A History of Latin America*, 6th ed., 37–51. Boston: Houghton Mifflin.

Kinzer, Stephen. 2013. *The Brothers: John Foster Dulles, Allen Dulles, and Their Secret World War*. New York: Times Books.

Kiyosaki, Robert, and Sharon Lechter. 2000. *Rich Dad, Poor Dad: What the Rich Teach Their Kids about Money That the Poor and Middle Class Do Not!* New York: Warner Business Books.

Klassen, Pamela. 2011. *Spirits of Protestantism: Medicine, Healing, and Liberal Christianity.* Berkeley, CA: University of California Press.

Klein, Malcolm. 1995. *The American Street Gang: Its Nature, Prevalence, and Control.* New York: Oxford University Press.

KPMG. 2010a. "ChildFund International, USA, Consolidated Financial Statements. June 30, 2010." http://www.childfund.org/media/publications/annual_reports/2010_Consolidated_Financial_Statement.aspx.

——. 2010b. "Compassion International Incorporated, Financial Statements. June 30, 2009 and 2010 (With Independent Auditors' Report Thereon)." http://www.compassion.com/multimedia/CPA-June-2010.pdf.

——. 2010c. "Consolidated Financial Statements: World Vision Inc. and Affiliates (With Independent Auditors' Report Thereon). World Vision, September 30, 2009 and 2010." http://www.worldvision.org/resources.nsf/Main/annual-review-2010-resources/$FILE/AR_2010AuditedFinancialStatement.pdf.

——. 2010d. "Save the Children Federation, Inc., Financial Statements. December 31, 2009. (With Independent Auditors' Report Thereon)." http://www.savethechildren.org/atf/cf/%7b9def2ebe-10ae-432c-9bd0-df91d2eba74a%7d/save-the-children-financial-statements-2009.pdf

LaHaye, Tim, and Jerry B. Jenkins. 1995. *Left Behind: A Novel of the Earth's Last Days.* Carol Stream. IL: Tyndale House.

Larios, Roxana. 2009. "Tratado entre EEUU y Centroamérica genera 3.650 empleos en Guatemala desde 2006." *Siglo Veintiuno,* July 2.

La Rue, Alan. 2006. "Interview with David Fischman." *ACAP Newsletter,* July.

Las Casas, Bartolomé de. 1992. *A Short Account of the Destruction of the Indies.* London: Penguin.

Latour, Bruno. 2004. "Why Has Critique Run Out of Steam? From Matters of Fact to Matters of Concern." *Critical Inquiry* 30, no. 2:225–48.

Latta, Samuel W. 1906. *Rest Houses for Railroad Men: How the Railroad Men Regard Such Conveniences.* New York: Welfare Department of the National Civic Federation.

Lauria-Santiago, Aldo, and Leigh Binford, eds. 2004. *Landscapes of Struggle: Politics, Society, and Community in El Salvador.* Pittsburgh: University of Pittsburgh Press.

Le Guin, Ursula K. 1975. "The Ones Who Walk Away from Omelas." In *The Wind's Twelve Quarters: Stories,* 275–84. London: Orion Books.

Levenson, Deborah. 2013. *Adiós Niño: The Gangs of Guatemala City and the Politics of Death.* Durham, NC: Duke University Press.

Levenson, Deborah, Nora Marina Figueroa, and Marta Yolanda Maldonado. 1988. *Por sí mismos: Un estudio preliminar de las "maras" en la Ciudad de Guatemala.* Cuadernos de investigación, no. 4. Guatemala: Asociación para el Avance de las Ciencias Sociales (AVANCSO).

Levine, Daniel H. 1995. "Protestants and Catholics in Latin America: A Family Portrait." In *Fundamentalisms Comprehended,* edited by Martin E. Marty and R. Scott Appleby, 155–78. Chicago: University of Chicago Press.

Lewis, Paul. 2000. "'Lectures or a Little Charity': Poor Visits in Antebellum Literature and Culture." *The New England Quarterly* 73, no. 2:246–73.

Li, Tania. 2007. *The Will to Improve: Governmentality, Development, and the Practice of Politics*. Durham, NC: Duke University Press.

———. 2010. "To Make Live or Let Die? Rural Dispossession and the Protection of Surplus Populations." *Antipode: A Radical Journal of Geography* 41, s1:66–93.

Llorca, Juan Carlos. 2006. "Reality TV Show Tries to Reform Ex-Gangsters." *Guardian*, February 4.

Lofton, Kathryn. 2011. *Oprah: The Gospel of an Icon*. Berkeley, CA: University of California Press.

Lomnitz, Claudio. 2008. "Narrating the Neoliberal Moment: History, Journalism, Historicity." *Public Culture* 20, no. 1:39–56.

Long, Charles H. 1994. "The Question of Denominational Histories of the United States: Dead End or Creative Beginning?" In *Reimagining Denominationalism: Interpretive Essays*, edited by Robert Bruce Mullin and Russell E. Richey, 99–105. New York: Oxford University Press.

López, Edgar. 2008a. "Americatel anuncia apertura de centro de servicios en Guatemala." *Siglo Veintiuno*, February 26.

———. 2008b. "Empresa NCO invertirá US$ 20 millones en nuevo centro de llamadas." *Siglo Veintiuno*, November 13.

———. 2008c. "Sector de telecomunicaciones adelanta ingreso en mercado televisivo." *Siglo Veintiuno*, March 10.

Loveman, Brian, ed. 2006. *Addicted to Failure: U.S. Security Policy in Latin America and the Andean Region*. New York: Rowman & Littlefield.

Luhrmann, Tanya. 2012. *When God Talks Back: Understanding the American Evangelical Relationship with God*. New York: Random House.

Lynch, Edward A. 1994. "The Retreat of Liberation Theology." *Homiletic and Pastoral Review*, February.

Madrid, Rony. 2011. *La vuelta al corazón en 40 días*. Guatemala City: Recursos para la Vida Real.

Mahmood, Saba. 2004. *Politics of Piety: The Islamic Revival and the Feminist Subject*. Princeton, NJ: Princeton University Press.

Manz, Beatriz. 1988. *Refugees of a Hidden War: The Aftermath of Counterinsurgency in Guatemala*. Albany: State University of New York Press.

———. 2005. *Paradise in Ashes: A Guatemalan Journey of Courage, Terror, and Hope*. Berkeley, CA: University of California Press.

Marion, Jean-Luc. 2012. *In the Self's Place: The Approach of St. Augustine*. Translated by Jeffrey L. Kosky. Stanford, CA: Stanford University Press.

Marshall, Ruth. 2009. *Political Spiritualities: The Pentecostal Revolution in Nigeria*. Chicago: University of Chicago Press.

———. 2010. "The Sovereignty of Miracles: Pentecostal Political Theology in Nigeria." *Constellations* 17, no. 2:197–223.

Martin, Dale B. 1990. *Slavery as Salvation: The Metaphor of Slavery in Pauline Christianity*. New Haven, CT: Yale University Press.

Martin, Emily. 1994. *Flexible Bodies: Tracking Immunity in American Culture from the Days of Polio to the Age of AIDS*. Boston: Beacon Press.

———. 1997. "Managing Americans: Policy and Changes in the Meanings of Work and the Self." In *Anthropology of Policy: Critical Perspectives on*

Governance and Power, edited by Cris Shore and Susan Wright, 183–200. London: Routledge.

Martini, Pablo Rodas. 2000. *Ante la titubeante política tributaria: El reto es trazar lineamientos de largo plazo.* Colección de educación fiscal no. 9. Guatemala: Facultad Latinoamericana de Ciencias Sociales (FLACSO)–Guatemala.

Marx, Karl, and Friedrich Engels. (1848) 2002. *The Communist Manifesto.* New York: Penguin.

Massumi, Brian. 2002. *Parables for the Virtual: Movement, Affect, Sensation.* Durham, NC: Duke University Press.

Matza, Tomas. 2009. "Moscow's Echo: Technologies of the Self, Publics, and Politics on the Russian Talk Show." *Cultural Anthropology* 24, no. 3:489–522.

Matzat, Don. 1990. *Christ Esteem: Where the Search for Self-Esteem Ends.* Harvest House.

Mayo, Elton. 1933. *The Human Problems of an Industrial Civilization.* New York: MacMillan.

Mazzarella, William. 2009. "Affect: What Is It Good For?" In *Enchantments of Modernity: Empire, Nation, Globalization,* edited by Saurabh Dube, 291–309. London: Routledge.

Mbembe, Achille. 2003. "Necropolitics." *Public Culture* 15, no. 1:11–40.

McCarthy, Anna. 2007. "Reality Television: A Neoliberal Theater of Suffering." *Social Text* 25, no. 4 (Winter):17–42.

McCreery, David, ed. 1994. *Rural Guatemala, 1760–1940.* Stanford. CA: Stanford University Press.

McGrath, Joanna, and Alister McGrath. 2002. *Self-Esteem: The Cross and Christian Confidence.* Rev. ed. Wheaton, IL: Crossway Books.

McKay, Ramah. 2012. "Afterlives: Humanitarian Histories and Critical Subjects in Mozambique." *Cultural Anthropology* 27, no. 2:286–309.

McQuaid, Kim. 1974. "The Businessman as Reformer: Nelson O. Nelson and Late 19th Century Social Movements in America." *American Journal of Economics and Sociology* 33, no. 4:423–35.

Melossi, Dario, and Massimo Pavarini. 1981. *The Prison and the Factory: Origins of the Penitentiary System.* London: MacMillan.

Melville, Herman. 1969. *Great Short Works of Herman Melville.* New York: Harper & Row.

Menaldo, Rolando Escobar, and Ana Maritza Morales. 2000. *Relación Estado-Contribuyente.* Colección de educación fiscal no. 4. Guatemala: Facultad Latinoamericana de Ciencias Sociales (FLACSO)–Guatemala.

Meskell, Matthew W. 1999. "An American Resolution: The History of Prisons in the United States from 1777 to 1877." *Stanford Law Review* 51:839–65.

Meyer, Birgit. 1999. "Commodities and the Power of Prayer: Pentecostalist Attitudes towards Consumption in Contemporary Ghana." In *Globalization and Identity: Dialectics of Flow and Closure,* edited by Birgit Meyer and Peter Geschiere, 151–76. Oxford: Wiley-Blackwell.

Meyer, Peter J., and Clare Ribando Seelke. 2013. *Central America Regional Security Initiative: Background and Policy Issues for Congress.* CRS Report

R41731, May 6. Washington, DC: Congressional Research Services. http:// www.fas.org/sgp/crs/row/R41731.pdf.

Miller, Perry. 1982. *The New England Mind: The Seventeenth Century.* Cambridge, MA: Harvard University Press.

Miller, Peter, and Nikolas Rose. 1988. "The Tavistock Programme: Governing Subjectivity and Social Life." *Sociology* 22:171–92.

Mills, Kenneth, and William Taylor, eds. 1998. *Colonial Spanish America: A Documentary History.* Wilmington, DE: Scholarly Resources.

Mittermaier, Amira. 2012. "Dreams from Elsewhere: Muslim Subjectivities beyond the Trope of Self-Cultivation." *Journal of the Royal Anthropological Institute* 18, no. 2:247–65.

Modern, John Lardas. 2007. "Ghosts of Sing Sing, or the Metaphysics of Secularism." *Journal of the American Academy of Religion* 75:615–50.

———. 2011. *Secularism in Antebellum America.* Chicago: University of Chicago Press.

Montaigne, Fen. 1999. "Deporting America's Gang Culture." *Mother Jones,* July/August. http://www.motherjones.com/politics/1999/07/deporting-americas-gang-culture-el-salvador.

Moodie, Ellen. 2010. *El Salvador in the Aftermath of Peace: Crime, Uncertainty, and the Transition to Democracy.* Philadelphia: University of Pennsylvania Press.

Moore, Donald S. 2005. *Suffering for Territory: Race, Place, and Power in Zimbabwe.* Durham, NC: Duke University Press.

Moreton, Bethany. 2007. "The Soul of Neoliberalism." *Social Text* 25, no. 3:103–23.

———. 2009. *To Serve God and Wal-Mart: The Making of Christian Free Enterprise.* Cambridge, MA: Harvard University Press.

Morris, Norval, and David Rothman, eds. 1998. *The Oxford History of the Prison: The Practice of Punishment in Western Society.* New York: Oxford University Press.

Moseley, Rachel. 2002. "Makeover Takeover on British Television." *Screen* 41, no. 3:299–314.

Murphy, Edward. 2004. "Developing Sustainable Peripheries: The Limits of Citizenship in Guatemala City." *Latin American Perspectives* 31, no. 6:48–68.

Nancy, Jean-Luc. 2008. *Dis-Enclosure: The Deconstruction of Christianity.* Translated by Bettina Bergo, Gabriel Malenfant, and Michael B. Smith. New York: Fordham University Press.

Negroponte, Diana Villiers. 2009. *The Merida Initiative and Central America: The Challenges of Containing Public Insecurity and Criminal Violence.* Foreign Policy at Brookings, Working Paper no. 3, May. http://www.brookings.edu/~/media/research/files/papers/2009/5/merida-initiative-negroponte/05_merida_initiative_negroponte.pdf.

Nelson, Diane M. 1999. *Finger in the Wound: Body Politics in Quincentennial Guatemala.* Berkeley, CA: University of California Press.

———. 2009. *Reckoning: The Ends of War in Guatemala.* Durham, NC: Duke University Press.

Nixon, Richard. 1971. "Remarks about an Intensified Program for Drug Abuse Prevention and Control, June 17." *American Presidency Project.* http://www.presidency.ucsb.edu/ws/index.php?pid = 3047#axzz1PCJydjl5.

Office of Immigration Statistics, United States Department of Homeland Security. 2006. *2004 Yearbook of Immigration Statistics.* http://www.dhs.gov/xlibrary/assets/statistics/yearbook/2004/Yearbook2004.pdf.

Office of Juvenile Justice and Delinquency Prevention, United States Department of Justice. 2013. "G.R.E.A.T.: Gang Resistance Education and Training." http://www.great-online.org/.

O'Neill, Kevin Lewis. 2005. "Writing Guatemala's Genocide: Truth and Reconciliation Commission Reports and Christianity." *Journal of Genocide Research* 7, no. 3:331–49.

——. 2010a. *City of God: Christian Citizenship in Postwar Guatemala.* Berkeley, CA: University of California Press.

——. 2010b. "The Reckless Will: Prison Chaplaincy and the Problem of Mara Salvatrucha." *Public Culture* 22, no. 1:67–88.

——. 2013. "Beyond Broken: Affective Spaces and the Study of American Religion." *Journal of the American Academy of Religion* 81, no. 4:1093–116.

O'Neill, Kevin Lewis, and Benjamin Fogarty-Valenzuela. 2013. "Verticality." *Journal of the Royal Anthropological Institute* 19, no. 2:378–89.

O'Neill, Kevin Lewis, and Kedron Thomas, eds. 2011. *Securing the City: Neoliberalism, Space, and Insecurity in Postwar Guatemala.* Durham, NC: Duke University Press.

Ong, Aihwa, and Stephen J. Collier, eds. 2005. *Global Assemblages: Technology, Politics, and Ethics as Anthropological Problems.* Oxford: Wiley-Blackwell.

Organization of American States. 2013. *The Drug Problem in the Americas.* Washington, DC: Organization of American States. http://www.oas.org/documents/eng/press/Introduction_and_Analytical_Report.pdf and http://www.oas.org/documents/eng/press/Scenarios_Report.pdf.

"Organized Crime in Central America: The Rot Spreads." 2011. *Economist,* January 20. http://www.economist.com/node/17963313.

Orsi, Robert A. 1982. *The Madonna of 115th Street: Faith and Community in Italian Harlem, 1880–1950.* New Haven, CT: Yale University Press.

Osteen, Joel. 2004. *Your Best Life Now: 7 Steps to Living at Your Full Potential.* New York: Warner Faith.

Ouellette, Laurie, and James Hay. 2008. *Better Living through Reality TV: Television and Post-Welfare Citizenship.* Malden, MA: Wiley-Blackwell.

Padilla, Felix. 1992. *The Gang as an American Enterprise.* New Brunswick, NJ: Rutgers University Press.

Pagden, Anthony. 1990. *Spanish Imperialism and Political Imagination.* New Haven, CT: Yale University Press.

"'Paisas' están transformándose en organización criminal, dice MP." 2012. *Prensa Libre,* August 29. http://www.prensalibre.com/noticias/justicia/Paisas-carcel-extorsion-grupo-criminal_0_763723886.html.

Panourgiá, Neni. 1995. *Fragments of Death, Fables of Identity: An Athenian Anthropography.* Madison, WI: University of Wisconsin Press.

Park, Robert E. 1926. "The Concept of Position in Sociology." Papers and Proceedings of the American Sociological Society no. 20. http://www.brocku.ca/MeadProject/Park/Park_1926a.html.

Parks, Magna. 2007. *Christians, Beware!: The Dangers of Secular Psychology.* Ringgold, GA: TEACH Services.

Patterson, Orlando. 1982. "Authority, Alienation, and Social Death." Chap. 2 in *Slavery and Social Death: A Comparative Study,* 35–76. Cambridge, MA: Harvard University Press.

Paul VI. 1967. *Populorum Progressio: Encyclical Letter on the Development of Peoples.* The Holy See, "The Holy Father," March 26. http://www.vatican.va/holy_father/paul_vi/encyclicals/documents/hf_p-vi_enc_26031967_populorum_en.html.

Peña, Elaine. 2011. *Performing Piety: Making Space Sacred with the Virgin of Guadalupe.* Berkeley, CA: University of California Press.

Peters, Philip. 2007. "Zagada Selects Transactel as Premier Guatemala BPO Member for Its Sphaero Alliance." PRWeb. News release, July 30. http://www.prweb.com/releases/2007/07/prweb543096.htm.

———. 2009. *Central America Contact Center & BPO Report 2010: An Expanding Bilingual Niche.* Coral Gables, FL: Zagada.

Petrella, Ivan. 2004. *The Future of Liberation Theology: An Argument and Manifesto.* Aldershot: Ashgate.

Pew Forum on Religion and Public Life. 2006. *Spirit and Power: A 10-Nation Survey of Pentecostals.* "Polling and Analysis," October. http://www.pewforum.org/files/2006/10/pentecostals-08.pdf.

Pisciotta, Alexander. 1994. *Benevolent Repression: Social Control and the American Reformatory-Prison Movement.* New York: New York University Press.

Plan International. 2010. "Plan: Worldwide Annual Review and Combined Financial Statements, 2010." http://plan-international.org/files/global/publications/about-plan/Plan Intl Annual RA2010.pdf.

Post, Emily. 1922. *Etiquette in Society, in Business, in Politics, and at Home.* New York: Funk & Wagnalls.

Povinelli, Elizabeth. 2002. *The Cunning of Recognition: Indigenous Alterities and the Making of Australian Multiculturalism.* Durham, NC: Duke University Press.

———. 2011. *Economies of Abandonment: Social Belonging and Endurance in Late Liberalism.* Durham, NC: Duke University Press.

Pratt, Mary Louise. 1986. "Fieldwork in Common Places." In *Writing Culture: The Poetics and Politics of Ethnography,* edited by James Clifford and George E. Marcus, 27–50. Berkeley, CA: University of California Press.

"Private Jails: Locking in the Best Price." 2007. *Economist,* January 25. http://www.economist.com/node/8599146.

Procacci, Giovanna. 1991. "Social Economy and the Government of Poverty." In *The Foucault Effect: Studies in Governmentality,* edited by Graham Burchell, Colin Gordon, and Peter Miller, 151–68. Chicago: University of Chicago Press.

Proyecto Interdiocesano de Recuperación de la Memoria Histórica (REMHI). 1998. *Guatemala, nunca más.* 4 vols. Guatemala City: Oficina de Derechos Humanos del Arzobispado de Guatemala (ODHAG). http://www.derechoshumanos.net/lesahumanidad/informes/guatemala/informeREMHI-Tomo1.htm.

Quirk, Matthew. 2008. "How to Grow a Gang." *Atlantic,* May 8. http://www.theatlantic.com/magazine/archive/2008/05/how-to-grow-a-gang/306760/.

Ralph, Laurence. 2014. *Renegade Dreams: Living through Injury in Gangland Chicago.* Chicago: University of Chicago Press.

Ranum, Elin Cecilie. 2006. "Pandillas juveniles transnacionales en Centroamérica, México y Estados Unidos: Diagnóstico nacional Guatemala." Mexico City: Centro de Estudios y Programas Interamericanos (CEPI) del Instituto Tecnológico Autónomo de México (ITAM). http://interamericanos.itam.mx/maras/docs/Diagnostico_Guatemala.pdf.

Redfield, Peter. 2005. "Doctors, Borders, and Life in Crisis." *Cultural Anthropology* 20, no. 3:328–61.

———. 2012. "Bioexpectations: Life Technologies as Humanitarian Goods." *Public Culture* 24, no. 1:157–84.

Reeves, Jimmie L., and Richard Campbell. 1994. *Cracked Coverage: Television News, the Anti-Cocaine Crusade, and the Reagan Legacy.* Durham, NC: Duke University Press.

Reinarman, Craig, and Harry G. Levine, eds. 1997. *Crack in America: Demon Drugs and Social Justice.* Berkeley, CA: University of California Press.

REMHI. *See* Proyecto Interdiocesano de Recuperación de la Memoria Histórica.

Restrepo, Jorge A., and Alonso Tobón García, eds. 2011. *Guatemala en la encrucijada. Panorama de una violencia transformada.* Geneva: Secretariat of the Geneva Declaration. http://www.genevadeclaration.org/fileadmin/docs/Guatemala_book/GD-Guatemala.pdf.

Rhodes, Lorna A. 2004. *Total Confinement: Madness and Reason in the Maximum Security Prison.* Berkeley, CA: University of California Press.

Ricoeur, Paul. 1984. *Time and Narrative.* Translated by Kathleen McLaughlin and David Pellauer. Vol. 1. Chicago: University of Chicago Press.

Riles, Annelise. 2000. *The Network Inside Out.* Ann Arbor, MI: University of Michigan Press.

Robbins, Joel. 2004a. *Becoming Sinners: Christianity and Moral Torment in a Papua New Guinea Society.* Berkeley, CA: University of California Press.

———. 2004b. "The Globalization of Pentecostal and Charismatic Christianity." *Annual Review of Anthropology* 33:117–43.

Roberts, Richard. 1999. *¡El poder ilimitado dentro de ti!* Translated by Edgar González. Tulsa, OK: Oral Roberts Ministries.

Rocha, José Luis. 2007. *Lanzando piedras, fumando "piedras": Evolución de las pandillas en Nicaragua 1997–2006.* Cuadernos de investigación de la Universidad Centroamericana no. 23. Managua: UCA.

Rodgers, Dennis. 2004. "'Disembedding' the City: Crime, Insecurity and Spatial Organization in Managua, Nicaragua." *Environment and Urbanization* 16, no. 2:113–23.

———. 2006. "Living in the Shadow of Death: Gangs, Violence, and Social Order in Urban Nicaragua, 1996–2002." *Journal of Latin American Studies* 38, no. 2:267–92.

Rodgers, Dennis, Robert Muggah, and Chris Stevenson. 2009. *Gangs of Central America: Causes, Costs, and Interventions*. Occasional Paper no. 23, May. Geneva: Small Arms Survey. http://www.offnews.info/downloads/SAS-OP23-Gangs-Central-America.pdf.

Rodríguez Barillas, Alejandro, and Gerardo Pérez Castillo. 2005. "Transparentando el Plan Escoba: Análisis de la estrategia policial en relación con las pandillas juveniles en Guatemala." *Revista Centroamericana justicia penal y sociedad* 22:11–84.

Rolsky, Louis Benjamin. 2012. "Charles H. Long and the Re-orientation of American Religious History." *Journal of the American Academy of Religion* 80, no. 3:750–74.

Romero, Oscar Arnulfo. (1988) 2004. *The Violence of Love*. Maryknoll, NY: Orbis Books.

Rosales, Carlos. 2012. "Prevention and Youth Are the Solution." *USAID Impact* (blog), August 17. http://blog.usaid.gov/2012/08/prevention-youth-are-the-solution/.

Rose, Nikolas. 1990. *Governing the Soul: The Shaping of the Private Self*. London: Routledge.

———. 1992. "Engineering the Human Soul: Analyzing Psychological Expertise." *Science in Context* 5, no. 2:351–69.

———. 1999. *Power of Freedom: Reframing Social Thought*. Cambridge: Cambridge University Press.

Rosen, Eva, and Sudhir Venkatesh. 2007. "Legal Innovation and the Control of Gang Behavior." *Annual Review of Law and Social Science* 3:255–70.

Rothman, David. 1971. *The Discovery of the Asylum: Social Order and Disorder in the New Republic*. Boston: Little Brown.

Rudnyckyj, Daromir. 2010. *Spiritual Economies: Islam, Globalization, and the Afterlife of Development*. Ithaca, NY: Cornell University Press.

Rumsey, John. 2008. "Guatemala: Right Place, Wrong Time." *Brazil Communications* (blog), November 10. http://www.johnrumsey.co.uk/wordpress/guatemala-right-place-wrong-time/.

Salvatore, Ricardo Donato, and Carlos Aguirre, eds. 1996. *The Birth of the Penitentiary in Latin America: Essays on Criminology, Prison Reform, and Social Control, 1830–1940*. Austin, TX: University of Texas Press.

Sanchez, Marcela. 2006. "Fighting Gangs with Reality TV." *Washington Post*, February 23.

Sanford, Victoria. 2003. *Buried Secrets: Truth and Human Rights in Guatemala*. New York: Palgrave MacMillan.

———. 2008. "From Genocide to Feminicide: Impunity and Human Rights in Twenty-First Century Guatemala." *Journal of Human Rights* 7:104–22.

———. 2012. *Violencia y genocidio en Guatemala*. Guatemala: F&G Editores.

Sassen, Saskia. 2001. *The Global City: New York, London, Tokyo*. Princeton, NJ: Princeton University Press.

Savenije, Wim. 2004. "La Mara Salvatrucha y el Barrio 18 St.: Fenómenos sociales transnacionales, respuestas represivas nacionales." *Foreign Affairs en Español* 4, no. 2:38–46.

———. 2007. "Las pandillas transnacionales o 'maras': Violencia urbana en Centroamérica." *Foro Internacional* 189, no. 3:637–59.

———. 2009. *Maras y barras: Pandillas y violencia juvenil en los barrios marginales de Centroamérica*. San Salvador: Facultad Latinoamericana de Ciencias Sociales (FLACSO)–El Salvador.

Scapp, Ron, and Brian Seitz, eds. 2006. *Etiquette: Reflections on Contemporary Comportment*. Albany, NY: State University of New York Press.

Schaefer, Donovan. 2013. "The Promise of Affect: The Politics of the Event in Ahmed's *The Promise of Happiness* and Berlant's *Cruel Optimism*." *Theory and Event* 16, no. 2.

Scheper-Hughes, Nancy. 1992. *Death without Weeping: The Violence of Everyday Life in Brazil*. Berkeley, CA: University of California Press.

Schielke, Samuli. 2008. "Boredom and Despair in Rural Egypt." *Contemporary Islam* 2, no. 3:251–70.

Schirmer, Jennifer. 1998. *The Guatemalan Military Project: A Violence Called Democracy*. Philadelphia: University of Pennsylvania Press.

Schlesinger, Stephen E., and Stephen Kinzer. 1999. *Bitter Fruit: The Story of the American Coup in Guatemala*. Cambridge, MA: Harvard University David Rockefeller Center for Latin American Studies.

Schmidt, Leigh. 2002. *Hearing Things: Religion, Illusion, and the American Enlightenment*. Princeton, NJ: Princeton University Press.

Schmitt, Carl. 2005. *Political Theology: Four Chapters on the Concept of Sovereignty*. Translated by George Schwab. Chicago: University of Chicago Press.

Sedgwick, Eve Kosofsky. 2003. *Touching Feeling: Affect, Pedagogy, Performativity*. Durham, NC: Duke University Press.

Seelke, Clare Ribando. 2009. *Mérida Initiative for Mexico and Central America: Funding and Policy Issues*. CRS Report R40135, August 21. Washington, DC: Congressional Research Service. http://www.fas.org/sgp/crs/row/R40135.pdf.

———. 2011. *Gangs in Central America*. CRS Report RL34112, January 3. Washington, DC: Congressional Research Service. https://www.hsdl.org/?view&did=11471.

———. 2013. *Gangs in Central America*. CRS Report RL34112, January 28. Washington, DC: Congressional Research Service. https://www.hsdl.org/?view&did=730334.

Seelke, Clare Ribando, and Kristin M. Finklea. 2014. *U.S.-Mexican Security Cooperation: The Mérida Initiative and Beyond*. CRS Report R41349, April 8. Washington, DC: Congressional Research Service. http://www.fas.org/sgp/crs/row/R41349.pdf.

Seelke, Clare Ribando, Liana Sun Wyler, and June S. Beittel. 2010. *Latin America and the Caribbean: Illicit Drug Trafficking and U.S. Counterdrug Programs*. CRS Report R41215, April 30. Washington, DC: Congressional Research Service. http://fpc.state.gov/documents/organization/142364.pdf.

"Seven Killed in Prison Gang Fight." 2008. *Los Angeles Times,* November 23.

Shanken, Andrew Michael. 2006. "Better Living: Toward a Cultural History of a Business Slogan." *Enterprise & Society* 7, no. 3:485–519.

Shaw, Clifford. 1930. *The Jack Roller: A Delinquent Boy's Own Story.* Chicago: University of Chicago Press.

Shaw, Clifford, and Henry McKay. 1942. *Juvenile Delinquency and Urban Areas.* Chicago: Routledge.

Shostak, Marjorie. 1981. *Nisa: The Life and Words of a !Kung Woman.* Cambridge, MA: Harvard University Press.

Sider, Gerald. 2006. "The Production of Race, Locality, and State: An Anthropology." *Anthropologica* 48, no. 2:247–63.

Sieder, Rachel. 2011. "Contested Sovereignties: Indigenous Law, Violence and State Effects in Postwar Guatemala." *Critique of Anthropology* 31, no. 3:161–84.

Sims, David. 2006. "The Right Balance for the Call Center: Somewhere between Prison and an Encounter Group." *Customer Interaction Solutions* 25, no. 5:48–50.

Skotnicki, Andrew. 2000. *Religion and the Development of the American Penal System.* Lanham, MD: University Press of America.

Slevin, Peter. 2010. "Deportation of Illegal Immigrants Increases under Obama Administration." *Washington Post,* July 26. http://www.washingtonpost.com/wp-dyn/content/article/2010/07/25/AR2010072501790_pf.html.

Smiles, Samuel. 1859. *Character.* New York: A.L. Burt.

———. (1866) 2002. *Self-Help.* 2nd ed. Oxford: Oxford University Press.

———. 1878. *Thrift.* London: John Murray.

———. 1880. *Duty.* London: John Murray.

Smith, Caleb. 2009. *The Prison and the American Imagination.* New Haven, CT: Yale University Press.

Smith, Carol A. 1984. "El desarollo de la primacia urbana en Guatemala." *Mesoamerica* 8:195–278.

———, ed. 1990. *Guatemalan Indians and the State, 1540 to 1988.* Austin, TX: University of Texas Press.

Sobrino, Jon. 1994. *The Principle of Mercy: Taking the Crucified People from the Cross.* Maryknoll, NY: Orbis Books.

Sohnen, Eleanor. 2012. *Paying for Crime: A Review of the Relationships between Insecurity and Development in Mexico and Central America.* Washington, DC: Woodrow Wilson Center/Migration Policy Institute, Regional Migration Study Group, December. http://www.migrationpolicy.org/pubs/RMSG-PayingforCrime.pdf.

Spergel, Irving. 1995. *The Youth Gang Problem: A Community Approach.* New York: Oxford University Press.

Spivak, Gayatri Chakravorty. 1988. "Can the Subaltern Speak?" In *Marxism and the Interpretation of Culture,* edited by Cary Nelson and Lawrence Grossberg, 271–313. London: MacMillan.

Sridhar, Archana. 2007. "Tax Reform and Promoting a Culture of Philanthropy: Guatemala's Third Sector in an Era of Peace." *Fordham International Law Journal* 31, no. 1:186–229.

Stanley, William. 1996. *The Protection Racket State: Elite Politics, Military Extortion, and Civil War in El Salvador*. Philadelphia: Temple University Press.

Steele, Shelby. 1990. "White Guilt." *The American Scholar* 59:497–506.

Steigenga, Tim. 2001. *Politics of the Spirit: The Political Implications of Pentecostalized Religion in Costa Rica and Guatemala*. Lanham, MD: Lexington Books.

Stern, Vivien. 1998. *A Sin against the Future: Imprisonment in the World*. Boston, MA: Northeastern University Press.

Stewart, Kathleen. 2007. *Ordinary Affects*. Durham, NC: Duke University Press.

Stoll, David, ed. 1990. *Is Latin America Turning Protestant? The Politics of Evangelical Growth*. Berkeley, CA: University of California Press.

———. 1993. *Between Two Armies in the Ixil Towns of Guatemala*. New York: Columbia University Press.

Struthers, Sally. 1987. "Christian Children's Fund Commercial." YouTube video. Uploaded October 26, 2009. http://youtu.be/ePENcrE_xcQ .

———. 1991. "Sally Struthers Commercial." YouTube video. Uploaded October 14, 2009. http://youtu.be/YeH14bh6ciU.

Struthers, Sally, and David Balboa. 1989. *Fitness Walking*. Los Angeles, CA: Prism Entertainment. Tape (VHS).

Struthers, Sally, and Joyce Virtue. 1979. *The Sally Struthers Natural Beauty Book*. New York: Doubleday.

Suarez, Julie, and Marty Jordan. 2007. "Three Thousand and Counting: A Report on Violence against Women in Guatemala." Fact-finding delegation report, September. Washington, DC: Guatemalan Human Rights Commission/USA. http://www.ghrc-usa.org/wp-content/uploads/2012/01/ThreethousandandCountingAReportonViolenceAgainstWomeninGuatemala1.pdf.

Swift, Jonathan. 1880. *Gulliver's Travels into Several Remote Regions of the World*. London: George Routledge and Sons.

Tatone, Michael. 2013. "Guatemala Murders Up 8% in 2013, Bucking Downward Trend." *InSight Crime: Organized Crime in the Americas*. http://www.insightcrime.org/news-briefs/guatemalan-murders-rise-president-starting.

Taylor, Charles. 1989. *Sources of the Self: The Making of Modern Identity*. Cambridge: Cambridge University Press.

Taylor, Frederick Winslow. 1911. *The Principles of Scientific Management*. New York: Harper & Brothers.

Terry, Fiona. 2002. *Condemned to Repeat? The Paradox of Humanitarian Action*. Ithaca, NY: Cornell University Press.

Thacker, Eugene. 2011. "Necrologies; Or, the Death of the Body Politic." In *Beyond Biopolitics*, edited by Patricia Clough and Craig Willse, 139–62. Durham, NC: Duke University Press.

Thomas, Kedron. 2012. "Intellectual Property Law and the Ethics of Imitation in Guatemala." *Anthropological Quarterly* 85, no. 3:785–814.

———. 2013. "Brand 'Piracy' and Postwar Statecraft in Guatemala." *Cultural Anthropology* 28, no. 1:144–60.

Thomas, William I., and Florian Znaniecki. 1918. *The Polish Peasant in Europe and America*. Boston: R.G. Badger.

Thoreau, Henry David. 1997. *Walden*. New York: Oxford University Press.

Thrasher, Frederic. 1927. *The Gang*. Chicago: University of Chicago Press.

Threadgold, Terry, and Frances Bartkowski. 1990. "The *Intervention* Interview." In *The Post-Colonial Critic: Interviews, Strategies, Dialogues*, edited by Sarah Harasym, 113–32. London: Routledge.

Ticktin, Miriam. 2011. *Casualties of Care: Immigration and the Politics of Humanitarianism in France*. Berkeley, CA: University of California Press.

Tolman, William Howe. 1900. *Industrial Betterment*. New York: Social Services Press.

———. 1912. *Hygiene for the Worker*. New York: American Book Company.

Transactel. 2009. "Bring Out the Power in You." Advertisement. *Prensa Libre*, July 16.

———. 2010. "Bring Out the Power in You." Advertisement. *Prensa Libre*, July 2.

———. 2012a. "Career Path." https://www.transactel.net/Career_path.

———. 2012b. "Our Values." https://www.transactel.net/Our_values.

Trivedi, Anjani. 2013. "How the American Privatized Prison Is Spreading Overseas." *Time*, August 23. http://world.time.com/2013/08/23/crime-pays-at-least-if-youre-a-private-prison-operator/.

Tsing, Ana. 2000. "Inside the Economy of Appearances." *Public Culture* 12, no. 1:115–44.

T. W. 2013. "Violence in Guatemala: Got to Admit It's Getting Better." *Economist. Americas View* (blog), January 22. http://www.economist.com/blogs/americasview/2013/01/violence-guatemala.

Tweed, Thomas. 1997. *Our Lady of the Exile: Diasporic Religion at a Cuban Catholic Shrine in Miami*. New York: Oxford University Press.

Tye, Larry. 1998. *The Father of Spin: Edward L. Bernays and the Birth of Public Relations*. New York: Crown.

United Nations Office on Drugs and Crime (UNODC). 2012. *Transnational Organized Crime in Central America and the Caribbean: A Threat Assessment*. Report, September. Vienna: UNODC. http://www.unodc.org/documents/data-and-analysis/Studies/TOC_Central_America_and_the_Caribbean_english.pdf.

———. 2013. "Intentional Homicide Count and Rate per 100,000 Population, by country/territory (2000–2012)." Global Study on Homicide. http://www.unodc.org/documents/data-and-analysis/statistics/crime/Homicide_statistics2012.xls.

Urciuoli, Bonnie. 2008. "Skills and Selves in the New Workplace." *American Ethnologist* 35, no. 2:211–28.

USAID. 2001. *Guatemala Tax and Investment Policy Reform Program: Fiscal Reform in Support of Trade Liberalization*. Washington, DC: USAID.

USAID Bureau for Latin America and the Caribbean, Office of Sustainable Regional Development. 2006. *Central America and Mexico Gang Assessment*. Washington, DC: USAID. http://pdf.usaid.gov/pdf_docs/PNADG834.pdf.

U.S. Department of State, Bureau of Western Hemisphere Affairs. 2007. "U.S. Strategy to Combat the Threat of Criminal Gangs from Central America and Mexico." Release, July 18. http://2001–2009.state.gov/p/wha/rls/89887.htm.

U.S. Senate Judiciary Committee. 2005. "Testimony of the Honorable Michael Chertoff." Presented at *Comprehensive Immigration Reform II* meeting of the full committee, 110th Congress, Washington, DC, October 18. http://www.judiciary.senate.gov/imo/media/doc/chertoff_testimony_10_18_05.pdf.

Valverde, Mariana. 1998. *Diseases of the Will: Alcohol and the Dilemmas of Freedom.* Cambridge: Cambridge University Press.

Vásquez, Manuel. 2011. *More Than Belief: A Materialist Theory of Religion.* New York: Oxford University Press.

Venkatesh, Sudhir. 2000. *American Project: The Rise and Fall of a Modern Ghetto.* Cambridge, MA: Harvard University Press.

Venkatesh, Sudhir, and Steven Levitt. 2000. "Are We a Family or a Business? History and Disjuncture in the Urban American Street Gang." *Theory & Society* 29, no. 4:427–62.

Visser, Margaret. 1991. *The Rituals of Dinner: The Origins, Evolution, Eccentricities, and Meaning of Table Manners.* New York: Grove Press.

Viviano, Frank. 2012. "A Vacation Goes South." *California.* http://alumni.berkeley.edu/news/california-magazine/summer-2012-north-south/vacation-goes-south.

Wacker, Grant. 2001. *Heaven Below: Early Pentecostals and American Culture.* Cambridge, MA: Harvard University Press.

Wallace, Scott. 2000. "You Must Go Home Again: Deported LA Gangbangers Take Over El Salvador." *Harper's Magazine,* August. http://harpers.org/archive/2000/08/you-must-go-home-again/.

Walton, Jonathan. 2009. *Watch This! The Ethics and Aesthetics of Black Televangelism.* New York: New York University Press.

Warren, Kay. 1998. *Indigenous Movements and Their Critics: Pan-Maya Activism in Guatemala.* Princeton, NJ: Princeton University Press.

Warren, Rick. 2002. *The Purpose Driven Life: What on Earth Am I Here For?* Grand Rapids, MI: Zondervan.

Washington Office on Latin America (WOLA). 2006. *Youth Gangs in Central America: Issues in Human Rights, Effective Policing, and Prevention.* Special Report, November. Washington, DC: WOLA. http://www.wola.org/sites/default/files/downloadable/Citizen%20Security/past/GangsReport_Final.pdf

Weber, Brenda. 2007. "Makeover as Takeover: Scenes of Affective Domination on Makeover TV." *Configurations* 15, no. 1:77–99.

———. 2009. *Makeover TV: Selfhood, Citizenship, and Celebrity.* Durham, NC: Duke University Press.

Wegenstein, Bernadette. 2007. "Introduction." *Configurations* 15, no. 1:1–8.

Wellman, James K., Jr., ed. 2007. *Belief and Bloodshed: Religion and Violence across Time and Tradition.* Lanham, MD: Rowman & Littlefield.

Werdegar, Matthew. 1999. "Enjoining the Constitution: The Use of Public Nuisance Abatement Injunctions against Urban Street Gangs." *Stanford Law Review* 51, no. 2:409–45.

West, Patrick. 2004. *Conspicuous Compassion: Why Sometimes It Really Is Cruel to Be Kind*. London: Civitas Institute for the Study of Civil Society.

Wexler, Laura. 1992. "Tender Violence: Literary Eavesdropping, Domestic Fiction, and Educational Reform." In *The Culture of Sentiment: Race, Gender, and Sentimentality in 19th-Century America,* edited by Shirley Samuels, 9–38. New York: Oxford University Press.

Whyte, William Foote. 1943. *Street Corner Society: The Social Structure of an Italian Slum*. Chicago: University of Chicago Press.

Williams, Marilyn T. 1991. *Washing "The Great Unwashed": Public Baths in Urban America, 1840–1920*. Columbus, OH: Ohio State University Press.

Williams, Philip, and Walter Knut. 1997. *Militarization and Demilitarization in El Salvador's Transition to Democracy*. Pittsburgh: University of Pittsburgh Press.

Williams, Raymond. 1977. "Structures of Feeling." Chap. 9 in *Marxism and Literature,* 128–35. New York: Oxford University Press.

Wilson, Maya. 2009. "Guatemala: Central American Crime Capital." Press release, February 9. Council on Hemispheric Affairs. http://www.coha.org/guatemala-%E2%80%93-central-american-crime-capital/.

Wilson, Richard, ed. 1997. *Anthropology and Human Rights: Culture and Context*. London: Pluto Press.

Wolseth, Jon. 2008. "Safety and Sanctuary: Pentecostalism and Youth Gang Violence in Honduras." *Latin American Perspectives* 35, no. 4:96–111.

Wood, Elisabeth Jean. 2003. *Insurgent Collective Action and Civil War in El Salvador*. Cambridge: Cambridge University Press.

World Vision Australia. 2013. "What Will I Write to My Sponsored Child?" http://www.worldvision.com.au/myworldvision/BuildingConnection/SendingLetters/WriteToSponsoredChild.aspx.

Worrall, John. 2003. "California Street Terrorism Enforcement and Prevention Act." In *Encyclopedia of Juvenile Justice,* edited by Marilyn D. McShane and Frank P. Williams III, 39–41. Thousand Oaks, CA: Sage.

Wydick, Bruce. 2013. "Want to Change the World? Sponsor a Child." *Christianity Today* 57, no. 5:20. http://www.christianitytoday.com/ct/2013/june/want-to-change-world-sponsor-child.html?paging=off.

Wydick, Bruce, Paul Glewwe, and Laine Rutledge. 2013. "Does International Child Sponsorship Work? A Six-Country Study of Impacts on Adult Life Outcomes." *Journal of Political Economy* 121, no. 2:393–436.

Yeats, William Butler. 1921. "The Second Coming (Slouching Towards Bethlehem)." In *Michael Robartes and the Dancer*. Churchtown, Ireland: Cuala Press. http://digital.library.villanova.edu/Item/vudl:40329.

Zechmeister, Elizabeth J., José Miguel Cruz, Susan Berk-Seligson, and Rodrigo Serrano-Berthet. 2013. "Crime, Violence, and Insecurity in Central America." Filmed February 28, 2013. Woodrow Wilson Center webcast, 1:56:34. Posted April 23, 2013. http://www.wilsoncenter.org/event/crime-violence-and-insecurity-central-america.

Zeiderman, Austin Gabriel. 2012. "Life at Risk: Governing the Future in Bogotá, Colombia." PhD diss., Stanford University. http://searchworks.stanford.edu/view/9688127.

Zilberg, Elana. 2004. "Fools Banished from the Kingdom: Remapping Geographies of Gang Violence between the Americas (Los Angeles and San Salvador)." *American Quarterly* 56, no. 3:759–79.

———. 2011. *Space of Detention: The Making of a Transnational Gang Crisis between Los Angeles and San Salvador.* Durham, NC: Duke University Press.

Zimring, Franklin E., Gordon Hawkins, and Sam Kamin. 2001. *Punishment and Democracy: Three Strikes and You're Out in California.* New York: Oxford University Press.

Zorbaugh, Harvey Warren. 1929. *The Gold Coast and the Slum: A Sociological Study of Chicago's Near North Side.* Chicago: University of Chicago Press.

Zovatto, Daniel. 2011. "2011 Latinobarometer: Central America: Pessimism Increases Hand in Hand with the Economic Crisis and Insecurity." *International IDEA News,* October–December. Posted November 30, 2011. Stockholm: International Institute for Democracy and Electoral Assistance. http://www.idea.int/americas/2011-latinobarometer-pessimism-increases.cfm.

Zylinska, Joanna. 2007. "Of Swans and Ugly Ducklings: Bioethics between Humans, Animals, and Machines." *Configurations* 15, no. 2:125–50.

Index

masturbation, 39, 153
Mateo (ex-gang member), xi, 1–7, 9–12, 18,
20–23, 25–31, 58–64, 89–95, 120–126,
151–157, 182–186, 189–193, 201–202,
204, 208n8, 209n9, 217n50
materialism, 81, 129, 142, 237n22
materiality, 11, 36, 50, 54, 57, 72, 87, 112,
123, 132, 141, 170, 179, 190, 226n35,
231n29
Matthew (disciple), 45–46
Maya. See indigenous
Mayo, Elton, 101
Mazzarella, William, 208n9, 232n38
McDonald's, 117
McKay, Henry, 75, 216n42, 226n29
megachurch, 72, 130, 229n17, 236n14. See
also church
Melville, Herman, 132, 237n22
Mérida Initiative, 16, 215n34
Mexican Boy (ex-gang member), 80, 86,
223n3
Mexico, 13, 16, 60, 160, 178, 215n34. See
also Mé;rida Initiative
Mexico City, 173
Miami, 108, 160–161, 193
middle class, 25, 38, 52, 56, 65, 73–74, 78,
88, 90, 98, 111–112, 129, 130, 132,
135, 137, 141, 151, 160, 224n11,
226n35, 235n8, 237n22. See also taste
migrant labor. See deportation; undocumented immigration
military, 10, 12–13, 15–16, 40–41, 151,
206n2, 212n18, 234n7, 245n1
Miller, Perry, 209n10
ministry, gang. See prison chaplaincy
miracle, 48, 62, 115, 168–169, 242n32
missionary, 45, 54, 71, 97, 99–101, 104,
128–129, 131, 135, 139, 141, 143–144,
187, 225n21
mob, 10, 14, 34, 36
modernity, 22, 37–39, 47, 52, 100–101,
175, 206n2, 207n7, 211n13, 219n10,
220n25, 224n19, 231n29, 235n8,
243n52, 244n59
Montt, Efrain Ríos, 13, 212n17
Moral Majority, 13
Morales, Pastor (prison chaplain), 33–36,
40–47, 54–55, 57
morality, 11, 18–19, 36–39, 44, 52, 55–56,
67–72, 76, 78–79, 84, 87, 97, 99–100,
104, 111–113, 116, 119, 123, 130, 132,
134–135, 139, 140–141, 168, 179, 185,
188, 190, 192, 216n41, 223n10,
225n28, 226n35, 236n14, 240n7. See

also affect; Christianity, undenominated;
manuals; materiality
morality play, 132
MS-13. See Mara Salvatrucha (MS-13)
multinational corporation. See corporation,
multinational
murder. See homicide

narrative, 5, 22, 30, 37, 40, 46–48, 50,
54–55, 66, 70–71, 73, 75, 77, 81, 83,
111, 134, 137, 145, 162, 170, 175, 180,
187, 202, 210n10, 211n13, 217n50,
224n16, 225n20, 241n21
negative. See attitude
Nelson, Diane, 170, 234n6, 243n45
neoliberalism, 19, 54, 76, 82, 97, 129, 159,
191, 208n8, 209n10, 222n38, 224n16,
230n24, 235n9
neo-Pentecostalism. See Pentecostalism
New York (ex-gang member), 74, 78–79, 81
New York City, 13, 15, 38, 89, 161, 223n3
Nixon, Richard, 160–161
North America, 37–39, 45, 50–52, 56,
66–67, 71, 75, 98–100, 123–124, 127,
129–130, 132, 137, 142, 144, 160,
201–202, 204, 210
Norwegian Cruise Line, 99

Obama, Barack, 15, 234n7
optimism, 48, 56, 68, 76–77, 85, 168, 174,
210n10, 237n22, 242n37. See also
attitude; hope; liberation theology;
temporality, future
Oslo Accord, 212n18
Osteen, Joel, 130, 236n14

Paisas, 33–34, 36, 40, 56, 218n2. See also
riots, prison
Panadero (ex-gang member), 85–86, 223n3
Panama, 98
panopticon, 38–39, 103, 220n25. See also
Foucault
past. See temporality
pastor. See Allende; Morales; prison
chaplaincy; streets
patience (Christian virtue), 23, 83–84, 97,
99, 106, 109, 117, 126, 188–189
Paul (Apostle), 67–68, 164. See also
conversion
Paul VI (pope), 244n57
Pavoncito (prison), 33, 35fig. 6, 36–37,
40–43, 48–49, 54–55, 103, 202, 218n2,
231n30. See also Boqueron; prison;
riots, prison